CROSSCURRENTS

Sixth Edition

CONTEMPORARY POLITICAL ISSUES

EDITED BY

MARK CHARLTON
ST. MARY'S UNIVERSITY COLLEGE

AND

PAUL BARKER
BRESCIA UNIVERSITY COLLEGE

NELSON EDUCATION

NELSON / EDUCATION

Crosscurrents: Contemporary Political Issues,
Sixth Edition

Edited by Mark Charlton and Paul Barker

Associate Vice President, Editorial Director:
Evelyn Veitch

Editor-in-Chief, Higher Education:
Anne Williams

Publisher:
Cara Yarzab

Acquisitions Editor:
Bram Sepers

Marketing Manager:
Ann Byford

Developmental Editor:
My Editor Inc.

Permissions Coordinator:
Shelley Wickabrod

Production Service:
ICC Macmillan Inc.

Copy Editor:
Cathy Witlox

Proofreader:
Barbara Storey

Manufacturing Coordinator:
Ferial Suleman

Design Director:
Ken Phipps

Managing Designer:
Katherine Strain

Cover Design:
Peter Papayanakis

Cover Image:
© Gail Mooney/Masterfile

Compositor:
ICC Macmillan Inc.

Printer:
Webcom

Library and Archives Canada Cataloguing in Publication

Crosscurrents : contemporary political issues / editors, Mark Charlton, Paul Barker. — 6th ed.

Includes bibliographical references
ISBN 978-0-17-610541-9

1. Canada—Politics and government—21st century—Textbooks. 2. Canada—Social policy—Textbooks. I. Barker, Paul, 1953- II. Charlton, Mark, 1948-

FC640.C76 2008   971.07
C2008-905032-0

ISBN-13: 978-0-17-610541-9
ISBN-10: 0-17-610541-7

Contents

Contributors

Michael Adams is a well-known pollster and author of numerous books on Canadian society and politics.

Ian Binnie is a justice of the Supreme Court of Canada.

Philip L. Bryden is dean of the Faculty of Law at the University of New Brunswick.

Michael Chong is a member of the Parliament of Canada for Wellington–Halton Hills.

Daniel Cohn is a professor of political science at York University.

Faron Ellis teaches politics at Lethbridge College, where he also serves as director of the Citizen Society Research Lab.

Thomas Flanagan is a professor of political science at the University of Calgary.

H. Patrick Glenn is a professor of law at McGill University.

Andrew Heard is a professor of political science at Simon Fraser University.

John von Heyking is a professor of political science at the University of Lethbridge.

John L. Hiemstra is a professor of political science at King's University College, Edmonton.

Peter Hogg is professor emeritus at Osgoode Hall Law School at York University.

Robert J. Jackson is a professor of political science at Carleton University.

Harold J. Jansen is a professor of political science at the University of Lethbridge.

Kenneth Jennings is a member of the Class of 2009 at the Dalhousie Law School.

Tasha Kheiriddin is the Ontario director of the Canadian Taxpayers Federation.

David Kilgour is a former member of Parliament for Edmonton–Strathcona.

Louis LeBel is a justice of the Supreme Court of Canada.

Wayne MacKay is a professor of law at the Dalhousie Law School.

John Major is a former justice of the Supreme Court of Canada.

Robert Martin recently retired from teaching law at the University of Western Ontario.

Daniel McGruder is a member of the Class of 2009 at the Dalhousie Law School.

Justice Beverley McLachlin is Chief Justice of the Supreme Court of Canada.

Hugh Mellon is a professor of political science at King's University College at the University of Western Ontario.

Jacquetta Newman is a professor of political science at King's University College at the University of Western Ontario.

Paul Nesbitt-Larking is a professor of political science at Huron University College.

John H. Redekop teaches political science at Trinity Western University.

Justice Mary Saunders is a member of the British Columbia Court of Appeal.

Tim Schouls teaches political science at Capilano College.

Roger Townshend is a lawyer specializing in Aboriginal issues.

Nelson Wiseman is a professor of political science at the University of Toronto.

Introduction

In the first edition of *Crosscurrents: Contemporary Political Issues,* we stated our desire to develop a collection of readings that would not only challenge students to think through a number of contemporary political issues but also foster in students an understanding of and tolerance for the views of others. To achieve this, we felt that a text structured in the form of a debate or dialogue on leading political issues provided an ideal format. We find it gratifying that a number of our colleagues have shared this goal and have used the previous editions in their introductory political science or Canadian politics courses.

CHANGES TO THIS EDITION

In preparing a new edition of *Crosscurrents,* we have maintained the basic structure and format of previous editions. The sixth edition addresses fifteen issues, somewhat fewer than previous editions, in response to requests to keep the new edition shorter. For each issue, an introduction provides the reader with the necessary background and places the subject in the context of more general principles of concern to the study of politics. Two essays then present conflicting viewpoints. Finally, a postscript offers a short commentary on the debate and suggests readings for students to explore the topic further.

From the comments of the reviewers, it is clear that *Crosscurrents: Contemporary Political Issues* is used in general introductory courses and in Canadian politics courses to about the same degree. Therefore, we have tried to select topics appropriate to both and have retained the public policy section, which covers a variety of issues. People who use the text in an introductory course may find the public policy section more helpful in the early part of such a course, which often deals with ideologies and concepts relating to rights and the role of the state in society.

A NOTE FOR FIRST-TIME USERS

In introducing the first edition of *Crosscurrents,* we set out our rationale for developing a reader using the debate format. We believe that the rationale for using this format for teaching introductory courses is as strong as ever and bears repeating for those who may be picking up this text for the first time.

There are three good reasons, we believe, for using the debate format. First, studies have shown that students learn and retain more information when they are engaged in an active learning process. Yet the reality in most Canadian universities is that students in introductory courses face ever larger class sizes, which militate against discussion and active student involvement. While students generally come to political science courses with a great deal of interest and enthusiasm, they frequently find themselves slipping into a pattern of simple note taking and passive learning.

Second, most introductory political science courses must of necessity address abstract principles and concepts and cover a great deal of descriptive material concerning processes and institutions. At the same time, students come to these courses expecting that they will discuss and debate what is going on in the chaotic world of politics. Unfortunately, it is often difficult for them to relate the debates of everyday political issues to the broader and more abstract principles encountered in their introductory courses. Without a reference point, discussions of contemporary issues may seem more like interesting "current events" digressions, with little direct relationship to the overall propositions being dealt with in the lectures.

Third, students frequently bring to their readings an uncritical awe of the authority of the published word. When confronted with a series of readings by the leading authorities on each subject, there is a strong temptation for students to think that the text presents the "final" word on the subject. They assume that further discussion and debate can add little new to the issue.

With these thoughts in mind, we have endeavoured to develop a collection of readings that will serve as a resource for a more interactive style of teaching, whether it be in classroom or tutorial discussion situations or in a more formal debate setting. Because of the flexibility of the format, *Crosscurrents* can be employed in the classroom in several ways.

(i) Some may wish to assign the chapters simply as supplementary readings reinforcing material covered in lectures, and to use them as points of illustration in classroom lectures or discussions.

(ii) The readings may be used as a departure point for essay assignments in the course. To encourage students to develop their critical skills, they could be asked to write an assessment of the arguments and evidence presented in one of the debates. Alternatively, students could select one side of the debate and write an essay developing their own arguments in favour of that view.

(iii) Others may wish to use the readings as a means of organizing weekly discussion sessions into a debate format. On each topic, two students may be asked to argue the case for opposing sides, and these arguments could be followed by group discussion. This format requires students to adopt a particular point of view and defend that position. Because the necessary background material is provided in the readings, this format is very easily adapted to large courses where teaching assistants are responsible for weekly tutorial sessions.

ACKNOWLEDGMENTS

We would like to express our appreciation to the many reviewers who offered very helpful comments and suggestions throughout the years: Tom Enders, Grand Prairie Community College; Karen E. Lochead, Wilfrid Laurier University; Gerry Boychuk, University of Waterloo; Andrew Heard, Simon Fraser University; Susan Franceschet, Acadia University; Darin Nesbitt, Douglas College; Alexandra Dobrowolsky, St. Mary's University; and John von Heyking, University of Lethbridge. We are particularly indebted to those authors who graciously agreed to write original essays or revise earlier ones specifically for this volume, as well as to the authors and publishers who have granted us permission to use their published work. In addition, we want to acknowledge the excellent support of Katherine Goodes of My Editor Inc. in helping us to bring this project to completion. The careful and detailed work of Susan Calvert, Director of Content and Media Production, and Cathy Witlox, Copy Editor, was also much appreciated. Finally, we would be remiss not to mention the patient support of our families, who, in their indirect ways, have contributed to this volume.

Mark Charlton, Calgary, Alberta
Paul Barker, London, Ontario

About the Editors

Mark Charlton is Vice-President Academic and a professor of political science at St. Mary's University College, Calgary, Alberta. Professor Charlton received his Ph.D. in political science from Laval University, where he studied as an Ontario–Quebec Fellow. He is author of *The Making of Canadian Food Aid Policy* (1992), editor of *Crosscurrents: International Relations* (2005), and co-author of *Thomson Nelson's Guide to Writing in Political Science* (2006). He has also published a number of articles in *International Journal, Études Internationales, Journal of Conflict Studies,* and the *Canadian Journal of Development Studies.*

Paul Barker teaches political science at Brescia University College, London, Ontario. Professor Barker received his Ph.D. from the University of Toronto. He is the author of *Public Administration in Canada* and has written articles on public policy that have appeared in *Canadian Public Administration, Canadian Public Policy,* and the *Canadian Journal of Law and Society.*

PART ONE

Is the Canadian Political Culture Becoming Americanized?

Can Native Sovereignty Coexist with Canadian Sovereignty?

Will Conservatism and the Conservative Party Fail?

Is the Canadian Political Culture Becoming Americanized?

✔ **YES**
PAUL NESBITT-LARKING, "Canadian Political Culture: The Problem of Americanization"

✘ **NO**
MICHAEL ADAMS, "Canada and the United States—Separated at Birth"

In the eyes of the world, Canada and the United States are very much alike. The two countries share a language, occupy the same continental space, and support the operation of free markets. The similarities between the two countries also extend to beliefs and attitudes about government—in other words, the political cultures of the two nations are comparable. Canadians and Americans both believe in a modestly sized public sector and exhibit reluctance to offer elected officials much leeway. Other countries may give government a large role, but not Canada and the United States.

But at the same time, some believe that the two countries are separated by differences in how they approach political life. Americans have been more suspicious of government than Canadians, a view revealed in their determination to ensure that political power is always separated and not concentrated. On the other hand, Canadians have been more positively disposed toward government; since Confederation, when the public sector was crucial to the birth of the nation, Canadians have seen purpose in government. For many Canadians, these contrasting attitudes are fundamental to the uniqueness of Canada. Inherent in the Canadian political culture are a sense of community and an appreciation of the value of collective efforts and public institutions. Such a pose curtails the often rapacious individualism found in purely liberal political cultures, the best example of which is that of the United States.

For those who see and cherish these differences, there are disturbing changes now taking place in the attitudes of Canadians toward government and public life. There is a declining trust in elected officials, and voters have become less attached to traditional parties and more enamoured of new vehicles of representation. Once valued public policies are now under attack, and the restriction or even downsizing of government has become an important goal. A belief in individual entitlement, fuelled in part by the Charter of Rights and Freedoms, has emerged as well, pushing aside more communitarian sentiments. For many, these and other developments mean only one thing: the Americanization of the Canadian political culture. The toleration, the sense of collective purpose, the respect for authority—all this and more is being lost. The way Canadians think about politics is changing, and it is a change to be regretted because it threatens to engulf Canada in what has been called the *possessive individualism* of the American political culture.

There are some, however, who believe that important differences in political culture continue to separate the two countries. One has only to look at the size of government today. In Canada, the public sector represents a little more than 40 percent of the total value of goods and services; in America, the percentage is almost 10 percent less. Then there are the public policies that emerge from government spending, another reflection of key differences. Canada continues to commit itself to universal health care, while the U.S. remains content with covering at-risk groups. The same story appears to pertain to other fields of policy, in which Canadians seemingly support aggressive government action and Americans favour little or no action. More generally, there is the perception that Canadians just think differently from the Americans when it comes to government. We still seem to prefer peace, order, and good government over life, liberty, and the pursuit of happiness.

In the readings, Paul Nesbitt-Larking argues that, indeed, the political culture of Canada is being Americanized. He also argues that this offers little cause for celebration, for it spells the end of what it means to be Canadian. Michael Adams, in an excerpt from his book *Fire and Ice*, avers that important differences still separate Canadians' and Americans' beliefs about government and the political process.

✔ **YES**

Canadian Political Culture: The Problem of Americanization
PAUL NESBITT-LARKING

Living next to you is in some ways like sleeping with an elephant; no matter how friendly and even-tempered the beast, if I may call it that, one is affected by every twitch and grunt. Even a friendly nuzzling can sometimes lead to frightening consequences.

–Pierre Trudeau, speech to the National Press Club, Washington, D.C., March 25, 1969

For a very long time, and certainly since the American Declaration of Independence in 1776, the destiny of Canada has been shaped through its complex interconnections with the political words and deeds of those other European descendants who live to the south of us. Canada is, and always has been, an American nation. Carved and crafted from a process of "defensive expansionism,"[1] in which the harsh wilderness of this northern part of the American continent was stitched together in east-to-west chains of settlement, often "in defiance of geography,"[2] Canada, in its very existence and longevity, is a major North American achievement. Less obviously, political and governmental life in Canada reflects two centuries of an ambivalent relationship with Americans and their way of life, in which Canadians have alternately incorporated and rejected American influences. Americans are a self-confident people who share a common heritage grounded in an evolving covenant to sustain the most perfect political system of freedom and opportunity. Through their enterprise and determination, Americans have translated the ideals of their founders into enormous economic, cultural, military, and political achievements. It is no idle boast to claim that the United States of America is the greatest nation on Earth.

When Americans are asked to name their "best friends" in the international community, most name the British; when they are asked with whom they conduct the most international trade, Japan is mentioned most often. These responses strike many Canadians as curious. Canada is in fact America's largest single trading partner,[3] and, when probed, a majority of Americans express a strong and genuine affinity toward Canadians. What these findings reveal is best expressed by former prime minister Pierre Trudeau in the above quotation: a combination of benign ignorance and careless presumption. Americans do not think much about Canada or Canadians at all, and when they do, they think of Canadians as Americans, with some curious characteristics, who happen to live in another place. Over the past two hundred years, Americans have made gracious and consistent overtures to Canadians to join them in their great republic, and they have

4

never been able to understand the apparent stubbornness with which a succession of Canadian leaders has resisted. American leaders have frequently regarded Canada as an odd little anomaly with its monarchical traditions and its chronic French–English tensions. Such Americans approximate Trudeau's elephants: they do not know their own strength and therefore are often unable to appreciate the damage or the offence they cause. Trudeau's tone is mild in its mockery, and it is possible to argue that his choice of animal attributes too much benevolence to the Americans. The American approach to Canada, as the U.S. has crafted its independent foreign policy throughout the past eighty years, might better be described as "bearlike" in its angry malevolence rather than elephantine in its passive tolerance. Whenever it is hungry, hurt, or under a perceived threat, the bear is prone to attack, lashing out against all who offend it or merely get in its way. While the Americans have uttered no serious threats to invade Canada since the late nineteenth century, they have interfered aggressively in our domestic and foreign affairs and, in so doing, have acted in ways that are at best insulting and undiplomatic and at worse in contravention of established international law and precedent. An egregious instance of undiplomatic interference is the ambassadorship of Paul Cellucci. Appointed by President George W. Bush, Cellucci was ambassador to Canada from 2001 to 2005. Using his ambassadorial role as a partisan bully pulpit, Cellucci lambasted Canadian governments for their domestic and foreign policy positions, far exceeding the bounds of normal diplomacy.

While it is possible to argue about the extent to which the American impact on Canada has been elephantine, bearlike, or both, it is indisputable that it has been of great magnitude. Our economy is dominated by American capital. American direct investment in Canada is currently about $274 billion (USD), and U.S.-based corporations own many of Canada's most profitable industries. Over 60 percent of all foreign direct investment in Canada comes from American corporations.[4] Since the 1950s, Canada's military strategy and structure have been shaped in deliberate synchronization with those of the United States through a series of bilateral and multilateral agreements. Military and geopolitical cooperation with the U.S.A. has intensified since 2006 under the Conservative administration of Prime Minister Stephen Harper. Whether we refer to it as "culture" or the "entertainment industry," Canada is dominated by American material. The vast majority of the movies or TV shows we watch or the magazines we browse through originate in the United States. In political terms, the American influence has also been profound. Many of our major political institutions have been deliberately shaped to reflect, if not entirely replicate, their American counterparts, including federalism, the Senate, the Supreme Court, and the Charter of Rights and Freedoms. Our political practices and processes have also come to approximate the American pattern in certain ways. In the early twentieth century, Canada adopted the American practice of selecting political leaders through holding large-scale party conventions; in recent decades, commentators have referred to the "presidentialization" of the role of Canada's prime minister. At the deepest level, many Canadians have been enthusiastic followers of the American way of political life and have come to admire American political values and beliefs. These Canadians have attempted to convince other Canadians of the superiority of the American way and to encourage them to incorporate American values into Canadian political parties, institutions, and practices. The struggle between those who value American political ideals and those who wish to preserve a distinctive Canadian set of ideals has been raging since the Declaration of Independence in 1776. In presenting the principal features of this ideological conflict throughout this paper, I shall explain why I believe Americanization is potentially so damaging to Canada and Canadians, and how eternal—or at least periodic—vigilance is the price of remaining Canadian.

POLITICAL CULTURE AND IDEOLOGY

Unlike most concepts in political science, "political culture" has a clear and definite beginning. The term was invented by Gabriel Almond and first used in an article in 1956.[5] Like other American political scientists of his era, Almond was determined to develop political analysis into a more rigorous and scientific discipline than it had been in the early decades of the century. The United States had emerged from the Second World War as the leading military, moral, and economic power in the world, with associated opportunities and dangers. In order to exert a meaningful influence on an unstable and rapidly changing environment, the American state required detailed and accurate analyses of political character in other parts of the world. Aware of the imprecision of existing accounts of political life in other countries, Almond adapted the "structural-functionalist" sociological framework of Talcott Parsons as a basis for developing a systematic understanding of political characteristics. Introducing political culture, he said: "Every political system is embedded in a particular pattern of orientations to political action. I have found it useful to refer to this as the political culture."[6] By this, he meant that it is possible to identify coherent and distinctive patterns of beliefs, values, and attitudes toward political institutions and practices among each of the world's political communities. Almond and his colleague Sidney Verba attempted to identify such political orientations among the citizens of England, Mexico, Germany, the United States of America, and Italy in *The Civic Culture*.[7] On the basis of their analyses of responses to survey data, Almond and Verba produced portrayals of the distinctive political cultures of each country based upon rigorous methodological techniques and consistent quantified measures.

Almond and Verba's study generated great interest and admiration and gave rise to over a decade of research based upon their model. The systematic study of political culture was undertaken in many countries, including Canada.[8] Despite its widespread success and acceptability, the approach also attracted its critics. Prominent among the criticisms were the following: that in its assumption of the civic perfection of the United States of America, the political culture approach provided an arrogant, partial, and distorted image of political values, beliefs, and attitudes in other countries; that there were serious methodological flaws inherent in attempting to capture something as deep, nebulous, and "holistic" as culture merely through adding up a series of quick responses to questions by individuals; and, perhaps most damning of all, that in the increasingly turbulent and conflictual years of the 1960s and early 1970s, the approach could offer little to explain mass discontent, institutional paralysis, sudden change, or socioeconomic breakdown. By the mid-1970s, the huge research industry generated by Almond had dwindled to almost nothing and political scholars turned their attention to other matters. In the Canadian case, the decline of interest in political culture was marked by a series of influential anti-American articles, reflecting a more general pro-Canadian assertiveness that was prominent at the time.[9]

Regrettably, in turning away from the "Americanized" version of political culture, the Canadian political science community abandoned a very important subfield of enquiry. With all its faults, the path-breaking work of Almond had alerted us to the importance of how people feel about political issues and how they make sense of their political experiences. In criticizing Almond and others for their failure to achieve the exacting standards of full scientific rigour, it is easy to overlook the obscurity of the concept of culture and the difficulties inherent in working with it. Raymond Williams referred to *culture* as one of the two or three most difficult words in the English language.[10] Ongoing disputes at the core of political science over the very meaning of *politics* itself attest to the continued controversies surrounding this concept. When politics and culture are put together in a composite concept, definitional difficulties are multiplied.

Despite these challenges, it is possible to adapt the core of meaning inherent in Almond's approach, adding to it insights derived from other scholars in the field. The central criticisms of Almond pertain to the manner in which the concept was (ab)used—both methodologically and ethically—rather than to the concept itself. In building on Almond, my own definition of political culture incorporates the following additional insights. First, political cultures should be seen as events as well as states of affairs; political cultures are generated, produced, reproduced, modified, and even transformed by people in their daily activities; people are strongly conditioned through their socialization to the symbolic worlds into which they are born and in which they grow up, but they also, in their turn, contribute to the reproduction of those symbolic orders. Second, political cultures are literally mundane or everyday; many of the political values, beliefs, attitudes, and symbols that we hold most dear are so taken for granted and unquestioned that we are often not aware of them. Third, I define *politics* more broadly than Almond, as the manner in which people come to decide on the appropriate distribution of valued resources, as well as on the making of those rules that govern us. The processes of politics are both cooperative and conflictual; politics happens everywhere there are things to be distributed and rules to be made. To summarize, political cultures happen as people, operating in an already constituted symbolic field of political cultural concepts and practices, convey to each other conceptions of the distribution and uses of valued resources and of the making of decisions and rules.

As I conceptualize them, political cultures are vague, nebulous, and shifting phenomena, and they are difficult to measure in any precise way. One of the most promising ways in which to explore political cultures is through the employment of the related concept of ideology. Political cultures consist of loose and semiformed ideas, beliefs, and feelings about political institutions and practices. Ideologies are partial appropriations from political cultures, arising from the conscious and deliberate attempts of the intellectual leadership of particular social groups (known as *ideologues*) to achieve a definitional monopoly of the political world that will be accepted by as many people as possible and that accords with the particular interests of their group. Ignoring the complexities and subtleties of political cultures and focusing on a narrow and self-interested band of values and beliefs, ideologues seek to convince others of the way things are, the way they ought to be, and, less obviously, the way it is possible for them to be. In so doing, ideologues hope that their "construction of reality" will convince others to effect political change in their favour. Ideologues employ a range of political movements and associations to achieve their ends, including political parties, political institutions, interest groups, the media, the bureaucracy, and the educational system.

Canadian political culture has provided fertile "clay" for a broad range of ideologues, who have attempted to mould and shape it according to their particular interests. Arguably the most important ideological struggle over the past two hundred years has been that between "individualism" and "communitarianism." Canadian political culture, in contradistinction to the American political culture, has managed to sustain a balance between these two principal ideological tendencies. As will become clear in the next section, another way of saying that communitarianism continues to be part of the Canadian equation is to say that Canadians have been consistently seduced by the promise of the American dream but have periodically drawn back in order to develop and sustain distinctive institutions and practices that counter American values.[11]

INDIVIDUALISM AND COMMUNITARIANISM

The quantitative approach to political culture, developed by Almond and his followers, did not recognize the importance of the ideological opposition between individualism and communitarianism. The reason for this is readily apparent: the model of political reality devised by Almond came from an ideological individualism so profoundly entrenched and successful that it had completely overwhelmed the American political culture. It rarely occurred to American students of political culture to think beyond the limits of their individualistic premises. The entire apparatus of methodology, questions, and comparisons among nations was premised upon this unquestioned individualism. It seems hardly surprising that when Almond and his colleagues applied their benchmarks, the United States routinely emerged as the most "perfect" political culture.

Students of political culture in Canada, however, have enjoyed full access to three other approaches to the study of political culture that have enabled them to reflect upon the Canadian experience of individualism versus communitarianism. These are the "fragments" approach, associated with Louis Hartz, Kenneth McRae, and Gad Horowitz[12]; the "historical-developmental" approach, best expressed in the synthesis offered by Seymour Martin Lipset[13]; and the more recent empirical attitudinal surveys of Michael Adams, Matthew Mendelsohn, and Edward Grabb and James Curtis, among others.[14] There are large-scale differences between the three approaches with respect to their theoretical presuppositions and method-ological approaches. What unites them, however, is their propensity to portray the evolution of Canadian political culture as an ongoing struggle between the American forces of possessive individualism on the one hand and the European forces of conservative order and socialist collectivism on the other hand. *Possessive individualism*, a phrase originating in the work of C. B. Macpherson, is a distillation of the essence of the pure ideology of individual property rights and freedom from interference, first developed in the work of John Locke.[15] The term *communitarianism* best combines the anti-individualistic impulses of traditional conservatism and socialism. As its name implies, communitarianism is a belief system that stresses both the logical and the moral necessity of thinking about political life in terms of the requirements of the community or the collectivity, rather than in terms of the isolated and abstracted individual. In considering those distinctively Canadian forces that have opposed possessive individualism throughout the past two centuries, communitarianism is best able to convey the alternating right-wing and left-wing critiques of American liberalism.[16]

The fragments approach to political culture argues that the principal "white set-tler" societies were established by ideologically homogeneous and cohesive colonies of Europeans, whose founding characteristics established the ideological parameters of those societies throughout the succeeding generations. Louis Hartz describes the powerful and pervasive force of liberal individualism in the United States, arguing that even in the twentieth century, its domination of the political culture can explain the early death of American socialism, the reluctant collec-tivism and populist character of the New Deal era, and the anticommunist vehe-mence of McCarthyism.[17] Kenneth McRae illuminates the importance of feudalism in the French-Canadian fragment, as well as loyalty to the British Crown among the English-Canadian fragment, in the establishment of a society in Canada that, while fundamentally sharing in the liberal individualistic ethos of the American political culture, exhibited elements of a political culture of cautiousness, moderation, gradualism, compromise, and order.[18] McRae also makes reference to the incursion of modest doses of left-wing culture with the settlement of parts of the Canadian west by later European fragments ideologically committed to socialism.[19] These themes are further amplified by Gad Horowitz in his seminal account of the development of ideologies in Canada. Horowitz goes much further than Hartz and McRae in pointing out the critical importance of the communitarian elements in Canada's historical development.[20] Horowitz also moves his analysis away from the Hartzian notion that the founding ideologies of the fragments "congealed" early and remained unchanged.

The manner in which historical developments, notably major events, shape the emergence of a political culture was explored in detail in the work of Seymour Martin Lipset. Over a thirty-year academic career from the 1960s to the 1990s, Lipset developed a comparative analysis of the political cultures of Canada and the United States. On the basis of his understanding of comparative patterns of settlement, formative historical events, such as the American Revolution and the Canadian "counterrevolution," and a broad array of sociological data on such matters as crime rates, divorce rates, and church attendance, Lipset came to concur with Horowitz that differences between the Canadian and American political cultures are profound indeed[21]:

> My central argument is that the two countries differ in their basic organizing principles. Canada has been and is a more class-aware, elitist, law-abiding, statist, collectivity-oriented, and particularistic (group-oriented) society than the United States. . . . The United States remained throughout the 19th and early 20th centuries the extreme example of a classically liberal or Lockean society, one that rejected the assumptions of the alliance of throne and altar, of ascriptive elitism, of mercantilism, of noblesse oblige, of communitarianism.[22]

While Lipset stressed the fundamentally liberal individualist character of both Canada and the United States and argued that, in the global context, "the two resemble each other more than either resembles any other nation,"[23] his framework of comparison, like mine, was between the two countries, and the distinctions are substantial enough to be noteworthy.

Recent empirical surveys of Canadian and American attitudes sustain the view that Canada is a more communitarian polity. Michael Adams's data reveal that, over the past decade, both Canadians and Americans have been shifting their attitudes away from support for traditional authorities toward greater individualism. However, Americans have moved strongly in the direction of possessive individualism, competitiveness, patriarchy, and exclusionary defensiveness. For their part, Canadians have diverged from the American path and shifted strongly toward socially oriented individualism, self-expression, and fulfillment through altruism and inclusiveness.[24] Both Adams and Edward Grabb and James Curtis highlight the important point that while the American South skews the United States toward its characteristic values of possessive individualism and exclusionary defensiveness, Quebec skews Canada toward socially inclusive individualism and a comfort with statism, secularism, and communitarianism. In a key table summarizing measures of individualism, Grabb and Curtis's data show that for three out of the four variables that achieve significant national differences, the United States is more individualistic. Moreover, the pattern of American individualism is as strong in the north as it is in the south.[25] Matthew Mendelsohn, in a summary of his findings, remarks that at the beginning of the twenty-first century, Canada remains "more collectivistic, more open to diversity, more supportive of state intervention, more deferential, and more prepared to find solidarity with people in other countries than its southern neighbour."[26] This is despite a decade of globalization, continental economic integration, federal and provincial neoliberal fiscal policies, and the consequent erosion of the Canadian welfare state.

Despite the historical pervasiveness of communitarian elements in Canada's political culture, and the eloquent passion of many of its supporters, possessive individualistic ideology is currently in global ascendancy.[27] If there is a communitarian response to these trends, it is to be found in the reactionary and defensively hostile impulses of religious and nationalistic fundamentalisms. Such social forces have grown in panic response to the rapid onset of a global economy and culture seemingly bereft of morality and meaning. Canadians have worked hard to sustain a more balanced and inclusive communitarian polity that celebrates diversity, openness, and polyethnic traditions. Given the current political landscape in the United States and beyond, such a balance seems increasingly challenging to sustain. In the next section, I turn my attention to the dangers for Canada associated with incorporating too much possessive individualism and narrow defensiveness: the problem of Americanization.

THE PROBLEM OF AMERICANIZATION

To speak of Americanization as a problem is not to adopt a narrowly ethnocentric, anti-American point of view. A large majority of Canadians were horrified at the attacks of September 11, 2001, in which thousands of innocent lives were lost, and chose to express their solidarity in empathetic support and acts of kindness. Canadians continue to express strong bonds of affection for Americans and an admiration for many aspects of the American way of life, notably the exuberant spirit of entrepreneurship. There is even a small minority of Canadians who would welcome a union of the two countries. Equally, not all Americans are defensive possessive individualists. American scholars, notably Robert Bellah and Robert Putnam, have adopted a critical perspective regarding the consequences of the early and monopolistic domination of individualist liberalism as the American creed and its continuing effects on the American polity. Equating individualism and libertarian freedom with "Americanism" itself has permitted the ideological intolerances of authoritarian populism and "witch hunts" and has discouraged forms of state-led and communitarian solutions to America's problems that have been made possible elsewhere. Globalization, in its economic, cultural, and militaristic forms, represents the universalization of Americanism in the form of global capitalism, global media, and American military presence overseas.

Americanism is rapidly becoming so dominant that communitarian ideological perspectives are in jeopardy. Ideologies in themselves do not die, but given the will and the opportunity, ideologues can so determine and shape political culture that a given people come to believe that only one ideological position is desirable or possible. A political culture can be so imbued with a particular ideological orientation that all others dwindle and fade. Once this is in process, political support for previously existing institutions, practices, and discourses that run counter to the interests of the prevailing ideology falls away. The institutions and practices of the Canadian nation-state have been built on the basis of a political culture characterized by some degree of communitarianism. Once these diminish beyond a certain point, Canada itself is in question. This point was grasped, in a work of brilliant insight, by conservative scholar George Grant, in 1965. In his *Lament for a Nation*, Grant understood that the uncritical adoption of American technocratic politics and economics, as well as the culture of populist consumerism, would undermine Canada to the point where its continued existence ceased to be relevant. He noted, "The impossibility of conservatism in our era is the impossibility of Canada."[28] Put simply, Grant was arguing that if nobody loves the country or regards the relationship between the generations as a communitarian trust, then the nation-state itself will become little more than a practical container. The subtitle of Grant's book is "The Defeat of Canadian Nationalism." There has never been a massive Canadian nationalism—at least not in English Canada—but there have been assertive moments of resistance to Americanization. The continued viability of Canada depends upon the capacity and willingness of Canadians to recognize those economic, cultural, and political signs of the eroding Canadian balance, and to work tirelessly in order to redress the imbalances.

For nearly two decades, Canada's principal political parties and political leaders have been actively promoting economic policies of Americanized possessive individualism. At the federal level, with the marginal exception of the early 1980s, when the Liberal Party attempted to forge a limited new "national policy," both Liberal and Progressive Conservative governments have driven the ideological agenda toward free-market solutions. As with the construction of any ideological perspective, the politicians have argued that their proposals are not merely sound but that they "have no choice." In the 1970s, the Liberals argued that too many demands had been made on the federal system and that it was impossible to continue to provide the kind of extensive and responsive public service that had developed throughout the 1950s and 1960s. They promoted monetary and fiscal policies that increased unemployment, facilitated a decrease in the public sector, and squeezed middle-class incomes through higher interest rates and taxes. In the 1980s, the Progressive Conservative Party pointed out that Canadians had been victims of fiscal irresponsibility, and they began to talk of the need to cut the national deficit. They continued the trend against communitarianism in Canada through their modest attempts at public sector cutbacks, their privatizations and deregulations, but mostly through their two free trade agreements and the introduction of the regressive Goods and Services Tax. The Progressive Conservative government hoped that these policies would stimulate noninflationary growth in the economy. In the 1990s, the emphasis on the national deficit intensified, and the Liberal Party perpetuated the trend toward Americanization, with its massive cuts to the federal public sector as well as cuts in transfer payments to the provinces. The radical downsizing of the federal government inevitably had an impact on the provinces. In some of them, notably Alberta and Ontario, right-wing governments went even further than the federal Liberal Party in radical reductions to the size and scope of the public sector on the basis of American-style populist individualism, promoting a generalized distrust of government and large-scale tax cuts designed to curtail redistributional policies.

In the 1990s, two new major parties came onto the federal scene. One of them, the Reform Party, which became the Canadian Alliance, was a strong proponent of possessive individualism and committed to further radical cuts in public spending. It advocated reductions in transfers to individuals and regions, large-scale tax cuts, and the diminution of the power of the federal state to enforce national standards. The Canadian Alliance and the Progressive Conservative Party united in 2003 to form the Conservative Party of Canada. Its new platform continued the general thrust of Canadian Alliance policies, calling for tax cuts, deregulation, and greater powers to the provinces. Of all the political parties and politicians in contemporary Canada, very few have been active promoters of policies to enhance the communitarian essence of Canada, or even to slow its decline. The Liberal Party under Prime Minister Paul Martin redressed the balance to some extent, restoring funds to public services, such as health, education, and social assistance; Canadian culture; Aboriginal peoples; and foreign aid. Despite these trends, however, the fiscal strategy of the Martin government simultaneously transferred massive resources and fiscal authority to the provinces while increasing military expenditure and cutting personal and corporate taxes. The combined impact of these measures was to jeopardize the longer-term revenue potential of the federal state, rendering it decreasingly able to act on behalf of Canadians and to devise renewed programs of national scope. Since the Canadian federal election of 2006, the Conservative government has accelerated these trends toward tax cuts, deregulation, and devolution of powers to the provinces. Moreover, the Harper administration has integrated Canada more directly into the American orbit by bringing Canada's foreign, defence, security, environmental, and trade policies into line with those of the Bush administration.

Behind the political parties have been the most important special interest groups. Many prominent corporate organizations, such as the Canadian Council of Chief Executives, the Canadian Federation of Independent Business, and the Canadian Taxpayers Federation, have actively promoted greater economic integration into the United States, as well as policies designed to cut the public sector and reduce taxes on the corporate elite. The corporate elite has been strongly supported by most of Canada's leading journalists, intellectuals, and academics. Some of them have, while attacking collectivism, continued to promote the rhetoric of a united Canada, which cherishes its distinctiveness. In this respect, they have offered some resistance to Americanization insofar as they have advocated the old-style orderly and conservative forms of "elite accommodation," through which Canada's distinctive communities are able to achieve a modus vivendi. In other words, they have advocated the kind of political arrangements that the Progressive Conservatives attempted to promote in the 1980s with the Meech Lake and Charlottetown accords. The ideals of such accords, based upon bilingualism and multiculturalism in a finely balanced Canada consisting of "a community of communities," continue to be supported at the highest levels. In modified form, such is the agenda of the current Liberal and Conservative parties.

The problem for Canada is that the refined and noble politics of cultural pluralism and mutual respect have been promoted through anachronistic and elitist political practices, from which most citizens have felt excluded. This is why Michael Adams and others have detected a growing wariness on the part of Canadians regarding traditional authorities. The politics of elite accommodation also runs directly counter to the anticollectivist impulses of economic possessive individualism. The cultural message of economic liberalism stresses narrowly defined rights, absolute freedom from restraint, and a rejection of those virtues associated with family, community, and society, such as love, tolerance, charity, duty, loyalty, and patriotism. There are signs that the hold of such qualities in the Canadian political culture is diminishing. An angry Canadian public rejected the Charlottetown Accord in 1992. The accord had been designed to provide a new compromise among Canadians in terms of their constitutional rights, as well as to restate the commitment of Canadians to a unified nationhood and distinctive national identity. Canadian voters punished the architects of the plan, the Progressive Conservative Party, by almost completely rejecting them in the federal election of 1993. In their place, English Canadians supported the Reform Party, while many Quebecers turned to the Bloc Québécois; both political organizations did not accept bilingualism and multiculturalism.

The decline in support for the traditional parties, the growing disrespect for politicians, the growth of support for narrowly defined single-issue political movements, and a generalized sense of the atomization of political society all point to a growing individuation of Canada's political culture.[29] The rapidly declining trust in Canada's political institutions, political parties, and politicians

14

is reported in Neil Nevitte's *The Decline of Deference*.[30] Nevitte's data demonstrate that "confidence in governmental institutions is declining while non-traditional . . . forms of political participation are increasing. In political matters, people are becoming less deferential, less compliant, more inclined to speak out . . . ."[31] Similar findings are reported by Harold D. Clarke and his colleagues in *Absent Mandate*, which also tracks Canadian public opinion in the 1980s and 1990s.[32] Clarke et al. report strong declines in partisan loyalty and attachment over these decades, in conjunction with growing disaffection, detachment, and negativity concerning politicians and parties.[33] Their final chapter is entitled "The Politics of Discontent," and a key feature of that chapter is their characterization of an "angry and cynical" electorate.[34] Concluding their work, Clarke et al. refer to the Canadian political situation as one of "permanent dealignment," by which they mean a consistently fragmented and volatile relationship between citizens and parties.[35] In the context of such permanent dealignment, communitarian attachments to persons and places become strained. Despite the fact that dealignment and disaffection can be dangerous to a political community, blind deference is no better. Deference is always a thin and brittle basis for a political community and is, in the final analysis, as damaging as possessive individualism. Disaffection and the decline of deference are, therefore, in some respects positive forces and represent the kind of assertive enhancement of political efficacy and political participation that Adams refers to as "the balance of individual autonomy with a sense of collective responsibility."[36] However, in contemporary Canada, the principal ideological forces that have picked up on the mood of popular anger and cynicism offer individuated solutions, which serve to amplify people's negativity, deepening and broadening their defensive possessiveness rather than encouraging their communitarian imaginations to seek new ways in which to invigorate the body politic. Canadian multiculturalism has come under siege from a barrage of antiterrorist discourses, the rebirth of strands of xenophobia, and the increased securitization of the Canadian state.

Canadians have demonstrated that they are not bound to the traditional political parties and that they are prepared to vote for new "antiparty" parties in numbers large enough to elect them the Official Opposition in the House of Commons. The Canadian Alliance represented an American-style populism that it made hegemonic in Western Canada. The Bloc Québécois offers the only true communitarian option in Canada, one that is, of course, grounded in demands for a distinctive and independent Quebec state to reflect the aspirations of the people of Quebec. To some extent, the success of Quebec nationalism is a reflection of the poverty of any true pan-Canadian national vision, either inside French Quebec or in the rest of Canada. Current political discourse in Canada is punctuated by the claims and counterclaims of single-interest groups, to which citizens are encouraged to adhere on the basis of their narrowly defined personal and individual desires. Among the most recent crop of such groups are gun owners angry about gun control, victims of crime angry about the lack of compensation in the criminal justice system, and religious traditionalists angry at the prospect of the right of civil marriage being extended to gays and lesbians. At present there is little to unite the various single-issue groups other than a shared belief in entitlement based on a conception of the state as a repository of goods and legal precedents that are "up for grabs."

The impact of the changing composition of Canada's political culture, as well as of the work of the ideologues of possessive individualism, has been acutely felt. Despite the efforts of small Canadian nationalist groups, such as the Council of Canadians, and an assortment of individuals, including some prominent politicians and journalists, the federal state has been radically Americanized in the past few decades: NAFTA and the GST are accomplished fact; Air Canada, Canadian National Railway, and Petro-Canada, corporations designed with explicit public and nation-building purposes, have been partially or totally privatized; major regulatory agencies, such as the Canadian Radio-television and Telecommunications Commission, have lost many of their regulatory powers; federal Crown corporations, notably the CBC, have suffered enormous budget cuts; and there have been radical reductions in the size and scope of the state. The effects of these cuts have reverberated in the quality of life at the provincial level: the "social safety net" has been lowered; universal provision of social services, which nurtures a communitarian ethos, has been rapidly replaced with "means-tested" and limited provision of social services, which targets and stigmatizes the poor; public systems of health care and education are being eroded to the point where partial privatization of so-called core or essential services seems highly probable; the gap between the rich and the poor is increasing as the middle class, which carried much of the burden of redistribution in the 1980s, becomes increasingly reluctant to share.

In furtherance of these trends, the liberal-individualistic message of radical decentralization is currently being hotly promoted by Canada's richest and most influential special interest group, the Canadian Council of Chief Executives. The Canadian Council of Chief Executives and the Conservative Party are both promoting a new Canada in which principal socioeconomic and political control is devolved to the provinces and in which there is little more than some vague sentiment to hold the country together. If there is radical decentralization in the future, those ties of common citizenship that bind us will fall away, and the already weak voices for Canada will become even weaker. There is growing evidence of parochial assertiveness and a "beggar-thy-neighbour" attitude among opinion leaders in Canada's more affluent provinces, Ontario and Alberta. As the voices for a pan-Canadian vision diminish, the logic of an independent Quebec state will increase. Once Quebec has gone, the remaining nine provinces and the territories will have very little left to hold them together. As they enter further into the liberal-individualistic ethos of free trade in the North American continent, an ethos buttressed by new World Trade Organization agreements that severely restrict the scope of sovereign states in controlling capital flows, so the patent absurdity of continued independence for a culturally fractured, socioeconomically divided, and geographically split Canada will become increasingly clear. We will have rationalized Canada out of existence.

CONCLUSION

Given the ideological assault of Americanizing possessive individualism on Canada's political culture, and the efficacy of that assault in terms of major changes in public policy, what is the prognosis for Canada? The spirit of self-centred individualism and defensive exclusionism does not bode well for the continued existence of Canada. Traditional conservatives would argue that any nation that has lost its sense of organic connectedness is in poor health. When the sentence "The West wants in" became the rallying cry for the foundation of the Reform Party, it was taken to mean that the western provinces wished to partake of the benefits and burdens of full and equitable citizenship. Regrettably, the sentence has come to be associated instead with a narrowly focused acquisitiveness, opportunistic rent-seeking, and an unwillingness to share natural advantages with those persons and regions less fortunate in the country. Under such circumstances, it seems improbable that the wealthier provinces, such as British Columbia, Alberta, and Ontario, will be able to see much sense in sustaining Canada as a unified nation-state. The deficit cutting and public-sector gutting economic policies of the Liberal Party and the Conservative Party are actively promoting this kind of fragmentation. And yet there do continue to be some modest signs of Canadian distinctiveness. As mentioned earlier, public opinion research reveals Canadians in the late 1990s to be more communitarian, statist, committed to social order, and supportive of public health care than Americans.[37] Moreover, it is always possible that the decline of public provision, the growing inequality, and the increasing immiseration of the poor will so offend the communitarian impulses of our political culture that Canadians will reject further trends toward possessive individualism.[38]

On the cultural front, there seems to be little patriotism or spontaneous love of country. There are occasional glimpses, such as when Canada won two hockey gold medals in the 2002 Winter Olympics. But other than these infrequent moments, it simply appears that few people care very much. Over a century ago, the French intellectual Ernst de Renan referred to a nation as an act of will, as "a daily plebiscite." There seems to be very little active will to nurture Canada. While it is possible to be reserved in one's patriotism, our continued silence in the context of accelerated Americanization is deafening. Not only is there an atmosphere of listless apathy about the nation, but also increasing numbers of English Canadians have exhibited an unwillingness to accept even the modest and unexceptional claim of Quebec to be a "distinct society." Such an uncompromising stance would be welcomed in the radically individualistic melting-pot homogeneity of the United States, but it makes little sense in Canada. It is possible that there are sufficient numbers of French Quebecers who could be persuaded to remain in a Canada of "two solitudes" united through mutual and distanced respect. The ultimate consequence of the logic of hard-line opposition to distinct society status is to drive those moderate Quebecers into the welcoming arms of the separatists.

Canada is in jeopardy. Our neighbours to the south have consistently stated that they would welcome Canada as a part of their great country. Such a solution might make sense. Here we might recall the sarcastic and self-pitying vitriol of George Grant, who said: "Perhaps we should rejoice in the disappearance of Canada. We leave the narrow provincialism and our backwoods culture; we enter the excitement of the United States where all the great things are done."[39] Such an eventuality would be a tragic loss to a world that desperately needs the model of polyethnic and multicultural tolerance provided by Canada. Perhaps, given the newfound assertive and anti-elite rebelliousness of Canadians, we will simply reinvent the country and craft something new, authentic, and beautiful. Maybe, in this globalized, postmodern age in which Canada's greatest claim to international distinctiveness is to be a country that is so tolerant of pluralities of differences among its own citizens that it really has no substantive core, Canada will actually become the first "post-nation": an address with no fixed identity, whose very openness will be an exemplar to the remainder of the world, whose new soft tribalisms will gradually infiltrate the remainder of the planet, including America, imbuing them with Canadianism and creating the ultimate global village.

NOTES

1. The phrase comes from H.G.J. Aitken, "Defensive Expansionism: The State and Economic Growth in Canada," in W.T. Easterbrook and M.H. Watkins, eds., *Approaches to Canadian Economic History* (Toronto: McClelland and Stewart, 1967), pp. 183–221.

2. W.A. Mackintosh, "Economic Factors in Canadian History," in Easterbrook and Watkins, eds., *Approaches*, p. 15.

3. United States International Trade Commission, *All Export Commodities/All Import Commodities*, Year-To-Date 2007, available at http://dataweb.usitc.gov/scripts/REPORT.asp. Accessed October 18, 2007.

4. Statistics Canada, *The Daily*, May 9, 2007, available at http://www.statcan.ca/Daily/English/070509/d070509a.htm. Accessed October 17, 2007.

5. Gabriel Almond, "Comparative Political Systems," *World Politics* 18 (1956), pp. 391–409.

6. Ibid., p. 396.

7. Gabriel Almond and Sidney Verba, *The Civic Culture* (Boston: Little Brown, 1963).

8. See Jon Pammett and Michael Whittington, eds., *Foundations of Political Culture: Political Socialization in Canada* (Toronto: Macmillan, 1976); Richard Simeon and David Elkins, "Regional Political Cultures in Canada," *Canadian Journal of Political Science* 7 (1974), pp. 397–437; John Wilson, "The Canadian Political Cultures: Towards a Redefinition of the Nature of the Canadian Political System," *Canadian Journal of Political Science* 7 (1974), pp. 438–483; Elia Zureik and Robert Pike, eds., *Socialization and Values in Canadian Society: Political Socialization* (Toronto: Macmillan, 1975).

9. Donald Smiley, "Must Canadian Political Science Be a Miniature Replica?" *Journal of Canadian Studies* 9 (1974), pp. 31–42; C.B. Macpherson, "After Strange Gods: Canadian Political Science 1973," in T.N. Guinsberg and G.L. Reuber, eds., *Perspectives on the Social Sciences in Canada* (Toronto: University of Toronto Press, 1974), pp. 52–76; Alan Cairns, "Political Science in Canada and the Americanization Issue," *Canadian Journal of Political Science* 8 (1975), pp. 191–234.

10. Raymond Williams, *Keywords: A Vocabulary of Culture and Society* (London: Fontana, 1976), p. 76.

11. This point is elaborated by Stephen Brooks, *Canadian Democracy: An Introduction*, 3rd ed. (Toronto: Oxford University Press, 2000), p. 34, who attributes a range of economic and cultural policies to a series of deliberate "refusals in the face of Americanizing pressures."

12. Louis Hartz, *The Founding of New Societies* (New York: Harcourt, Brace and World, 1964); Kenneth McRae, "The Structure of Canadian History," in Louis Hartz, *The Founding of New Societies*, pp. 219–274; Gad Horowitz, "Conservatism, Liberalism, and Socialism in Canada: An Interpretation," *Canadian Journal of Economics and Political Science* 32 (1966), pp. 143–171.

13. Seymour Martin Lipset, *Continental Divide: The Values and Institutions of the United States and Canada* (New York: Routledge, 1990).

14. Michael Adams, *Fire and Ice: The United States and Canada and the Myth of Converging Values* (Toronto: Penguin, 2003); Matthew Mendelsohn, *Canada's Social Contract: Evidence From Public Opinion*. Discussion Paper P101. Public Involvement Network, Canadian Policy Research Networks (November 2002); Edward Grabb and James Curtis, *Regions Apart: The Four Societies of Canada and the United States* (Toronto: Oxford University Press, 2005).

15. C.B. Macpherson, *The Political Theory of Possessive Individualism* (London: Oxford University Press, 1962). The dominance of possessive individualism in the American tradition has been well established in the key political cultural contributions to American society, notably Alexis de Tocqueville, *Democracy in America* (New York: Doubleday, Anchor, 1969); Louis Hartz, *The Liberal Tradition in America* (New York: Harvest, 1955); David Riesman, *The Lonely Crowd: A Study of the Changing American Character* (New Haven: Yale University Press, 1962); Robert N. Bellah, Richard Madsen, William M. Sullivan, Ann Swidler, and Steven M. Tipton, *Habits of the Heart: Individualism and Commitment in American Life* (New York: Harper and Row, 1986); and Robert Putnam, *Bowling Alone: The Collapse and Revival of American Community* (New York: Simon and Schuster, 2000).

16. Sylvia Bashevkin, "The Politics of Canadian Nationalism," in Paul Fox and Graham White, eds., *Politics: Canada* (Toronto: McGraw-Hill, 1995), pp. 40–47.

17. Hartz, *The Founding of New Societies*, pp. 107, 111–112, 119.

18. McRae, "The Structure of Canadian History," p. 239.

19. Ibid., p. 270.

20. Horowitz, "Conservatism, Liberalism and Socialism in Canada," p. 148.

21. General interpretations of the comparatively communitarian character of Canada, proffered by McRae, Horowitz, and Lipset, are rejected by Janet Ajzenstat and Peter J. Smith, "Liberal-Republicanism: The Revisionist Picture of Canada's Founding," in idem., eds, *Canada's Origins: Liberal, Tory, or Republican?* (Ottawa: Carleton University Press, 1995), pp. 1–18. Not only do they claim that there is little Tory conservatism in the Canadian political tradition, but they go further in regarding the Upper and Lower Canadian establishments of the nineteenth century as fundamentally "liberal," and their principal rebel opponents, such as Mackenzie and Papineau, as "civic republican." While this is not the place to engage in detailed debate with Ajzenstat and Smith, I am in fundamental disagreement with their characterizations. Not only do they ignore the abundant evidence of elitist, ascriptive, affective, and particularistic practices on the part of the governing classes, but they also promote the idea that "civic republicanism" is "antiliberal." The ideology is better interpreted, by Louis Hartz among others, as "left" or radical liberalism. While it is true that Mackenzie and Papineau "scorn . . . the nineteenth-century liberal constitution" (p. 8), the basis of their opposition is not antiliberalism, but antiauthoritarianism. There is little evidence to support the claim that the nineteenth-century rebels were against the basic principles of possessive individualism. Their rallying cry was not for the abolition of capitalism but for responsible government and genuine democratic rights.

22. Lipset, *Continental Divide*, p. 8.

23. Ibid., pp. 214, 219, 225. Neil Nevitte has recently produced comparative survey data to illustrate the fact that, in the context of the advanced industrial nations, Canada and the United States are often closer to each other than to any other nations. He goes further and argues that Lipset's claims that Canadians are more deferential, law-abiding, and passive than Americans are not supported in his data. See Neil Nevitte, *The Decline of Deference* (Peterborough: Broadview Press, 1996), pp. 105–106.

24. Adams, *Fire and Ice*, pp. 39, 97, 123.

25. Grabb and Curtis, *Regions Apart*, p. 181.

26. Mendelsohn, *Canada's Social Contract*, p. 1.

27. The historical tradition of communitarianism and collectivism is mentioned in numerous sources, including Rand Dyck, *Canadian Politics: Critical Approaches* (Toronto: Nelson, 1996), p. 286; Michael Whittington and Richard Van Loon, *Canadian Government and Politics: Institutions and Processes* (Toronto: McGraw-Hill Ryerson, 1996), p. 99; and Brooks, *Canadian Democracy*, pp. 52–55.

28. George Grant, *Lament for a Nation* (Toronto: McClelland and Stewart, 1965), p. 68.

29. Peter Dobell and Byron Berry, "Anger at the System: Political Discontent in Canada," in Fox and White, *Politics: Canada*, pp. 4–9; Maclean's/Decima polling data, *Maclean's*, January 2, 1995.

30. Nevitte, *The Decline of Deference*, pp. 56, 79, 267, 291. Nevitte uses his data to interpret recent changes in the Canadian political culture as evidence of a general move toward postindustrial, postmaterialist, and postmodern values, pervasive throughout the West, and he specifically downplays the "Americanization" thesis. Nevitte's method of calculating the degree of "Americanization," outlined in footnote 2 on

page 314 of his book, is designed to assess the "cultural lag" thesis that Canadian value changes lag behind those of the United States. Nevitte takes a series of dimensions in which he measures the change in both Canadian and American values from 1981 to 1990. One of these dimensions is "confidence in government institutions." According to Nevitte's data, "confidence in government institutions" declined from 49.6 percent in 1981 to 31.8 percent in 1990 in the United States, a decline of nearly 18 percentage points. In Canada, the comparable change was from 36.9 percent in 1981 to 29.4 percent in 1990, a decline of 7.5 percentage points. Using his calculus of "cultural lag," Nevitte declares Canada to be the leader of the trend in 1990 (Table 9-2, p. 292). The fact that the U.S. figure in 1990 more closely approximates the Canadian figure in 1981 than the Canadian 1990 figure approximates the American 1981 figure—Nevitte's criterion for Canada as the cultural leader—is, in my opinion, inadequate as a measure of the degree of Americanization. It is, of course, possible to argue that the Americans are becoming more like Canadians. However, it seems equally plausible to postulate that the profound loss of confidence, tracked in the American data, has a more moderate, yet still substantial, echo effect in Canada.

31. Ibid., p. 267.

32. Harold D. Clarke, Jane Jenson, Lawrence LeDuc, and Jon H. Pammett, *Absent Mandate: Canadian Politics in an Era of Restructuring*, 3rd ed. (Vancouver: Gage, 1996).

33. Ibid., pp. 22, 61, 65, 67.

34. Ibid., pp. 176–180.

35. Ibid., p. 185.

36. Adams, *Fire and Ice*, p. 123.

37. Footnote 12. See also George Perlin, "The Constraints of Public Opinion: Diverging or Converging Paths," in Keith Banting, George Hoberg, and Richard Simeon, eds., *Degrees of Freedom: Canada and the United States in a Changing World* (Montreal and Kingston: McGill-Queen's University Press, 1997), pp. 71–149.

38. For data in support of these claims, refer to Statistics Canada, *Canada at a Glance, 2000* (available at http://www.statcan.ca), "Persons with Low Income after Tax." The percentage of Canadians with low incomes declined only marginally from 3,744,000 in 1993 (13.1%) to 3,163,000 in 2001 (10.4%). Given the economic boom of this era and the conservatism of the measure (*after*-tax income), the failure to deal with poverty is troubling. The failure was particularly pronounced among children. In 2002, 35 percent of female-headed sole-parent families had low incomes according to Statistics Canada. A United Nations report on *Child Poverty in Rich Nations* (2000) calculated the Canadian child poverty rate at 15.5 percent. More detailed—and disturbing—data on child poverty are contained on the Campaign 2000 website (http://www.campaign2000.ca), which states in its 2004 report that more than a million Canadian children continue to live in poverty and shows an increase in child poverty between 1989 and 2000. This is despite pledges made by all major Canadian political figures in the late 1980s to eradicate child poverty by 2000.

39. Grant, *Lament*, p. 8

✗ NO

Canada and the United States— Separated at Birth
MICHAEL ADAMS

Canada's history has been dominated by three great themes: building a nation and holding it together, providing a growing list of services to the Canadian people, and managing our relations with the United States.

At the time of the American Revolution, Canada was a collection of British colonies that remained under the protection of the British crown rather than join the republican experiment launched by the thirteen colonies to the south. Thanks to that revolution, we even inherited some American Tories who stood loyal to the British Empire and migrated north.

To put it in a social values context, the American colonists rejected the traditional authority of the British crown while the Canadian colonists deferred to it, or, in the case of Quebec, fashioned a pragmatic compromise between the authority the British won on the Plains of Abraham in 1759 and that of the Roman Catholic Church.

From the late eighteenth century until 1867, the northern colonies remained under British rule, although increasing numbers of colonists demanded that their governments be more responsible to them than to the colonial administrators in Britain and their agents here. Some firebrands even instigated rebellions—one in Upper Canada (Ontario) in 1837 and another in Lower Canada (Quebec) in 1837 and 1838. These were revolts against an elite of appointed officials, not revolutions against the British regime, and in neither case was there significant loss of life. Early Canadians valued a liberty based on order over a freedom derived from the chaos of mob rule, which they believed prevailed in the new republic to the south.

Whereas America was conceived in violent revolution, the Canadian colonists were counter-revolutionaries whose cautious leaders were unable to negotiate the compromises necessary for their reluctant Confederation until 1867, nearly a century after the American colonies broke from Britain. While the Canadian colonies were slowly and laboriously brokering a larger union, America was deadlocked over slavery, lurching unrelentingly toward—and ultimately embroiled in—a bloody civil war that took the lives of 620,000 soldiers representing 2 percent of the population at that time, or nearly 6 million Americans in today's terms.

In his Declaration of Independence, Thomas Jefferson dedicated his country to the ideals of life, liberty, and the pursuit of happiness. Not to be outdone in the evocative slogan department, a century later Canada's Fathers of Confederation could see no higher pursuits than peace, order, and good government.

The early experience of the two countries also differed in a way that haunts America still. The southern colonies had developed an economy based on slavery, an institution the United States retained (with increasing reluctance in a number of quarters) until the Civil War in the 1860s. The Canadian economy had little use for slaves or indentured workers on plantations for cotton or any other crop. As a result, the gradual abolition of slavery by Upper Canada's first governor, John Graves Simcoe, after 1793 and later by the British government was a non-issue for Canada, except to make this country a refuge for American slaves who were able to escape their servitude via the Underground Railroad prior to Abraham Lincoln's Emancipation Proclamation of 1863. The American Dilemma, as Swedish sociologist Gunnar Myrdal aptly termed that country's legacy of slavery in his 1944 book of that title, continues to express itself today—often tragically for the large proportion of African-Americans who live in poverty and under threat of violence even amid the affluence of the world's richest country.

The American Constitution also infamously guaranteed the right of its citizens to bear arms. The Second Amendment was once understood to be a provision granting militias the power to overthrow illegitimate governments through the use of force, but it has recently been recast as the codification of the God-given right of every man, woman, and toddler to pack heat. Canada's Constitution contained no such right, and the consequences for each country are palpable to this day. Americans kill themselves and each other with the use of firearms at ten times the rate Canadians do.

America's revolutionaries, many of whom were Deists, agnostics, or even atheists, separated Church from State. Their forebears, the Puritans, had departed Britain in search of freedom to practise their religion. In founding their own communities in the New World, the Puritans were not in turn overly generous to those with dissenting theologies: Tocqueville notes that the criminal codes of some early communities included long passages copied verbatim from Leviticus and Deuteronomy. Nevertheless, 150 years later, the U.S. Bill of Rights enshrined the principle of religious freedom for Puritans and all others, declaring in the First Amendment that "Congress shall make no law respecting an establishment of religion, or prohibiting the free exercise thereof."

The Canadian colonies, on the other hand, inherited the British tradition of direct state involvement in religion. After the British conquest of Quebec in 1759-60, the British not only allowed Roman Catholics to practise their religion, but, with the 1774 Quebec Act (designed to keep Quebecers loyal as the American colonies threatened open revolt), ceded to the Church the responsibility for the education of Catholic children. Meanwhile in Upper Canada, Governor John Graves Simcoe attempted to implement Anglicanism as the state religion, but failed in the face of religious pluralism in the colony. The British North America Act of 1867 entrenched in Canada's Constitution the Catholic Church's control over the education of Catholics in Quebec and elsewhere in the country. This provision sought to reciprocate similar rights granted to Protestants. America's constitutional separation of Church and State and its more market-driven approach to religion has contributed to much higher rates of religious belief and practice than we now see in countries like Canada and the United Kingdom.

- anti-Americanism

Another difference in the founding ideologies of the two countries was the orientation to citizenship. The American revolutionaries envisioned their country as the Biblical "City upon a Hill," a shining beacon for all who shared the Enlightenment ideals of free speech, religion, and commerce as well as progress, science, and rationality. People from all nations of the world would be welcome to cast off the chains of feudalism and migrate to the home of the brave and the land of the free. Out of many, there would be one, *E Pluribus Unum*, a proud American living in one nation, and, since the 1950s when the Pledge of Allegiance was updated, "under God." Some might argue that this ideal of unity and ultimate sameness has not been honoured from the outset, beginning with the exclusion of all but property-owning Caucasian males from the voters' list in America's first presidential election in 1789, a group that formed less than 10 percent of the population.

In spite of many gaps between the ideal and the reality that seem obvious to us today, Americans have generally honoured their self-evident truths by welcoming migrants from around the world to join their melting pot, to become unhyphenated Americans willing to join the struggle for success and to send their sons to fight and if necessary die for their new country even against their former homelands.

Canada, by contrast, had no aspiration to mould an archetypal Canadian out of its three founding nations—French, English, and Aboriginal—or subsequent waves of newcomers from every corner of the planet. Each of the founding groups found themselves in their own enclaves. In the case of the Aboriginals, relocation was often forced and to be followed by various abuses; in the case of the French in Quebec, the enclave has always enjoyed considerable sovereignty. Sociologist John Porter characterized Canada in 1965 as a Vertical Mosaic, with the descendants of the English and the Scots at the top of the socioeconomic hierarchy. According to Porter, all groups lived more or less peaceably in their communities, whatever their position in the pyramid, but had little to do with one another—a place for everyone and everyone in his or her place. In 1945 novelist Hugh MacLennan characterized English- and French-speaking Canada as Two Solitudes; this even in his native Montreal, where each comprised about half the population of what was then Canada's largest metropolis. The ethnic hierarchy of Canada today bears little resemblance to the descriptions of 1945 or even 1965, and the ideology of multiculturalism has promoted more positive attitudes toward racial and ethnic minorities north of the border than the melting pot creed has in the republic to the south.

The seeds of this compartmentalized but generally peaceful society are to be found in large part in the gradual decision by the British after their defeat of the armies of France on the Plains of Abraham in 1759 to allow 60,000 French habitants to retain their language and religion rather than attempt their assimilation into what were then very small Anglo-Saxon colonies in Canada. By the mid-nineteenth century, when the English-speaking Canadian provinces were more populous, so too, thanks to the "revenge of the cradle," was Quebec's French-speaking minority, which was able to successfully resist further calls for assimilation (most famously that of Britain's Lord Durham in 1839, who saw the absorption of the French as a solution to the "two nations" that he found "warring within the bosom of a single state"). The subsequent union of Canada East (Quebec) and Canada West (Ontario) ultimately proved unworkable. But the Confederation of those two colonies, as well as New Brunswick and Nova Scotia in 1867 and subsequently six others, has proven more lasting (although certainly not without its shaky moments).

When Quebec awoke in the 1950s from its traditional deference to the Church and Anglo-Saxon commercial hegemony, it launched a "Quiet Revolution," with the election of Jean Lesage's Liberals in 1960, to assert greater political control within its own borders. The response by the federal government was a Royal Commission on Bilingualism and Biculturalism, the latter concept soon extended to Multiculturalism when the one-third of Canadians whose ancestors had come from countries other than France and the United Kingdom demanded acknowledgement. The result was the official recognition of Canada's linguistic duality and multicultural heritage—the political birth of modern Canada—and the formal entrenchment of one of the most significant differences between Canada and the United States, one that has become more, not less, important over the past half-century. No government in the United States has ever adopted a policy of bilingualism (except the commonwealth of Puerto Rico, where English-Spanish bilingualism was imposed through military force in 1902), even though up to a third of the population in states like California, Texas, and Florida are Spanish-speaking. Nor is it conceivable that a state could negotiate separation from the other forty-nine. Canada, like the former Soviet Union, has acknowledged in its 1999 Clarity Act that a province can legally secede under certain conditions.

Federalism is the political institution that accommodates the centrifugal forces of Canada's regions, allocating responsibility for education and the delivery of social and health services to the provinces. In contrast, the parliamentary system that Canada inherited from the British has become hierarchical and quasi-authoritarian. Canadian governments rarely get a majority of the votes, but our first-past-the-post, single-member district electoral system usually gives the party with the most popular support across the country the majority of the seats, and a majority government can pretty well do what it wants: increase taxes, negotiate a free trade agreement with the United States, put in place a tax on goods and services, privatize Crown corporations, implement strong gun control legislation, legalize abortion, establish a national medicare program.

Canada now spends 45 percent of its gross domestic product on government services, which is close to the average for the countries of the European Union. The United States, by contrast, spends 35 percent—including double the amount spent by the entire European Union on defence.

Part of the reason Canada has more activist government than does the United States is our governments' ability to act decisively within their areas of jurisdiction when they have parliamentary majorities—which is most of the time. Canada's British parliamentary system gives majority governments the power to do things that are popular, but more importantly to implement policies they believe to be necessary but unpopular—policies that may cause their defeat in the next election, but that are rarely reversed by the next government. The infamous Goods and Services Tax imposed by the Conservative government in 1990 was a major factor in its defeat in 1993, but the Liberals elected on the promise to rescind the tax recanted and were rewarded with re-election in 1997 because the voters had become inured to the new tax on consumption.

The Americans, in contrast, devised a system of government designed to balance power among the executive, legislature, and the judiciary so as to limit government. In times of national crisis, the president and commander-in-chief could wage war, but for the most part the government of the United States operates by consensus and compromise. It takes an extraordinary domestic crisis like the Great Depression of the 1930s or a reform-minded surge of idealism as in the 1960s for the country and its institutions to coalesce around national programs like Social Security (income support for the elderly), the 1964 Civil Rights Act, Medicare (health care for the elderly), and Medicaid (health care for the poor). Often in America it is the judiciary that initiates significant change, as in *Brown v. Board of Education* (1954), which desegregated schools in Topeka, Kansas, and *Roe v. Wade* (1973), which guaranteed a woman's right to abortion. Much of the rest of the time, the country seems content that politics be a game played in an opaque world of behind-the-scenes tradeoffs between politicians who are constantly running for re-election and the lobby groups who fund their campaigns.

Canadian democracy is certainly vulnerable to the charge of elitism, even authoritarianism, but it is more democratic than the U.S. system if judged on the basis of predictable policy outcomes. Despots too can deliver predictable outcomes, of course, but with no democratic recourse. In Canada, majority governments can quickly adapt to reflect public opinion, or can dare to resist public opinion, making unpopular decisions in the hope that their judgments will prove wise over the long term—and that today's risky policy initiative will be the seed of tomorrow's public consensus (and hopefully "tomorrow" rolls around before the next election). If a government makes an unpopular decision that remains unpopular for long enough to bring about its electoral defeat, a subsequent government can always rescind the decision. The Canadian system of government, I would claim, does a better job of reflecting the considered judgment of the people and therefore keeping them engaged in the political process than does that of the United States.

The United States is renowned for the direct democracy that the Progressives inspired at the turn of the twentieth century and that is given expression in the myriad plebiscites and referenda we see on state-wide ballots every two years. But these forms of democracy have not proven themselves to be superior to or more democratic than representative democracy; they overly simplify political choices (forcing yes/no binaries) and are often preceded by impenetrable preambles that are so complex voters turn off and don't vote at all. Furthermore, plebiscites and referenda tend to align majorities against minorities ands invite private corporations and interest groups to spend lavishly when their self-interest is threatened. Such direct democracy looks to me more like mob rule than the considered judgment of the people that one would hope for in a democracy. American practice is a far cry from the occasional use of referenda in Canada on major constitutional issues like secession.

Canadian parties have platforms and policy positions that they usually try to implement once in office. The Mulroney Conservatives ran for re-election in 1988 on the single issue of implementing the historic free trade agreement they had negotiated with the United States. They were re-elected, albeit with only 43 percent of the popular vote, and then proceeded to carry out one of the most important policy initiatives, certainly from a symbolic point of view, in modern Canadian history. Can there be a better case for the legitimacy and effectiveness of Canada's system of representative government than the election of 1988, an election that truly represented the future to the present? By the mid-1990s, three-quarters of Canadians told pollsters they supported North American free trade that by then included Mexico.

Limited government is a cornerstone of America's political institutions and is tightly yoked to the country's founding ideology. The periods of activist government—at the turn of the twentieth century, in the 1930s, and in the 1960s and early 1970s—should be seen as aberrations. The neo-conservatism of the past two decades, beginning with Ronald Reagan's inauguration, should be viewed as a return to the norm. "New" Democrat Bill Clinton was least successful when he tried to be a liberal activist, as in the case of gays in the military or when pushing his wife's leftist notions of universal health insurance. He was at his zenith when, in league with "moderate" Republicans, he dismantled "welfare as we know it," the 1996 reform reducing American welfare rolls by one-third—a literal triage of America's poor. Americans have far less tolerance for state-sponsored dependence than do Canadians and Europeans, with the curious exception of the elderly, whose Social Security entitlement (kept cozy in its much ballyhooed "lock box") is a sacred cow that even the most right-wing conservative Republican dare not question.

Orientation to religion, government institutions, and founding ideology. These three factors fundamentally differentiate Canada and the United States, and this has long been the case. But these foundations have expressed themselves in the latter part of the twentieth century in some unanticipated ways. First let us look at the present realities that we or a French count might have anticipated 200 years ago. The United States has become the greatest nation on earth. It is the world's dominant economic and military power, and the leading innovator in the new information and biotechnologies. It is still the only nation on earth capable of mounting a concerted effort in exploring at the same time the human genome and the solar system. Its citizens have, on average, the highest standard of living on the planet, nearly half of the world's billionaires (242 out of 538 cited by *Forbes* in 2002) even after the dotcom/telecom implosion, and 60 percent of its millionaires, the largest elite ever known in history.

Certainly the growing gap in social values between our two countries during the 1990s (see Figure 1) must be at least partly attributable to America's emerging, after the collapse of the Soviet empire, as the world's only superpower, perhaps the most powerful ever to have existed on earth. This unique new status has reduced America's need to forge multilateral alliances against a powerful and threatening state adversary and encouraged the U.S. to revert to the more aggressive unilateralism it demonstrated in its conquest of the American West and in President Munroe's nineteenth-century doctrine proclaiming America's right to control affairs in the western hemisphere, a doctrine that came to seem implicitly writ large over the entire planet. Toward the close of the last century, American exceptionalism was becoming the realpolitik of globalization. Although the foreign-policy swagger that was evident during George W. Bush's first term has been checked by the chaos in Iraq (and the obvious overstretching of the U.S. military), America remains uniquely powerful both militarily and culturally. This exceptional position, I believe, will act to further differentiate the values of the United States from those of the rest of the developed world.

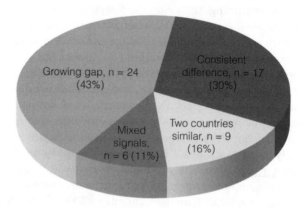

FIGURE 1

CANADA–US COMPARISON OF 56 COMPARABLE VALUES 1992–2000

Source: Environics

History is very much with us. The violence that was America is America. The moralism—good guys, bad guys, right and wrong, you're either with us or against us, establish moral superiority, wait for provocation, and then blow them away—that was America remains America. In the first decade of the twenty-first century, we have an American government that, however challenged by the consequences of its actions in Iraq and Afghanistan, retains a sense of righteous zeal that is not up for negotiation. America's allies are not its counselors; they are relegated to toeing the line, some enthusiastically, others resentfully.

Canada and the countries of Europe try to balance market forces with public policy, to reconcile the tendency for the rich to get richer and create an all but impenetrable elite with a social welfare state and policies to redistribute income from the haves to the have-nots. Such countries recognize individual rights but try to balance them with the rights of collectivities. These societies are more likely than Americans to realize that individuals can have too much freedom and that freedoms can be exercised irresponsibly by individuals to their own and others' detriment. Canadians put greater value than Americans on peace, order, and good (read activist) government. This is the aspiration of a conservative people, as opposed to the eighteenth-century liberalism that appealed to the American revolutionaries.

The diseases of an all but untrammeled individualism are, of course, not without their desirable counterpoints. America is a more dynamic society than Canada, more creative, more innovative, more exciting, and more fun. According to *The Economist* 700 of the world's 1,200 leading scientists work in the United States; these are the people we rely on to find the cure for cancer, the antidote for AIDS, and the key to Alzheimer's, and to best the long list of diseases that afflict people in every part of the planet.

Some of the sites at which Canada's difference from the U.S. is most apparent are, somewhat surprisingly, our cities. In examining the size and density of the communities in which we live, we find that a counterintuitive evolution has taken place. Canada, as any schoolchild knows, is the world's second largest country after Russia, but in terms of population contains a modest 30 million or so. The U.S. is a large country too, the world's fourth largest, but numbers roughly 300 million people.

What is astonishing is that in spite of all this vast northern space, Canadians are huddled in relatively few large urban centres, mostly a few kilometres north of the Canada–U.S. border. More than a third of Canadians live in one of three metropolitan areas: Toronto, Montreal, or Vancouver. In contrast, America's three largest metropolitan areas, New York, Los Angeles, and Chicago, represent only 16 percent of the United States population.

Canada is a more urban country than the United States. It is also more multicultural. Whereas 11 percent of Americans are foreign born, the figure for Canada is 18 percent. Moreover, a large proportion of America's foreign born are from Mexico; in Canada they are drawn from virtually everywhere on the planet, with very large populations being East and South Asian.

As in the United States, first- and second-generation immigrants tend to congregate in cities where entry-level jobs, now often in the service sector, are located and where they are more likely to find support from previous waves of immigrants from their homelands.

What is fascinating about Canada's cities is their cosmopolitan livability, their relatively low rates of crime and interracial and inter-ethnic conflict. Toronto is arguably the world's most multicultural city, but has a murder rate only slightly higher than fifty years ago when it was predominantly Anglo-Saxon. The homicide rate in Metro Toronto has increased slightly from 1.4 per 100,000 in the 1959–61 period, when its population was approximately 1.5 million, to 2.2 per 100,000 in the 1999–2001 period, when its population had grown to approximately 2.6 million. Compare this with murder rates in major U.S. cities: in 1999 rates per 100,000 in New York City, Chicago, and Los Angeles were 8.9, 22.7, and 11.6 respectively. In the U.S. capital of Washington, D.C., the rate was a whopping 46.4 per 100,000, in contrast to only 0.36–three murders–in 2001 in Canada's capital of Ottawa where, thankfully in this case, nothing much ever happens.

Canada's history of multiculturalism and the pattern of development that led to its urbanism have rendered its three great cities as models of vibrant and peaceful multicultural coexistence throughout the world.

It is interesting indeed that these two New World nations have each won the sweepstakes in two international competitions: the Americans for the highest standard of living on the planet and the Canadians for the best quality of life. The Americans have done this by being motivated by the notion of individual achievement; the Canadians by balancing individual autonomy with a sense of collective responsibility. We are each twenty-first-century expressions of the ideas of our ancestors and the institutions they built. America honours traditionally masculine qualities; Canada honours qualities that are more traditionally feminine. America honours the lone warrior fighting for truth and justice, the father who is master of his lonely house on the prairie, and a few good men planting the Stars and Stripes on a distant planet. Canada honours compromise, harmony, and equality. Americans go where no man has gone before; Canadians follow hoping to make that new place livable.

The founding ideas and institutions of each country have given rise to unanticipated consequences. I have found Americans to be more deferential to institutions than Canadians. This is counterintuitive. I have found Canadians to be less anomic, aimless, and alienated from their society than are Americans, who are nominally a more religious people. This too is counterintuitive. And, perhaps most surprising, I have found Canadians to be a more autonomous people than Americans, less outer-directed and less conformist. This too is contrary to the stereotype of Americans as a nation of individualists.

Canadians, however, have found themselves throughout their history to be in an interdependent world. After the Conquest of the French by the British army on the Plains of Abraham in 1759, it was decided by the authorities not to vanquish or assimilate the Quebec colonists but to accommodate their collective aspirations to preserve their religion, language, and culture. In the nineteenth century, when America suffered a bloody civil war over slavery, Canada experienced a few rebellions, but in the end negotiated compromises that eventually led to Confederation in 1867. Good never triumphed over evil in Canada. Rather, opposing forces, often more than two, fighting over geography, religion, language, or the spoils of power, eventually came to some sort of accommodation—usually with little loss of life, especially when compared with the U.S. Civil War and the near annihilation of Aboriginals as Americans settled the West.

Our founding ideas, our institutions, and then the experience of building our two nations have been very different: one by conquest, the other by compromise. This Canadian penchant for going halfway rather than fighting it out to see who's left standing expressed itself in the twentieth century with the recognition that Canada was not only bilingual but also multicultural. And now, with the establishment of the new northern jurisdiction of Nunavut (one of whose official languages is Inuktitut), Canada is formally recognizing multilingualism as well.

Thus, in Canada, the culture of accommodation that has been our sociohistorical tradition expresses itself today as social liberalism, multiculturalism, multilingualism, multiple faiths and spiritual paths, and sometimes even as cultural fusion or hybridization. In its most postmodern form, it can exist as an openness to flexible, multiple expressions of individual personality, the leading edges of which are the flexibility of gender, age, and cultural identities. Demography as destiny is the vestige of a bygone era.

It is fascinating to see a country evolve from such deep deference to hierarchical authority to such widespread autonomy and questioning of authority—yet in the process not descending into chaos. Canadians are no longer motivated by duty, guilt, noblesse oblige, or fear of social sanction if they do not conform to group norms. Their kinder, gentler balance of freedom and equality, and of the public and the private domains, has created a tolerant, egalitarian society that enjoys freedom from potential catastrophe, danger, and violence that many on this planet envy, including many Americans.

In my nightmares, I may see the American fire melting the Canadian ice and then dream of the waters created by the melting ice drowning the fire, but this will not happen—at least not in our lifetimes. The two cultures will continue side by side, converging their economies, technologies, and now their security and defence policies, but they will continue to diverge in ways that most people in each country, I believe, will continue to celebrate.

POSTSCRIPT

In his essay, Paul Nesbitt-Larking paints a picture that must be familiar to many. Government restraint, strident interest groups, growing public intolerance and anger—these are signs of the times. And Nesbitt-Larking argues, convincingly, that these are all manifestations of the growing Americanization of Canadian political life. Canada has always battled the threat of Americanization, and now it faces the prospect of finally losing this protracted war. Yet, it may be possible that Nesbitt-Larking exaggerates his case. Canada still has a national health care program; the United States does not. Canada still has a disciplined political process; the United States does not. And Canada still has a sense of community; the United States does not. Moreover, recent surveys—uncovered by Nesbitt-Larking—reveal that Canadians remain different from Americans in their basic attitudes.

Nesbitt-Larking can be challenged in another way. Perhaps the changes taking place are what Canadians want, and they may be considered to be beneficial. One of these changes is a weakening of the deferential attitude Canadians hold toward leaders and political elites. As Nesbitt-Larking admits, this development can be seen in a positive light. Perhaps the costs of Americanization are acceptable in view of the development of a more vibrant and democratic polity in Canada. What is happening is not really the Americanization of Canada but rather the democratization of a nation held back by vestiges of traditional conservatism.

Michael Adams nicely reminds readers of the differing origins of Canada and the U.S. and their impact on political culture. He also presents evidence that permits one to hold that the effects of these differences largely remain: government is still larger in Canada, the political process still reflects the British heritage, and Canadians still resist the attempt to build a monolithic polity built on strictly liberal beliefs. But doubts linger. Adams likens Americans to lonely warriors fighting for justice, Canadians to a peaceful people in search of compromise. Maybe in earlier years, but Canada has recently committed men and women to fighting a counterinsurgency war in Afghanistan. The peacekeeper has become literally a warrior, possibly a signal that Canadians now view political life in a different—a more American—light.

For students wishing to pursue the debate, it is first necessary to gain a general overview of Canadian political culture. For this, one would do well to read David V.J. Bell, *The Roots of Disunity: A Study of Canadian Political Culture,* 2nd ed. (Toronto: Oxford University Press, 1992) and Nelson Wiseman's more recent *In Search of Canadian Political Culture* (Vancouver: UBC Press, 2007). Shorter treatments of Canada's beliefs about politics include David V.J. Bell, "Political Culture in Canada," in Michael S. Whittington and Glen Williams, eds., *Canadian Politics in the 21st Century,* 7th ed. (Scarborough: Thomson Nelson, 2008); Stephen Brooks, "Political Culture in Canada: Issues and Directions," in James P. Bickerton and Alain-G. Gagnon, eds., *Canadian Politics,* 4th ed. (Peterborough: Broadview Press, 2004); and Neil Nevitte and Mebs Kanji, "New Cleavages, Value Diversity, and Democratic Government," in James P. Bickerton and Alain-G. Gagnon, eds., *Canadian Politics*, 4th ed. (Peterborough: Broadview Press, 2004). An examination of the American political culture is also appropriate, for which Herbert McCloskey and John Zaller's *The American Ethos: Public Attitudes toward Capitalism and Democracy* (Cambridge: Harvard University Press, 1984) would be suitable. A text that gives a more nuanced view of the possessive or competitive individualism of Americans is Richard J. Ellis, *American Political Cultures* (New York: Oxford University Press, 1993).

Students should then consult comparative studies of American and Canadian political cultures. Such studies include Gad Horowitz, *Canadian Labour in Politics* (Toronto: University of Toronto, 1968), ch. 1; Seymour Martin Lipset, *Continental Divide: The Values and Institutions of the United States and Canada* (New York: Routledge, 1990); Richard M. Merelman, *Partial Visions: Culture and Politics in Britain, Canada, and the United States* (Madison: University of Wisconsin Press, 1991); and George Perlin, "The Constraints of Public Opinion: Diverging or Converging Paths?" in Keith Banting, George Hoberg, and Richard Simeon, eds., *Degrees of Freedom: Canada and the United States in a Changing World* (Montreal and Kingston: McGill-Queen's University Press, 1997). More recent works include Michael Adams, *Fire and Ice: The United States and Canada and the Myth of Converging Values* (Toronto: Penguin, 2003) and Edward Grabb and James Curtis, *Regions Apart: The Four Societies of Canada and the United States* (Toronto: Oxford University Press, 2005). An even more recent text of some relevance is Andrew Cohen, *The Unfinished Canadian: The People We Are* (Toronto: McClelland and Stewart, 2007), which contains a critique of Adams's thesis on the differences separating Canadians and Americans. *available online*

A large part of the debate revolves around changes in the political culture of Canada. For an important work on this subject, students should read Neil Nevitte, *The Decline of Deference* (Peterborough: Broadview Press, 1996) as well as Neil Nevitte, ed., *Value Change and Governance in Canada* (Toronto: University of Toronto Press, 2002). As for manifestations of these changes in the operation of the Canadian political system, the following texts and readings are important: Harold Clarke et al., *Absent Mandate: Canadian Electoral Politics in the Era of Restructuring*, 3rd ed. (Toronto: Gage, 1996); Alan Cairns, *Charter Versus Federalism: The Dilemmas of Constitutional Reform* (Montreal and Kingston: McGill-Queen's University Press, 1992); Reg Whitaker, "Canadian Politics at the End of the Millennium: Old Dreams, New Nightmares," in David Taras and Beverly Rasporich, eds., *A Passion for Identity*, 3rd ed. (Scarborough: Nelson Canada, 1997); and Hamish Telford and Harvey Lazar, eds., *Canada: The State of the Federation 2001: Canadian Political Culture(s) in Transition* (Montreal and Kingston: McGill-Queen's University Press, 2002).

Can Native Sovereignty Coexist with Canadian Sovereignty?

✔ **YES**
ROGER TOWNSHEND, "The Case for Native Sovereignty"

✗ **NO**
THOMAS FLANAGAN, "Native Sovereignty: Does Anyone Really Want an Aboriginal Archipelago?"

In Canada, the subject of Aboriginal rights has never been high on the political agenda. Most Canadians have a vague awareness of the deplorable living conditions on many Indian reserves, but that is about all. The demands of Native people for land, greater autonomy, and even self-government have received little notice. More "immediate" issues such as constitutional reform, Quebec separatism, western alienation, or free trade with the United States have usually pushed Native issues off the list of urgent public issues.

However, the dramatic events surrounding the Oka crisis of 1990 did more to change public perceptions of Native issues than any other single event. Reacting to municipal plans to expand a local golf course onto traditional Native lands, armed Mohawk Warriors began erecting barricades in an effort to stop the work. The protest soon escalated into a full-scale confrontation between the Quebec provincial police and Mohawk Warriors, in which one police officer was killed. Soon a second set of barriers was erected on the Kahnawake reserve near Montreal as a demonstration of support. As the situation appeared to become more violent, Quebec Premier Robert Bourassa called in the Canadian armed forces to restore order to Oka. For the first time in twenty years, Canadian troops were deployed against fellow citizens.

For federal and Quebec officials, the issue was straightforward. The Mohawks, in using arms and barricades to press their case, had broken the law and needed to be brought to justice like any other citizens who had committed illegal acts. Land claims and other grievances would be settled only when arms were surrendered and the lawbreakers brought to justice. But the Mohawks rejected this view. It was not just the matter of land claims that was at stake. It was, the Warriors claimed, a question of sovereignty. The Mohawks occupied sovereign territory that had never been surrendered to any British or Canadian government. Thus, the Mohawks had every right, as any other sovereign nation, to take up arms to defend themselves. It was the police and army who were acting illegally.

At the heart of Native grievances is the *Indian Act*, 1867, which set the tone for successive federal government dealings with Native people. Under this act, elected Indian band councils, not traditional political institutions, deal with the Department of Indian Affairs and Northern Development. Band councils are granted limited powers, but all financial decisions are ultimately subject to the approval of the minister responsible for Indian Affairs. Thus, sovereignty remains undivided and concentrated in the hands of Ottawa. Band councils are like fledgling municipal governments, able to exercise only those powers specifically delegated to them.

Native leaders have long argued that this relationship is humiliating and paternalistic. The real aim of the *Indian Act*, they argue, has been to use the band councils as an instrument for destroying traditional Native institutions and for assimilating and integrating Native people into the larger Canadian society. For moderate Native leaders, the solution has been to negotiate some greater delegation of powers to the band councils. But for a growing number of Native leaders this is not enough. Only when the full sovereignty of Indian nations is recognized will Native people be able to overcome their degrading colonial status.

In the wake of the Oka crisis, Native issues were suddenly given a more prominent place on the Canadian political agenda. The government of Brian Mulroney appointed a royal commission on Aboriginal questions and gave Native leaders an increasingly prominent role in discussions leading up to the constitutional proposals of 1992. The Charlottetown Accord appeared to address many Native concerns. The accord included a recognition of the inherent right of Aboriginal people to self-government and the commitment to make these Aboriginal governments one of three orders of government along with Ottawa and the provinces. Federal and provincial governments would have committed themselves to negotiating self-government agreements with those Native bands that wished to do so, while a series of future First Ministers' Conferences were promised to give ongoing consideration to Aboriginal constitutional issues.

However, many remained skeptical of the accord. Non-Native critics wondered what a third order of government meant. What form would Native self-government take? How would it mesh with the notion of a sovereign Canada? At the same time, many Native people felt that the accord had not gone far enough. After all, the accord stated that Aboriginal laws could not be inconsistent with those Canadian laws that are deemed essential to the preservation of peace, order, and good government. This was hardly a recognition of Native sovereignty.

With the defeat of the referendum, many of the questions surrounding the issue of Native sovereignty were left unresolved. In October 1996, the Royal Commission on Aboriginal Peoples published its five-volume report. Although the commission made more than four hundred specific proposals, the report has quietly passed from public attention. This complacency was due in part to the lukewarm response of the Liberal government, which stated that the estimated

$30-billion cost of implementing the report's recommendations was too great to accommodate in the present economic circumstances. Instead, the Liberal government introduced the First Nations Governance Act, which the government stated was designed to ensure financial and political accountability and to "modernize" the old *Indian Act*. Many Native groups opposed the pending legislation, arguing that, rather than being a step forward, the legislation would in fact turn Aboriginal communities into the equivalent of municipalities and open the door to the expansion of provincial powers in Native affairs. When Parliament was prorogued in December 2003, the First Nations Governance Act was allowed to die on the order paper and has not since been reintroduced.

In the following essays, two specialists in Native issues debate the meaning of Native sovereignty and its relationship to the concepts of a sovereign Canada. Roger Townshend, a lawyer who has done extensive work on Native land claims and Aboriginal constitutional issues, sets out the case for Native sovereignty. Thomas Flanagan of the University of Calgary argues that the demand for Native sovereignty as it is posed by Native leaders is incompatible with the continued existence of Canada.

✔ **YES**
The Case for Native Sovereignty
ROGER TOWNSHEND

There is a great divide in perceptions between Aboriginal people in Canada and non-Aboriginal people. The average non-Aboriginal Canadian takes as self-evident the legitimacy of the Canadian state and its jurisdiction over Canadian territory. The average Aboriginal person, on the other hand, views much of the power exercised by the Canadian state as illegitimate, oppressive, and infringing on Aboriginal governance powers. To the extent that non-Aboriginal Canadians are aware of this perception among Aboriginal people, they are likely bewildered by it and have trouble seeing either a reasonable basis for it or any practical ways in which such a view could be acted on. Yet it is precisely this divergence of views that has caused and will continue to cause confrontations in the political arena, such as those regarding constitutional amendments, and confrontations on the ground, such as at Kanesatake (Oka), Ipperwash, and Caledonia.

Although non-Aboriginal Canadians rarely question the legitimacy of the Canadian state, most thoughtful people would likely be distressed at how flimsy the logical justification for Canadian sovereignty indeed is. There is no question that, prior to European contact, Aboriginal nations in North America had stable cultures, economies, and political systems, and that many (if not all) of these were of amazing sophistication in adaptation to their environment. What is sometimes not recognized is that different Aboriginal nations had cultures and economies that were vastly different from one another. They still are.[1] However, European peoples were often blinded by preconceived notions of Aboriginal culture and mistook difference from European lifestyles for inferiority. Some Euro-Canadians still do. But to view as inferior cultures that, for example, had the technology and organization to hunt whales on the open ocean, build large permanent houses, or create sophisticated political confederacies is surely untenable.[2]

Pre-contact Aboriginal nations unmistakably exercised full control or "sovereignty" over their traditional lands, although in somewhat different ways than did European nations. It would be arrogant and ethnocentric to recognize only a European model of political organization as capable of possessing sovereignty. It would also be deeply ironic, since European political theorists took a significant interest in the Haudenosaunee (Iroquois) confederacy and its structure influenced the drafters of the U.S. Constitution (the latter was acknowledged by the U.S. Senate in 1987).[3]

In their initial contact with Aboriginal nations, Europeans generally treated them as allies or as enemies, but in any event, as nations to be treated as equals with European states. How then did this change? International law then and now recognized changes in sovereignty based on conquest, discovery and settlement, or treaty. There is nothing in Canadian history that could qualify as a conquest in the international law sense. Treaties with Aboriginal nations fall into two rough categories. There are "peace and friendship" treaties, which, if anything, reinforce the concept of the equal nationhood of Aboriginal nations. There are also treaties that read as land transactions, which by their silence concerning matters of jurisdiction would seem to provide little help in rooting a claim that they are a source of Canadian sovereignty. Furthermore, there are vast areas of Canada where there are no historic treaties whatsoever. Thus, the invocation of treaties is wholly unsatisfactory as a foundation of Canadian sovereignty. What is left is the doctrine of discovery and settlement. The difficulty with this is that it was intended to apply only to lands that were vacant. Its initial application to a claim of European jurisdiction required the step of considering the Aboriginal people as legal nonpersons. In fact, the "discovery" of the Americas sparked lengthy theological and judicial debates in Europe about whether indigenous people indeed were or should be treated as humans. Thus, the only justification for Canadian sovereignty (inherited from British sovereignty) that has an air of reality to it requires, as a precondition, a judgment that Aboriginal people are not really human for legal purposes. This is surely repugnant to thinking Canadians.[4]

Despite the logical flimsiness of its assertion of sovereignty, the British (and later the Canadian) state, after an initial period of nation-to-nation dealings, has treated Aboriginal people as subjects and indeed as less than equal subjects. Since the onset of European settlement, Canadian "Indian" policy has been aimed at assimilating Aboriginal people into Canadian society. This integration was to be achieved on an individual level and preferably by entry into the working-class level of society. Efforts of Aboriginal people to interact as a group with Canadian society or to integrate at a non-working-class level of Canadian society met with suppression. For example, for many years an Aboriginal person who graduated from university automatically ceased to be an "Indian" in the eyes of the federal government. The policy of assimilation came to a head in 1969 with the notorious White Paper, which called for the termination of "Indian" status. This document was resoundingly rejected by Aboriginal people and in fact became the catalyst for the creation of Canada-wide Aboriginal political organizations. This policy of assimilation has been a complete and utter failure. The political resistance of Aboriginal peoples to assimilation into Canadian society has never been stronger. Most Aboriginal people, in a fundamental way, view the Canadian government as a foreign government and not one that is "theirs." This should hardly be shocking, since it was only in 1948 that the Inuit gained the right to vote in federal elections and in 1960 that status Indians living on reserves were given this right. Neither have Aboriginal communities lost their social, cultural, and economic distinctiveness. The Canadian government has tried long and hard to change this, but it has failed. Its attempts have only created much human misery. The residential school system, where Aboriginal children were separated from their families, forbidden to speak their language or practice their religion and culture, and were physically, psychologically, and sometimes even sexually abused, is one of those attempts. Another attempt was the criminalizing of traditional Aboriginal religious ceremonies. Also, the Aboriginal traditional economy has in many parts of the country been seriously impaired both by the environmental effects of development activities and directly by legislation restricting hunting rights. Yet the attachment of Aboriginal people to the land remains unbroken.[5]

So what options are open? The dismal social conditions in which many Aboriginal people in Canada live are the result of failed assimilationist policies of the Canadian government. Most Aboriginal people firmly believe that the political key to a better future is the recognition of jurisdiction of Aboriginal governments. This must be a jurisdiction that goes well beyond a municipal-government type of jurisdiction, which would allow and encourage the development of new types of structures that would reflect the distinct cultural, political, economic, and spiritual aspects of Aboriginal society. This must be a jurisdiction that is provided with sufficient resources to be viable. It would indeed mean a fundamental restructuring of the institutions of the Canadian state or, perhaps more accurately, a rolling back of the jurisdiction of the Canadian state to allow Aboriginal institutions to flourish. It is this approach that could allow for a just and peaceful coexistence of Aboriginal peoples in the Canadian state.

The defeat of the proposed constitutional amendments in 1992 was a missed opportunity to begin to pursue this path. These amendments were rejected by the majority of both non-Aboriginal and Aboriginal people. However, it must be realized that they were rejected for very different reasons. The rejection of the Charlottetown Accord by non-Aboriginal people seems to have little to do with the Aboriginal proposals in the accord. To the extent that these were a factor, non-Aboriginal Canadians were probably disposed to view them as giving too much to Aboriginal peoples. Most Aboriginal people, on the other hand, rejected the accord because it was too small a step in the direction they wanted to go.

It is puzzling that the idea of Aboriginal sovereignty should be so threatening to non-Aboriginal people. The very nature of the Canadian political system involves a division of powers between federal and provincial governments. It is but an easy step in theory to implement another order of government and provide for an appropriate division of powers. This would not be a challenge to the very essence of Canada, since the sharing of jurisdictional powers between different government institutions is already part of the essence of the Canadian state. Canadian sovereignty is also leaking at the other end with increasing globalization and trade agreements. It becomes confusing, then, why Canada should be unwilling to share jurisdiction with Aboriginal governments if it is indeed willing to modify its sovereignty with relation to the provinces and also at the international level. Nor would the idea of Aboriginal sovereignty within a federal state be an uncharted course. In the United States, a country hardly known for being progressive, it is an established legal doctrine that Indian tribes are "domestic dependent nations." The implementation of this concept extends to separate tribal justice and court systems.

Many non-Aboriginal Canadians may be troubled by the idea of Aboriginal sovereignty, since they feel that Aboriginal people should be able to achieve their social and economic goals by participation as individuals within Canadian society. This misses the entire point of Aboriginal difference. Most Aboriginal cultures have a distinctive and tangible collective nature that goes well beyond the sum of the individuals that constitute them and that would be destroyed by assimilation on an individual basis. The failure of many non-Aboriginal Canadians to appreciate this reflects only that liberal individualism is such a pervasive ideology in Canadian society that it is barely recognizable as an ideology at all and often viewed as ultimate truth. This appears to be the position taken by Thomas Flanagan in the opposing article. He uses "liberal democracy" as a touchstone. The definition of "liberal democracy" has contentious points, but the sense in which Flanagan appears to be using it, and in which I am using it for the purpose of this article, is a political system in which individual rights are considered paramount and equality is measured as formal equality of agency (that is, as the lack of state restraint on an individual's actions) rather than measured by whether the result of political and economic forces leads to substantively equal results. The economic aspect of a "liberal democracy" in this sense is an unrestrained free market, which by this definition is the pinnacle of economic equality, despite resulting in extremes of wealth and poverty.

By definition, a group with a culture that differs in significant points from liberal individualism cannot be accommodated within a purely individualistic framework, particularly when any integration with a larger society can take place only on an individual basis. It is true that a society that permits or encourages interaction on a collective basis is not a "liberal democracy" in the sense explained above. In this sense, many Canadians are not "liberal democrats" and few nations are "liberal democracies."[6]

The point is, a "liberal democracy" is not an acceptable political structure for most Aboriginal people. Fortunately (in my view), Canada has never been a "liberal democracy" in a strong sense. As Flanagan notes, French–English duality and ethnic diversity (both of which include collective aspects) challenge the basis of "liberal democracy." For that matter, whether or not "liberal democracy" is a meaningful term is questionable, since the concepts of liberalism and democracy can come into sharp conflict (for example, when a majority wishes to suppress rights of a minority).

Others may view the kind of structural diversity advocated in this article to be impractical. As Flanagan admits, it is not unprecedented—he cites the Ottoman Empire as an example. There are also analogies less unfamiliar to Canadians—the position of Indian tribes in the U.S. system is one.

The practicality of political structures that could accommodate Aboriginal diversity was studied extensively by the Royal Commission on Aboriginal Peoples. The commission operated from 1991 to 1996, collected thousands of briefs, generated tens of thousands of pages of transcripts of hearings, and commissioned an extremely comprehensive set of research papers. The commissioners included a retired Supreme Court judge and a Quebec Superior Court judge. The report of the commission is more than 3,200 pages long. The underlying research papers are many times that long.

The commission recommended sweeping changes to relations with Aboriginal peoples. The report sets out the following:[7]

- First, Aboriginal nations have to be reconstituted.

- Second, a process must be established for the assumption of powers by Aboriginal nations.

- Third, there must be a fundamental reallocation of lands and resources.

- Fourth, Aboriginal people need education and crucial skills for governance and economic self-reliance.

- Finally, economic development must be addressed if the poverty and despondency of lives defined by unemployment and welfare are to change.

The commission emphatically saw the needs for political restructuring and social initiatives as mutually dependent—neither could succeed without the other. The commission also went into great detail about processes and structures. For example, it saw the right of self-determination as vested in Aboriginal nations, not individual local communities (e.g., First Nations). The commission made detailed recommendations about how such nations could be encouraged to reconstitute, for example, as aggregations of local communities. It also suggested a number of options for the integration into this structure of off-reserve and urban Aboriginal people. This vision of fairly sizable Aboriginal nations having the right of self-determination responds to concerns about the practicality of hundreds of First Nations or similar communities, some very small, having powers similar to those of provinces. With the issuance of the commission's report, it should no longer be enough for those opposing Aboriginal self-determination to simply object that hundreds of small Aboriginal communities could not possibly be able to be self-governing, except perhaps in the municipal sense. To be made fairly, any such objections need to engage with the many and detailed recommendations of the commission about how to make Aboriginal self-determination work.

The alternatives to recognizing Aboriginal jurisdiction must be examined realistically. The commission also looked at this question in considerable detail and concluded that the economic cost of doing nothing exceeded, in the long term, the cost of implementing its recommendations.[8] Flanagan's alternative is to do more consistently what the Canadian government has been trying to do for a century. This has failed utterly and has created much suffering and resentment in the process. What is there to lose in trying something different? Demands for the recognition of Aboriginal jurisdiction are not going to go away. If "legitimate" avenues for advancing these demands are shut down, other means may be sought. The continued peace and security of Canada may well depend on accommodating Aboriginal jurisdiction.

Respect for the cultural distinctiveness of Aboriginal people requires the recognition of institutional forms of Aboriginal governments, with sufficient resources to exercise jurisdiction meaningfully. The sad history of the treatment of Aboriginal people by the Canadian state also cries out for redress in the form of recognition of Aboriginal sovereignty. Such recognition should not be viewed as completely impractical or as entailing the very destruction of the Canadian state.

NOTES

1. See, for example, the descriptions of five distinct pre-contact Aboriginal cultures in *Report of the Royal Commission on Aboriginal Peoples* ("*RCAP*") 1 (Ottawa: Minister of Supply and Services, 1996), pp. 46–90.

2. For whaling practices, see, for example, G. Monks, A. McMillan, and D. St Claire, "Nuu-chah-nulth whaling: Archaeological insights into antiquity, species preferences, and cultural importance," *Arctic Anthropology*, 2001. Aboriginal nations on the Pacific coast built large permanent houses (*RCAP* 1, p. 73). The Haudenosaunee (Iroquois) had a sophisticated political confederacy (*RCAP* 1, pp. 52–61). Thomas Flanagan, in the article opposite, characterizes pre-contact Aboriginal cultures as "Neolithic" hunting–gathering societies, incapable of possessing sovereignty. "Neolithic," if understood in the technical anthropological sense of agricultural peoples settled in large villages with domesticated plants and animals, fairly accurately describes the economies of some pre-contact Aboriginal cultures. "Hunting–gathering" (if interpreted to include fishing) describes the economies of some others. However, "Neolithic hunting–gathering society" is a contradiction in terms. See, for example, P. Driben and H. Herstein, *Portrait of Humankind: An Introduction to Human Biology and Prehistoric Cultures* (Boston: Pearson Custom Publishing, 2002), pp. 347–351. Further, Flanagan appears to be using anthropological vocabulary in a value-laden way to disparage Aboriginal cultures and has ignored the fundamental rejection by anthropology of any kind of ethnocentrism, including conceptual ethnocentrism (Driben and Herstein, p. 359).

3. See *RCAP* 1, p. 53 and related endnotes, and Dale Turner, *This Is Not a Peace Pipe: Towards a Critical Indigenous Philosophy* (Toronto: University of Toronto Press, 2006), p. 34.

4. For more detail on the international law aspects of this, see, for example, O. Dickason, "Concepts of Sovereignty at the Time of First Contact," in Dickason and Green, eds., *The Law of Nations and the New World* (Edmonton: University of Alberta Press, 1989). See also a brief summary in *RCAP* 1, pp. 43–46.

5. For more examples of the failure of the policy of assimilation and Aboriginal resistance to it, see, for example, Diane Engelstad and John Bird, eds., *Nation to Nation: Aboriginal Sovereignty and the Future of Canada* (Concord: House of Anansi Press, 1992), and the revised edition by John Bird, Lorraine Land, and Murray MacAdam, eds. (Toronto: Public Justice Resource Centre and Irwin Publishing, 2002).

6. The U.S. would amount to a liberal democracy in this sense, although "liberal democrat" in U.S. political parlance means something completely different.

7. *RCAP* 5, pp. 2–3.

8. *RCAP* 5, pp. 23–89.

✗ **NO**

Native Sovereignty: Does Anyone Really Want an Aboriginal Archipelago?

THOMAS FLANAGAN

"...words are wise men's counters, they do but reckon by them: but they are the money of fools...."

–Thomas Hobbes, *Leviathan* (1651), I, 4

In the spirit of Hobbes, we should be clear on what we are talking about before we try to debate Native sovereignty. I have elsewhere defined *sovereignty* as "the authority to override all other authorities." More specifically, it is

... a bundle of powers associated with the highest authority of government. One is the power to enforce rules of conduct.... Another is the power to make law, [also the power of] raising revenue, maintaining armed forces, minting currency, and providing other services to society. In the British tradition, sovereignty also implies an underlying ownership of all land.... Finally, sovereignty always means the power to deal with the sovereigns of other communities as well as the right to exercise domestic rule free from interference by other sovereigns.[1]

That is the abstract meaning of *sovereignty* in the vocabulary of political science. In this sense, it is a conceptual property of the states that make up the international state system. Almost all of the entities that possess sovereignty are members of the United Nations (192 members in 2007).

In this frame of reference, sovereignty can pertain only to states. It makes no sense to speak of sovereignty unless there is, as in the classical definition of the state, an organized structure of government ruling over a population within defined territorial boundaries. Native societies in what is now Canada did not possess sovereignty before the coming of the Europeans; neither the concept nor the underlying institutions were part of the Neolithic cultures of their hunting–gathering societies. Of course, hunting–gathering societies have political processes that assign rank and dominance within communities and involve conflict between communities, but the political processes of stateless societies are not the same thing as statehood and sovereignty.

As a way of increasing their political leverage in contemporary Canada, Native political leaders have adopted the classical language of statehood to describe their communities. What used to be called bands or tribes are now called "nations," and these nations are said to have possessed sovereignty from the beginning and to possess it still.[2] This strategic use of language has served Native leaders well in their struggle for greater power within the Canadian polity, but politically effective assertions should not be confused with intellectually persuasive analysis.

When Native leaders in Canada now claim to possess sovereignty, they typically mean one of two things, each of which is related to a particular political situation. In what follows, I will argue that both of these meanings are incompatible with the continued existence of Canada and the maintenance of essential Canadian political traditions. It is not that words alone can destroy Canada; words in themselves do not accomplish anything. But words such as *Native sovereignty* are the verbal symbols of political projects that cannot be reconciled with Canadian institutions.

1. Some Native leaders, for example those from the Mohawk communities of Kahnawake and Kanesatake in Quebec, speak of sovereignty in the robust sense described above, that is, the international sense. They hold that the Mohawks on their territory constitute a sovereign, independent state not part of Canada or the United States. This sovereign state should be admitted to the United Nations and in other respects become part of the international community. A Mohawk elder told the Royal Commission on Aboriginal Peoples in March 1993, "You have no right to legislate any laws over our people whatsoever. Our lands are not yours to be assumed. You are my tenant, whether you like it or not."[3] Many times since then, some (not all) Mohawks have acted as if Canadian law did not apply to them, as in the occupation, beginning in 2006, of a construction project in Caledonia, Ontario.[4]

   While I respect the honesty of this position, I do not take it seriously as a political proposition. In the ten provinces, Canada has over six hundred Indian bands living on more than 2,200 reserves, plus hundreds of thousands of Métis and non-status Indians who do not possess reserves. These scattered pieces of land and disparate peoples are not going to be recognized as independent sovereign states, now or ever. They are simply not viable as sovereign states paying their own way and defending their interests in the international community. Nor is there any practical way to weld them into a single sovereign state. Native peoples are deeply divided by language, religion, customs, and history and in no way constitute a single people. They are not seeking emancipation from the tutelage of Indian Affairs in order to lose their identity in some supra-tribal bureaucracy.

2. The concept of sovereignty, as originally formulated by the philosophers Jean Bodin and Thomas Hobbes, was thought to be a set of powers located in a single seat of authority—perhaps the monarch, perhaps the parliament, but in any case one sovereign. However, sovereignty can also be divided. Indeed, the classical definition of *federalism* implies a system of divided

sovereignty, in which two levels of government each have shares of sovereign power guaranteed in a constitution that cannot be changed unilaterally by either level of government acting alone. In such a context, it is at least verbally meaningful to speak of giving Native peoples a constitutionally entrenched share of sovereign authority.

This is more or less the political theory contained in the failed Charlottetown Accord. According to that document, "[t]he Constitution should be amended to recognize that the aboriginal peoples of Canada have the inherent right of self-government within Canada," and Aboriginal self-governments should be recognized as "one of the three orders of government in Canada."[5] Although the terms *federalism* and *sovereignty* were not used, the most straightforward way to interpret the scheme proposed by the Charlottetown Accord was as an extension of divided sovereignty in a federal system from two to three levels. Although none of the details were worked out, the accord would have endowed Aboriginal self-governments with many of the attributes of provinces: an entrenched constitutional basis of authority, participation in constitutional amendment procedures, representation in the Senate, a role in fiscal federalism, broad legislative jurisdiction, and so on.

Even though the Charlottetown Accord was defeated in a 1992 referendum and never adopted, its proposal for a limited form of Aboriginal sovereignty cannot be dismissed on a priori grounds. There is no self-evident reason that federalism must be based on only two levels of government. Why not a "third order"? There are in fact many reasons why not, but they are more practical than conceptual.

As mentioned above, there are in Canada over 700,000 status Indians belonging to more than six hundred bands on more than 2,200 reserves scattered across all provinces. No one has proposed a workable mechanism by which this far-flung archipelago could be knit together into a single level of government. On the contrary, it was widely assumed in the debate on the Charlottetown Accord that the focus of self-government would be the band, or perhaps small clusters of closely related bands organized into tribal councils. Indeed, one of the widely touted advantages of the third order of government is its alleged flexibility, which would allow different bands or groups of bands to have their own institutions of government, criminal justice systems, schools, and so on.

But surely realism must intervene at some point. We are talking about six hundred bands with an average population of little more than a thousand, many located on small, remote pieces of land without significant job opportunities, natural resources, or economic prospects. There would be virtually no revenue base, let alone a pool of human skills necessary to operate modern public services. How are such small, isolated, and impoverished groups of people supposed to support and operate an untried system of government incorporating a degree of complexity not seen since the Holy Roman Empire of the Middle Ages?

This is only the initial objection. Hard as it would be to harmonize 2,200 reserves into a workable third order of government in a multi-tiered federal system, the problem is actually much more difficult than that. At any given time, about half of Canada's status Indians live off reserve. They reside almost everywhere in the rest of Canada, from remote wilderness areas to the city centres of Vancouver, Toronto, and Montreal. In addition to status Indians, there are several hundred thousand (the true number is impossible to ascertain) Métis and non-status Indians, that is, people of partly Indian ancestry who are not registered under the *Indian Act* but have some degree of identity as Native people. A small number of Métis live in territorial enclaves (the Métis settlements of northern Alberta), but most are mixed in with the general population of Canada. Again, there is every conceivable kind of social situation. There are Métis hunters, trappers, and fishermen in the northern forests; Métis farmers on the Prairies; and Métis business owners, professionals, and workers in Winnipeg and other major cities.

How could one create a third order of government embracing all Aboriginal people, as the Charlottetown Accord purported to do, when most of these people do not live in defined territories? Since no one, thank God, was talking of forcibly relocating populations to create separate territories, the only other approach would be to create a racially defined system of government for Aboriginal people no matter where they live.

There is a historical model for such a system, namely the Ottoman Empire that ruled the Middle East and southeastern Europe from the fifteenth century until it was dismembered after the First World War. Throughout this immense territory, members of numerous Christian churches (Maronite, Coptic, Chaldean, Greek Orthodox, Armenian Orthodox, etc.) lived alongside the adherents of several Islamic sects (Sunni, Shi'ite, Druze, etc.). There were also important Jewish populations in most parts of the empire. Ethno-religious communities were allowed a substantial degree of autonomy, including not only religious freedom but also their own systems of private law, regulating matters such as marriage, family, and inheritance within their separate communities.

It was in some ways an admirable system, ruling a colourful, polyglot population for five centuries—no mean achievement in itself. But I doubt it is a model Canadians want to imitate, for it was in no sense liberal or democratic. There were no elections or other institutions of representative government. The sultan was theoretically an autocrat, but in fact rule was carried out by the imperial bureaucracy. The empire existed to collect taxes, keep internal order, and wage war against the neighbouring Persian, Russian, and Austro-Hungarian empires.

Like all liberal democracies, Canada is based on an entirely different set of political principles, most notably the twin concepts of the rule of law and equality under the law. The legal equality of all citizens is what makes democracy possible. As John Stuart Mill argued cogently in his *Considerations on Representative Government*, people cannot participate peacefully and cooperatively in one political system unless they feel themselves part of a single community: "Free institutions are next to impossible in a country made up of different nationalities."[6] A territorial definition of the polity is essential to the existence of liberal democracy. Political and civil rights must be contingent on residence within a specific territory, not membership in a specific race or ethnic group.

Admittedly, Canada as a liberal democracy is challenged by the linguistic cleavage between English and French as well as the ethnic diversity of our Aboriginal and immigrant populations. But, at least prior to the Charlottetown Accord, the solutions toward which we groped were always liberal democratic ones based on legal equality within defined territorial jurisdictions. The French fact in Canada was recognized by creating the province of Quebec, which, although it happens to have a French majority, is a province similar in principle to all the others. The same is true of the largely Inuit province of Nunavut. It is a territory within which an Inuit majority controls a liberal democratic system of government, not an Inuit ethnic polity.

The Aboriginal self-government provisions of the Charlottetown Accord would have changed this by authorizing an ethnically defined third order of government to sprawl across existing territorial jurisdictions. It was a departure from, not an extension of, our federal system of liberal democracy. It is so incompatible with our system that it probably would not have worked at all. But to the extent that it had any effect, it would have encouraged the segmentation of Native people. Wherever there were appreciable numbers of Indians and Métis in our cities, they would have been encouraged to develop their own schools, welfare agencies, justice systems, elective assemblies, and other paraphernalia of government. Instead of being encouraged to take advantage of the opportunities of Canada's urban society and economy, as so many immigrants from the Third World are now doing, Native people would have been led to withdraw further into a world of imaginary political power and all too real dependence on transfer payments.

Finally, even if they could have been made to work in their own terms, the Aboriginal self-government provisions of the Charlottetown Accord would have set up unacceptable pressures to create segmented arrangements for other groups. In addition to setting up the third order of government across the country, the accord provided for unique Aboriginal participation in national political institutions: Aboriginal senators, possibly with a "double majority" veto over legislation on Aboriginal matters[7]; Aboriginal members of the House of Commons;[8] and Aboriginal nominations to the Supreme Court, as well as a special advisory role for an Aboriginal Council of Elders.[9] It would not have been long before other groups demanded similar treatment: women's organizations, visible minorities, the disabled, gays and lesbians, and so on. Indeed, demands of this type were heard during the referendum on the accord. Reservation of Senate seats for women was a major issue in certain provinces, notably British Columbia; and Joe Clark promised to revisit the situation of the disabled once the accord was passed. Even if Canada's liberal democracy could have survived the distinct society for Quebec and the third order of government for Aboriginals, it could not survive if every identifiable group set out to entrench its political power in the Constitution. It would be the end of equality before the law, and ultimately of liberal democracy itself.

Up to this point, the tone of my essay has been unavoidably negative, because I was asked to argue the negative side in a debate about Native sovereignty. Let me take the opportunity in closing to state my views in a more positive way.

Status Indians in Canada have certainly failed to thrive under the regime of the *Indian Act* and the Department of Indian Affairs. Bureaucratic socialism has been a failure wherever it has been tried, whether in Eastern Europe or North America. In my view, Indian bands should receive full ownership of their reserves, with the right to subdivide, mortgage, sell, and otherwise dispose of their assets, including buildings, lands, and natural resources. This more efficient regime of property rights would accelerate the trend to Aboriginal entrepreneurship that is already evident on some reserves. Politically, reserves should assume the self-government responsibilities of small towns or rural municipalities. What happens afterward should be up to them. This kind of devolution of power is already possible under federal legislation; it has taken place in a few cases, such as the Sechelt band of British Columbia, and is being negotiated by other bands across the country. It does not require an elaborate metaphysics of sovereignty.

However, a large and ever-increasing majority of Native people do not live on reserves and never will, except for occasional visits. For this majority, neither self-government nor sovereignty can have any meaning except to the extent that they, as Canadian citizens, participate in the government of Canada. For them, the political illusion of self-government is a cruel deception, leading them out of, rather than into, the mainstream of Canadian life. Their future depends on fuller participation in the Canadian society, economy, and polity. They are, for all intents and purposes, internal immigrants, and for purposes of public policy, their problems are fundamentally the same as those of other recent immigrants.

It is now thirty years since Pierre Trudeau became prime minister of Canada. One of his government's early projects was the famous White Paper on Indian affairs, which articulated an approach similar to the one stated here, namely to encourage the social, economic, and political integration of Natives into Canadian society. Sadly (as I see it), Native leaders totally rejected the White Paper and set off along the opposite path of emphasizing separate institutions and political power, pursuing the elusive goals of land claims, Aboriginal rights, self-government, and sovereignty. As far as I can tell, thirty years of this political approach have produced hardly any beneficial results. There are more Native politicians and lawyers than there used to be, but economic and social conditions seem to have improved very little. We still read every day about unemployment rates of 90 percent on reserves, of Third World standards of housing and health, of endemic alcoholism, drug addiction, violence, and family breakdown.

What the black economist Thomas Sowell has written of the United States is equally true of Canada:

> Political success is not only relatively unrelated to economic advance, those minorities that have pinned their hopes on political action—the Irish and the Negroes, for example—have made some of the slower economic advances. This is in sharp contrast to the Japanese-Americans, whose political powerlessness may have been a blessing in disguise, by preventing the expenditure of much energy in that direction. Perhaps the minority that has depended most on trying to secure justice through political or legal processes has been the American Indian, whose claims for justice are among the most obvious and most readily documented.... In the American context, at least, emphasis on promoting economic advancement has produced far more progress than attempts to redress past wrongs, even when those historic wrongs have been obvious, massive, and indisputable.[10]

More concisely, but in the same vein, the Tsimshian lawyer and businessman Calvin Helin has written, "It is time for indigenous people to stop dwelling on the rancorous injustices of the past ... we cannot do anything about history. Our actions now, however, can impact the future."[11]

Helin's words point in the direction of a different understanding of sovereignty, as when political philosophers talk about "popular sovereignty" or economists talk about "consumer sovereignty." These usages refer not to statelike systems of organized authority but to people making decisions for themselves, either as groups (popular sovereignty) or as individuals (consumer sovereignty). They are more or less synonymous with "self-determination."[12] As Helin argues, Native people have to take control of their own lives. They have to find and hold jobs, get better education for their children, and run their own communities more openly and efficiently. None of this requires an elaborate apparatus of government and vocabulary of sovereignty; it is more a matter of change at the individual level.

Native people probably don't value my advice, because I'm not a Native person and haven't experienced what they've experienced. So let me close by quoting Calvin Helin again:

> Aboriginal citizens must take ownership of [their] problems and assert control over their own destinies. We must look immediately to opportunities that are available to generate our own sources of wealth and employment that ultimately could lead to the Holy Grail of rediscovered independence and self-reliance. It is time to re-take control of our lives from government departments, bureaucrats, and the Indian Industry. To do this, we have to create our own wealth, develop a focused strategy to educate youth, and control our own purse strings. Reasserting control with a strategic plan for

moving forward should ultimately lead to more basic personal happiness. The object is to ensure that larger numbers of Aboriginal people are leading more enriched, rewarding lives. Wealth (or money), although needed to provide opportunities, in itself is not the goal, but only a means to this greater end. Successfully implemented, this process in turn should pay huge economic and social dividends for Canada as a country.[13]

NOTES

1. Mark O. Dickerson and Thomas Flanagan, *An Introduction to Government and Politics: A Conceptual Approach*, 7th ed. (Toronto: Thomson Nelson, 2006), pp. 30–31.

2. See Menno Boldt and J. Anthony Long, "Tribal Traditions and European-Western Political Ideologies: The Dilemma of Canada's Native Indians," *Canadian Journal of Political Science* 17 (1984), pp. 537–553; Thomas Flanagan, "Indian Sovereignty and Nationhood: A Comment on Boldt and Long," ibid., 18 (1985), pp. 367–374; Boldt and Long, "A Reply to Flanagan's Comments," ibid., 19 (1986), p. 153.

3. Debbie Hum, "Ottawa Has No Right to Impose Its Law on Natives: Mohawk," *The Gazette* (Montreal), March 18, 1993.

4. *Wikipedia*, "Caledonia Land Dispute," available at http://en.wikipedia.org/wiki/Caledonia_land_dispute.

5. Charlottetown Accord, s. 41.

6. John Stuart Mill, *Considerations on Representative Government* (Chicago: Henry Regnery, 1962; first published 1861), p. 309.

7. Charlottetown Accord, s. 9.

8. Ibid., s. 22.

9. Ibid., s. 20.

10. Thomas Sowell, *Race and Economics* (New York: David McKay, 1983), p. 128.

11. Calvin Helin, *Dances with Dependency: Indigenous Success through Self-Reliance* (Vancouver: Orca Spirit Publishing and Communications, 2006), p. 264.

12. Terry L. Anderson, Bruce Benson, and Thomas E. Flanagan, eds., *Self-Determination: The Other Path for Native Americans* (Stanford, CA: Stanford University Press, 2006).

13. Helin, *Dances with Dependency*, p. 39.

POSTSCRIPT

The main purpose of the article by Roger Townshend is to demonstrate that Native claims to sovereignty have a strong historical and moral basis. Moreover, the author argues that there is plenty of room to accommodate broader notions of Native sovereignty that would not lead to the destruction of the Canadian state as Thomas Flanagan suggests. Nevertheless, even if we accept his argument, there still are a number of nagging practical questions that remain. Would all of the more than 600 tribal bands in Canada be given equal sovereign status? Or would sovereignty be granted to some kind of pan-Indian confederation? Would such a body constitute a third level of government as envisaged in the Charlottetown Accord? If sovereignty is recognized, and outstanding land claims resolved, would federal and provincial governments, preoccupied with deficit reduction measures, simply withdraw access to all services currently provided? Would small and dispersed Indian bands be able to fund and staff the social, economic, and governmental programs that self-government would necessitate?

One intriguing response to some of these questions has been put forward by Thomas Courchene and Lisa Powell in a volume entitled *A First Nations Province* (Kingston: Institute of Intergovernmental Affairs, 1992). They suggest that instead of creating a third order of government, a First Nations province could be created that would represent Native aspirations, providing the powers, institutions, and ability to carry out intergovernmental relations in largely the same manner as provinces presently do.

The notion of a third level of government was taken up by the Royal Commission on Aboriginal Peoples. In its final report, the commission recommended that an Aboriginal order of government, which would coexist with the federal and provincial orders of government, be recognized. According to the commissioners, "The governments making up these three orders are sovereign within their own several spheres and hold their powers by virtue of their inherent or constitutional status rather than delegation. They share the sovereign powers of Canada as a whole, powers that represent a pooling of existing sovereignties" (p. 244). Although the commission found that Aboriginal communities may choose from one of three different models of Aboriginal government, it recommended that a House of First Peoples be created as a third chamber of Parliament. The House of First Peoples would have power to veto certain legislation that "directly affect[s] areas of exclusive Aboriginal jurisdiction . . . or where there is a substantial impact of a particular law of Aboriginal peoples" (p. 418). Although Aboriginal responses to the report were positive, government complacency and the ongoing preoccupation with unity issues relating to Quebec have ensured that these recommendations have largely been ignored. Some fear that it will take further Oka crises to put the issue of Native sovereignty back at the top of the public policy agenda.

Not everyone sympathetic to Native concerns feels that these demands should be pressed in terms of claims to sovereign statehood. For example, Menno Boldt and J. Anthony Long point out that sovereignty is really a Western European concept based on notions of territoriality and hierarchical authority that are foreign to traditional Native culture. In their article "Tribal Traditions and European-Western Political Ideologies: The Dilemma of Canada's Native Indians," *Canadian Journal of Political Science* 17, no. 3 (September 1984), pp. 537–555, Boldt and Long argue that reliance on the concept of sovereignty has led many Native leaders to reinterpret their own history in a selective way that actually legitimizes European-Western philosophies and conceptions of authority: "The legal–political struggle for sovereignty could prove to be a Trojan Horse for traditional Indian culture by playing into the hands of the Canadian government's long-standing policy of assimilation" (p. 548).

Although Native issues have been ignored for so long, a number of excellent books on the subject have appeared in recent years. *Pathways to Self-Determination: Canadian Indians and the Canadian State*, edited by Leroy Little Bear, Menno Boldt, and J. Anthony Long (Toronto: University of Toronto Press, 1984) is a useful set of essays (many written by Native leaders) for beginning to explore these issues. *Nation to Nation: Aboriginal Sovereignty and the Future of Canada*, edited by John Bird, Lorraine Laud, and Murray MacAdam (Concord: House of Anansi Press, 2001), contains a series of thirty essays that deal with the issues surrounding sovereignty, land claims policy, and Native/non-Native relations. Also useful are the following volumes: J. Frideres, *Native People in Canada: Contemporary Conflicts*, 3rd ed. (Scarborough: Prentice-Hall, 1988) and B. Morse, *Aboriginal Peoples and the Law: Indian, Métis and the Inuit Rights in Canada* (Don Mills: Oxford, 1984). Another good resource, Tim Schouls's recent book, *Shifting Boundaries: Aboriginal Identity, Pluralist Theory, and the Politics of Self-Government* (Vancouver: University of British Columbia Press, 2003), focuses on the importance of the question of formation and protection of Aboriginal identity to the notion of self-government.

Perhaps the most detailed resource on this issue is the five-volume Report of the Royal Commission on Aboriginal Peoples. Especially useful on the issues of sovereignty and self-government is the volume titled *Restructuring the Relationships* (Ottawa: Report of the Royal Commission on Aboriginal Peoples, Volume 2, 1996). For a critical perspective on the issue of Native sovereignty, see Melvin Smith, *Our Home and Native Land?* (Victoria: Crown Western, 1995).

Two of Canada's noted political scientists have published books on Aboriginal policy from quite different perspectives. Tom Flanagan published *First Nations? Second Thoughts* (Montreal and Kingston: McGill-Queen's University Press, 2000), which sets up to refute what he sees as the primary "myths" surrounding the debate over Aboriginal rights. Alain Cairns, in *Citizens Plus: Aboriginal Peoples and the Canadian State* (Vancouver: University of British Columbia Press, 2000), looks at ways in which the gap between Aboriginal people and non-Aboriginal people can be bridged in a way that respects the distinctive needs of First Nations peoples. While he thinks that Aboriginal nations will not opt for a form of sovereign independence that exceeds their capacity to govern, Cairns encourages Canadians to seek ways to improve the living conditions of Aboriginals and give them greater control over their daily lives while recognizing that a certain degree of integration into modern society, an option he calls "citizens plus," is essential. Cairns concludes, "So the choices that we have to make for territorially based nations are the nature and extent of Aboriginal self-government and how we organize our common life in the areas beyond the reach of self-government" (p. 212). For an assessment of Cairns's argument, see Heidi Libesman, "In Search of a Postcolonial Theory of Normative Integration: Reflections on A.C. Cairns' Theory of Citizens Plus," *Canadian Journal of Political Science* (December 2005).

Will Conservatism and the Conservative Party Fail?

✔ **YES**
NELSON WISEMAN, "Going Nowhere: Conservatism and the
Conservative Party"

✘ **NO**
FARON ELLIS, "Twenty-First Century Conservatives Can Succeed"

In 2003, members of the Progressive Conservative Party and the Canadian Alliance party agreed to combine their forces to create a new national political party. The two representatives of conservatism in Canada would be replaced by one single entity called the Conservative Party of Canada. Not surprisingly, the new party subscribed to beliefs and principles associated with modern conservative thinking. Government would be small; elected officials would be accountable; and individual rights and freedoms would be emphasized. Progressive social policies, such as health care and the environment, would be respected, but the well-being of the country would rest on the efforts of individual Canadians and not on government.

The genesis of the Conservative Party lay in developments that took place in the preceding decade. The Progressive Conservatives historically had been the standard-bearer of conservatism in Canada. But in the late 1980s, the Reform Party rose in an attempt to more accurately represent those with conservative views (and to better serve interests in the West). The two parties tangled in federal elections, each frustrated in the belief that the other had divided the conservative vote. The result was easy victories for the Liberal Party of Canada. Faced with this situation, efforts were made to unite the two parties of conservatism. Initial efforts managed only to alter the makeup of the Reform Party and to give it a new name (the somewhat awkward Canadian Reform Conservative Alliance, shortened to Canadian Alliance). Eventually, the endeavour to unite the right led to serious discussions between the leaders of the two conservative parties and the creation of the Conservative Party of Canada. Canada would now have a single, united party dedicated to conservative principles and ready to govern.

The question was whether Canadians were ready to accept conservatism and its representative. Early indications have suggested that Canadians might be willing to give the two a chance. In the 2004 federal election, the new Conservative Party won 99 seats and helped force the ruling Liberals into a minority situation, and in the 2006 election the Conservative Party of Stephen Harper won a minority government with 124 seats. The rather quick ascendancy of the new party is impressive, but the difficulty of the Conservative government in translating the minority situation into a majority one—especially in light of the seeming disarray of the federal Liberal Party—points to a reluctance on the part of the country to embrace the party of modern conservatism. It seems that the election of a minority Conservative government at the federal level has not resolved the issue of whether modern conservatism has a future in Canada, but rather has only made it a more interesting question to ponder.

In the minds of some, Canada has never been and for the foreseeable future will never be suited to conservatism and conservative parties. In the past, conservatism was less hostile to government than its modern counterpart and more willing to respect traditions. But it largely lost out to the emerging liberalism and its focus on individualism and progressive policies that challenged past practices. In this environment, the Progressive Conservative Party experienced mostly failure and had to watch the triumphant Liberal Party of Canada become the nation's governing party. Modern conservatism differs from the old conservatism and indeed reflects some of the attributes of classical liberalism (for example, small government and a focus on economic freedoms). However, it seems that the country has moved on and is embracing a liberalism that provides for active government and that has little time for those with qualms about same-sex marriages, easy access to abortion services, and state support for regulated child care. In other words, modern conservatism fits uneasily, if at all, into the Canadian reality. Accordingly, the Conservative Party faces only disappointment.

There are others, however, who feel differently and believe that Canada is ready for a party that advocates limits on government and that reminds people of the importance of traditional institutions such as the family and church. The challenge is to ensure that the party plays to its strengths and resists the temptation of the Liberals' way—which is to be all things to all people. It must also ensure that extremists in the party—those who wish to use the state to impose moral choices on the citizenry—are unable to wield much power or gain much notice.

In the readings, Nelson Wiseman, a professor of political science at the University of Toronto, argues that modern conservatism and the Conservative Party have little future in Canadian politics. Faron Ellis, a political scientist at Lethbridge College, makes the case that Canada is fertile ground for modern conservatism and that the Conservative Party can position itself to take advantage of this situation.

✔ **YES**

Going Nowhere: Conservatism and the Conservative Party
NELSON WISEMAN

This is a tale of two quite different conservative philosophies and two quite dissimilar Conservative parties that share the same labels but differ in thought and development. According to our story, one variant of conservatism has failed and the other soon will. The fortunes of both conservative parties are related to the shortcomings of the conservative ideologies that have infused them. The denouement to this account is—alas for conservatives and Conservatives—the continuing hegemony of liberalism and the Liberal Party in Canadian politics.

To be sure, the Conservative Party has had its moments in the sun. It racked up the largest majorities in Canadian history in 1958 and 1984 and tenuously triumphed in the 2006 election. Flickering periods of Conservative success have been relatively brief, best seen as temporary interregnums between long periods of Liberal Party rule. Conservatives, serving as a default option for the electorate, have prevailed when the Liberals have faltered. The conservative impulse, in both its older manifestation and its newer incarnation, is a minoritarian one in Canada. The overarching mainstream ideology—liberalism—has been the principal guide in Canadian political thought. The periodic, transitory victories of the Conservative Party have come as reactive jerks to an otherwise popular Liberal Party when it appears arrogant and tired. Chastened by the electorate from time to time, the Liberals have consistently bounced back in a way that they did not in Britain, where the social democratic Labour Party displaced them. Canada's Liberals have also been more effective in capitalizing on Canada's changing social composition than have the Conservatives.

The older Canadian conservative tradition and Conservative Party are those of the nineteenth century. Genetically rooted in British conservatism or Toryism, early Canadian conservatism was a reaction to American revolutionary liberalism. The conservative creed—carried to Canada by decamped and expelled American Loyalists—was expressed earlier, in a Gallic manifestation, by French Canada's quasi-feudal structures and ideological disposition. Conservatism was reinforced by the War of 1812 and by Britain's imperial control of British North America's political and economic systems: thus, the early influence of a high Tory right in the form of Upper Canada's Family Compact and Lower Canada's Chateau Clique. In French Canada—which appeared more like pre-liberal, pre-revolutionary Old France than Europe's liberal, revolutionary New France—the ultramontane Roman Catholic establishment came to hold sway a few decades after the Conquest. It deferred to British leadership in matters of state (the Church opposed Papineau's 1837 rebellion against the English) and economy (it preached the virtues of subsistence farming for the *habitants* and denigrated worldly materialism). In exchange for its fealty to the British Crown, the conservative clerical class was left at the commanding heights of French Canada's separate, segregated culture and society. It was a mutually reinforcing division of labour: the economically dominant British—driven by a possessive individualist outlook—tended to industry, trade, and commerce protected by a strong, centralized state, while the economically subordinate French Canadians looked inward with pride for spiritual, religious inspiration to preserve their traditional conservative ways. Canada's founders were America's anti-revolutionary liberals—those with a Tory streak buttressed by their British connection—working with French conservatives.

The new conservatism—and the new Conservative Party—are that of the early twenty-first century. Unlike the old conservatism, it is not at all repelled by America. Proximity and attraction to America's evolving neoliberalism (known as "neoconservatism" there) pollinate the new conservatism. Both Canadian liberalism and the new Canadian conservatism have drawn heavily on American thought and models, while the older conservatism and Conservative Party had greater British impetus. Post-Loyalist American farmers carried American liberal ideas of freedom, equality, and individualism when they pioneered the western reaches of Upper Canada in the early nineteenth century. Later, early twentieth-century American farmers transplanted then-current American notions when they homesteaded the western reaches of the prairies. Canadian liberalism was buttressed by a massive influx of many radical nineteenth-century Britons who had experienced the rise and success of the anti-Tory, liberal British Reform Party. Upper Canada's population exploded from 77,000 in 1811 to 952,000 by 1851. British liberalism, streaked by conservatism, was sustained by the opportunities afforded by Canada's expanding frontier economy, where land was free or cheap. Liberalism grew and further eclipsed conservatism because, while Old World social structures such as rigid class divisions and a state-sanctioned church could be wistfully imitated, they could not maintain their early hold. They were not native to, nor an organic part of, the North American reality and came to be rejected. Other Canadian realities, however, favoured some Old World notions, such as a strong state. That was indispensable to the settlement of the Canadian West and the building of a national economy and culture using Crown corporations.

Modern conservatism rejects the liberal Keynesian paradigm that took hold after the Second World War. In the Keynesian schema, the state endeavoured to guide macroeconomic supply and demand, society's gross production and consumption. It did so by manipulating the levers of fiscal policy, public-sector spending, and taxation. Modern conservatism, in contrast, seeks unfettered free-market practices by shrinking the state, accommodating *laissez-faire*, privatizing state enterprises, deregulating, liberalizing trade regimes, outsourcing state functions to profit-motivated contractors, and cutting back social entitlements.[1] The agenda of the new conservatism is offloading and downsizing government activities. The focus is not on what the state can do to manage the economy but on what private enterprise, acting freely, can do to boost it. The state's potential role as social engineer in the form of affirmative action programs for disadvantaged groups is ridiculed and rejected. On some social issues, such as abortion and gay marriage, however, the new conservatism's partisans are divided.

Times change, ideas evolve, political parties reinvent themselves, and new groups of Canadians appear as older ones fade and die off. Although the polity is always in flux, successful institutions, ideologies, and political parties outlive their competitors and shift with the changing temper of the times. The weakness of the federal Conservatives is, in part, a product of political geography: the key to winning federal power is to capture the larger cities. There, the Liberals have consistently dominated since the 1960s. In most provinces, in contrast, the road to provincial power is to win the rural and outlying districts, where Conservatives have been more successful.[2] The key to winning the votes of the ever-changing electorate has been to change with it. An example is the success of Ontario's provincial Progressive Conservatives during their unmatched dynasty of 42 consecutive years of power between the 1940s and 1980s. They had the ability to change as Ontarians changed. That party's formula was to bridge the old Ontario and the new Ontario, maintaining its Anglo-Saxon rural/small town supporters while augmenting them with those in the growing, more ethnically and ideologically diverse metropolitan centres. The party was by turns—sometimes simultaneously as need be—"progressive" and "conservative,"[3] a contradictory formula that worked. In contrast, the federal Conservatives and their conservatism, for the most part, have played the role of handmaidens or followers in the political and policy arenas rather than trailblazers. The opponents of conservatism successfully characterized the party and its ideas as reactionary, as a perpetrator of an inegalitarian status quo that serves established interests.

THE OLD CONSERVATISM

Classical conservatism, as articulated by Edmund Burke, had a tiny leftist tinge to it, in that it was receptive to change so long as society's fundamental institutions were preserved. In this view, organic change—where the polity's components worked together harmoniously for the beneficial maintenance of the whole system—was natural and welcome. Fundamentals were to prevail over innovations when they clashed. This older strand of conservatism harked back to the wisdom of the ages. There is a quaint, archaic flavour to it. It warns of the dangers of experimentation and cautions people to do and think as their forebears did. It sees man as born flawed, he and his world as imperfect. Classical conservatism (known in its British manifestation as Toryism and expressed as a form of quasi-feudalism in early French Canada) knitted together a number of interconnected and reinforcing principles. They included, in addition to an adherence to tradition, the importance of maintaining social order through a strong authority, an authority that demanded and deserved deference. Order required protecting the weak as well as the strong. It meant a strong, centralized, and authoritative—but not necessarily big—government. Classical conservatism was less optimistic about human nature than liberalism and placed less faith in government's wisdom and planning abilities than socialism urged.

Classical conservatism embraced hierarchical institutions as guarantors of stability. These institutions—such as the Crown, the church, the military, and the patriarchal family (and other hierarchies like corporations and universities)—were organized and understood to provide reinforcement and direction to the community's common interests. Such institutions worked as partners, in collaboration; they neither competed with each other nor were internally driven. In this cosmology, political society is a hierarchically structured organic-corporatist-communitarian entity composed of unequal classes—some more privileged than others—all sanctioned by heredity and tradition and relating to each other cooperatively. It was a compassionate conservatism in that, out of a sense of *noblesse oblige*, society's privileged were duty-bound to protect and aid the poor and less fortunate. Classical conservatism's collectivist and elitist elements were considered natural as well as necessary bulwarks against revolutionary chaos, class conflict, and fearful anarchy. The old conservatism thus viewed democracy's stirrings and unshackled individual freedoms with suspicions of "mobocracy."

The creation of the modern Canadian state was a conservative triumph over liberalism in that market logic—absorption by the American economic behemoth—was resisted on nationalist grounds. Politics trumped the economic allure of continental integration. Nevertheless, the old conservatism was always a minoritarian impulse in the political culture; it infused Canadian liberalism but did not displace it as the dominant outlook. The state's Tory institutions were deployed in the interests of liberal acquisitiveness and economic expansion. The old conservatism, for example, underwrote private enterprise at public expense for national economic development and "national purpose"[4] in projects like the Canadian Pacific Railway.

Joe Clark made much of the old conservatism's notion of community, describing Canada as a "community of communities." Even Brian Mulroney, who preached an aggressive market liberalism and reversed the Conservatives' protectionist posture vis-à-vis the United States, came to describe Canada's universal social programs as a "sacred trust" not to be violated, for they were "a cornerstone of our party's philosophy."[5] Socialists, however, had first championed such programs while old conservatives opposed their implementation by welfare liberals. Perhaps one of the last gasps of old conservatism came on the eve of the 2003 merger of the old Progressive Conservative Party and the Canadian Alliance. Lowell Murray, a Progressive Conservative senator and former Mulroney cabinet minister, wrote that, as a Progressive Conservative,

> We believe that government's job is to provide stability and security against the excesses of the market. Democratic politics must define the public

interest and ensure it always prevails over more private ambitions. To that extent the forces of technology and globalization need to be tamed.... Reform [the new] conservatism which is what the Alliance [party] practises relies on people's fear of moral and economic decline.... It spoils all the good arguments for the market economy by making a religion of it, pretending there are market criteria and market solutions to all of our social and political problems.[6]

The Old Conservative Party

John A. Macdonald's old Conservative Party was undeniably successful; it won five of Canada's first six elections. The party, however, floated on the shaky foundations of a shifting coalition of forces rather than being constructed on solid pillars. Indeed, the very first Conservative government was actually a Liberal–Conservative one, bringing together anti-American Tories and Montreal-based English Canadian financiers and business liberals seeking to build an economic empire via railway construction. This alliance drew on the support of Quebec's conservative *Bleus* and some of Canada West's Reformers who were also tied to railway interests. The old Conservatives' triumphs lay in Macdonald's skills in organizing and dispensing bureaucratized patronage: some Conservative constituency associations operated like employment agencies where individual party activists formally applied for government positions, trading on their financial or campaigning contributions. Such procedures were considered normal and legitimate, based on the idea that "to the victor belongs the spoils."[7] Wilfrid Laurier's Liberal machine proved equally adept at using the glue of patronage. Notwithstanding its brokerage orientation, the old Conservative Party differed from the Liberal Party in that it was the carrier of what there was of the old conservatism.

The old Conservative Party's undoing was its failure to continue to broker successfully between British and French on issues of language and religion. French Catholic Quebec was upset with Métis leader Louis Riel's execution and the suppression of French language schooling in New Brunswick, Ontario, and especially Manitoba. The party became identified as fiercely Protestant and British. Quebec was lost to the party as it further distanced itself from the Québécois on issues of international empire, war, and conscription. The Conservatives could thus not muster enough support in Quebec to win more than four seats in any of the four elections between 1917 and 1926; they won none in 1921. Six decades later, the story had not changed much. Only two seats in Clark's governing caucus in 1979 were from Quebec and, in 1980, only one. The party did not select a French Canadian leader (Jean Charest) until it was in its death throes in the 1990s. John Diefenbaker's Conservative victory in 1958 and Mulroney's landslides in the 1980s were false indicators of Conservative viability in Quebec. The party benefited from the fleeting tactical acquiescence of Quebec's old and new nationalists, the Union National and the Parti Québécois, as well as, in Mulroney's case, the provincial Liberals.

Another source of the Conservatives' undoing was, paradoxically, their most notable policy accomplishment: the National Policy of 1879. The construction of a Trans-Canada railway, the settlement of the West, and the imposition of tariffs facilitated the development of central Canada's nascent industrial economy. The tariff, a regionally discriminatory transportation policy, as well as the power of financial institutions associated with the Conservatives of Montreal's St. James Street and Toronto's Bay Street, turned the West against the party. It became a Liberal stronghold and a wellspring for third-party protest (in the form of the Progressives, Social Credit, and the CCF). R.B. Bennett's Conservatives held power during the Depression and came to be blamed for it. Diefenbaker swept the West in 1958 in part because his populism and background were so different from those of the leaders who preceded him, like Ontario's Colonel George Drew. The party had anointed a progressive, populist Westerner, John Bracken, as its leader during the Second World War, but the country was not prepared to switch leaders then or in the war's aftermath. The challenge to the ruling Liberals then was from the left (the CCF) rather than the right. Bracken's singular contribution to the party was to change the "Conservative" brand to "Progressive Conservative," but the party did not live up to its new billing.

The chronic electoral weakness of the old Conservative Party was evidenced in the thirty elections between 1896 and the party's last outing in 2000: it won nine of them, but in only six did it win a majority of seats. In all three elections that returned Conservative minorities, the party attracted fewer voters than the Liberals. The "government party," the Liberals, have held office in parts of all but 27 of the past 111 years. The old Conservatives served as the natural "opposition party." A telling sign of their vulnerability came in Canada's first multiparty election in 1921: they ran third behind the upstart, the loosely organized Progressives, who themselves became a dilapidated annex of the Liberals. In all three elections between 1993 and 2000, the old Conservatives, claiming that they were the only "national" alternative to the Liberals, ran last in a five-party system. The relatively few Conservative victories in the twentieth century were more rebuffs for the perceived shortcomings of Liberal regimes rather than support for Conservative mandates. In only four of the 26 elections since 1921 have the Conservatives won with wide national support.

Unlike parties of principle like the Progressives, CCF-NDP, Social Credit, Reform Party, and Canadian Alliance, the old Conservative Party styled itself, like the Liberal Party, as a brokerage party. Its strategy was to build a tent large enough to hold Canadians from all strata of society. It operated as a cadre party—deferring to its leader and his coterie on major issues of policy. No Conservative convention or policy gathering debated or endorsed free trade or the GST before their institution by the leader. Gaining a few seats and a higher vote share is deemed a victory by a small party like the NDP, but Conservatives measured their leader by a higher standard: outright victory. The more they found themselves relegated to the opposition benches, the more a mindset of defeat and self-destructive tendencies set in. A "Tory Syndrome"[8] took hold, in which a weak election performance led Conservative partisans to attribute failures to their leader, thus weakening him and his ability to take the party forward.

As a near perpetual opposition party, the old Conservatives projected the image of naysayers with little or no experience in fashioning public policy or responsibility for public administration. More often than not, the party's MPs appeared uncoordinated in their opposition roles, some working at cross-purposes with their leader. When they occasionally did hold office, as in the Meighen, Bennett, Diefenbaker, and Clark years, they offered incoherent and unsynchronized policy direction or struggled with crises beyond their control (the Depression and sky-rocketing oil prices in the 1970s).

The Mulroney Conservative victories in the 1980s were the fruit of a tenuous alliance of Western Canadian rural, fiscal, and social conservatives on the one hand and Quebec nationalists on the other. There had always been substantial Conservative support in Ontario and the Maritimes—the very creatures of Loyalism—but it had not been sufficient to propel the party to power. Quebec's francophone Conservatives were an *ersatz* phenomenon, first and foremost nationalists whose nationalism transcended any liberal-conservative-socialist cleavage, such as that of English Canada. Once Quebecer Mulroney left the stage, the party plummeted in the province from 63 seats in 1988 to one in 1993 and reverted to its longstanding marginal position.

Sociodemographic change eroded the historic bases of support for the old Conservative Party in English Canada. The Maritimes' constantly shrinking share of the population in the twentieth century made the region count for less and less. Loyalist and early post-Loyalist rural Ontario was transformed into an increasingly urban, multicultural, kaleidoscopic society. The Liberals benefited. The outcome of the four minority elections between 1957 and 1965 reflected that change: southern, metropolitan Ontario's swing seats determined whether Conservatives or Liberals would come out on top, as the rest of the country was in a state of electoral stasis with few seats changing hands. Immigrants, soon naturalized as citizens, were more favourably disposed to the Liberals, as was a rising class of young, upwardly mobile, urban professionals. These groups saw Liberal immigration and urban policies as more positive than those of the Conservatives. Old Tory Toronto, once a Conservative stronghold, became a Liberal bastion. The Conservatives' battles against bilingualism and the maple leaf flag (they fought to retain the Red Ensign with its Union Jack) did not res-onate with either Quebecers or Ontario's newer ethnic minorities. The Liberals reinforced their standing with these groups, and the Conservatives weakened theirs, on issues such as multiculturalism, affirmative action programs, and social policy. The old Conservatives represented the old Canada, disproportion-ately those of British ethnic descent, Protestant, and rural/small town. They could not shake that image.

THE NEW CONSERVATISM

The new conservatism is a modern variant of the old liberalism. The new conservatism or neoliberalism gives priority to the individual over the community in the economic sphere. Immense business corporations are seen as individuals. Community is defined atomistically as the sum of its self-governing, equally free-willed individuals. Margaret Thatcher captured this sentiment with her observation, "There is no such thing as society." The new conservatism, unlike the old conservatism, is loath to use the state to protect the public good or for broad community interest at the expense of the private freedoms—the negative liberties—of its autonomous individuals. An exception is made for the state's war-making and police functions. The new conservatism depicts society as a one-class citizenry rather than as a society of unequal classes, as both Tories and socialists do. Thus, the new conservatism favours the mechanics of an individual-based participatory form of democracy; it embraces the use of referenda and the potential recall of elected representatives, seeing representatives as delegates charged with communicating, unmediated, their electors' views. It does not see politicians, as Burke and the old conservatism did, as trustees elected to exercise their personal judgment of what is best, and held to account in elections on the basis of stewardship.

The new conservatism views the state as a constantly renewed and voluntary arrangement among contemporaries. This jettisons the old conservatism's conceptualization of state and society as an inherited ancient bond that links past, present, and future generations. The new conservatism claims to move on popular impulse, operating on the principle that society is a compact among equal citizens. Hierarchical and monarchical institutions—like an appointed upper house and the Crown's residual prerogatives exercised by the prime minister—are condemned as outdated remnants of the old conservatism. The new conservatism lambastes the old conservatism for offering an unreal, inferior understanding of the existing socioeconomic order and how it should work. The old conservatism is indicted as a reactionary vision of the future.

The new conservatives, however, are divided on the moral, as opposed to economic, sphere of human behaviour. The same-sex marriage issue demonstrates their division. Libertarian conservatives tolerate traditionally proscribed acts— homosexuality, abortion, suicide, drug use, etc.—so long as such behaviour is freely chosen. Social conservatives have kept the faith with old conservatives in the moral sphere. Unlike libertarians, they believe government must not remain neutral on moral issues. Social conservatives look to government to preserve and promote traditional values and institutions such as the traditional family and to do so in the schools, the law, and the media. They condone teaching religion in schools as part of education's bedrock function. In contrast, libertarians would leave the teaching of religious doctrines to the educational marketplace. Social conservatives are also distinguished by their positions on issues such as fetal rights, capital punishment, and criminal sentencing. It is a comment on its evolution that the old

Conservative Party, by the 1990s, had come to look at abortion and gay rights more favourably than the new conservatives in the Reform/Alliance party, which upheld the moral cudgels of the old Canada.

Where the libertarian and social conservative tendencies of the new conservatism merge is on rejection of state intervention in economic matters, except for state intervention in support of private enterprise. Their common objective goes beyond "shrinking the state" to reducing its very capacity to act. They would place much of the traditional public policy agenda beyond the reach of government and, consequently, beyond the reach of citizens who may wish to have their government steer a more collectivist course. The new conservatives would limit the instrumentality of government in pursuit of social justice objectives because they are wedded to free-market solutions. This dampens the prospect for public embrace of the new conservatism because Canadians have become inured to and expect government action in the liberal reform tradition. Preoccupation with individual and corporate rights towers over considerations of social and economic justice for the new conservatives. But, "Like nature itself, the market order knows neither justice nor injustice," writes Cy Gonick. "Social obligation, the idea of solidarity between self and community, has no place . . ." in this logic.[9]

Nationalism is a litmus test differentiating the old and new conservatism. Tory conservatism expressed itself in a certain anti-Americanism. David Orchard, the anti–free trade crusader, carried its banner in his bid for the old Conservative Party leadership in 1998 and 2003. Red Tories and old-style Burkean Tories had been nationalist communitarians who opposed class struggle but promoted a national identity to counter American influence. Liberalism and the Liberals, in contrast, had not been philosophically or historically linked to statism or collectivism until Pierre Trudeau led them. The closer the new Conservative Party moves toward contemporary American conservatism, the farther away it moves from the Tory nationalism that had informed the old Conservative Party. The last Conservative leader who underlined the links between his party and its British Conservative Party roots was Robert Stanfield; he cited both Burke and the pioneering British Tory factory legislation of the nineteenth century as part of Canadian conservatism's legacy.[10]

The New Conservative Party

There is no single genesis for the new Conservative Party: origins include some elements of the populist agrarian revolt of the 1920s, the Social Credit phenomenon of the 1930s, the appearance of the Reform Party in the 1980s, and the demolition of the old Conservative Party in the 1990s. Initially, prairie populism was diametrically opposed to the old conservatism and old Conservative Party. Social Credit, preaching the virtues of monetary reform, wedded it with messianic evangelicalism. Its logo was a green Christian cross on a white background. Preston Manning, the founding Reform Party leader, is the godson of Social

Credit's founder, "Bible" Bill Aberhart. Manning's father, Ernest, took over Aberhart's immensely popular *Back to the Bible Hour* radio broadcasts and served as Alberta's premier for a quarter-century. Reflecting and leading the transmutation of Social Credit, he went from serving as Alberta's anti-bank provincial treasurer in the 1930s to director of the Canadian Imperial Bank of Commerce in the 1960s. In that decade, he called for a merger of Conservative and Social Credit partisans into a new Conservative party that stressed "Social Conservative ideals and principles." He wrote of "the responsibility of governments to give first consideration to human beings as individuals (as persons) rather than to human beings in the aggregate." He defined the family as the "most fundamental unit of human association" and pointed to the public's "spiritual resources" and "the Sovereignty of God." The "Social Conservative," wrote Manning, "will speak of a 'society of great individuals,' before he will speak of a 'great society,'"[11] a term used by welfare liberals in the American Democratic administration at that time.

Social Credit faded and disappeared as the elder Manning recommended, but the younger Manning resurrected the division among conservatives in the 1980s with the Reform Party. The spark for its ignition was the blatant favouritism shown by Mulroney's old Conservatives for Quebec's aerospace industry at the expense of Manitoba's. Reform smashed the old Conservatives' base in English Canada beyond the Atlantic region. The policy inclinations of Reform's activists, however, limited the party's appeal. A survey of the party's 1992 Assembly—attended by the elder Manning who termed it a "crusade"—showed that 96 percent of delegates agreed that courts were too lenient with criminals, 99 percent agreed that government ought to reduce its deficit as much as possible, 96 percent thought the welfare state made people less willing to look after themselves, 98 percent opposed a constitutional veto for Quebec, and 97 percent opposed increased government efforts to further multiculturalism.[12] Reform (and its successor, the Canadian Alliance) competed with the old Conservatives for the same minoritarian right-wing vote, with failing results for both of them, especially the Conservatives. Some policy convergence facilitated their merger. Electoral arithmetic compelled it. In 1997, the economic and fiscal planks in the old Conservative and Reform platforms were near carbon copies. Where they differed was on Quebec, bilingualism, immigration, institutional reform, and "morality" issues. In the 2000 election, Joe Clark's old Conservatives somewhat tempered their market liberalism. They spoke of social safety nets and equalization payments because Atlantic Canada was their only remaining base.

The base of the new Conservative Party, like its predecessor party and Reform/Alliance, continues to be the West and English Canada's rural/small town districts. In its first outing, the new party proved to be less than the sum of its parts: the combined vote for the two older parties had been nearly 38 percent in 2000, but the new merged party garnered less than 30 percent in 2004. Chronic weakness in large cities and irrelevance in Quebec were fatal shortcomings, as cities account for increasing numbers of Canadians. The 2004 results speak for themselves: of fourteen major urban centres for which Elections Canada broke out the vote,[13] the new Conservatives led the popular vote in only three (Calgary, Edmonton, and St. John's). In four centres (Halifax, Montreal, Vancouver, and Victoria), they were beaten by the NDP as well as the Liberals. In the largest city, Toronto, they won no seats and drew no more votes than the NDP. The combined vote for the Bloc Québécois and the NDP nearly equalled the vote for the Conservatives. In the Conservatives' 2006 election victory, they were shut out in Toronto, Montreal, and Vancouver.

Data (excluding Quebec) drawn from the 2004 Canadian Election Study reveal the new Conservative Party's limited growth potential. In the 2000 election, the old Conservatives led as voters' second-choice party, but the new Conservatives badly trailed both the Liberals and the NDP on this score in 2004. Nearly half of respondents agreed that "Stephen Harper is just too extreme." Public opinion overwhelmingly supported increased government funding for health care and education. There was less public support for cutting personal taxes (the Conservatives' signature policy) than for increasing social housing. The ratio of Liberal-to-Conservative supporters was more than three-to-one among the steadily growing numbers of members of visible minorities. The Conservatives trailed the NDP among this group as well. The Conservatives did have the lead among self-described religious fundamentalists (over half) and (nearly half of) Protestants. Nevertheless, the party did gain about the same vote level (outside Quebec) as the Liberals.[14] The billion-dollar gun registry boondoggle and the "sponsorship" scandal in the run-up to the election discredited the Liberals in the eyes of many voters.

THE FUTURE: GOING NOWHERE

Even after the scandals that rocked the Liberals and the internecine disputes between the Jean Chrétien and Paul Martin wings of that party, the Conservatives fell short in the 2004 election. In the 2006 election, they eked out a plurality of seats and formed a minority government but only lurched ahead of the Liberals after the RCMP launched an investigation into a leak of Liberal government tax policy. The Conservatives benefited more from the failings of the Liberals than by virtue of their own behaviour or philosophy. The prospects of their becoming a majority government are poor unless they make substantial gains in metropolitan Canada and Quebec. They continue to be overwhelmed by the other parties and Canada's liberal–social democratic ethos.

A majority election victory for the new Conservative Party would be but a necessary, not sufficient, condition for the new conservative philosophy to prevail. As new Canadians settle in the new Canada of cosmopolitan, polyethnic, metropolitan cities, the Conservatives' old Canada base—rural/small town, Protestant English Canada—continues to shrivel. The Conservatives have strength and substantial potential in English Canada's suburbs, the exurban areas encircling the cities' cores, and in Quebec's rural nationalist heartland. That was demonstrated during the Mulroney years. The party may yet capitalize on that potential but, if it does, it will likely be for a relatively brief period—the Conservative stretch in office from 1984 to 1993 was atypical.

In power, Stephen Harper's Conservative government has behaved very much like the Liberals. After the Conservatives denounced the Liberals as spendthrifts, their first two budgets increased program spending by more than 7 percent annually at a time that inflation was running near 2 percent. After dismissing climate change and the Kyoto Protocol as a socialist fraud, Harper described global warming as "perhaps the greatest threat to confront the future of humanity today."[15] After beating the war drums on Canada's role in Afghanistan, the Conservative government turned to a former Liberal foreign minister for direction and announced it would defer to Parliament's wishes. Nearly two years after their minority victory in 2006, the Conservatives stood lower in most polls than on election night and trailed the Liberals in all regions of the country save the prairies. Women especially were wary of them, and a majority of Canadians opined that Harper was "too right wing" and a George Bush lackey.[16]

"Canada is not yet a conservative or Conservative country," wrote Tom Flanagan, a Harper confidante and the 2004 Conservative national campaign director. Notwithstanding the Conservative victory in 2006, "neither the philosophy of conservatism nor the party brand comes close to commanding majority support."[17] Citing Burke, Flanagan preached the need for Harper's government to pursue "moderation," "inclusion," and "incrementalism." This simultaneously revealed a lingering touch of the old conservatism, the need to imitate Liberal ways as the way to electoral success, and the minoritarian status of conservatism and Conservatism— old and new.

Conservatism and the Conservative Party have had an embedded place in Canada's political culture, but the new conservatism of the late twentieth and early twenty-first centuries appears to be a passing phenomenon. So long as Canadians invest in defining themselves by who they are not—Americans—and so long as the new conservatism is driven by similar ideas and demographic forces to those in the U.S., the appeal of the new conservatism is limited. The new Conservative Party's prospects brighten only when they behave like the opportunistic Liberals did.

NOTES

1. Stephen McBride and John Shields, *Dismantling a Nation: The Transition to Corporate Rule in Canada,* 2nd ed. (Halifax: Fernwood, 1997), p.18, and John Shields and B. Mitchell Evans, *Shrinking the State: Globalization and Public Administration "Reform"* (Halifax: Fernwood, 1998).

2. Timothy L. Thomas, "An Emerging Party Cleavage: Metropolis vs. the Rest," in Hugh G. Thorburn and Alan Whitehorn, eds., *Party Politics in Canada,* 8th ed. (Toronto: Prentice-Hall, 2001), ch. 30.

3. John Wilson, "The Red Tory Province: Reflections on the Character of the Ontario Political Culture," in Donald C. MacDonald, ed., *The Government and Politics of Ontario,* 2nd ed. (Toronto: Van Nostrand Reinhold, 1980).

4. Reg Whitaker, *A Sovereign Idea: Essays on Canada as a Democratic Community* (Montreal and Kingston: McGill-Queen's University Press, 1992), p. 20.

5. Quoted in Colin Campbell and William Christian, *Parties, Leaders, and Ideologies in Canada* (Toronto: McGraw-Hill Ryerson, 1996), p. 52.

6. Lowell Murray, "Don't Do It, Peter," *The Globe and Mail,* June 23, 2003.

7. Gordon T. Stewart, "Political Patronage under Macdonald and Laurier, 1878–1911," *American Review of Canadian Studies* 10, no. 1 (1980).

8. George C. Perlin, *The Tory Syndrome: Leadership Politics in the Progressive Conservative Party* (Montreal and Kingston: McGill-Queen's University Press, 1980).

9. Cy Gonick, *The Great Economic Debate* (Toronto: James Lorimer, 1987), p. 130.

10. Robert L. Stanfield, "Conservative Principles and Philosophy," in Paul Fox and Graham White, eds., *Politics: Canada,* 8th ed. (Toronto: McGraw-Hill Ryerson, 1995), pp. 307–311.

11. E.A. Manning, *Political Realignment* (Toronto: McClelland and Stewart, 1967), pp. 65–70.

12. Keith Archer and Faron Ellis, "Opinion Structure of Party Activists: The Reform Party of Canada," *Canadian Journal of Political Science* 27, no. 2 (June 1994), Table 5, pp. 295–297.

13. Elections Canada, "Election Night Results," available at http://enr.elections.ca/Major Centres_e.aspx. Accessed on November 3, 2004.

14. Elisabeth Gidengil and Neil Nevitte, "Something Old, Something New: Preliminary Findings of the 2004 Canadian Election Study," seminar presentation, University of Toronto, October 22, 2004.

15. Quoted by Lawrence Martin, "Unlike George, Steve Keeps God to Himself," *The Globe and Mail,* July 5, 2007.

16. Gloria Galloway, "The Harper Paradox," *The Globe and Mail,* August 28, 2007, and Canadian Press, "Liberals Still Even with Tories After Weeks of Bad News," press release, October 3, 2007.

17. Tom Flanagan, *Harper's Team: Behind the Scenes in the Conservative Rise to Power* (Montreal and Kingston: McGill-Queen's University Press, 2007), p. 275.

✗ NO
Twenty-First Century Conservatives Can Succeed
FARON ELLIS

In order that our free will may not be extinguished, I judge that it could be true that fortune is the arbiter of half our actions, but that she lets the other half, or nearly that, be governed by us.

—Niccolo Machiavelli, *The Prince* (1513) XXV

Included in Machiavelli's message to sixteenth-century princes is advice that contemporary political parties should heed: although they cannot control their entire fate, they can control some. By making provisions to help withstand the ravages visited upon them upon them by their opponents, they are better armed to accomplish their goals: to guide public policy, voters, and public discourse toward their objectives and away from their opponents'. For conservatives, this includes establishing a set of core principles that, after considerable compromise by all the disparate and divergent interests that make up the loosely knit Canadian conservative movement, they can agree to champion as the best way to achieve some of their objectives. For the new Conservative Party of Canada, the overall task is similar, but complicated by the structural requirement of building those common objectives into an organization capable of fulfilling its purpose: to successfully compete for votes in a manner that affords it the opportunity to form a national government and implement conservative principles.

Ideologically, Canadian conservatism has been composed of an often fractious, complex mix of seemingly contradictory ideological streams. Elements of Toryism, business liberalism, nationalism, and populism, among others, have all enjoyed periods of support,[1] making Canadian conservatism, like most ideologies, a very amorphous entity. The new Conservative Party, on the other hand, is a political party, and parties are first and foremost organizations. As organizations operating within a larger institutional context, parties have different demands placed on them than do movements or ideologies. As such, parties are subject to different pressures for accommodating the wide variety of perspectives that underpin their overall ideological constituency. They are also subject to standards of compromise and cooperation that are unique to them as organizations. Parties must inevitably make decisions about what constitutes their core ideology, values, or principles. They must determine how much of each competing sub-ideology will be represented and how far the party will go in accommodating more peripheral elements. Attempting to accommodate too many peripheral elements often comes at the expense of fulfilling the party's ultimate purpose: successfully competing for votes.

The founding liberal-pluralist political culture in this country dictates that Canadian parties cannot afford to become too ideologically doctrinaire in either their policies or their leadership selection, at least not if their intentions are to form a national government. To a certain extent, this is what three-time Harper campaign manager Tom Flanagan expresses in his "Ten Commandments" of Conservative campaigning.[2] In particular, he advocates *moderation* because "Canada is not yet a conservative or Conservative country."[3] Citing game theory, he reminds Conservatives that if they veer too far to the right of the median voter, they will not win elections. In agreeing that the Conservatives cannot be seen as straying too far, it is important to remember that the Liberal Party of Canada demonstrated throughout the last half of the twentieth century that a party need not command majority support in elections to effectively govern for years on end.[4] Note also Flanagan's somewhat hopeful use of the term *yet*. He does not say that Canada will never be a conservative or Conservative country, only that it is not *yet* one. In order to move the median voter closer to conservatism, Flanagan advocates an *incrementalism* in which conservatives must be satisfied with making progress in small, practical steps. In allowing that "sweeping visions have a place in intellectual discussion," he is unequivocal that they are "toxic in practical politics."[5]

There is considerable truth contained in Flanagan's analysis. In particular, it is true that practising politicians must effectively mediate competing political demands much more so than do even the most practically minded academics writing from the somewhat detached isolation of the ivory towers. Also, minority governments must be particularly cautious, given their precarious existence. But it is also important to remember that neither can parties become so amorphous, or unfocused, as to be devoid of any tangible identity onto which voters can grasp and thereby attach their often transient partisan and voting loyalties. All parties must attempt to define their identities positively, with some substance, and on their own terms, or risk surrendering that opportunity to their opponents, who are likely to do so negatively and on much less favourable terms. New parties and leaders face even greater challenges along this dimension than do established parties and leaders. It is therefore even more important for the former to establish an identity that is of their own creation, prior to attempting to broker a coalition large enough to form a government. It is my contention that a libertarian-conservative core identity—based on a limited state that promotes not only economic liberty but also moral and social liberty—offers the best prospects for success for conservatives and the new Conservative Party.

Similarly, we can begin by conceding half, or nearly that much, of Professor Wiseman's argument. For he is correct in his assertion that the new Conservatives will fail if they continue to pursue an old Canada vision with values rooted in the nineteenth century and that survive primarily in rural Canada. He is also correct in his assertion that conservatism will continue to be at best a default option for voters who tire of corrupt or arrogant Liberal governments if Conservatives continue to be united by no greater principles than their mutual distaste for Liberal regimes. As long as conservatives refuse to embrace the overriding, mainstream, libertarian political culture of contemporary Canada, including the ascendancy of pluralism and individual rights, Conservatives will continue to suffer from a schizophrenia that will expose their unreadiness to govern. To deny that liberalism is the foundation of Canadian political culture, and is here to stay, is a prescription for failure. Simply attempting to rebuild previously failed coalitions would be as irrational as it has been unproductive.

But the continuing hegemony of liberalism in Canada need not necessitate continued Liberal Party hegemony. As Wiseman correctly concedes, the Canadian Liberal Party has become at best a liberal-social-democratic pretender. To that we can add overly statist. In their quest to provide continuing rationale for a strong national government, and federal powers more generally, Liberals have been fond of providing Canadian voters with statist responses to most social, economic, and political issues, real or imagined. In the process, the federal Liberals have become so illiberal that they can no longer legitimately claim the mantle of liberty's defenders. These conditions all but necessitate a libertarian-conservative response to Liberal Party electoral hegemony.

It is here where Conservatives can succeed. By consistently following a few simple principles, albeit most involving tough choices, considerable courage, and tremendous resolve, Conservatives can build a new, mainstream party around a core set of libertarian-conservative principles that will make their party capable of consistently competing for power. This will require a leap of faith for some. But as the evidence and rationale that follow will demonstrate, accommodating Canadian liberalism's new manifestations in a complex, urban, pluralistic polity is not as radical a transformation for the new Conservatives as it may first appear. The libertarian core of both the former Reform and Alliance parties, as well as the disparate remaining non-Tory elements of the Progressive Conservative Party, has several common foundational elements upon which a more grand party can be built—and to which many mainstream voters can be recruited. Quite clearly, the Stephen Harper–led Conservative government has attached itself to some of these principles in the short term. What remains to be seen is whether or not Conservatives have the vision and discipline to build an enduring political institution upon these foundations.

VARIOUS KINDS OF CONSERVATISM

All the forms of conservatism that have emerged in all the federal and provincial party systems over the years can be distilled down to three:

1. Toryism of the nineteenth century—combining a reverence for tradition with support for state maintenance of an ordered and structured society—that in various incarnations sputtered through the twentieth century.

2. Libertarian conservatism in the form of nineteenth-century liberalism—with its emphasis on economic liberty, free markets, capitalism, and a limited state—that reappeared in the late twentieth century as neoconservatism or neoliberalism.

3. Social conservatism of the nineteenth century—with its emphasis on traditional, primarily religious moral values and opposition to advancing liberal-pluralism—that manifested itself in the late twentieth century as the religious right.

Innumerable hybrids of one or more elements of each have appeared in the various parties, movements, and factions that have called themselves conservative over the past 150 years.

The most important dimensions of conservatism at the beginning of the twenty-first century revolve around the relative unity of conservatives in support of fiscal conservatism and the need for dismantling late twentieth-century state-sponsored, "left-wing," social engineering public policy. There exists, however, a wide gulf between libertarian and social conservatives on moral issues, and each has recently taken up a common cause with populists in an effort to improve their fortunes. Each errs in doing so, but for different reasons, which shall be elaborated upon later.

Conservatives should relegate Toryism, with its accompanying statism, to the dustbin of history or to the Liberals and their socialist allies. Social conservatism should be tolerated, in the same manner in which all competing ideas should be tolerated. It should not, however, be adopted as part of the defining identity of the national Conservative Party. Hybrids should also be rejected for practical and strategic reasons; most important among these is the propensity for hybrids to be so amorphous that they provide conservatism's enemies with frequent, numerous opportunities to distort and mischaracterize the Conservative Party. Only by defining a core libertarian-conservative identity will the new Conservatives find the ideological consistency necessary to become an electorally successful, enduring national coalition capable of being more than a temporary default option for voters who tire of corrupt or arrogant Liberal regimes.

REFLECTIONS ON THE WISEMAN "DOOMED TO FAILURE" THESIS

Many grains of truth are contained in Nelson Wiseman's review of Canadian conservative history. Like most undergraduate students of Canadian politics, I was introduced early to the Hartz–Horowitz "Tory touch" fragment thesis and to Wiseman's application of the thesis to the study of Canadian prairie political culture.[6] Both continue to serve as exemplary readings when conceptualizing and teaching Canadian political culture, as much for their utility in engendering critical thinking as for their other virtues. The thesis posits that political cultures in new societies are primarily fragments cast off from the European ideological dialectic. Separated from the original dialectic, new societies lose the impetus for change and remain frozen fragments of the prevailing ideology that existed at the time of their founding. Having been founded when liberalism dominated, Canadian and American political cultures are primarily liberal. But because Canada contained a quasi-feudal French element as well as an English Tory element, the Canadian political culture, although primarily liberal, is touched with Toryism, thereby making a synthesis to socialism a possibility. Because a full critique of the thesis is outside of the parameters of this debate, I will direct readers to previous rebuttals and restrict my comments to how this historical thesis impacts on the contemporary debate about the future of conservatism and the Conservative Party of Canada.[7]

Initially, pining for the virtues of a mythical Toryism, while at the same time portraying all libertarian elements of conservatism as inherently vicious, is in keeping with the standard statist attack on the "new right." It is typically the purview of hostile academics and media pundits, but not necessarily that of Canadian voters. It is no coincidence that the death of the Progressive Conservative Party, and by default the "Tory touch" mythology, was bemoaned far more by the former than the latter. After all, without a party vehicle to which the myth can remain attached, the Tory element of the dialectic appears more difficult to substantiate, and the Marxist tautological house of cards begins to collapse. In effect, without Toryism the desired end state of socialism becomes unattainable. Liberalism's triumph as the final political culture leaves Toryism a relic of the past, and socialism a never to be achieved fantasy. But the next generation of Marxist academics need not despair. They will likely find enough anti-American and statist Toryism within the Liberal Party of Canada to keep the myth alive.

The fact that a wide variety of left-wing pundits see so much to mourn in the death of the Progressive Conservative Party should give Conservatives cause for celebration. For it was the Tory element of the coalition that failed conservatism in the 1980s and has been at least partially responsible for keeping them from succeeding since. Conservatives should bid a fond farewell to the vanguard of former Progressive Conservative "red Tories" and rejoice at the prospect of extinguishing them and their fellow travellers from amongst their ranks.

Secondly, it is correct to assert that if the new Conservatives remain geographically anchored in the West and rural ridings, they are likely destined to perpetual opposition. But history need not dictate a predetermined future. Canadian voters are characterized by a number of traits, and among these is their well-deserved reputation for vote switching.[8] The persistent shattering, rebuilding, or creating anew of electoral coalitions and partisan alignments is one of the most enduring features of Canadian party systems.[9] Not only do Canadian voters regularly realign their partisan attachments in tectonic shifts that shatter the old order, they also exhibit a high degree of vote switching between non-monumental elections. Wiseman implies this when he states that Toronto used to be a Conservative bastion but is now a Liberal fortress. While downtown Toronto ridings may represent tough electoral territory for the Conservatives for some time to come, opportunity awaits them in the suburbs of central Canadian cities, primarily with voters who tire of bearing an increasingly disproportionate burden for the multiplicity of statist schemes designed to address issues that affect them only marginally, or not at all. Many are current Liberal party voters, and evidence abounds to suggest that the Liberal coalition, although consistently the largest, is increasingly the most susceptible to erosion. While the Conservatives brought 83 percent of their 2004 voters back to them in the 2006 election, the Liberals retained only 53 percent of their 2004 voters. Further, the 2006 pattern is not simply a temporary manifestation of the Liberals' current misfortunes. Since 1993, the Liberals have consistently retained less than two-thirds of their former voters between elections while the Reform-Alliance-Conservative parties have consistently retained over 80 percent of their voters.[10] This alone should give pause to those who believe the Conservative coalition would be most susceptible to fracturing under various hypothetically altered electoral or party competition scenarios.

With that said, if the new Conservatives do not succeed in defining a libertarian vision for these voters but instead allow their opponents to define conservatism as inhospitable to the collective ambitions of central Canadian suburbanites, Conservatives will not succeed. Opponents will attempt to use simplistic but often effective guilt-by-association tactics, such as those marshalled against the Reform Party (familial: what former Alberta premiers Aberhart and Manning stood for in the 1930s is equivalent to what Preston Manning stood for in the 1990s),[11] the Canadian Alliance (operational: Stockwell Day is beholden to the religious right), and the new Conservatives (conspiratorial: Stephen Harper is an American Republication clone). Attempting to equate what Preston Manning advocated in the 1990s to what his father or Aberhart were advocating in the 1930s and 1940s stretched credibility too far to be significantly effective.[12] But Day's use of social conservative activists and their organizational muscle in his Alliance leadership campaigns legitimized the "too scary" stigma, adding significantly to his inability to establish a positive public image of his own making.[13] And although Harper's electoral prospects suffered from the "vast right-wing conspiracy" attacks more in the 2004 election[14] than in 2006,[15] the overall political problem remains: conservatism's opponents have been more successful at defining conservative parties' identities than have conservatives. The "reactionary agents of their own privilege" case has been repeatedly made, and it has repeatedly stuck. When supported by frequent, often outlandish public comments made primarily but not exclusively by undisciplined members of Parliament, images of Reform and the Alliance emerged that often didn't mesh with members' and voters' core values. In both cases, the parties tended to be mischaracterized as much more socially conservative, more pro-American, and more anti-French than were either their memberships or their voting bases.[16]

Professor Wiseman's selective use of the attitudinal data that Archer and I collected at the 1992 Reform Assembly is instructive on these points. He correctly points out that virtually all Reform delegates thought the federal government should seek to reduce its federal deficit as much as possible—neither a surprising nor unreasonable finding given the fact that the federal government was continuing to borrow between $30 and $40 billion annually on its way to building a half-trillion-dollar national government debt. As such, he quite correctly characterizes Reformers as fiscal conservatives. But little evidence exists to support the characterization of Reform as anti-abortion and therefore upholding the "moral cudgels of the old Canada." In fact, Reformers held solidly libertarian positions, not social conservative positions, on the abortion choice issue. By a two-to-one margin, 1992 Reform delegates stated they were pro-choice (61.5 percent agreed abortion is a private matter to be decided by a woman, 30.9 percent disagreed, and 7.5 percent were uncertain).[17] Opinion structure among delegates attending the Alliance's only convention in 2002 was also clearly pro-choice and not significantly different from Reform (56.2 percent agreed, 34.8 percent disagreed, and 9 percent were uncertain).[18] Delegates to the 2005 Conservative convention adopted as policy by a margin of 55 percent to 45 percent the most libertarian position possible by committing the party to not restrict abortion choice.[19] Post-convention survey results indicate that majorities of Conservative delegates in all provinces except Saskatchewan were pro-choice.[20]

These and similar mischaracterizations aptly demonstrate the challenges that Reform and the Alliance encountered and that the new Conservatives have only begun to address: the ability to positively define a vision for conservatism before the many entrenched interests—who correctly view conservatism as a threat to their state-sponsored privilege—define conservatism's public image negatively. The fact that their opponents' tactics are as predictable as they are transparent makes that task somewhat easier for the new Conservatives than it was for Reform or the Alliance.

Finally, despite his general characterization of libertarian conservatives as atomistic hedonists with no collective consciousness, and the corresponding implication that socialists have a monopoly on what constitutes social justice, Wiseman is correct to state that conservatives tend to be relatively united on economics but divided on moral matters. More problematic is his inclusion of "the role of the state" on his list of "conservatives' common objectives." While it is true that general agreement exists about reducing the state's capacity to excessively engage in socialist economic engineering, the various factions within conservatives are bitterly divided over the state's role in legislating moral issues—a point Wiseman concedes about the moral divisions but not about the state's role in defining or regulating moral decision making.[21]

The problem for libertarian conservatives, and many voters who are intrigued by but have not yet voted for conservative parties, is their suspicion that social conservatives want to use the coercive power of the state to replace left-wing economic social engineering with right-wing moral engineering. Libertarian conservatives are as opposed to the latter as they are to the former. They share these sentiments with growing legions of Canadian voters who have become either suspicious of or hostile to forty years of statist public policy, and the corresponding price tag, but have repeatedly demonstrated that they are more distrustful of right-wing moral engineering than they are of left-wing social engineering. Which brings us to the choice Conservatives now face: which type of party and which vision of conservatism are they prepared to champion to the Canadian voter?

The contention here is that a libertarian-conservative vision within the mainstream of Canadian liberalism offers the most effective long-term strategy for Conservative success. While I will not presume to prescribe to the Conservative Party what specific policy measures it should adopt, I will offer a few suggestions as to the direction its policy positioning should take as the party continues to define its identity and its new electoral constituency. I'll also review and evaluate a selection of the initial steps the party has taken toward (or away from) achieving that goal. Initially, Conservatives need to fill the policy void with clear, articulate, and consistent fiscally conservative, non-statist economic policy. Secondly, they need to define a libertarian core vision that includes drawing a line in the sand across which social conservatives will not be allowed to drag the party. And most importantly, they must avoid the populist trap by setting clear limits on the party's planned use of populist decision-making mechanisms.

ESTABLISHING LEGITIMATE FISCAL CONSERVATIVE CREDENTIALS

For Conservatives, the federal government's successes in battling the evils of annual deficits should not be considered a victory in the war on socialist fiscal policy. Nor should they be satisfied with simply using unanticipated surpluses to marginally reduce the national debt. They must present Canadians with a comprehensive, bold, and clearly fiscally conservative economic platform, part of which must include substantial, broadly based middle-class income tax cuts. To date, the Harper government has not delivered. Spending increases in its first two budgets rivalled those of the previous three Liberal budgets.[22] Despite rhetoric to the contrary, the government has not delivered broad-based income tax cuts. Finance Minister Jim Flaherty has instead offered up a two percent reduction in the GST and a series of selective, "boutique" tax cuts in an attempt at winning over targeted minority populations of voters. But in order to finance these minor reductions, and the laudable further reductions in business taxes announced in the government's October 2007 *Economic Statement*, Canadians' personal tax burden is projected to rise to its highest level in fifteen years by 2012–13.[23] This is far from satisfactory, given the prominence fiscal conservatism plays in uniting the various conservative factions.

In using targeted tax cuts as a means to achieving strategic, short-term electoral gain, the Conservatives have failed to provide a central vision for a limited state that most of its core supporters agree should underpin a conservative economic agenda. Although the Harper government should be given credit for not being reckless, and thereby partially inoculating itself against charges of extremism or harbouring a radical right economic agenda, its fiscal policies have not been nearly bold enough to meet even minimum expectations from its core electoral base. Conservatives should rise to the challenge of living up to their rhetoric about "Canadians being overtaxed" and provide meaningful evidence that they take their slogans seriously. If public opinion is not yet fully onside with this agenda, it is incumbent upon Conservatives to convince more voters of the wisdom contained in their vision rather than shirk from it and yield the economic agenda to their competitors. Conservatives should emulate past successes where they have led rather than followed public opinion on fiscal conservative matters. The battles against deficits and the fights to achieve free trade should serve as reminders of how voters have handsomely rewarded politicians who demonstrate leadership.

Conservatives must also be cautious about being further distracted in their economic policy development by national unity or regionalism issues. Most importantly, they must resist the temptation to adopt "special case" exemptions from the limited-state agenda for the sake of vote buying in Quebec or Atlantic Canada. The mobilization strategy for Quebec and the East should be based on the conviction of principle and the consistency and comprehensiveness of the vision rather than opportunistic piecemeal regional graft. Dedication to the rule of constitutional law, including respect for the division of federal powers, is consistent with a libertarian, non-statist approach to economic issues, and this approach already appears to be paying dividends for the Conservatives in Quebec. It is also consistent with an overall agenda of reducing centralized social engineering and in support of provincial equality and autonomy. Corporate welfare in the form of subsidies to regionally based industries, hugely disproportionate equalization asymmetry, and regionally structured employment insurance rules should be as anathematic to Conservatives as are billion-dollar gun registry bureaucracies and affirmative-action agendas.

The Harper Conservatives have made some incremental progress in attempting to bring symmetry back to the federal government's fiscal relations with the provinces, although they have done so at the cost of significantly increasing total transfers— ostensibly under the guise of fulfilling an election commitment to end the fiscal imbalance with the provinces, but nevertheless at significant cost to their fiscal conservative credentials. The government plans a return to per capita funding for social, education, and health transfers, and has made equalization richer for most receiving provinces while providing transitional options for provinces with increasing resource revenue. But even here, Conservatives should be learning about the perils of drifting too far away from fiscal conservative principles in attempting to accommodate provincial populations and their politicians. Despite being able to choose the most lucrative of several options, Newfoundland and Labrador Progressive Conservative premier Danny Williams has used his interpretation of the new equalization rules to bolster his ongoing battles with Ottawa, a strategy that includes actively campaigning against reelecting federal Conservatives. Furthermore, when Quebec premier Jean Charest used his province's new federal largesse to promise an additional $700 million in tax cuts to Quebec voters, few members of the federal Conservative cabinet and caucus could effectively account for the optics—at worst, that the federal government was engaging in a blatant Quebec provincial vote buying scheme, and at a minimum, that it was complicit in a scheme that led to taxpayers outside of Quebec footing the bill for tax cuts in that province that would not yet be enjoyed in the rest of the country.

DEFINE THE CORE LIBERTARIAN IDENTITY

Conservatives should adopt social and moral policies that are consistent with their economic positions. That is, if Conservatives can justify the legitimacy of limiting the state from excessively interfering in Canadians' economic lives, they should also be able to justify with equal conviction the legitimacy of limiting the state from excessively interfering in the most private aspects of Canadians' personal lives. By boldly articulating the moral legitimacy of individual liberty, the rule of law, political freedom, responsive and accountable governing institutions, and free political expression, Conservatives can succeed in defining an identity for themselves that is consistent, principled, and enduring.

Social conservatives need to be assured that they are welcome in the coalition,[24] but they need to be reminded that the planned dismantling of left-wing social engineering will not be accompanied by a corresponding increase in right-wing moral engineering. Ensuring that this libertarian core philosophy is established early in the formative years of the new party, and clearly communicated, is both honourable—in that it will allow social conservatives to make informed decisions about their participation—and necessary in order to attract moderate voters who are still repelled by the possibility of a social conservative hidden agenda. Social conservatives need to understand that, by remaining within the mainstream of the Conservative coalition, they are likely to achieve about half of what they want, or nearly that much. But social conservative zealots who refuse to defer to party policy or who plan to continue championing their moral causes at the expense of the greater electoral good of the party should be thoroughly, swiftly, and efficiently extinguished from the ranks of the Conservative Party.

The Conservative Party made great strides toward libertarian principles and away from social conservative principles at its 2005 policy convention.[25] The Harper government quickly followed up with its tactically brilliant and strategically adroit handling of the same-sex marriage issue. Given that opinions amongst party activists were running three-to-one against same-sex marriage,[26] and Harper had committed to campaign in support of those opinions during his speech to the party's first policy convention, he had little option but to include opposition to the Liberals' same-sex marriage legislation in his 2006 election platform. But the way in which he approached the issue should be considered a textbook example of how to achieve both short-term tactical electoral advantage and long-term strategic positioning. In announcing on the first day of the 2006 election campaign that the Conservatives would hold a free vote on the same-sex marriage issue, Harper achieved the former by defusing the issue early and strengthened his credibility by further inoculating the party against charges of harbouring hidden agendas on other social conservative issues such as abortion. But even more impressive was the decision to hold a free vote on the issues, virtually guaranteeing that the motion would be defeated and the Conservatives could put the issue behind them. The transparency of the tactical decision was obvious to all but the most zealous social conservatives. To further ensure that the motion would not succeed, it was written to include enough seemingly contradictory provisions to allow MPs on either side of the issue to vote against it based on one or another of its provisions. When the parliamentary vote was held in December of 2006, Conservative MP support was sufficiently muted that the caucus was correctly accused of "merely going through the motions" of fulfilling an election promise.[27] The prime minister then put the issue to rest by declaring that the "decisive result" had determined the issue once and for all and that he did not anticipate "reopening this question in the future." To further ensure that the matter was indeed settled, Harper poured cold water on any notions that he would consider a compensatory motion to strengthen religious freedoms. Ardent social conservatives such as the Canadian Family Action Coalition were predictably outraged and reacted to the government's "betrayal" of social conservatism with declarations that "their" party had abandoned them. Those reactions enhanced an already successful strategy by further distancing the Conservatives from organized social conservative interests and their overall agenda.

Libertarian conservatives should follow up on this successful political strategy by making an articulate case for the moral legitimacy of pluralism. Although Canadian conservatives have succeeded in making their opposition to state-sponsored programs well known, because their opposition extends to programs that are targeted at identifiable groups, they have been much less successful at defending themselves against charges that their lack of support for government sponsorship of specific groups equates to hostility toward the groups themselves. It is here where libertarians have failed Canadian conservatism most: by not countering the charges of intolerance with a staunch defence of the diversity that is by definition a necessary component of pluralism.

Liberal-pluralism entails a diversification of power and the existence of a plurality of organizations that are both independent and noninclusive. Central to this is a limited state that leaves individuals free to voluntarily enter into multiple associations with others. But it is more. Pluralism entails not only the recognition and articulation of diversity or differentiation; it assumes a particular belief content that contains its own morally authoritative claim on legitimacy. In other words, pluralism is a normative as well as a descriptive concept. Pluralism asserts that not only do differences exist but also that difference itself is a moral good. Difference rather than likeness, dissent instead of unanimity, and choice above conformity are all fundamental to pluralism. Advocating for the liberty to voluntarily enter into noninclusive associations without state interference requires the recognition of competing associations with which one chooses not to associate. Libertarians need to further argue that these choices and associations are private and that the state should not be making decisions about which groups are to be publicly sponsored and which are not. But in advocating for private choice, a diversity of competing perspectives is assumed. Libertarians owe it to conservatism to firmly establish that Conservatives are as supportive of diversity and choice in private moral matters as they are supportive of private religious or economic associations. Libertarians must begin to vigorously counter all charges to the contrary from both within and outside of the conservative movement. Again, Harper has taken the lead on this issue, albeit in an incremental way. Careful attention should be paid to his speeches, particularly those given to international audiences. When a prime minister who either writes for himself, or at a minimum provides final approval of every word in his speeches, delivers addresses that are increasingly peppered with libertarian terminology (*pluralism, rule of law, freedoms*, etc.), one can be certain that this is both intentional and instructive about the future course of a Harper-led Conservative government.[28]

AVOID THE POPULIST TRAP

Both social conservatives and libertarians have periodically attached themselves to populism. In the late twentieth century, the various elements of conservatism created a populist trap that had the effect of limiting their electoral success. Social conservatives frequently embraced populism in the naïve hope that direct democracy mechanisms would somehow help them stem the tide of an increasingly secular, liberal political culture. Libertarians, although philosophically opposed to social conservative moralizing, don't fear the consequences of putting their differences to the test of a populist dispute resolution mechanism. The combination of the two doesn't usually represent a threat to libertarians on the policy front. Libertarians know that under most direct democracy scenarios, they will come out winners when the mainstream liberal-pluralist political culture expresses its collective will in favour of rights, autonomy of individuals, freedom of choice, and liberty. Even a referendum on same-sex marriages today would likely at worst face even odds. A vote on abortion would be a slam dunk in favour of choice. But in not fearing the outcome of populist decisions, libertarians too often and too easily surrender their legitimate concerns about the potential for majority tyranny. By legitimizing the populist dispute resolution mechanism, libertarians legitimize the majoritarian principles contained in them, and thereby legitimize the potential for the suppression of individual rights, autonomy, choice, and liberty, so long as it is done democratically. Libertarians should stop surrendering to populist expediency and begin a concerted defence of libertarian-pluralism.

Populism has also been thought to offer Conservatives an escape clause from having to take firm stances on moral issues, so as not to alienate one or the other key elements of the contemporary coalition. And herein lies the populist trap. It is a function of both excessive cleverness and an unwillingness to adopt firm positions on divisive policy domains. By substituting populist direct democracy decision-making mechanisms for firm policy stances, conservatives institutionalize unknowns into their parties' platforms and their identities. By definition, direct democracy contains a quality of the unknown. For if a party's policy platform dictates the eventual public policy outcome, the direct democracy decision-making exercise is meaningless. Likewise, institutionalizing direct democracy decision-making severely restricts the party from taking firm positions on controversial issues when needed, most importantly during election campaigns. Both create uncertainty in the minds of voters. No one can say for sure what the party stands for because, prior to consulting the people, it does not know where it stands. More importantly, the institutionalized uncertainty affords the party's opponents ample opportunity to fill in the unknowns with negatives, especially when supported by the often-extreme utterances of undisciplined party members. It also serves to deny other conservatives the ammunition needed to defend their positions with any certainty, clarity, or conviction. No party can afford to turn over definition of its own identity to its opponents. New parties with high levels of unknown quantities can afford it the least.

The populist trap plagued Reform in its attempt to expand its base outside of Western Canada. It helped turn much of the Alliance's 2000 election campaign into a fountain of comedic material and political ridicule. Harper has so far successfully avoided building a populist trap of his own making—witness the noticeable lack of advocacy for a referendum to resolve the same-sex marriage or abortion issues—but to some extent he has suffered from a residual populist trap hangover from the Reform–Alliance era. It stalled the new Conservatives momentum in the 2004 election and quite possibly was the single biggest issue to forestall their ascension to government at that time. Since then, Harper has increasingly adopted a classical libertarian position when discussing populism.[29] His September 2007 speech to the United Nations Council on Foreign Relations is instructive both for its critical, at times hostile, treatment of populism as well as for its messaging. At one point, he all but equated "political populism and authoritarianism." And while the content of the speech was primarily directed toward Latin American nations, he concluded by admonishing the Americans in his audience that this is not simply a problem for the developing countries of the

Americas. "[T]here is nowhere in the hemisphere that those forces [populism, nationalism, and protectionism] can do more real danger than those forces in the United States itself," and by extension, also in Canada.[30] This speech provides the best example to date of the real Stephen Harper, at least in as much as it is illustrative of his thinking and public pronouncements while he was an opposition MP and while he served as president of the libertarian National Citizens Coalition.[31]

The Conservative Party would be wise to carefully consider their leader's words and intentions and limit their proposed use of referenda to only constitutional or other grand institutional changes. Free parliamentary votes can remain a symbolic aspect of the overall platform but should not be fallen back on so frequently that it delegitimizes using the "whip" when important, often divisive matters of core principle need to be implemented. As the Harper government has demonstrated, its members of Parliament and other party officials must exercise the discipline necessary to act as a cohesive organization, thereby providing Canadians with the assurances that they are competent enough to continue governing. Ideological populists, and those willing to use populism as an excuse for lack of such discipline, should be told, respectfully but firmly, that their opinions would be better expressed through an advocacy group than from within a party organization, and their presence within the Conservative Party should be extinguished.

As part of this process, Conservatives must judiciously avoid the temptation to enlist help from mercenary interest groups: social conservative, populist, or otherwise. The most undisciplined of all associates, they will tarnish the party's image and will abandon the party when their most zealous pursuits are not realized. Their potential for short-term electoral help is dwarfed by the detriment they will cause to the long-term objectives of establishing a broadly based coalition built upon a libertarian core. And once associated with their causes, it is difficult for any party to overcome the negative impression that will have been implanted in the minds of many voters. Trying to extricate the negativity by purging itself of these associations at a later date will likely also prove futile. Few elections have been won on the slogan, "You can trust us . . . now that we have turned on our former friends."

CONCLUSION

By defining its own identity centred on a comprehensive, consistent libertarian core identity, conservatives and the new Conservative Party have begun the process of building the foundations for an enduring and competitive national political party. Instead of denying the continued progression of liberal-pluralism in Canada, Conservatives can succeed by championing individual liberty, pluralism, choice, and a limited state. By eschewing both left-wing social engineering and right-wing moral engineering, by standing in defence of liberty in moral as well as economic affairs, Conservatives can define a place for conservatism in the mainstream of Canada's liberal-pluralist political culture. If carefully organized and executed with discipline, the Conservative Party of Canada has the opportunity to end Liberal Party hegemony and establish itself as a legitimate governing party for the twenty-first century.

NOTES

1. For a concise introduction to these and other issues involving ideology and parties in Canada, see Faron Ellis and Heather MacIvor, *Parameters of Power: Canada's Political Institutions,* Brief Edition, (Toronto: Nelson, 2008); in particular, chapters 1, 4, and 5.

2. For a list of "Ten Commandments for Conservative Campaigning," see Tom Flanagan, *Harper's Team: Behind the Scenes in the Conservative Rise to Power* (Montreal and Kingston: McGill-Queen's University Press, 2007). Important among Flanagan's "Ten Commandments" are unity, moderation, incrementalism, and policy.

3. Ibid., p. 278.

4. In the last half of the twentieth century, only in 1949 (49.2 percent) and 1953 (48.8 percent) did the Liberals approach majority popular vote territory. In most of their other election victories, they garnered less than 45 percent of the popular vote.

5. Flanagan, *Harper's Team,* p. 282.

6. For concise versions of each, see Gad Horowitz, "Conservatism, Liberalism and Socialism in Canada: An Interpretation," pp. 90–106, and Nelson Wiseman, "The Pattern of Prairie Politics," pp. 351–368, both in Hugh G. Thorburn and Alan Whitehorn, eds., *Party Politics in Canada,* 8th ed. (Toronto: Prentice Hall Canada, 2001).

7. See Nelson Wiseman, "Canadian Political Culture: Liberalism with a Tory Streak," pp. 56–67; and Janet Ajzenstat and Peter J. Smith, "The 'Tory Touch' Thesis: Bad History, Poor Political Science," pp. 68–75; both in Mark Charlton and Paul Barker, eds., *Crosscurrents: Contemporary Political Issues,* 4th ed. (Scarborough: Thomson Nelson, 2002).

8. See Harold D. Clarke, Jane Jenson, Lawrence Le Duc, and Jon H. Pammett, *Absent Mandate: Interpreting Change in Canadian Elections,* 2nd ed. (Toronto: Gage Educational Publishing Company, 1991).

9. See R.K. Carty, "Three Canadian Party Systems: An Interpretation of the Development of National Politics," in Hugh G. Thorburn and Alan Whitehorn, eds., *Party Politics in Canada,* 8th ed. (Toronto: Prentice Hall Canada, 2001), pp. 16–32, and R.K. Carty, William Cross, and Lisa Young, *Rebuilding Canadian Party Politics* (Vancouver: UBC Press, 2000).

10. For evidence, see Ellis and MacIvor, *Parameters of Power, Brief,* ch. 5, in particular the table entitled "Canada by the Numbers 5.4: Voter Loyalty 1988–2006," p. 198.

11. See Sydney Sharp and Don Braid, *Storming Babylon: Preston Manning and the Rise of the Reform Party* (Toronto: Key Porter, 1992). For a critique of these early analysts, see Tom Flanagan, *Waiting for the Wave: The Reform Party and Preston Manning* (Toronto: Stoddart Publishing Co., 1995).

12. Faron Ellis and Keith Archer, "Reform at the Crossroads," in Alan Frizzell and Jon H. Pammett, eds., *The Canadian General Election of 1997* (Toronto: Dundurn Press, 1997), pp. 111–133.

13. Faron Ellis, "The More Things Change . . . The Alliance Campaign," in Jon H. Pammett and Christopher Dornan, *The Canadian General Election of 2000* (Toronto: Dundurn Press, 2001), pp. 59–89.

14. Faron Ellis and Peter Woolstencroft, "New Conservatives, Old Realities: The 2004 Election Campaign," in Jon H. Pammett and Christopher Dornan, eds., *The Canadian General Election of 2004* (Toronto: Dundurn Press, 2004), pp. 66–105.

15. Faron Ellis and Peter Woolstencroft, "'A Change of Government, Not a Change of Country': The Conservatives and the 2006 Election," in Jon H. Pammett and Christopher Dornan, eds., *The Canadian Federal Election of 2006* (Toronto: Dundurn Press, 2006), pp. 58–92.

16. For an analysis of Reform opinion structure, see Faron Ellis, *The Limits of Participation: Members and Leaders in Canada's Reform Party* (Calgary: University of Calgary Press, 2005). For a comparison of attitudes of party members in Canada with specific analysis of ideological divisions, see William Cross and Lisa Young, "Policy Attitudes of Party Members in Canada: Evidence of Ideological Politics," *Canadian Journal of Political Science* 35, no. 4 (December 2002), pp. 859–880.

17. See Keith Archer and Faron Ellis, "Opinion Structure of Party Activists: The Reform Party of Canada," *Canadian Journal of Political Science* 27, no. 2 (June 1994), pp. 277–308.

18. Faron Ellis, "Canadian Alliance Party Profile: Results of the 2002 Alliance Convention Delegate Study," Citizen Society Research Lab Seminar Series, March 15, 2005, Lethbridge College.

19. See Conservative Party of Canada, "Results of the March 17–19, 2005, Founding Policy Convention," forthcoming.

20. Faron Ellis, "Conservative Party Profile: Results of the 2005 Conservative Party Convention Delegate Study," Citizen Society Research Lab Seminar Series, November 9, 2007. Overall, 55.5 percent agreed abortion is a matter of private choice, 38.1 percent disagreed, and 6.4 percent were uncertain.

21. See Cross and Young, "Policy Attitudes of Party Members," for a comparison of differences between Alliance and PC members' attitudes.

22. See Department of Finance, *2007 Budget: A Stronger, Safer, Better Canada*, available online at http://www.budget.gc.ca/2007/index_e.html.

23. See Dale Orr, "1: Income Tax Cuts," *National Post*, November 15, 2007, FP15, and his more detailed Global Insight Canada analysis of the federal government's October 2007 *Economic Statement*, and the statement itself, available online at http://www.fin.gc.ca/budtoce/2007/ec07_e.html.

24. For further thoughts on these matters, see Flanagan's "Ten Commandments," (1) Unity and (3) Inclusion, in *Harper's Team*, pp. 277–281.

25. See Ellis and Woolstencroft, "A Change of Government," pp. 62–65.

26. The formal vote on the issue at the 2005 Montreal convention resulted in 74 percent of delegates voting to uphold the traditional definition of marriage.

27. Janice Tibbetts, "Same-sex Debate's Over, Harper Says: MPs Soundly Defeat Motion 175–123," CanWest News Services, December 8, 2006.

28. See, for example, Stephen Harper, "Prime Minister Harper Signals Canada's Renewed Engagement in the Americas," speech delivered in Santiago Chile, July 17, 2007; or "Prime Minister Harper Concludes Meetings with CARICOM Leaders," Bridgetown, Barbados, July 19, 2007. Both these and many other of the prime minister's speeches are available in multimedia format on the government's web pages at http://pm.gc.ca.

29. Noted are the exceptions of using a referendum in attempting to legitimize its plans for ending the barley components of the Canadian Wheat Board's monopoly and Harper's musings about supporting an NDP motion to hold a referendum on abolishing the Senate.

30. Stephen Harper, "PM Addresses the Council on Foreign Relations," New York, September 25, 2007, available online at http://pm.gc.ca.

31. Harper served first as vice-president (1997) and then as president (1998–2002) of the National Citizens Coalition, a libertarian-conservative advocacy organization that has as its slogan "More freedom through less government."

POSTSCRIPT

In his article, Nelson Wiseman sees only dim prospects for modern conservatism and the Conservative Party in Canadian politics. Though there are many reasons for this expected fate, the main one appears to be that modern conservatism is out of step with the beliefs of most Canadians. The tendency of the Harper government to act in a manner quite similar to its Liberal predecessors is seemingly only one manifestation of this assertion. Yet the claim can be questioned. In Wiseman's view, most Canadians supposedly believe in government that takes a leading role in shaping society and providing services, but the past decade or so has witnessed the government cutting both spending and taxes—an action consistent with conservatism and the platform of the Conservative Party. Wiseman also points to what many think to be the Achilles heel of the Conservative Party—namely its potential to support reactionary or extreme stances on moral issues. But the party has so far been able to steer well clear of positions that would limit access to abortion services or marginalize gays and lesbians. And as for Wiseman's belief that certain elements of the electoral map—large cities, certain regions of the country—are beyond the grasp of the Conservative Party, it can be argued that Canadians are more than capable of switching their allegiances. Nothing in Canadian politics is set in stone.

For his part, Faron Ellis is much more positive about the chances of conservatism and the Conservative Party. Indeed, it seems that Conservatives need only be themselves and electoral success will come their way, a belief partially fulfilled with the results of the most recent federal election. But, as with Wiseman, there are questions. Ellis says that Conservatives and their party should stick to an economic platform that finds little favour with "special case" funding for the likes of Quebec and Atlantic Canada. However, the electoral success of the Conservative Party rests in part on breakthroughs in these regions, so to say no to their requests appears self-defeating. Ellis is also tough on social conservatives and the populists who wish for more direct democracy—both must be clearly secondary to the libertarian element of the Conservative Party. Ellis's stance here would certainly make things easy for the party, but some might argue that in effectively simplifying the essence of the Conservative Party, he also ignores important aspects of its makeup. In other words, to win, the Conservative Party must almost deny itself, or at least parts of it. Finally, Ellis subscribes to the belief that the Conservative Party should for the time being embrace a position of moderation and incremental policy changes. He feels this will be sufficient to move the Canadian electorate in the right direction, but it may just as likely cause the Conservative Party to stagnate and become little different from the Liberal Party.

For an understanding of the new Conservative Party of Canada, one might start with Faron Ellis and Peter Wollstencroft's contribution in Jon H. Pammett and Christopher Dornan, eds., *The Canadian General Election of 2004* (Toronto: Dundurn Group, 2004). This article discusses the origins of the party and contains references to documents necessary for appreciating the position of the Conservative Party. A follow-up to this article is another piece by Ellis and Wollstencroft, in Jon Pammett and Christopher Dornan, eds., *The Federal General Election of 2006* (Toronto: Dundurn, 2006). For a more detailed examination of the Conservative Party and its electoral experiences, students should see Tom Flanagan, *Harper's Team: Behind the Scenes in the Conservative Rise to Power* (Montreal and Kingston: McGill-Queen's University Press, 2007). This exciting text also includes much on what is central to the debate on the fate of conservatism and the Conservative Party, namely the appropriate strategy for the new Conservative Party. Flanagan has also written two other interesting articles on this Conservative strategy: Tom Flanagan, "Solidifying Gains," *Literary Review of Canada,* December 2006, and Tom Flanagan, "In Defence of Going Slow," *National Post* (September 28, 2007), A21 (a longer version of which appears in the online journal *C2C: Canada's Journal of Ideas* 1, no. 2).

With this understanding of the party, students might wish to back up and acquire a better picture of the overall party system in Canada, as well as predecessors to the Conservative Party. For these insights, Hugh Thorburn and Alan Whitehorn's *Party Politics in Canada,* 8th ed. (Toronto: Prentice-Hall Canada, 2001), is the place to go. R. Kenneth Carty, William Cross, and Lisa Young's *Rebuilding Canadian Party Politics* (Vancouver and Toronto: UBC Press, 2000) helps to sort out the past, present, and possible future of party politics in Canada. Also useful is James Bickerton and Alain-G. Gagnon, "Political Parties and Electoral Politics," in James Bickerton and Alain-G. Gagnon, eds., *Canadian Politics*, 4th ed. (Peterborough: Broadview Press, 2004). For some deep history on conservative parties in Canadian politics, a good source is Dan Azoulay, *Canadian Political Parties: Historical Readings* (Toronto: Irwin Publishing, 1999).

The debate addresses not only the Conservative Party but also the ideology of conservatism. For information on conservatism and the competing ideologies in Canadian politics, a good place to start is Colin Campbell and William Christian, *Parties, Leaders, and Ideologies in Canada* (Toronto: McGraw-Hill Ryerson, 1996). There are also some useful chapters on this topic: David Bell, "Political Culture in Canada," in Michael Whittington and Glen Williams, eds., *Canadian Politics in the 21st Century,* 7th ed. (Scarborough: Thomson Nelson, 2008); Raymond Bazowski, "Contrasting Ideologies in Canada: What's Left? What's Right?" in James Bickerton and Alain-G. Gagnon, eds., *Canadian Politics*, 3rd ed. (Peterborough: Broadview Press, 1999); and Neil Nevitte and Mebs Kanji, "New Cleavages, Value Diversity and Democratic Governance," in James Bickerton and Alain-G. Gagnon, eds., *Canadian Politics*, 4th ed. (Peterborough: Broadview Press, 2004). Nelson Wiseman's new book, *In Search of Canadian Political Culture* (Vancouver: UBC, 2007), should also be consulted, as should Travis Smith's insightful article on conservative thinking: Dr. Travis D. Smith, "Why Canada Needs Conservatives, Though It Tends to Imagine Otherwise," *C2C: Canada's Journal of Ideas* 1, no. 1.

A number of books have been written about conservative parties in Canadian politics that preceded the formation of the Conservative Party of Canada. These include Jeffrey Simpson, *The Discipline of Power: The Conservative Interlude and the Liberal Restoration* (Toronto: MacMillan, 1980); George Perlin, *The Tory Syndrome: Leadership Politics in the Progressive Conservative Party* (Montreal and Kingston: McGill-Queen's University Press, 1980); Tom Flanagan, *Waiting for the Wave: The Reform Party and Preston Manning* (Toronto: Stoddart, 1995); Trevor Harrison, *Of Passionate Intensity: Right Wing Populism and the Reform Party of Canada* (Toronto: University of Toronto Press, 1995); and Faron Ellis, *The Limits of Participation: Members and Leaders in Canada's Reform Party* (Calgary: University of Calgary Press, 2005).

PART TWO

Is the Canadian Charter of Rights and Freedoms Antidemocratic?

Should the Federal Government Play a Leading Role in Health Care?

Is the Recognition of Quebec as a Distinct Nation a Positive Step for Canada?

Is the Canadian Charter of Rights and Freedoms Antidemocratic?

✔ **YES**
ROBERT MARTIN, "The Canadian Charter of Rights and Freedoms Is
Antidemocratic and Un-Canadian"

✘ **NO**
PHILIP L. BRYDEN, "The Canadian Charter of Rights and Freedoms Is
Antidemocratic and Un-Canadian: An Opposing Point of View"

Do terminally ill patients have the right to a doctor-assisted suicide? Should women have unrestricted access to abortion without fear of criminal penalty? Does freedom of expression include the right to produce and distribute pornography? Are Sunday shopping regulations a violation of freedom of religion? Should people be able to marry same-sex partners? All of these questions raise difficult issues regarding the relationship between individual citizens and their government. In essence, they each pose the same questions: What civil rights does an individual have, and how are they to be protected from the intrusive arm of the state?

In choosing to establish a system of parliamentary government on the "Westminster model," the founders of Canada adopted a British solution to this problem. Parliament would be supreme and would act as the ultimate guarantor of individual rights and freedoms. This solution reflects an implicit trust in both Parliament and the basic democratic values of civil society. It assumes that civil liberties are so deeply ingrained in the national political culture that parliamentarians and citizens alike would never seriously consider using the power of government to infringe upon them. Public opinion and tradition would act as a powerful constraint against any violation of the fundamental civil and political liberties that are considered to be an inherent part of a democratic system. With the establishment of a federal system in Canada, courts were given the task of deciding whether federal and provincial legislatures were acting within their respective jurisdictions, not whether their actions violated civil and political liberties. There was no perceived need to give such rights special judicial protection that put them outside the reach of legislators.

Not everyone was happy with this solution. They pointed to a long history of both provincial and federal governments' trampling of the rights of citizens. In the early part of this century, British Columbia passed laws denying Asians the right to vote in provincial elections. During the Second World War, the federal government arbitrarily seized the property of Japanese Canadians and placed them in internment camps without due process of law.

These experiences, and others, convinced many Canadians that greater protection of civil rights was needed. The Americans provided an alternative solution: define the rights of citizens in a written constitutional document that is beyond the reach of the legislature. The courts, through the power of judicial review, can then pass judgment on whether the legislation passed by a government infringes on civil liberties. John Diefenbaker began to move Canada in this direction in 1960, when his government passed the Canadian Bill of Rights. But this bill was simply an act of Parliament and applied only to the federal government. As a result, Canadian courts made only limited use of the Bill of Rights.

With the adoption of the Canadian Charter of Rights and Freedoms as part of a larger constitutional package, the government of Pierre Trudeau brought in a new era in 1982. With the entrenchment of the Charter in the Canadian Constitution, not only were Canadians given an explicit definition of their rights, but also the courts were empowered to rule on the constitutionality of government legislation.

There is little doubt that the adoption of the Charter has significantly transformed the operation of the Canadian political system. Since the adoption of the Charter, the Supreme Court of Canada has been involved in virtually every issue of any great political significance in Canada. As a result, there has been a growing public awareness about the potential "political" role that the Supreme Court now plays in the lives of ordinary Canadians. Increasingly, Canadians define their needs and complaints in the language of rights. More and more, interest groups and minorities are turning to the courts, rather than the usual political processes, to make their grievances heard. Peter Russell has described the dramatic impact of the Charter on Canadian politics as having "judicialized politics and politicized the judiciary."

Has the impact of the Charter been a positive one? Has the Charter lived up to its promise to enhance Canadian democracy through the protection of civil liberties? Robert Martin, a former law professor at the University of Western Ontario, feels that the impact of the Charter has been largely a negative one. In particular, he argues that the Charter has had an antidemocratic effect on the country and has accelerated the Americanization of Canada. In contrast, Philip Bryden, dean of the Faculty of Law at the University of British Columbia, argues that the Charter plays an essential role in protecting and enhancing the quality of Canadian democracy.

YES

The Canadian Charter of Rights and Freedoms Is Antidemocratic and Un-Canadian
ROBERT MARTIN

INTRODUCTION

On April 17, 1982, the Canadian Charter of Rights and Freedoms became part of our Constitution. Everyone who has written about the Charter agrees its effect has been to change profoundly both our politics and the way we think. Most of the commentators have applauded these changes. I do not.

I believe the Charter has had decidedly negative effects on Canada. It has contributed to an erosion of our democracy and of our own sense of ourselves. It is time for a serious and critical stocktaking.

Let me be clear that I am not suggesting the Charter itself has actually *done* any of this. A central problem with the Charter has been its contribution to our growing inability to distinguish between the concrete and the abstract. The Charter is simply words on a piece of paper. What I will be addressing are the uses to which the Charter has been put by human beings. I will look at the antidemocratic effects of the Charter and then turn to an analysis of its un-Canadian character.

THE CHARTER IS ANTIDEMOCRATIC

By their nature, constitutions express a fear of democracy, a horror that the people, if given their head, will quickly become a mindless mob. As a result, constitutions, all constitutions, place enforceable limitations on the powers of the state and, more particularly, on the lawmaking authority of the people's representatives.

Prior to 1982, the Canadian Constitution did contain such limitations. Our central constitutional document, the British North America Act of 1867, divided lawmaking authority between Parliament and the provincial legislatures and, thereby, limited that authority. But these limitations were purely functional. The authority to make laws about education, for example, rested with the provinces. Ottawa could not make laws about education, and if it attempted to do so, the attempt could be struck down by the courts. The courts had no authority to tell the provinces how to exercise their authority over education, to tell them what kind of laws they should make about education.

This is what changed in 1982. The federal division of powers remained, but for the first time, substantive limitations were placed on lawmaking authority. The judges were given the power to strike down laws that, in their opinion, were inconsistent with the Charter.

It is crucial to understand basic distinctions between legislators and judges. Any Canadian citizen over the age of eighteen is eligible to be elected to Parliament or a provincial legislature. Elected members are directly accountable to their constituents. They must face reelection at least once every five years. By way of contrast, to become a senior judge in Canada, you must be a lawyer, and you must have been one for ten years. You are appointed until age seventy-five through a closed process that a former chief justice of Canada described as "mysterious," and you are made constitutionally independent, directly accountable to no one.

The defining feature of representative democracy in Canada has been that it is up to the elected members of our legislatures to resolve issues of social, economic, and political policy, subject, of course, to the approval or disapproval of the people, which is expressed at periodic elections. This has changed since the adoption of the Charter. Judges can now overturn deliberate policy decisions made by the elected representatives of the people where those decisions do not accord with the way the judges interpret the Charter. This is undemocratic. Some of our commentators call this "counter-majoritarian," but the phrase is pure obfuscation.

We seem to be experiencing great difficulty today in grasping this simple truth about the antidemocratic nature of judicial review of legislation. One explanation for our difficulty is that we have forgotten that liberalism and democracy are not the same thing. Liberalism is about individual rights, about the ability of individuals to do as they please without interference from the state. Liberalism makes protection of the autonomy of the individual more important than the promotion of the welfare of the collectivity. Democracy is, and always has been, about the interests of the collectivity, about majority rule, about power to the people.

There is an inherent and irreconcilable tension between liberalism and democracy. This tension has always been built into our political system, a system that is ordinarily described as liberal democracy.

The Charter is a liberal document. It sets out fundamental notions about the rights of the individual that have always been at the core of liberalism. More to the point, the Charter has led to a shift in emphasis in Canadian liberal democracy. The balance has been tilted in favour of liberalism and away from democracy.

Members of the judiciary, led by the Supreme Court of Canada, have shown little restraint in arrogating to themselves a central policymaking role. In 1984, they conferred upon themselves the distinction "guardian of the Constitution." They haven't looked back.

Our judges have not hesitated to substitute their views of acceptable or desirable social policy for those of our legislators. When the judges have not agreed with the policy decisions of our elected representatives, they have invalidated the legislation that expresses those decisions. But the judges have been prepared to go further. They have shown themselves willing to write legislation, to even go to the point of imposing financial obligations on the state.

The willingness to interfere with the traditional policymaking functions of legislatures has not been restricted to the courts. Administrative tribunals now sit in judgment on the validity of legislation, and boards of inquiry set up under human rights acts rewrite legislation and create new legal responsibilities for individuals.

We have become more and more inclined to seek to resolve the central questions agitating our society in the courtroom, rather than through the political process. The result of this is to surrender to lawyers control of the social agenda and of public discourse.

In a similar vein, the Charter has given a great boost to interest-group politics. Indeed, an active judicial role and interest-group politics seem made for each other.

Interest-group politics is antidemocratic in two respects. It erodes citizenship, the essential precondition to democratic politics. People are induced to define themselves according to their race or sex or sexual preference or some other ascriptive criterion, rather than as citizens. And, in practice, interest-group politics has meant seeking to use the courts as a means of short-circuiting or bypassing democratic processes.

The Charter has thus, in an institutional sense, had an antidemocratic effect. But it has also reinforced ideological currents that are antidemocratic. The most important of these stem from our growing obsession with "rights."

Our fascination with rights has been central to a process through which we seem to have come to prefer the abstract over the concrete. "Rights" appear to be more attractive than real things such as jobs or pensions or physical security or health care. We have been persuaded that if we have "rights" and these "rights" are enshrined in a constitution, then we need not concern ourselves with anything else. It is difficult to describe as "democratic" a public discourse that avoids addressing actual social and economic conditions.

Rights discourse itself encourages antidemocratic tendencies. The inclination of persons to characterize their desires or preferences as "rights" has two unfortunate results. First, there is an inevitable polarization of opposing positions in any debate. And, second, the possibility of further discussion is precluded. If you assert that something is your "right," my only possible response is, "No, it isn't."

Finally, the interest in rights has done much to promote individualistic and, therefore, antisocial ways of thinking. My impression is that many people view their rights as a quiver of jurisprudential arrows, weapons to be used in waging the ceaseless war of each against all.

THE CHARTER IS UN-CANADIAN

It is difficult to imagine any single event or instrument that has played a more substantial role in Americanizing the way Canadians think than has the Charter. The Charter clearly did not begin this process, but it has, since 1982, been central in it.

The basis for my assertion about the Americanizing effects of the Charter is a recognition that, historically and culturally, the Charter is an American document. This truth is seldom adverted to. As a technical drafting matter, the Charter, it is true, was the creation of Canadian lawyers. But the document's roots lie elsewhere. The idea of enshrining the rights of the individual in a constitution and then protecting those rights through judicial intervention is uniquely American. It may well be a good idea, but no one who had the slightest acquaintance with our history could call it a Canadian idea.

"Life, liberty, and the pursuit of happiness" are not simply words in the Declaration of Independence; they are essential notions defining the American experience. Up until 1982, the central Canadian notions were profoundly different. Our social and constitutional watchwords were "peace, order, and good government."

That has changed. I now teach students who are convinced that we did not have a Constitution, that we were not a proper country until we adopted the Charter. We have worked diligently to abolish our own history and to forget what was once our uniqueness. We are now told that the Charter is a basic element in defining what it means to be Canadian. And many Canadians do appear to believe that we can understand ourselves through our approach to the constitutional protection of rights.

The Charter has promoted our Americanization in other ways besides helping persuade us that we don't have a history. We have, as has already been noted, become more individualistic in our thinking and in our politics over the last decade. Again, it would be foolish to see the Charter as the only cause of this, but it is noteworthy that the first decade of the Charter saw an increase in the concrete indications of social alienation—crime, marital breakdown—as well as in more subtle forms—incivility, hostility, and so on. There was a time when one had a palpable sense, on crossing the border, of entering a different society. This is no longer true.

The Charter has led us to forget our uniqueness as Canadians and to disregard our history. It has had an incalculable effect in Americanizing both the way we think and the way we see ourselves. We have become incomparably more individualistic. Our collective sense of ourselves, and our idea of responsibility for each other and the society we share, has been seriously weakened.

Like Americans, we now believe there must be a legal remedy for every social ill. Like Americans, we put "me" first.

CONCLUSION

Many Canadians have contrived to forget that most of the things that once made Canada a fine country—physical security, health care for all, reasonably honest and competent government, sound education—came about through the political process, not as gifts from beneficent judges.

The fact is that, during the period the Charter has been part of our Constitution, ordinary Canadians have seen a steady erosion of their standard of living. Unemployment is high and rising. Social services, health care, and pensions are threatened. Not only has the Charter not been of any help in preventing this erosion; it has served to distract our attention from what has been going on.

The great beneficiaries of the Charter have been the lawyers. They are consulted on issues of public policy, they pronounce on the morality or desirability of political and social beliefs and institutions, their advice is sought in a vast array of situations. The number of lawyers grows exponentially as does the cost of retaining their services.

The Charter has, to judge by media commentators, become the basis of our secular religion. And the lawyers are the priests. At some time, Canadians will decide to take control of their agenda back from the lawyers. That is when we will begin to give serious thought to repealing the Charter.

✗ NO

The Canadian Charter of Rights and Freedoms Is Antidemocratic and Un-Canadian: An Opposing Point of View

PHILIP L. BRYDEN

Robert Martin's essay launches a two-pronged attack on the Canadian Charter of Rights and Freedoms. The Charter is, according to Professor Martin, both antidemocratic and un-Canadian, and the sooner we Canadians come to our senses and realize that our lawyers have hoodwinked us into believing that the Charter is a good thing, the better off all of us (except maybe the lawyers) will be. My own view is that Professor Martin's essay presents a caricature of both the Charter and modern Canadian democracy, and that when we put the Charter in a more realistic light, we will see that the Charter can, and does, make a valuable contribution to Canada's democratic system of government.

The more powerful of Professor Martin's criticisms is his argument that we should get rid of the Charter because it is antidemocratic. Its attraction is that it contains a germ of truth. Like most half-truths, however, it hides more than it reveals.

In its simplest terms, the argument that the Charter is antidemocratic rests on the superficially plausible idea that if nonelected judges are empowered to overturn the decisions of elected politicians, the document that gives them this power must be antidemocratic. The usefulness of the argument lies in its reminder to us that the greatest challenge for a court that has the kind of authority granted by our Charter is to interpret the vague but meaningful generalities on which this authority rests—ideas such as freedom of expression, fundamental justice, and equality—in a way that is consistent with our commitment to democratic government. Where the argument begins to mislead is when its proponents assume that because some judges have had difficulty meeting this challenge in the past, the whole enterprise is doomed to failure.

More specifically, two myths that underpin the notion that the kind of judicial review created by our Charter is inherently antidemocratic need to be exposed. The first myth is that the decisions of our elected legislators and the will of the majority of the electorate are one and the same. Democratic government as it is currently practised in Canada bears little resemblance to the workings of the Athenian polis or a New England town meeting. That observation is neither a disavowal of our current system of representative democracy nor an assertion that the way we presently govern ourselves stands in no need of improvement. It is, however, a reminder that when skeptics examine the record of judicial review using our Charter and point out some court decisions that deserve criticism, we should be evaluating that judicial performance against the reality of parliamentary government in Canada today and not against some romanticized portrait of government of the people, by the people, and for the people.

The second (and ultimately more damaging) myth is that majority rule is, or ought to be, all that modern democratic government is about, and it is in perpetuating the myth that "there is an inherent and irreconcilable tension between liberalism and democracy" that Professor Martin makes his most serious error. My point is not simply that we need a Charter to protect us from the tyranny of the majority, though I think it is dangerously naïve to believe that our fellow citizens are somehow incapable of tyranny. Rather, I want to suggest that democratic government as we should (and to a significant extent have) come to understand it in Canada consists of a complicated web of commitments to each other, only one of which is the commitment to government that in some meaningful way reflects the will of the people.

A belief that important decisions can be taken only after a free and public discussion of the issues, a willingness to abide by a set of rules that govern the way we make authoritative decisions, an acceptance of significant constraints on the use of force—these and many other commitments, some contained in the Charter and others not, are not mere side effects of modern Canadian democracy. They lie at the very heart of democratic government in Canada. And they are part of the reason that the Canadian system of government—notwithstanding all its shortcomings—is respected by people around the world.

This is, I freely acknowledge, a liberal conception of democratic government. Moreover, I recognize that there are other visions of democracy—the kind of Marxist democracy practised by Chairman Mao's Red Guards during the Cultural Revolution, for example—that leave no room for special protection of those who are not able to identify themselves with the will of the majority. For very good reasons, however, Canadians have accepted a liberal notion of democracy, and our commitment to this version of the democratic ideal was firmly in place long before we adopted the Charter.

The real issue is not whether placing some constraints on our legislators is inherently antidemocratic—it isn't. Instead, we ought to ask whether Canadian judges using the Charter can play a useful role in enhancing the quality of our democracy. The answer to this question is not obvious, but I believe that our judges can play such a role, and that by and large our experience during the first few years of the Charter bears this out.

Robert Martin leaves the impression that the Charter has fundamentally undermined the power of our elected representatives to shape the laws that govern our society. If we take a closer look at both the structure of the Charter and the judicial record in interpreting the Charter, however, I find it very difficult to see how that impression can be substantiated.

Because of the types of rights it does (and does not) guarantee, the Charter has little relevance to large and important areas of our political life, notably economic and foreign policy. The judiciary did not bring us free trade with the United States—our political leaders did. And our elected representatives, not our judges, will decide the shape of any new trade pact we may enter into with the

United States and Mexico. Our elected representatives decided to commit our troops in the Persian Gulf War, and they, not our courts, will decide what role we play in other trouble spots around the world.

Where the Charter has had some potential to conflict with social policy, our judges have tended to be rather reluctant to accept claims that individual rights should override important governmental interests. Thus, our Supreme Court has decided that provincial Sunday closing laws reasonably limit freedom of religion and that Criminal Code prohibitions on hate speech and obscenity are acceptable constraints on freedom of expression. We may or may not agree with the wisdom of these and other decisions upholding the right of our politicians to pass laws that place reasonable limits on our constitutionally protected rights and freedoms, but this is certainly not the record of a judiciary that is attempting to undermine democratic government in Canada.

This is not to say that Charter litigation is meaningless because the government always wins. Our courts have made important decisions upholding the rights of refugee claimants, of people accused of crimes, of women, gays and lesbians, and many others. Once again, many of these decisions have been controversial, but I believe they have raised our sensitivity to the concerns of people whose interests are not always well represented through our political process. And in so doing, I would argue, they have enhanced the quality of Canadian democracy.

Professor Martin seems to believe that the Charter has undermined our sense of ourselves as a collectivity and contributed to the rise of a political life that is alternatively characterized by narrow interest-group politics or pure selfishness. To the extent that this description of contemporary Canadian politics has an aura of authenticity about it, however, I think it confuses cause and effect. The popularity of the Charter (indeed much of the need for a Charter) arises from the fact that Canadians understand the diversity of their interests and want to incorporate into their democratic system of government a recognition of the vulnerability of some of those interests.

This diversity of interests was not created by the Charter, and getting rid of the Charter is not likely to usher in a return to a mythical golden age of harmony and communitarian spirit. Throughout our history, Canadians have recognized and sought to give legal protection to our diversity on regional, linguistic, religious, and other grounds, and I suspect that only someone from Ontario could imagine characterizing this as an erosion of citizenship.

Again, the problem of the fracturing of our sense of ourselves as a political community that Professor Martin identifies is a real one, and it is a challenge for supporters of the kind of political ideals that the Charter represents to realize their goals in a way that does not irreparably undermine other political values that are important to us. What Professor Martin fails to do, in my view, is make a convincing case that it is not possible for us to meet this challenge or that it is not worthwhile for us to try to do so.

Professor Martin's second criticism of the Charter is that it is un-Canadian, by which he seems to mean that the Charter contributes to the "Americanization" of Canadian political life. It would be foolish to deny the influence of the United States Bill of Rights on both the content of the Charter and the political will that animated its adoption. In my view, however, Professor Martin is wrong in his attempt to characterize the Charter as a species of cuckoo in the Canadian political nest that seeks to supplant domestic institutions and traditions with unsavoury ideas from south of the forty-ninth parallel.

In response to Professor Martin, I would begin with the rather obvious point that even if some of the important ideas embedded in the Charter were imported into Canada from abroad, so is much of the rest of the apparatus of Canadian government. Canada's parliamentary and common law traditions were imported from England; our federalism was imported (albeit in a substantially altered form) from the United States in 1867; and our civil law traditions were imported from France. In each instance we have made these traditions our own, in some instances by performing major surgery on them in the process.

The Charter itself follows in this tradition of domesticating foreign political ideas and structures. For example, a central element of the American Bill of Rights is the protection of the right to private property. The drafters of the Canadian Charter (wisely in my view) decided that our normal political processes were adequate for the protection of the rights of property owners and that judges should not be given this responsibility under the Charter. In addition, the Charter recognizes certain rights of French and English linguistic minorities, expresses a commitment to our multicultural heritage, and contains approaches to equality and other rights that set it off as a document that is quite distinctive from the American Bill of Rights. The Charter's roots may lie in American soil, but the tree that springs up from those roots is distinctively Canadian.

The more subtle but significant point on which Professor Martin and I disagree is that he seems to use the term "Americanization" as a sort of shorthand for most of what he doesn't like in contemporary Canadian political life. No doubt there are plenty of Canadians who prefer the kind of life we had in the 1970s (or the 1950s for that matter) to the kind of life we have today. What is unclear to me, however, is how unemployment, family breakdown, the consequences of massive public-sector debt for our social welfare programs, and the other things that trouble Professor Martin about life in Canada in the twenty-first century can be laid at the door of the Charter.

In fairness, Professor Martin does not ascribe these social ills to the Charter itself, but he says that the Charter has "served to distract our attention from what has been going on." If the Charter has served to distract Canadians from thinking about the problems of high unemployment and threats to the continued viability of our present schemes for delivering social services, universal health care, and pensions, this is certainly news to me. And I dare say it would come as news to those who took part in the 1993 federal election campaign that revolved around these very issues. Professor Martin is probably correct when he states that the Charter is not going to be of much help in addressing these problems, but nobody ever claimed that it would. More important, we shouldn't assume that because the Charter doesn't address these important problems, the issues the Charter does address are somehow insignificant.

The Charter does not represent the sum of Canadian political life, any more than the American Bill of Rights represents the sum of political life in the United States. From a political science standpoint, what the Charter represents is a special way of addressing a limited range of issues that we feel are unlikely to get the kind of attention they deserve in the ordinary process of electoral politics, and a formal commitment to ourselves that the ideals such as freedom, justice, and equality that the Charter enshrines deserve a special place in our democratic political life. I think this was a commitment that it was wise for us to make in 1982, and that Canadians are right to be proud of this new and distinctive feature of our democracy.

POSTSCRIPT

The debate between Robert Martin and Philip Bryden on the Charter of Rights and Freedoms dates back to 1994. Robert Martin has more recently expanded his critique of both the Charter and the role of the Canadian Supreme Court in a strongly written book entitled, *Most Dangerous Branch: How the Supreme Court Has Undermined Our Law and Democracy,* (Montreal and Kingston: McGill-Queen's University Press, 2004). In this book, Martin writes, "As someone who is committed to the maintenance of constitutional democracy, I cannot avoid seeing the Court as a collection of arrogant and unprincipled poseurs, largely out of control."

But Martin is not the only one to express serious reservations about the impact of the Charter on Canadian political life. One of the most caustic critiques of the Charter has been written by Michael Mandel. In his book *The Charter of Rights and the Legalization of Politics in Canada* (Toronto: Wall and Thompson, rev. ed. 1994), Mandel argues that the Charter has led to the "legalization of politics in Canada." Because the scope of interpretation of the Charter is very broad, judges make highly political decisions. They are not just interpreting the law according to some technical, objective criteria but are actually making the law, usurping the role traditionally reserved only for elected legislators. Because of the high cost of litigation, the legalization of politics, according to Mandel, leads to a conservative, class-based politics that works against socially disadvantaged groups.

Like Martin, Seymour Lipset, a noted American sociologist, argues that the Charter threatens to erase the cultural differences between Americans and Canadians by transforming Canada into a "rights-centred" political culture. See his *Continental Divide* (New York: Routledge, 1990). Christopher Manfredi argues that part of this Americanizing influence is reflected in the frequency with which Canadian judges cite American precedents when making their decisions.

Because of the growing importance of the Charter to Canadian politics, there has been a steady flow of books on this subject in recent years. In addition to the works cited above, students will find the following helpful: Rainer Knopff and F.L. Morton, *Charter Politics* (Scarborough: Nelson, 1992); Patrick Monahan, *Politics and the Constitution: The Charter, Federalism and the Supreme Court* (Toronto: Carswell, 1987); and David Beatty, *Putting the Charter to Work* (Montreal and Kingston: McGill-Queen's University Press, 1987). A book written by a civil rights activist who supports Philip Bryden's arguments is Alan Borovoy's *When Freedoms Collide: The Case for Our Civil Liberties* (Toronto: Lester & Orpen Dennys, 1988). See also Janet Hiebert, *Charter Conflicts: What Is Parliament's Role?* (Montreal and Kingston: McGill-Queen's University Press, 2002); Christopher Manfredi, *Judicial Power and the Charter, Canada and the Paradox of Liberal Constitutionalism,* 2nd ed. (Toronto: Oxford University Press, 2001); Peter McCormick, *Supreme at Last: The Evolution of the Supreme Court of Canada*

(Toronto: Lorimer, 2000); and Rory Leishman, *Against Judicial Activism: The Decline of Freedom and Democracy in Canada* (Montreal and Kingston: McGill-Queen's University Press, 2005).

If we accept Martin's argument that we should be concerned about the impact of the Charter, what can be done? Is Martin's closing suggestion that many Canadians may begin thinking about repealing the Charter a likely outcome? Perhaps a more likely development is that Canadians will begin to take a more careful look at the record of individual judges and to demand more say in their appointment. The question of whether Parliament should review the appointment of Supreme Court judges is taken up in Issue Eight.

Should the Federal Government Play a Leading Role in Health Care?

✔ **YES**
ANDREW HEARD AND DANIEL COHN, "The Federal Government Should Stay Involved: The Case for a Strong Federal Role in Health Care"

✘ **NO**
PAUL BARKER, "The Case against a Strong Federal Role in Health Care"

Federalism is a form of government that divides powers and responsibilities between national and regional governments. The intent behind selecting this type of governing arrangement is to increase the chances that local differences are respected while simultaneously allowing for the achievement of country-wide goals. At first glance, it may seem that the two levels of government would operate independently, each looking after their respective duties. But in reality, they often interact in the making of public policies. The lack of clarity in a nation's constitution, the refusal of policies to fit easily into legislative categories, and the sheer competitiveness of governments are some of the factors that lead to a high degree of interdependence in federal states. In light of this quality, there is a continuous struggle to sort out the roles of federal and provincial governments. Some areas of policy will, eventually, fall mostly to national governments (e.g., national security) and others to provincial ones (e.g., education). But with some policies, there will be disagreement and confusion over who should assume prominence. In Canada, this last situation prevails in relation to health care.

The Canadian health care system (or medicare) offers comprehensive physician and hospital care to all citizens at no direct cost. It is an impressive policy accomplishment and often ranks as the most important public issue in the minds of Canadians. For this reason alone, it is felt that the federal government should take a leading role in the area of health care—medicare is truly a national program and appreciated as such by all Canadians. Supporters of a strong federal role also point to the need for a single authority to offer direction on reforms to the health care system. Medicare needs to continually change to ensure that Canadians are able to receive effective health care, and some believe that the federal government is best positioned to orchestrate the introduction of necessary reforms. In addition, the Canadian health care system has become an important symbol of Canadian values, a situation that also seems to argue for a strong federal presence.

There is, however, a view that suggests that it is unwise for the federal government to assume a lead role in health care. One reason for this is legal: health care is largely a provincial responsibility. The rule of law, an important element in any constitutional democracy, would be allegedly weakened without the provinces directing medicare. A further argument against a strong federal role is that the health system would perform better with the provinces largely in charge. Medicare is in reality ten provincial plans (plus three territorial ones) knitted together by a commitment to principles contained in a piece of federal legislation called the *Canada Health Act*. Accordingly, the provinces have much more experience with health care and much more expertise as well. More generally, it is felt that the national government ought to be spending its time on matters that are more clearly national in scope.

There are also some who feel that the two orders of government should share duties when it comes to health care. It might be said that this is the way it has been done in the past. The federal government sets out the broad principles of health care and provides much needed financial assistance, while the provinces administer the health care plans. A closer look, however, at the history of medicare shows that there has always been a lead player in health care, whether it was the federal government in the initial stages of medicare or the provinces in more recent years. In the past few years, the federal government appears to be attempting to reassert itself. Through various health care accords and a national commission, it has sought to play a guiding role in the reform of the Canadian health care system. The question for this debate is, in a way, whether this recent development bodes well for health care in Canada.

In the readings, Andrew Heard and Daniel Cohn, two political scientists at Simon Fraser University, claim that the Canadian health care system requires a strong hand from the federal government. Paul Barker, one of the editors of *Crosscurrents*, makes the case against a strong presence for Ottawa in health care.

✔ YES

The Federal Government Should Stay Involved: The Case for a Strong Federal Role in Health Care
ANDREW HEARD AND DANIEL COHN

Health care is one of the most important areas of public policy. Canada's system of provincial-run single-payer, universal health insurance plans (popularly known as medicare) enjoys widespread and stable long-term public support.[1] Included in this public judgment is the belief that the maintenance of medicare is a joint responsibility of the federal and provincial governments.[2] Our medicare system has become an important symbol of Canadian identity. Opinion polling conducted in 2005 found that 85 percent of Canadians believed that eliminating public health care would fundamentally change the nature of Canada.[3] The universal and comprehensive medical care that all Canadians are entitled to is one of the most visible differences between Canadian and American cultures.[4] From its public proposal in 1945 through to today, the federal government has played a lead role in creating and guiding medicare. While provincial premiers have taken turns protesting the federal government's invasion of "exclusive" provincial jurisdiction, a brief analysis shows that the federal government is completely justified in taking a lead role. Far from being an invader, it is simply continuing to protect a system it helped develop decades ago. At its heart, medicare in Canada draws its strength from providing basic medical care for all Canadians, regardless of which province they happen to live in. The federal government has an important role to continue to shape and protect this national treasure.

Some historical context is vital to understanding the reasons the federal government plays a substantial role in health care, and also why that role is on solid constitutional ground. When the Fathers of Confederation settled on a division of powers between the national and provincial governments, the guiding principle was that the federal government would be responsible for most important issues, and the provinces would deal with matters of more "local and private concern." Health care then was still very primitive, with only the most rudimentary care available; indeed, it was well into the twentieth century before contact with a doctor was actually likely to improve one's chances of survival. At the time of Confederation, most hospitals were run by religious orders, with a few others set up by other charitable groups or municipalities. The *Constitution Act, 1867* gave the provinces jurisdiction over charities, hospitals, and insane asylums, while the new federal government gained control over marine hospitals and quarantine. These are the only direct references to health care in the formal constitutional documents. All that the provinces were explicitly granted in 1867 was the right to keep an eye on the churches and municipalities that ran the few small hospitals existing at the time. In addition, the provinces were responsible for licensing physicians, as a consequence of their juris-diction over "property and civil rights"; civil rights in this context meant one's rights in property, and not the idea of civil liberties we think of today.

Canadian society responded to such profound disruptions in the twentieth cen-tury as the Great Depression and World War II with new ideas about the role of the state to foster the social welfare of its citizens. The original division of powers between the federal and provincial governments in the *Constitution Act, 1867* proved unable to adapt to the new social and economic realities of the twentieth century. First, the Great Depression showed the necessity of providing people with some insurance against unemployment. The courts ruled that this was a provin-cial responsibility because of their control of most employment contracts, but the provinces simply did not have the financial resources to implement employment insurance. As a result, the *Constitution Act, 1940* was passed to enable the fed-eral government to take responsibility for this area of public policy. Similarly, the post–World War II era saw the acceptance of a universal pension scheme and sup-plemental benefits as a way to care for senior citizens. Again, the provinces had constitutional responsibility without the practical ability to provide these benefits. A constitutional amendment was passed in 1951 to allow the federal government to create the Canada Pension Plan, and another in 1964 authorized it to provide Old Age Benefits; these amendments preserved provincial jurisdiction as well, because Quebec preferred to launch its own version of these schemes. Thus, the context of the period in which medicare was first created was an era of increasing federal government responsibility for social welfare programs—with the full agreement of the provincial governments at the time. Far from being a constitu-tional invader, the federal government was welcomed by many as a white knight.

Without federal policy leadership, it is doubtful that most Canadians would have public health insurance today, as the provinces proved very reluctant as a group to be policy innovators. While Saskatchewan's CCF-NDP governments are popularly given credit for "inventing" medicare, it must be pointed out that Canadians would have had a complete public health insurance plan at the end of World War II if the provinces had accepted the proposals that Ottawa put forward in 1945. Instead, they walked out of the post-war reconstruction conference. Rebuffed when it first raised the topic of public health insurance, the federal gov-ernment offered to subsidize the creation of universal, single-payer, provincially run hospital and diagnostic services insurance in 1957, as well as insurance for physician bills in 1966, only after support for each measure had reached critical mass in provincial capitals and with voters.[5]

In order to evaluate the merits of the federal government's role in health care policymaking, we must first identify medicare's actual character and scope. Canada's system of provincially run, single-payer, universal health insurance plans is not a coherent countrywide program, nor does it represent the full extent of public involvement in the financing of health care. Rather, it should be seen as the backbone of a framework within which each province has designed its own system for financing and delivering health care. This framework provides provincial governments with unparalleled autonomy in designing their own health care systems. In a recent study of health care policymaking in federations, K.G. Banting and S. Corbett found that all of the federal governments that they studied played some role in structuring health care, and that Canada had the most decentralized health care policymaking process among the countries studied.[6]

In order to qualify for the full value of the transfers that provinces are entitled to under the Canada Health Transfer,[7] they must abide by the five conditions of the *Canada Health Act*. These govern the way that they manage and finance physician, hospital, and diagnostic services:

- Universality: All permanent residents of the province must be eligible to join the plan.

- Comprehensive: All medically necessary services must be insured. In practice, there is no agreed list of services. Rather, it has been left up to each province to determine what is and is not medically necessary (subject to objections from the federal health minister).[8]

- Accessibility: Services must be reasonably available, and there can be no out-of-pocket charges to patients for those services covered by a provincial plan. Initially, only hospital and diagnostic services were covered by this ban on user fees. However, the *Canada Health Act* extended this ban to physician services. This act also specifically gave the federal minister the power to reduce a province's subsidy by one dollar for each dollar of user fees that it allowed.

- Portability: The plan must provide coverage for members travelling outside of their province.

- Public Administration: The plan must be run by an agency responsible to the provincial legislature on a not-for-profit basis.

As noted above, in comparative terms, Canadian provinces have a great deal of autonomy. However, even the five terms noted above are less stringent than they would first appear. The federal government has only rarely found provinces to be so far out of compliance as to warrant penalties in the form of deductions from their transfer payments.[9] The power exercised by successive federal governments to ensure compliance with these terms has been so light it has raised questions from the auditor general of Canada.[10] In fact, since 1977, provinces have not even been required to spend the money sent to them by Ottawa, or the supporting tax powers that Ottawa has given them (through programs such as the Canada Health Transfer and its predecessors) on the provision of health care. For the financing and delivery of health care goods and services other than physician, hospital, and diagnostic services—important items provided outside of hospitals such as dentistry, optometry, physiotherapy, nursing homes, and elder and home care—even the loose rules of the *Canada Health Act* do not apply.

It has been suggested that Ottawa is trying to play a greater leadership role now that it is flush with budget surpluses. A good example is the 2000 first ministers' health accord. This deal provided some money "string-free," but also set aside some money that provinces could use only for the purchase of new "health technology." While many thought this meant the provinces were compelled to use the money to buy more state-of-the-art diagnostic equipment so as to cut queues, in fact any equipment used in the health care system was eligible, including lawn mowers.[11] Therefore, it is a bit difficult to argue that the federal role should be reduced further, as Canadian provinces already have more autonomy than subnational jurisdictions in other major federations, and the rules that constitute the existing, minimal federal framework tend to be enforced very moderately and with great discretion.

A federal role is also required because the provinces have proven reluctant to manage health care. When Saskatchewan created its physician insurance plan in the early 1960s, doctors went on strike to protest the loss of professional autonomy that they felt would result. The strike ended with an agreement that set the terms for the subsequent spread of provincial physician insurance plans. Provincial governments would be responsible for overall funding but would leave professional management of care in the hands of physicians, who would work (for the most part) as private entrepreneurs, billing the province on a fee-for-service basis. Those who wanted could "opt-out" and bill their patients directly either for the same fee set by the province or an additional amount. In these cases, the patient would apply to the province for reimbursement at the provincially set rate. As concern moved from building provincial health systems in the 1950s and 1960s to placing them on a more financially sustainable footing in the 1970s and 1980s, the provinces proved unwilling to make the tough choices needed to control health costs, because it would involve confronting the medical profession and other powerful interest groups.

What started as a concession to ease the concern of a few doctors became a means for provinces to avoid managing their health care systems and a potential threat to health care accessibility. This was exacerbated in 1977 when Ottawa agreed to grant the provinces more leeway in how they managed their health care systems. Instead of being reimbursed 50 cents on the dollar for providing services Ottawa approved of, provinces received a block grant to spend as they wished. Therefore, if the provinces could not keep costs under control, they, not Ottawa, would be responsible for the extra costs. User fees provided a loophole that would allow provinces to avoid managing their problems or paying the price for their inability to manage: if the physicians' fee chart was kept artificially low, the patient—not the province—was on the hook for the extra costs. In some provinces, there were substantial problems accessing care without user fees. Most notable in this regard was Ontario, where more than half of all anesthesiologists and more than one-third of obstetricians were extra-billing. It was at this point that Ottawa stepped in and banned extra-billing with the introduction of the *Canada Health*

Act. It is worth pointing out that the decision to ban user fees for physician, hospital, and diagnostic services was seen as so essential that the *Canada Health Act* received unanimous support in the House of Commons on final reading.[12]

This pattern has been repeated on other occasions as well, with the majority of provinces refusing to make the tough decisions necessary to manage their health care systems until Ottawa takes some determined action that compels the provinces to face their problems. The most recent example of this is the wave of hospital rationalizations that swept the provinces during the 1990s and the early years of the new millennium. Although some provinces, such as Alberta, acted on their own, most did less than they could have done until confronted with the cuts to transfers implemented by the federal budgets in 1994–95 and 1995–96. Given that the majority of provinces are reluctant to either innovate or manage their health care systems, a minimal federal health policy framework is necessary to ensure provinces maintain the key features of the program, let alone modify it so as to take better account of the reality of modern health care by providing universal access to home care and pharmaceutical coverage.

It is also worth pointing out that the national consensus exhibited when the *Canada Health Act* was unanimously passed by the House of Commons appears to be holding firm. When Prime Minister Harper's Conservatives came to power, many feared that the five principles embedded in the *Canada Health Act* might be watered down or simply ignored (especially the prohibition on user fees). After all, as leader of the right-of-centre National Citizens Coalition, Prime Minister Harper had urged his home province of Alberta to take complete control over health policy and simply ignore the terms of the *Canada Health Act.*[13] Yet, the Conservatives have been in power for more than a year, and no changes to the act have been proposed, and none appear on the horizon. In fact, both the prime minister and Health Minister Tony Clement have sided with opponents of Alberta's government when it tested the waters on policy changes that would have violated the act.[14] As with the Mulroney Conservatives, who supported the passage of the *Canada Health Act* while in opposition, and the Diefenbaker Conservatives, who appointed the Royal Commission, which recommended that provincial hospital insurance be extended to cover physician bills in the 1960s, today's Tories seem to have concluded that Ottawa has an important role to play in health care policymaking and that reducing this role does not make sense.

Finally, health care is both an expensive and extensive activity, representing a relatively consistent 10 percent annual share of Canada's gross domestic product. In today's dollars, health spending is about $160 billion when including both public and private expenses. If health care's share of the gross domestic product were to rise, Canada's international economic competitiveness could be undermined. Because the maintenance of this competitiveness is a major concern and responsibility of the federal government, Ottawa has no choice but to take a hand in health policy and not simply restrict its role to financier of provincial policy. This is especially the case in that medicare provides Canada with a competitive advantage over the United States in many vital industries, including automobile manufacturing. Even with the rapid increase in natural resource prices that has occurred in recent years, automobile manufacturing is still Canada's number two source of export earnings after oil and natural gas.[15]

With an appreciation of the actual nature and extent of the federal government's role in health care, one can examine the constitutional grounds for this role. Some provincial leaders trumpet health care as the "exclusive jurisdiction" of the provinces and feel that any federal involvement violates the Constitution. Like many good myths, this view has some real basis in fact. Indeed, the opening words of section 92 of the *Constitution Act, 1867* declare: "In each Province the Legislature may exclusively make Laws in relation to Matters coming within the Classes of Subject next hereinafter enumerated. . . ." This statement is followed by a list of areas of public policy, including charities, asylums, and hospitals. Some believe that this is conclusive evidence that the federal government is treading on provincial toes by daring to legislate on insured medical treatments. However, there are two crucial pieces of the puzzle that must also be fitted into the picture before one can draw proper conclusions on the subject.

First, the whole constitution is much more than just the literal words found in the documents comprising the formal Constitution of Canada. If those documents were to be taken literally, then the federal government would be fully entitled to exercise its powers of reservation and disallowance to veto any provincial legislation to which it objected. While the constitutional documents list certain areas of public policy as the "exclusive" jurisdiction of one level of government or the other, the modern reality is that just about every area of public policy is affected by the activities of both levels of government. For example, the federal government has "exclusive" jurisdiction to legislate on criminal law, but major changes are almost always discussed first with the provincial governments in an effort to get a consensus of support before amending the Criminal Code. A complex pattern of interaction among all governments is sustained right across the policy spectrum.

Secondly, modern Canadian federalism depends to an enormous extent upon "fiscal federalism," which has origins in the formal Constitution but has developed into a much broader and more substantive framework through intergovernmental agreements. These arrangements have allowed the provincial governments to implement important policies that would otherwise have remained only possibilities within the provinces' theoretical jurisdiction. The profound differences in economic activity across this country mean that Canadians would have vastly different provincial public services if the provincial governments relied exclusively on the income generated within their provinces. A belief in the basic equality and worth of Canadians fostered the development of a succession of financial schemes to transfer money from the federal government to the provinces so that Canadians across the country would receive roughly similar benefits. At various times, those federal funds have accounted for up to half of some provincial budgets. Without funding from Ottawa, Canadians living in several provinces would almost certainly still not have comprehensive medical coverage. There is simply no way that the poorer provinces could have afforded to implement the medicare programs that are so appreciated by all Canadians today.

The main federal involvement in medicare is the transfer of money to the provinces, with some conditions attached, rather than legislation aimed purely at regulating insured medical services. The conditions, as we discussed above, are aimed at maintaining some common benefits for Canadians across the country. The crux of the debate then really revolves around the constitutionality of these conditional grants.

There are two basic grounds for justifying the federal government's ability to set some conditions on the grants given to the provinces. The first is the notion of the "federal spending power." In its essence, this idea suggests that the federal government is free to make gifts to the provinces and to attach some conditions upon the receipt of those gifts. While there is some debate over the extent of the federal spending power, there can be little doubt about its basic constitutionality. In *Reference re Canada Assistance Plan* (1991), the Supreme Court of Canada upheld the basic ability of the national Parliament to create conditional block grants and to alter their terms unilaterally.[16] A key point for the court was that the federal legislation principally sets the terms under which federal money can be transferred and does not attempt a broader regulation of a provincial matter. The *Canada Health Act* would appear to satisfy this approach to the federal spending power. The only real "enforcement" under the act is the withholding of federal funding, and actual enforcement is sporadic and limited.[17] If a provincial government were to violate any one of the five main conditions of the *Canada Health Act*, the federal government *may* withhold funds after consulting with the provincial government; the withholding is discretionary. The only mandatory withholding of funds is provided in the case of a province that permits extra-billing; the federal government's contribution for health care is reduced on a dollar-for-dollar basis. The *Canada Health Act* might be constitutionally vulnerable if the provinces could establish that the impact of the federal legislation negated their ability to exercise their policy powers on the matter.[18] However, the provincial governments are ultimately free to pursue their own policies if they are prepared to substitute their own revenue for the money that the federal government would otherwise donate. As a result, the act seems to be consistent with the Supreme Court's view that federal legislation under the spending power must concern conditions of dispensing its own funds and not attempt a broader, independent regulation of provincial matters.

It is important to note, too, that Canadians support the federal government's power to attach conditions to its health care transfers. While 72 percent of Canadians in 2004 believed that the federal government was not paying its fair share of health care, 67 percent believed that new federal spending should come with conditions rather than letting provincial governments administer the funds as they see fit.[19] Admittedly, this poll contradicts the findings in other surveys that have asked more generic questions about whether the provincial governments should be able to spend health care funds according to their own priorities; in most of these polls, respondents favoured provincial autonomy. Nevertheless, it is revealing that when Canadians were asked to focus specifically on the federal government's role, such a strong majority believed that the federal government should direct how new funds are spent.

The other possible constitutional justification relies on the POGG power, which the courts have interpreted to flow from the opening words of section 91 of the *Constitution Act, 1867* that empower the federal government to "make laws for the Peace, Order, and Good Government of Canada." In an enduring contradiction, the courts have declared this statement to mean that the federal government may pass laws that would normally be in provincial jurisdiction, when the plain English reading of this whole clause seems to explicitly preclude federal legislation on matters listed in section 92 as belonging to the provincial legislatures. As bizarre as this may seem, it is nonetheless an important doctrine of the Constitution and has been developed by the courts for well over a century now.

The federal Parliament may, in two general sets of exceptional circumstances, pass laws that would normally be matters for the provinces. The first is in times of emergency, but this does not apply to health care. The other set of circumstances is when there is a matter of "national concern" or with "national dimensions" involved. Both of these could possibly apply to the *Canada Health Act*. Health care is so vital to Canadian society that the most basic tenets of public health insurance need to be set nationally. If some provinces strayed from the agreed programs, the viability of the coast-to-coast coverage of all Canadians could be seriously threatened. Minor provincial variations could be tolerated, but any significant deviation would undermine medicare. In the case of extra-billing, some doctors charging small amounts would not threaten public health care, but many doctors charging substantial fees would be a very different stress. Events in the early 1980s showed how quickly extra-billing could spread to defeat the basic premise of public health care. By 1983, 62 percent of anesthetists and 39 percent of obstetricians in Ontario were charging their patients significant amounts for any operations they performed.[20] In particular regions of Ontario, every single member of a medical specialty was extra-billing, charging fees that could reach as high as $400 for the delivery of a baby. While many doctors waived fees for their poorest patients, such a situation presented other people with an expensive outlay for health care. What was supposed to be a universal program of health care funded from insurance premiums and tax dollars soon threatened to degenerate into a patchwork across the country; in most provinces all insured services remained free, but in others the extra-billing meant that Canadians living in those provinces faced significant charges for basic health care and hospital treatment.

Had the federal government not intervened in 1984 and the trend of extra-billing continued, the medicare system might not have survived into the twentieth-first century in a form we would recognize.

These circumstances might possibly meet the test laid down by the Supreme Court of Canada in the *Crown Zellerbach* case.[21] In that decision, the court held that federal legislation could be enacted under the POGG power on matters of provincial jurisdiction if provincial inaction or inability would lead to the collapse of a particular regulatory scheme. The corollary of this position could occur if one or more provinces willfully pursued contrary policies that seriously undermined a public policy in which there was a real national interest. The real-world experience of provincial innovation with extra-billing indicates that the medicare system might require federal legislation if it is to survive.

In conclusion, it is both desirable and constitutional for the federal government to play a substantial role in health care. Canadians deeply value the comprehensive medicare programs that insure everyone across the country for a comprehensive range of treatments, as well as ensuring that their coverage moves with them across the country. Federal grants have permitted all Canadians to enjoy relatively comparable levels of health care that simply could not have been achieved without the federal government. A 2003 Ekos poll found that, in the public's eyes, the single most important aspect of the Canadian health care system was equal access to health care for all Canadians.[22] While there are still differences in treatment and waiting times from province to province, those differences pale in comparison to what might exist without the lead role taken by the federal government. Provincial autonomy in health care still exists; any province could pursue its own objectives if it is prepared to fund medicare itself. So far, at least, provincial governments have decided to abide by the collective vision of health care that successive federal governments have defended. Even the richest provinces have concluded it is better to abide by the national policy preferences. It is important to note, too, that provincial autonomy does not necessarily mean advancements in health care. The track records of some provincial governments in experimenting with extra-billing in the 1980s and hospital closures in the 1990s and early 2000s demonstrate that provincial innovations can have a very negative impact on health care. Neither does the participation of the federal government stifle policy development. Organ donation and prescription drugs are just two of the many areas where federal, provincial, and territorial governments are working collaboratively to develop better public policy for all Canadians. It is important to note that it is the provinces and territories themselves that wish to see such partnerships. It is not a case of Ottawa trying to muscle in on their turf.[23] Ultimately, the federal–provincial dynamic provides a system of healthy checks and balances that depends upon a national consensus to survive. Medicare is a unique policy area that accommodates differences in provincial political cultures while transcending them at the same time. Medicare was created thanks to the leadership shown by the federal government and that role is needed just as much today.

NOTES

1. Matthew Mendelsohn, *Canadians' Thoughts on Their Health Care System: Preserving the Canadian Model through Innovation* (Ottawa: Commission on the Future of Health Care in Canada, 2002).

2. Antonia Maioni, "Federalism and Health Care in Canada," in Keith G. Banting and Stan Corbett, eds., *Health Policy and Federalism: A Comparative Perspective on Multi-Level Governance* (Montreal and Kingston: McGill-Queen's University Press, 2002), p. 177.

3. Stuart N. Soroka, "Canadian Perceptions of the Health Care System" (Toronto: Health Council of Canada, 2007), p. 23.

4. Peter C. Newman, "Remembering Pierre Berton," *Maclean's Magazine* (December 13, 2004), pp. 36–38.

5. D. Cohn, "The Canada Health and Social Transfer: Transferring Resources or Moral Authority?" in P.C. Fafard and D.M. Brown, eds., *Canada: The State of the Federation, 1996* (Kingston: Queen's University Institute of Intergovernmental Affairs, 1996), pp. 169–171.

6. K.G. Banting and S. Corbett, "Health Policy and Federalism: An Introduction," in K.G. Banting and S. Corbett, eds., *Health Policy and Federalism: A Comparative Perspective on Multi-Level Governance* (Montreal and Kingston: McGill-Queen's University Press, 2002).

7. From 1977 to 2005, there were three different federal transfers to the provinces for the nominal support of medicare and to which the terms of the *Canada Health Act* applied after it passed in 1984. From fiscal 1977/78 to 1996/97, there was the Established Program Financing (EPF) transfer, which funded medicare and post-secondary education. In the 1995/96 budget (effective 1996/97), this was merged with the Canada Assistance Plan (CAP), which funded social programs, including the cost of medical and health services for low-income families not covered by medicare (called "extended health" services), to create the Canada Health and Social Transfer (CHST). In the 2004/05 budget, the CHST was split into the Canada Health Transfer and the Canadian Social Transfer.

8. This has led to federal–provincial disputes as to what should be covered. The most persistent case surrounds the unwillingness of some provinces to fund abortion services. See Laura Eggerson, "Abortion Services in Canada: A Patchwork Quilt with Many Holes," *Canadian Medical Association Journal* 164 (March 20, 2001), pp. 847–849.

9. K.G. Banting and R. Boadway, "Defining the Sharing Community: The Federal Role in Health Care," in H. Lazar and F. St-Hilaire, eds., *Money, Politics and Health Care: Reconstructing the Federal–Provincial Partnership* (Montreal and Kingston: The Institute for Research on Public Policy and the Institute of Intergovernmental Relations, 2004), pp. 15–16.

10. Auditor General of Canada, *Status Report of the Auditor General of Canada to the House of Commons* (Ottawa: Office of the Auditor General of Canada, September 2002), ch. 3.

11. L. Priest, "Fund for Medical Machines Buys Lawn Tractors," *The Globe and Mail* (April 2, 2002), p. A1.

12. S. Heiber and R. Deber, "Banning Extra-Billing in Canada: Just What the Doctor Didn't Order," *Canadian Public Policy* 13, no. 1 (1987), pp. 62–74; M. Begin,

"Revisiting the Canada Health Act: What Are the Impediments to Change, A Speech to the Institute for Research on Public Policy" (Montreal: Institute for Research on Public Policy, February 20, 2002); Joseph Magnet and Sandra Rodgers-Magnet, "Medicare Under Siege," *The Globe and Mail* (December 29, 1983), p. A7.

13. S. Harper, T. Flanagan, T. Morton, R. Knopff, A. Crooks, and K. Boessenkool, "The Alberta Agenda [An open letter to the Hon. Ralph Klein, Premier of Alberta]," *Policy Options* (April 2001), pp. 16–17.

14. D. Walton and B. Curry, "Alberta Backs Off Private Medicare Blueprint," *The Globe and Mail* (April 21, 2006), p. A1

15. Industry Canada, "Trade Data Online Database," available at http://strategis.gc.ca/sc_mrkti/tdst/engdoc/tr_homep.html. Accessed on November 1, 2007; D. Hakim, "This Year Ontario May Pass Michigan in Making Vehicles," *New York Times* (November 27, 2004), p. C1.

16. *Reference re Canada Assistance Plan* [1991] 2 *Supreme Court Reports*, p. 525.

17. Sujit Choudhry, "The Canada Health Act and the Social Union: The Need for Institutions," *Osgoode Hall Law Journal* 38 (2000), p. 39.

18. Dale Gibson, "The Canada Health Act and the Constitution," *Health Law Journal* 4 (1996), p. 1.

19. Soroka, "Canadian Perceptions of Health Care," p. 35.

20. Magnet and Rodgers-Magnet, "Medicare Under Siege."

21. *R. v. Crown Zellerbach* [1988] 1 *Supreme Court Reports*, p. 401.

22. Ekos Research Associates, "Romanow Tracking Poll (November 2004)," available at http://www.ekos.com/admin/articles/Romanow24Nov2003.pdf. Accessed on March 17, 2005.

23. The Canadian Council for Donation and Transplantation, *Enhancing Tissue Banking in Canada: Phase I Sustainability* (Edmonton: The Canadian Council for Donation and Transplantation, 2007), pp. 1–4; Conference of Provincial/Territorial Ministers of Health, "News Release: Health Ministers Continue Working on the National Pharmaceuticals Strategy" (July 5, 2006), available at http://www.scics.gc.ca/cinfo06/830882004_e.html. Accessed on November 1, 2007.

✗ NO

The Case against a Strong Federal Role in Health Care
PAUL BARKER

A major issue in Canada is whether the federal government should take the lead in the area of health care. There is great concern about the Canadian health care system itself, but a related concern is which level of government should assume the dominant position in ensuring that Canadians receive effective health care services. In the past, the federal government has been central to the introduction of hospital and physician programs, the core elements of the publicly funded health care system in Canada known as medicare. More recently, it has reached agreements with the provinces that require the latter to introduce health care reforms that are consistent with the wishes of the federal government. Some are comfortable with the federal government in this role and believe that a service as important to all Canadians as health care requires a great deal of direction from the centre. Not only will this increase the chances of ensuring that all parts of the country have access to medically required care, but it will also confirm health care as an important symbol of Canadian citizenship and values.

There are others, however, who are uneasy with a strong federal presence in the area of health care. They believe that such a presence may violate the country's Constitution, which authorizes the provinces to handle most aspects of health care. The federal government has authority to act on public health matters and to provide health services to specific groups. But legal responsibility for the major elements of the Canadian health care system—hospital care, physician services, community-based care, and prescription drugs—rests with the provinces. Those who find little favour in a major federal role in health care also believe that the goal of providing high quality care will be best achieved by allowing the provinces to head the effort at reforming health care services. The sheer experience and expertise of the provinces, garnered through three decades of directly administering their health plans, almost alone make the case for this argument. A final contention is that a strong federal role in health care draws the national government away from a concern more pressing than health: the security of the country. Canada needs a national government able to guide it in a world that is increasingly volatile and decidedly unsympathetic to nations unprepared and poorly equipped. Implicit in this last argument is the notion that medicare should become more of a health care program and less of a symbol of Canadian beliefs and values.

LEGAL ARGUMENT

The legal argument against the primacy of the federal government in health care relies on two considerations. One is that such a role may violate the terms of the Constitution. The written Constitution places the great bulk of responsibility for health care with the provinces, yet federal actions in this area take little notice of the division of powers. The other consideration is that a strong federal presence offends the spirit of the Constitution and its treatment of health care. Even if a constitutional challenge to aggressive federal actions in health care were to fail, it could still be argued that a strong federal role takes insufficient heed of the intent of the Constitution to have the provinces carry the brunt of the load in the field of health care.

Provisions in the Canadian Constitution and accompanying judicial review suggest that responsibility for the Canadian health care system lies mostly with the provinces. Section 92(7) of the *Constitution Act, 1867* states the provinces have legislative responsibility for hospitals, and case law has interpreted other heads of provincial powers as giving the provinces authority over such matters as the regulation of doctors, the training of health professionals, and the operation of social insurance plans. It thus seems fair to conclude that "[w]hen it comes to health, the provinces hold the front lines."[1] However, it would be wrong to argue from this that a federal presence is obviously unconstitutional, for there are powers in the Constitution that give authority to the federal government to act in the area of health. The most important of these is the federal spending power, which allows the federal government to transfer funds to the provinces and place conditions on the use of these funds as long as these conditions fall short of an attempt, in effect, to regulate in an area of provincial jurisdiction. Many believe that federal conditional grants for health—which have formed the basis for Ottawa's involvement in medicare—respect the limits of the federal spending power.[2] They allow the federal government to shape activities in health care without crossing the line by attempting to effectively legislate elements of provincial health plans. The question of the constitutionality of the federal actions hinges in part on the veracity of this claim.

It seems clear that traditional federal conditional grants for health care are safe from any constitutional challenge. These grants simply stipulate that the provinces follow some quite general requirements in return for receiving financial assistance from the federal government. For instance, the provinces should endeavour to ensure that their plans offer a "comprehensive" set of services and are "universal" in the sense that all residents are covered. Similarly, residents must have "reasonable" access to health care services, and efforts ought to be made to make health benefits "portable" and administered on a non-profit basis. All of these conditions or requirements give the provinces some flexibility in the management of their plans (or stipulate requirements that no government would do otherwise even in the absence of the stipulations). But other aspects of the federal role paint a different picture. The *Canada Health Act,* a piece of federal legislation, outlines the aforementioned general conditions, but it also includes a further condition: namely, the provincial plans prohibit hospital user fees and physician charges at point of service. This prohibition is achieved by reducing federal grants to the provinces equal to the amount of user fees and physician charges levied in the province; a province that levies, for example, two million dollars in hospital user fees loses the same amount in federal funding. This condition, unlike the other conditions in the federal legislation, appears to be more precise in its aim and more determined to shape a particular aspect of provincial plans—in other words, there is no room for flexibility, and hence this condition takes on the character of a regulatory activity. Recent federal–provincial accords also suggest that the federal government has become more specific in its requests. In the accords, the provisions state that new monies must be spent on particular areas (e.g., primary health care, home care), and some even go so far as to require the purchase of particular items relating to health care (diagnostic imagining machines).[3] As with the prohibition on charges and fees, these too appear to be an attempt to regulate health care through the provinces and hence constitute an unconstitutional use of the federal spending power.

A defence against this last claim can be made based on a distinction between compulsory regulation and voluntary regulation.[4] Clearly, a federal law that forces the provinces to do something within the latter's jurisdiction or directly regulates a matter that is a provincial responsibility would be in violation of the Constitution. This is compulsory regulation. But it is argued that the use of the federal spending power in health care does not engage in this type of regulation. Rather, it engages in a voluntary form of regulation—here, the provinces can either accept or reject the health care conditions. Admittedly, a rejection of federal conditions means less or even no federal money, but still the absence of compulsion is apparent. The problem with this line of defence is that there is an element of compulsion. In light of the high cost of health care, the provinces really have no choice: they must gain access to the federal funds and hence must observe the accompanying conditions. It is an offer the provinces are unable to refuse.

The second consideration in the legal argument against a strong federal role is that such a role is inconsistent with the spirit or overall intent of the Constitution. An impressive number of heads of power in section 92 of the *Constitution Act, 1867* place most of the responsibility for health care services with the provinces. These heads include property and civil rights, matters of a local or private nature, and management of hospitals. Accordingly, surveys of constitutional responsibility of health care inevitably conclude that the overall aim of the Constitution is to allow the provinces to take the lead in health care. Some might argue that this is an artifact of circumstance, that the Fathers of Confederation would have allocated powers differently if they had been able to foresee the import of health care to the nation. But the centrality of the provinces is also a product of judicial review, which is of much more recent vintage. And for some legal scholars, it makes sense to place responsibility with the provinces—the drafters of the *British North America Act* were more prescient than we give them credit for.[5] A primary federal role thus seems out of place, for the relevant law and the accompanying spirit appear determined to give the provinces pride of place in the area of health care. Of course, it is possible that a strong federal role might be ruled consistent with the letter of the law. The federal spending power, for instance, might be invoked to support aggressive federal actions in the area of health care, and there is case law to back up such an interpretation. In this guise, the spending power means that Ottawa "may attach to any grant or loan any conditions it chooses, including conditions it could not directly legislate."[6] But surely this is equivalent to engaging in an end run on the Constitution, an activity that hardly respects its spirit.

Recent developments supply some evidence for revealing how the spirit of the law goes unrecognized. In 2001, the federal government set up a commission to study the future of health care without any provincial participation in its activities. As Richard Simeon says, it seems strange to examine medicare without the inclusion of government entities most identified with health care.[7] Not surprisingly, the report of the commission talks insistently about the need for federal leadership and a strong presence at the centre.[8] In 2003, the federal and provincial governments agreed to an accord stipulating that new federal monies had to be spent on particular areas, and a year later another accord followed the same line of development.[9] As mentioned already, the accords can be seen in violation of the letter of the law. But perhaps the greater injury is to the spirit, because the accords reverse the process that is to be expected: the federal government submits its plans, and the provinces inevitably accept them. The provinces have attempted to introduce their own plans for reform into the proceedings, but these have been summarily rejected. The accords also made provision for a national body—the Health Council of Canada—whose main task is to monitor the implementation of the provisions contained in the accord of 2003. This, too, represents a failure to appreciate the intent of the Constitution, for the council endeavours to track the behaviour of the provinces and report on any shortfalls. More ambitiously, it also seeks to provide some leadership on issues it deems important to the health of Canadians (for example, waiting lists). The council, while well intentioned, fails to respect the fact that it is the provinces that are largely responsible for the maintenance and development of the Canadian health system. Supporters of the council are quick to point out that the council includes members from provincial governments, but the fact is that the federal government initiated the proposal without effusive support from the provinces (and, indeed, Quebec and Alberta refused to accept the body). As with many developments in health care, the council was a price that the provinces had to pay in order to get federal funding.

POLICY ARGUMENT

Any federal state seeks to establish arrangements between the two levels of government in order to produce the best policies and programs possible. The legal division of powers is one such arrangement. But sometimes a state's constitution fails to allocate responsibilities in a way that provides for good public policy, and a disjunction between the legal and desired division of roles emerges. In this situation, a need to supplement or amend the legal structure becomes evident. However, with respect to health care in Canada, no such disjunction exists. As shown, the Canadian Constitution places responsibility squarely with the provinces, and, as will be shown now, this is an allocation that contributes to an effective and equitable health care system in Canada. A strong federal leadership role in health care is thus not only inconsistent with the Constitution but also detracts from the effort to produce good health care programs in Canada.

The policy argument against a strong federal role in health care begins with a consideration of claims made in favour of giving the provinces primacy in formulating and implementing health care programs. In a federal state, the policy role of the national government can be derived from an attempt on the part of central authorities to address the failings of the provinces; such an exercise thus requires first an understanding of the benefits of leaving policy to the provinces.[10] There are at least three reasons for believing that the aim of producing good health care policy will be best met by strong provincial leadership. One reason is that the provinces are better positioned than the federal government to determine the differing health care preferences of individual Canadians across the country. Although all Canadians wish for an effective health care system, they may differ in how this is best achieved. Some may feel that a strong hospital sector is necessary to achieve this end, while others may prefer a more community-based approach. Similarly, the provinces may differ on the appropriate decision-making structures in relation to health care—nearly all provinces have set up regional health authorities, but the membership, structure, and duties of these bodies are not the same across the country.[11] The fear associated with a strong federal role is that the national government will be insensitive to these differing preferences in its attempt to offer a national health care system; a major attraction of federalism is its capacity to reflect the diversity of a nation, yet a too-strong national government can nullify this quality.

A second and related reason is that the provinces are better informed on what it takes to build a workable health care system. The greater expertise stems from the past thirty years of making and carrying out health care programs. During these years, the federal government has participated in making the Canadian health care system a success, but its role has largely been related to providing for conditional grants—not running health care programs. It has been the banker of health care, not the maker. A case might be made that the federal government is not at an informational disadvantage in the early stages of developing a country's health care system, but medicare in Canada has long left this stage of development and now finds itself in a period of renewal, which requires a level of expertise derived from close experience working with health care programs. Such challenges as reorganizing the delivery of primary health care (including the redefining of responsibilities of health care workers), rationalizing the supply of hospital services, and determining the efficacy of medical procedures are hardly suited for an order of government with little familiarity with the intricacies of health care services. Moreover, the informational requirements also extend to an appreciation of the political dynamics associated with health care reform. It is not enough to know what has to be done: success in health care also depends on knowing how it is to be done. And, again, the provincial governments are better positioned to understand the local politics of health care.

A third and final reason for provincial primacy in health policy is that it increases the chances of policy experimentation. A strong federal role does not necessarily rule out experimentation, but a strong provincial role guarantees a country with ten laboratories in which to test new ideas. The attraction here is that one or two provinces may experiment with a proposed change in health care and not put the entire health care system in harm's way. If the innovation tests well, the other provinces can elect to incorporate it into their health care systems; if it fails, then little damage is done. A famous U.S. Supreme Court justice nicely captures the essence of this third benefit of provincial primacy:

> It is one of the happy incidents of the Federal system that a single coura-geous state [or province] may, if its citizens choose, serve as a laboratory, and try moral, social, and economic experiments without risk to the rest of the country.[12]

At present, there is evidence of the desire of some provinces to experiment. Among these provinces, Alberta is arguably the most ambitious. It believes that medicare would benefit if the private sector were more greatly involved in health care through the provision of necessary health care services. The province has also believed at times that various types of direct patient charges might ease the pres-sure on provincial health care plans. Most experts find little research to support such initiatives, but the latter have not been thoroughly tested in Canada. Experimentation can help eliminate the uncertainty about privatization and do so without incurring the possibility of injury to the entire Canadian health care system.

The preceding suggests that substantial policy benefits arise from giving the provinces primacy policy over health care. It is also true, however, that this same arrangement can lead to some costs. Any significant differences in provincial health care programs may dissuade some Canadians from moving from one province to another—for example, to take a new job. This would be an undesirable development, because a smooth-functioning market needs people to use their skills in the most productive way. A province may also make decisions that have unwanted effects on other provinces; for instance, it may refuse to provide full health care coverage to residents visiting from other parts of the country. The aforementioned costs are associated with losses in efficiency in that provincial decisions on health care may have negative effects on the allocation of scarce resources in the country. But the more important cost might be in relation to equity and the aim of any nation to instill an element of fairness in its provision of public services throughout the country. Provinces acting on their own without central direction may produce a health system that fails to provide all Canadians with a set of roughly comparable health care services. Considerations of fairness suggest that it is appropriate that health care programs—in either their structure or effect—be fairly similar across Canada. Unity considerations also come into play at this point: a country with widely disparate levels of services may produce tensions and animosities between regions that threaten the viability of the country.

All of these possible costs point toward the need for a federal role that reduces the prevalence of the difficulties created by the provinces. But this need not be a strong role. What is required here is what the federal government has done in the past, which is to set out some general conditions that remind the provinces of their commitment to making medically necessary health care accessible to all Canadians. And the emphasis here is on a *gentle* reminder, for the provinces mostly act as one in relation to the broad strokes of health policy (though, as mentioned, differences in details may appear). A perusal of provincial health plans reveals a great deal of similarity in terms of their basic contours, and a review of provincial planning for the future again reveals similar thinking (reform of physician and hospital care, more community-based services, greater emphasis on promotion and prevention). In the past couple of years, the federal government has felt it necessary to become more aggressive in monitoring the provinces and to make available monies only for certain services and programs. But many of these services and programs have been under consideration by the provinces for several years. There is, in other words, no need for a federal role in health care policy that goes beyond the general conditions contained in the *Canada Health Act*. And even if provincial plans were to diversify more in the future, an argument could still be made for limiting Ottawa's role. Canadians may decide that the benefits of differentiation more than compensate for the loss in comparability. Alberta may begin to charge patients directly, Quebec may pursue more aggressively its use of for-profit imaging clinics, and Ontario may lean heavily on nurse practitioners to solve its perceived shortage of doctors—and Canadians may accept these developments with little notice. The balance between achieving similar health plans and allowing the provinces to go their own way has historically been in favour of the former, but this balance is not set in stone. Indeed, opinion surveys show that Canadians are willing to try new ways of delivering and financing health care.[13]

PHILOSOPHICAL ARGUMENT

The philosophical argument against a strong federal role in health care is that such a role draws the national government away from its core duties and in particular its primary role of providing security for the nation. Accordingly, *philosophical* in this context refers to the well-known belief in liberal philosophy that the key obligation of any national government is to provide for stability. Under certain circumstances, when peace and stability reign, a national government can afford to concern itself with matters unrelated to security. But most of the time, discussions of national leadership typically relate to the development of foreign and defence policies that protect a nation against aggressors. At present, Canada is in need of this kind of leadership, but it is not clear that its national government is meeting this need. Ultimately, the philosophical argument against Ottawa taking the lead in the reform of the Canadian health care system is that it is needed more elsewhere.

In allocating powers in a federal state, there is little disagreement about assigning responsibility for national security to the central government. If there is any issue that has countrywide dimensions and surmounts regional differences, it is security and the literal survival of the nation. The *Constitution Act, 1867* reflects this belief by giving Ottawa authority over such matters as the military, navy, militia, and overall defence of the country. There is also little argument that this issue must be a primary concern—if not *the* primary concern—of any national government. Without security and the provision of some kind of order, there can be no basis for a workable society. As Thomas Axworthy writes, "... we should never forget that the first principle of the state is to promote the human security of our own citizens. ..."[14] Despite this understanding, there are signs that the federal government is falling short of carrying out its most important duty.

One sign is the questionable capacity of Canada to defend itself against potential threats to its security. Once, Canada had one of the largest armed forces in the world, but now they are a pale shadow of their former selves. Andrew Cohen writes that Canada's armed forces "are among the weakest in the industrialized world" and notes that our expenditures on defence measured in terms of their share of GDP rank seventeenth among the nineteen members of the North Atlantic Treaty Organization.[15] Not surprisingly, Canada finds itself hard-pressed to deal with terrorism both in and outside its borders, and its contributions to addressing other international threats are disappointing. In the eyes of its allies, its intentions are good, but its capabilities are woeful—Canada is "a kind of well-meaning Boy Scout."[16] Another sign is the decline in its ability to conduct relations with other countries. As with its armed forces, the Canadian foreign service was once a presence in world affairs, but now that time is gone. Maintaining the security of the nation relies not only on armaments but also on men and women skilled in the arts of diplomacy. Unfortunately, Canada appears largely without the necessary diplomatic and conceptual skills for navigating the world of international politics.

Arguably the most dispiriting sign is the inability of the national government to define a role for Canada in the post–Cold War era. At times, this inability seems to stem from a desire to withdraw from world affairs, to have no real role, and to rely on others to sort out the complexity of international relations. But other times, it appears as a failure to apply the necessary attention to an important issue. The national government understands the need to undertake such a role, for only it can provide the necessary framework for addressing the security of Canada. However, its priorities appear to lie elsewhere, in health care and other domestic issues. In the 2004 federal election, the prime minister declared that the number one priority of a Liberal government would be health care and that reducing waiting times represented the "litmus test" of his government's most important commitment.[17] In other words, the federal government would direct it energies toward ensuring that Canadians do not have to wait as long for health care services. With this kind of sentiment, there should be little wonder about the absence of an articulated position for Canada to take in world affairs. Ensuring that Canadians have timely access to health care is important, but it should not be the primary preoccupation of a national government.

Some believe there is much exaggeration about the failings of the national government in the area of defence and foreign policy. There are indications that the federal government is aware of the threat of terrorism—for example, it has directed additional funds to this area and passed new anti-terrorist legislation—and the state of the armed forces is not as bad as some claim. Even so, the actions of the federal government may still seem wanting. For a national government to carry out its duty to defend the country, it is not enough to provide a defence of the citizenry. This role, if fully exercised, can also be used to give definition to a nation. Cohen, for one, believes a decision on part of the federal government to reengage itself in world affairs would have a uniting effect:

> What we do abroad will enrich us at home. For a country forever wondering if it has a future, indeed doubting if it has one, the new Canadian internationalism could become an instrument of pan-Canadian unity, taking us beyond the boundaries of language and race and region, drawing on all elements of a truly diverse society.[18]

Of course, it is contended that this is exactly what the federal government is doing with health care, using it to give definition and unity to Canada. Moreover, it is also believed that a withdrawal of the federal government from a leadership position in health care would put at risk the nation-building capability of this public program. But as suggested, greater involvement in foreign affairs can accomplish the same purpose while at the same time ensuring the security of the nation. For those who believe that the commitment to health care is too deep-rooted to be so easily replaced, it has to be remembered that the universal health care system has been a part of Canada for only the past thirty or so years.[19] What also has to be remembered is that it is the underlying values of government programs that are important and not the programs themselves. Medicare has served admirably in reminding Canadians of what is means to be a Canadian, but other programs can perform this function just as well.

There is also the possibility that lessening the importance of health care to Canadians may actually be beneficial in a further sense. The reform of health care at times requires actions that appear threatening to medicare (for example, closing hospitals or de-insuring certain services), and elected officials may be reluctant to take such actions in the glare of public attention on health care. The fact that major adjustments to health care involve the participation of first ministers also points to the highly charged atmosphere in which health care reform takes place. A less emotive setting might lead to better health care policy. The de-emphasis of health care could also provide a related benefit, which is to give provincial governments more room in which to allocate their revenues. The national importance of medicare, especially in recent years, has led to provincial budgets that pay a lot of attention to health care and look less favourably on other significant responsibilities. It is often claimed that medicare underpins the notion of Canada as a sharing community. But sometimes it appears as if the emphasis on health care only forces governments and the electorate to concentrate on health and to neglect other activities that make a contribution to Canadian life.[20] The fear is that the underlying sentiment here is not one of sharing, but almost a desperate determination to ensure that one's own health care needs are met.

MOST RECENT DEVELOPMENTS

Most recent developments suggest a federal government more willing to act in a manner that respects both the legal preeminence and policy expertise of the provinces in the area of health care. These same developments also indicate that Ottawa may pay more attention to matters of security and less to health care. On being elected in 2006, the government of Stephen Harper pursued a promise of patient wait-time guarantees by which provinces would set a reasonable wait time for specified procedures and arrange for care elsewhere if this time were exceeded.[21] However, it proceeded cautiously on this matter in light of provincial demands for additional federal funding to finance the guarantees; the tepid embrace of the guarantees also reflected the beliefs of the prime minister, who felt that "the federal government should live up to its financial commitments but should otherwise let the provinces exercise their constitutional jurisdiction [in health care]."[22] Eventually, by April 2007, the federal government and the individual provinces and territories had come to an agreement on a patient wait-times guarantee. In exchange for new federal assistance, each of the provinces (and territories) would set out wait-time guarantees for one of the designated priority fields in health care by 2010.[23] Some criticized the arrangement, saying that the provinces picked areas where they had already recorded progress on wait times—put differently, the agreement did little to accelerate the movement toward bettering access to necessary care.[24] But in truth it was a prudent agreement, one that underlined provincial control over health care and accepted that provinces had a better appreciation of health care challenges than did the federal government.

A more sensible federal approach to health care recently can also be seen in the reaction of Ottawa to provincial health initiatives. In 2006, the Alberta government announced a new health plan containing some noteworthy proposals. One proposed allowing doctors to practise in both the public and private health care systems, while another authorized the purchase of private insurance for medically required care; still another stressed the need to consider reducing the number of services insured under the medicare system.[25] In the past, similar provocations on the part of Alberta had led to an aggressive federal government demanding a withdrawal of the proposals (or actions) and threats of withholding of federal funds on the grounds that the *Canada Health Act* had been violated. However, this time the federal government, as with the guarantees, acted more cautiously. The federal health minister said he would have to look at the proposals carefully and see whether they fit with the aforementioned federal legislation.[26] The prime minister then followed up with a letter to the premier of Alberta, arguing that the province's proposals would generate some unwelcome outcomes.[27] A short time later, the Alberta government withdrew its proposals.

At the same time, the Quebec government announced some new health measures in response to an earlier decision of the Supreme Court of Canada. The court had ruled the province's prohibition on the purchase of private health insurance to be in violation of the Quebec Charter of Rights; the fear was that the decision would open up the floodgates in Quebec to the development of a parallel private health care system accessible only to the well-off. The response of the Quebec government was to provide immediate access to private insurance, but only for specified procedures, which could be provided only by doctors operating outside the provincial health plan. It also set out a health care guarantee by which patients could secure care in a private facility in cases where wait times in the public system exceeded a certain period of time.[28] The actions of the Quebec government amounted to an attempt "to lift the ban on private insurance without undermining the public health system."[29] Watching these developments in Quebec, the federal government might have been tempted to assume an aggressive stance, one that placed the entire emphasis on the protection of the public health care system and strict adherence to the *Canada Health Act*. But Ottawa understood that the courts had placed the province in a difficult situation and that the Quebec government had to be accorded some flexibility.

Another telling development is evidence of little direct federal action in the provinces. This can admittedly be interpreted in various ways, but a plausible interpretation is that these provinces are achieving some important health care changes without any substantial federal intervention. Take Ontario, for example. It has completely revamped the institutional structure for the planning, financing, and management of major health services. Under the new system, the Ministry of Health has devolved responsibility for the financing and delivery of hospital care, home care, community-based care, and other services to fourteen regionally based structures. The expectation is that the decentralization of decision-making will lead to a provision of care more sensitive to actual needs of communities. At the same time, the central ministry of health has been reformed to assume a role that emphasizes planning and evaluation, in the hope of providing for a more efficient and directed health care plan.[30] The province has also achieved impressive reductions in wait times for various services, and a similar level of success has been recorded in attempts to create primary care groups. The latter development has also witnessed the greater use of health care professionals who complement the work of physicians, a significant accomplishment in light of the traditional resistance to doctors to this kind of setup.[31] These developments in Ontario reflect recent financial contributions of the federal government, but they also remind us of the expertise in health care administration found at the provincial level.

A final recent development relates to the earlier argument about the need for the federal government to reset its priorities and focus more on security matters and less on areas of provincial jurisdiction. According to one expert on security, Canada remains a "bit player" in world affairs, but there are nevertheless some positive signs in this field.[32] In the past few years, the federal government has attempted to articulate a new and more prominent role for Canada in international relations; the days of letting other countries take the lead appear to be coming to an end. The most apparent result of this change in thinking has been Canada's effort in Afghanistan, where Canadian troops have been engaged in full-scale battles against insurgency groups. The federal government has also budgeted for more financial resources to be directed at defence and has already impressed experts with purchases of much-needed trucks, ships, and aircraft.[33] More generally, the federal government is paying more attention to defence and foreign affairs. Perhaps the best indication of this is the effort that Prime Minister Harper has directed toward foreign relations. "Well, I've said one of the big surprises I have had on the job has been the degree to which international affairs occupies my time, my workload, and my actual responsibilities. . . ."[34]

CONCLUSION

For the most part, the federal role in health care in Canada has been to provide the provinces with financial assistance, with the stipulation that provincial health plans observe some general conditions. This is a role that recognizes the primacy of the provinces in health care. The provinces are allowed to shape their plans with little interference from federal authorities, a situation consistent with the constitutional framework and with the requirements of sound public policy. It also increases the chances that the national government will concern itself with truly national matters and not be distracted by issues that can be handled by the other order of government. Accordingly, a strong federal role in health care upsets traditional arrangements for health care and puts at risk the benefits of these arrangements. At present, some feel that the challenges facing the health care system require federal leadership; Ottawa needs to use its spending power (and financial resources) to force the provinces to make the necessary reforms in their health care plans. But the policy benefits of such action will be negligible—the provinces are better positioned to reform medicare—and it will be contrary to the spirit of the Constitution. Moreover, a strong federal role in health care reform will draw the national government away from its true purposes.

NOTES

1. Andre Braen, "Health and the Distribution of Powers in Canada," in Tom McIntosh, Pierre-Gerlier Forest, and Gregory P. Marchildon, eds., *The Governance of Health Care in Canada* (Romanow Papers, Volume III) (Toronto: University of Toronto Press, 2003), p. 30.

2. See, for example, Peter Hogg, *Constitutional Law of Canada,* Loose-leaf Edition (Toronto: Thomson Carswell, 1997), p. 6.8.

3. First Ministers' Meeting—Communiqué on Health (September 11, 2000); 2003 First Ministers' Accord on Health Care (February 5, 2003).

4. Hogg, *Constitutional Law of Canada,* p. 6.8.

5. Braen, "Health and the Distribution of Powers in Canada," p. 42.

6. Peter Hogg, quoted in Keith Banting and Robin Boadway, "Defining the Sharing Community: The Federal Role in Health Care," in Harvey Lazar and France St-Hilaire, eds., *Money, Politics and Health Care: Reconstructing the Federal–Provincial Partnership* (Montreal and Kingston: The Institute for Research on Public Policy and the Institute of Intergovernmental Relations, 2004), p. 6.

7. Richard Simeon, "We've Tied the Commission's Hands," *The Globe and Mail* (April 13, 2001), p. A13.

8. Commission on the Future of Health Care in Canada, *Building on Values: The Future of Health Care in Canada* (November 2002), ch. 2.

9. First Ministers' Meeting, *A 10 Year Plan to Strengthen Health Care* (September 2004).

10. Robin Boadway, "The Folly of Decentralizing the Canadian Federation," *Dalhousie Review* 75, no. 3 (Winter 1996), pp. 333–334.

11. Carolyn Tuohy, *Accidental Logics: The Dynamics of Change in the Health Care Arena in the United States, Great Britain, and Canada* (New York: Oxford University Press, 1999), p. 98.

12. Harvey Rosen et al., *Public Finance in Canada,* 2nd ed. (Toronto: McGraw-Hill Ryerson, 2003), p. 166.

13. Matthew Mendelsohn, *Canadians' Thoughts on Their Health Care System: Preserving the Canadian Model through Innovation* (Saskatoon: Commission on the Future of Health Care in Canada, June 2002), pp. 9–13.

14. Thomas Axworthy, "Choosing Canada's Role in the World," *National Post* (October 16, 2004), p. RB1.

15. Andrew Cohen, *While Canada Slept: How We Lost Our Place in the World* (Toronto: McClelland & Stewart, 2003), p. 27.

16. Michael Ignatieff, quoted in J.L. Granatstein, *Who Killed the Canadian Military?* (Toronto: Harper Flamingo Canada, 2004), p. 179.

17. Liberal Party of Canada, *A Fix for a Generation: The Paul Martin Plan for Better Health Care* (2004).

18. Cohen, *While Canada Slept*, p. 203.

19. Michael Bliss, "The Great Myths of Medicare," *National Post* (September 7, 2004), pp. A1, A9.

20. In Ontario, for example, the expenditures of the provincial government are coming close to representing nearly half of all *program* expenditures.

21. Conservative Party of Canada, *Stand Up for Canada: Federal Election Platform*, 2006, p. 30.

22. Tom Flanagan, *Harper's Team: Behind the Scenes in the Conservative Rise to Power* (Montreal and Kingston: McGill-Queen's University Press, 2007), p. 79.

23. Andrew Mayeda, "Tories Claim Victory on Wait Times," *National Post* (April 5, 2007), p. A4.

24. "There's Nothing to These Waiting-time Guarantees," editorial, *The Globe and Mail* (April 6, 2007), p. A12.

25. Government of Alberta, *Health Policy Framework*, February 2006.

26. Gloria Galloway, "'We're Studying It,' Ottawa Says," *The Globe and Mail* (March 1, 2006), p. A4.

27. Brian Laghi, "PM Warns Klein of Gaps in Care, Queue Jumping in Health Plan," *The Globe and Mail* (April 8, 2006), p. A9.

28. Government of Quebec, *Guaranteeing Access: Meeting the Challenges of Equity, Efficiency and Quality, Consultation Document* (Government of Quebec, February 2006).

29. Rheal Seguin, "Quebec Government Walked Fine Line to Shape Health Plan," *The Globe and Mail* (February 18, 2006), p. A7.

30. John Ronson, "Local Health Integration Networks: Will 'Made in Ontario' Work?" *HealthCare Quarterly* 9, no. 1 (2006).

31. W. Michael Fenn, "Reinvigorating Publicly Funded Medicare in Ontario: New Public Policy and Public Administration Techniques," *Canadian Public Administration* 49, no. 4 (Winter 2006), pp. 541–44.

32. J.L. Granatstein, *Whose War Is It? How Canada Can Survive in the Post-9/11 World* (Toronto: Harper Collins, 2007), p. 205.

33. Janice Gross Stein and Eugene Lang, *The Unexpected War: Canada in Kandahar* (Toronto: Viking Canada, 2007).

34. "Looking Back at a Year in Power," *National Post* (February 6, 2007), pp. A18–19. The speaker is, of course, the prime minister.

POSTSCRIPT

In a calm and measured way, Andrew Heard and Daniel Cohn show why many believe the federal government ought to play an important role in health care in Canada. Ottawa was integral to the introduction of medicare, and it has been essential to pushing reluctant provinces into adopting necessary health care changes. It has also been there when the very survival of medicare seemed at risk. For those who fear that the federal government may be treading all over the Constitution, Heard and Cohn argue convincingly that such fears are unfounded. There are, however, a few spots in which the two authors might be more convincing. They say that the provinces are not up to the task of making necessary reforms, yet one wonders whether the provinces are truly incapacitated. The two also state that the provinces are free to reject federal transfers if they dislike the attached conditions but acknowledge that these transfers are essential to the well-being of many provinces. Heard and Cohn are also impressed with the fact that the provinces possess a great deal of autonomy in comparison with sub-national states in other federations. But it fails to follow that this opens the door for a stronger federal presence in Canada. Perhaps the Canadian provinces are just better able to handle health care than their counterparts located elsewhere.

In his effort, Paul Barker is concerned that a strong national role will run roughshod over the spirit of the Constitution if not the actual provisions and judicial interpretations. He also seems impressed with the ability of the provinces to make sound health policies and thinks that a strong federal role leads to the neglect of more proper duties of the federal government. All of this is perhaps worthy of consideration, but the arguments are vulnerable. As Barker admits, the legal case against a strong federal role seems to rest largely on the rather shaky grounds that somehow the spirit of the Constitution—which is not really defined—is somehow violated. He also thinks a strong provincial role is necessary to preserve different approaches to the delivery and financing of health care but later on says that provincial health plans are largely similar. Do we really need to preserve the possibility of differences when few differences actually appear in provincial plans? As for his belief that a strong federal role leads to the neglect of the security of the nation, it omits the possibility that a federal government might be able to do both. His claim that medicare should assume less importance seems misguided: Canadians believe strongly in this program and seem less than willing to give it up as a symbol of this country's beliefs and values. Barker also appears impressed with the stance of the Harper government on health care and concurrent developments in the provinces. Yet, there appears to be a palpable fear that medicare is once again losing its way without a strong federal presence (especially on the matter of wait times) and that recent provincial initiatives—such as Ontario's regional authorities—may well fall short of expectations. Finally, Barker seems all too eager to see federal-provincial relations in health care as a clash of titans, but Heard and Cohn show that the two orders of government are capable of cooperative actions.

Students interested in this issue might begin with articles that provide an overview of federalism and health care in Canada: Antonia Maioni and Miriam Smith, "Health Care and Federalism," in Francois Rocher and Miriam Smith, eds., *New Trends in Canadian Federalism,* 2nd ed. (Peterborough: Broadview Press, 2003); Antonia Maioni, "Health Care," in Herman Bakvis and Grace Skogstad, eds., *Canadian Federalism: Performance, Effectiveness and Legitimacy,* 2nd ed. (Toronto: Oxford University Press, 2007); and Alan Davidson, "Dynamics without Change: Continuity of Canadian Health Policy," *Canadian Public Administration* 47, no. 3 (Fall 2004). Two additional pieces might also be consulted for a close-up view of recent developments relating to the federal role in health care: Gerard Boismenu and Peter Graefe, "The New Federal Tool Belt: Attempts to Rebuild Social Policy Leadership," in *Canadian Public Policy* 30, no. 1 (2004), and Tom McIntosh, "Intergovernmental Relations, Social Policy and Federal Transfers after Romanow," *Canadian Public Administration* 47, no. 1 (Spring 2004). Gerard Boychuk has also written some articles that bring us up to date on federal–provincial relations and health care: Gerard Boychuk, "The Chretien Non-Legacy: The Federal Role in Health Care Ten Years On ... 1993–2003," in Lois Harder and Steve Patten, eds., *The Chrétien Legacy: Politics and Public Policy in Canada* (Montreal and Kingston: McGill-Queen's University Press, 2006); Gerard Boychuk, "Patience! ... Wait Time Guarantees and Conservative Health Care Policy," in G. Bruce Doern, ed., *How Ottawa Spends 2007–2008: The Harper Conservatives—Climate of Change* (Montreal and Kingston: McGill-Queen's University Press, 2007); and Gerard Boychuk, "How Ottawa Gambles: Rolling the Dice in Health Care Reform," in G. Bruce Doern, ed., *How Ottawa Spends, 2005–2006: Managing the Minority* (Montreal and Kingston: McGill-Queen's University Press, 2005). The next step is to examine how the Constitution treats health care, and for this, one should refer to Peter Hogg, *Constitutional Law of Canada: Student Edition 2007* (Toronto: Carswell, 2007), chs. 6 and 32; Andre Braen, "Health and the Distribution of Powers in Canada," in Tom McIntosh, Pierre-Gerlier Forest, and Gregory P. Marchildon, eds., *The Governance of Health Care in Canada* (Toronto: University of Toronto Press, 2004); and Dale Gibson, "The Canada Health Act and the Constitution," *Health Law Journal* 4 (1996).

To participate in this debate, students need to understand the policy implications of assigning health to one level of government or another. Robin Boadway and his colleagues have provided a useful framework for addressing this most important issue: Robin Boadway, "Recent Developments in the Economics of Federalism," in Harvey Lazar, ed., *Canada: The State of the Federation 1999/2000* (Montreal and Kingston: McGill-Queen's University Press, 2000), and Keith Banting and Robin Boadway, "Defining the Sharing Community: The Federal Role in Health Care," in Harvey Lazar and France St-Hilaire, eds., *Money, Politics and Health Care:*

Reconstructing the Federal-Provincial Partnership (Montreal and Kingston: Institute for Research on Public Policy and the Institute of Intergovernmental Relations, 2004). Allan Maslove also provides some direction on this issue as well: Allan Maslove, "National Goals and the Federal Role in Health Care," in National Forum on Health, *Canada Health Action: Building on the Legacy: Striking a Balance between Health Care Systems in Canada and Elsewhere* 4 (Ottawa: Her Majesty the Queen in Right of Canada, 1998), and Allan Maslove, "Health and Federal-Provincial Financial Arrangements: Lost Opportunity," in G. Bruce Doern, ed., *How Ottawa Spends, 2005-2006: Managing the Minority* (Montreal and Kingston: McGill-Queen's University Press, 2005). For differing views on the actual impact of allocating major responsibility for health care to one level of government or the other, students should consult the following publications: Gregory P. Marchildon, *Three Choices for the Future of Medicare* (Ottawa: Caledon Institute of Social Policy, April 2004); Michael Rachlis, *The Federal Government Can and Should Lead the Renewal of Canada's Health Policy* (Ottawa: Caledon Institute of Social Policy, February 2003); Commission on the Future of Health Care in Canada, *Building on Values: The Future of Health Care in Canada Final Report* (Saskatoon: Commission on the Future of Health Care in Canada, November 2002), ch. 2; various chapters in Tom McIntosh, Pierre-Gerlier Forest, and Gregory P. Marchildon, eds., *The Governance of Health Care in Canada* (Toronto: University of Toronto Press, 2004); Antonia Maioni, "Decentralization in Health Policy: Comments on the ACCESS Proposals (and comments by John Richards)," in Robert Young, ed., *Stretching the Federation: The Art of the State in Canada* (Kingston: Institute of Intergovernmental Relations, 1999); and Thomas J. Courchene, *Redistributing Money and Power: A Guide to the Canada Health and Social Transfer* (Toronto: C.D. Howe Institute, 1995), ch. 5.

In his article, Barker argues for a federal government that spends more time on security policy and less on health care. For sources on the state of Canada's foreign and defence policies, students might look at the following: Andrew Cohen, *While Canada Slept: How We Lost Our Place in the World* (Toronto: McClelland & Stewart, 2003); J.L. Granatstein, *Who Killed the Canadian Military?* (Toronto: HarperFlamingo Canada, 2004); and the February 2005 issue of *Policy Options*. These sources are largely critical of Canada's attempts to provide sound arrangements for the security of the country. Different interpretations of Canada's relations with the rest of the world include Jennifer Welsh, *At Home in the World: Canada's Global Vision for the 21st Century* (Toronto: HarperCollins, 2004); Laura Macdonald, "In the Shadow of the Superpower: Beyond Canada's Middle Power Image," in Michael Whittington and Glen Williams, eds., *Canadian Politics in the 21st Century* (Toronto: Thomson Nelson, 2004); Andrew Cooper, "Canadian Foreign Policy after September 11: Patterns of Change and Continuity," in James Bickerton and Alain-G. Gagnon, eds., *Canadian Politics*, 4th ed. (Peterborough: Broadview Press, 2004); and the set of articles in Janine Brodie and Linda Trimble, eds., *Reinventing Canada: Politics of the 21st Century* (Toronto: Prentice-Hall, 2003). The most recent treatments of Canada's foreign and defence policies include J.L. Granatstein, *Whose War Is It? How Canada Can Survive in the Post-9/11 World* (Toronto: Harper Collins, 2007), and Janice Gross Stein and Eugene Lang, *The Unexpected War: Canada in Kandahar* (Toronto: Viking Canada, 2007).

Finally, an appreciation of the history of medicare in Canada is required. For this, one should read Malcolm G. Taylor, *Health Insurance and Canadian Public Policy: The Seven Decisions That Created the Canadian Health Insurance System* (Montreal and Kingston: Institute of Public Administration of Canada, 1978). There are more recent histories available, but Taylor's work is magisterial in its telling of the story of medicare. For an up-to-date review of the Canadian health care system, see Gregory Marchildon, *Health Systems in Transition: Canada* (Toronto: University of Toronto Press, 2006).

Is the Recognition of Quebec as a Distinct Nation a Positive Step for Canada?

✔ **YES**
MICHEL SEYMOUR, "Quebec and Canada at the Crossroads: A Nation within a Nation"

✗ **NO**
Michael Chong, "Canada as One Nation"

Debates about the nature of the Canadian political community, and Quebec's role in it, have long been a national preoccupation among Canadians. This debate took on new life in 2006 on the eve of the twenty-fifth anniversary of the Charter of Rights and Freedoms. Prime Minister Stephen Harper was visiting Quebec City on June 23 in order to join Quebecers in celebrating their "Fête nationale." A reporter asked Harper whether his participation in Quebec's "national" holiday was an indication that he accepted the idea that Quebec is a nation. The prime minister dismissed the question, quipping that any debate over Quebec as a nation was merely "semantic" and "doesn't serve any purpose."

The issue may well have not gone further if a federal Liberal leadership campaign was not underway. A few days after Harper's remarks, Michael Ignatieff, a candidate in the leadership race, stated in a speech that Quebec is indeed a nation. His policy platform issued a few months later called for an amendment to the Canadian constitution in order to recognize the "national status of Quebec."

Ignatieff's position stirred up a renewed debate on the status of Quebec. His two principal rivals, Stéphane Dion and Bob Rae, expressed reluctance to reopen any constitutional negotiations, suggesting that such a move would be bound to end in embarrassing failure like previous such attempts.

But once the issue had been raised, it was difficult to curtail further debate. The Quebec wing of the Liberal party passed a motion making the recognition of Quebec as a nation the official policy of the Liberal party. In November, the Bloc Québécois, seeking to both exploit the divisions within the Liberal party and embarrass the Conservatives, announced that it would table a motion in the House of Commons effectively recognizing Quebec as a nation.

Not wanting to be caught in a no-win situation, Prime Minister Stephen Harper decided to act preemptively by introducing his own resolution to Parliament recognizing the Québécois as "a nation within a united Canada." Harper's move proved to be a strategically shrewd one. The opposition parties, including the Bloc, supported the resolution, leading to its easy passage in the House of Commons. The Liberals withdrew their own resolution without its being debated. Ignatieff had one of his key platform issues stolen from him, and the Bloc Québécois failed to score any telling points against either the Conservatives or Liberals.

While the immediate political dangers surrounding the issue subsided, the incident focused attention once again on the fact that the concept of *nation* remains a highly contentious one in Canada. The debate continues as to whether it is better to think of Canada simply as one nation or as a nation that contains within itself other nations.

In the following readings, we encounter two different perspectives on this issue. Both authors note the multiple ways in which the idea of a nation can be viewed. Michel Seymour, a philosopher at the University of Montreal, sees no contradiction between considering Canada a nation and recognizing the existence of Quebec as a nation within it. In contrast, Michael Chong, a member of Parliament from Ontario, argues that we should think of Canada as one nation of 33 million citizens.

✔ **YES**

Quebec and Canada at the Crossroads: A Nation within a Nation
MICHEL SEYMOUR

[. . .] I wish to argue that there is no such thing as an entirely objective nation that could be described as if it were a scientific phenomenon to be investigated like we investigate atoms or galaxies. Nations involve important subjective features, such as national consciousness and the will to live together. Whether we use an ethnic, civic, cultural, diaspora or sociopolitical concept of the nation, it must be emphasised that any legitimate account must not treat it as if it were an entirely objective phenomenon. It is to a very large extent subjective. A group cannot constitute a nation unless there is a certain national consciousness entertained by a large number of individuals within the population. These individuals must represent themselves as forming a nation in order to become one. This self-representation not only involves a description of itself as a nation but also an expression of what it wants to become as a nation.

I said that nations incorporate some crucial subjective features, but becoming a nation is not something that a group can improvise; it is not only a matter of will, and we must not immediately recognise a group as a nation just because that group suddenly decides that it is to become a nation. In each case that I have discussed so far, there are subjective and objective features involved. For instance, I have argued that civic nations are countries and this is certainly an objective feature. I have also suggested that language, culture and history form relatively objective features that can play a role in the creation of the cultural nation. In the case of the sociopolitical nation, I have used notions such as national majorities and national minorities, and these notions can receive sociological characterisations. So it would be wrong to suggest that a group becomes a nation as soon as it represents itself as a nation. Nations, after all, are not just imagined communities, *pace* Benedict Anderson (1983).[1]

It must also be emphasised that the self-representation crucially involved in the very concept of the nation should not be construed as a mere belief that one belongs to this or that nation. It would be circular to try to define the concept of the nation by invoking as a constitutive element the belief that there is such a nation. We would then be presupposing the concept we wish to define. Of course, we could also want to claim that nations, as social entities, exist only when individuals entertain beliefs involving the concept of the nation. The ontological reality of nations would then be explained merely by recourse to the presence in the minds of individuals of a certain conceptual item. We would then be arguing for a fictionalist account of the nation, since its ontological reality would then be reduced to the occurrence of a concept in the minds of certain individuals. In order to avoid a circular definition and a fictional explanation, it is important to specify the self-representations without using the concept of a nation. For instance, the concept of an ethnic nation requires people to perceive themselves as being of the same ancestral origin. The concept of a cultural nation rejects that last feature, but requires that each individual perceive herself as assimilated to the same linguistic, cultural and historical group. A civic nation supposes that each individual represents herself as part of the same country. And a sociopolitical nation supposes that each individual represents herself as part of a political community containing a majority of individuals who also happen to be the majority of individuals in the world who share the same language, culture and history.

I said that a self-representation is a crucial element involved in the existence of a nation, but this should not be confused with national sentiment. Individuals are very different in their emotional allegiances. The importance of particular group affiliations may vary from one person to the other and may vary through time even for a single individual. We all have different affective links and different ways of ordering the importance of our group affiliations. This emotional or affective ranking is not relevant for determining whether we belong to this or that nation. I may belong to a nation even though I fail to experience any national sentiment or any national pride. Individuals may fail to consider their national affiliation as a 'primary good' in Rawls' sense.[2] Nevertheless, they can still be part of a particular nation, for they entertain the relevant self-representation.

A MULTINATIONAL CANADA

[...]Since nations are at least in part subjective, and since there are many concepts of the nation, one can expect that different concepts could be used by different communities and could contribute to a different national self-representation. And the obvious conclusion is that we must tolerate these different national identities and self-representations, and afford them all a political recognition in the public sphere.

We can turn that point into a philosophical argument. Let us suppose that we accept, as a first premise, the principle of the intrinsic value of cultural diversity (or its instrumental value relative to the human species).[3] Let us also accept as a second premise what I have called a conceptual pluralism. If we add, as a third premise, the claim that nationhood is at least in part a matter of self-representation and then also note, as an empirical observation, that many different populations entertain different self-representations involving different concepts of the nation, then we must accept, in conclusion, a fundamental principle of tolerance. This conclusion is a crucial normative claim that should be kept in mind in what follows. It is a background assumption that I am going to take for granted in what I have to say concerning the Canadian case.

So let me now turn to an application of these ideas to the Canadian case. We must be aware that, in Canada, there are different populations representing themselves as nations in different ways and with different concepts. I leave aside for the sake of simplicity Aboriginal nations and the Acadian nation and I shall discuss only the case of Quebec and Canada. By restricting my considerations to the relations between Canada and Quebec, I do not mean to suggest that the Aboriginal nations are less important. It is only for methodological reasons that I choose to concentrate on Quebec and Canada. The Acadian nation is according to my account a purely cultural nation, while Aboriginal peoples within Canada belong to different categories. They may be ethnic nations, sociopolitical nations or diasporas.

Quebeckers used to represent themselves as members of a purely cultural French Canadian nation, and they now see themselves as part of a Quebec nation understood in the sociopolitical sense. As far as English Canadians are concerned, there are some who think that Canada is a post-national community of communities.[4] Others think of Canada as a multination state composed of many different cultural or sociopolitical nations. According to that view, there would be an English Canadian nation.[5] But the majority now thinks of Canada as constituting a single civic nation. The Canadian nation for them is the country as a whole.[6]

QUEBEC AS A SOCIOPOLITICAL NATION

Let me just say a few words about the Quebec sociopolitical nation, since the sociopolitical nation is apparently a fairly new and original conception. Even if there are French-speaking Canadians living outside Quebec who roughly share the same language, history and culture, they are less numerous than those living inside Quebec. Francophones living outside Quebec form a 'national minority', i.e. an extension of the French national majority within Quebec. French Canadians living outside Quebec do not represent themselves just as any other minority. They form an 'historical minority', that is, they are a part of what used to be one of the 'two founding peoples of Canada'. This is why they must be considered as a national minority of French Canadians. However, the French Canadian nation no longer exists, for it has been replaced by a cultural Acadian nation within the province of New Brunswick and by a Quebec nation within Quebec. And so the French Canadian founding people no longer exists, for it has paved the way to new forms of national consciousness emerging within New Brunswick and Quebec. Be that as it may, French Canadians living outside Quebec form a national minority that must be respected as such.

Now since the francophones who are living inside Quebec form a majority, and since they are also the majority of those individuals who, around the world, share the same language, history and culture, they are what I call a 'national majority'. So the Quebec nation can be understood as a political community, containing a national majority of French Quebeckers, a national minority of Anglo-Quebeckers and individuals having, for instance, Italian, Jewish, Greek, Portuguese, Haitian, Lebanese or Latino-American national origins.

According to that view, we cannot automatically include the members of the eleven Aboriginal nations that we find on the territory of Quebec within the Quebec nation because these groups also contain national majorities. They are part of the Quebec state and Quebec is in that sense a multinational state containing the Quebec nation and the eleven Aboriginal nations (comprising a population of 74,000 individuals). The members of these Aboriginal nations may be described as Quebec citizens in the juridical sense, but they are not part of the Quebec nation as such, for they are part of other nations (ethnic, sociopolitical or diaspora nations). These eleven nations might eventually be part of a Quebec 'nation' understood in the civic sense, if Quebec ever becomes a sovereign state, but they would still be distinct nations (within an encompassing nation).

The same remarks apply to the Quebec nation within Canada. It is part of a larger political community, but it constitutes a distinct nation. It can be treated as part of the Canadian nation only if we use the word in a civic sense, but it still constitutes a distinct nation in the sociopolitical sense. Canada cannot be understood as a sociopolitical nation containing a national majority of Canadians and a national minority of Quebeckers, for Quebeckers are not a national minority at all, in the strict sense of being 'the extension of a neighbouring nation'. They are perhaps a 'national minority' only in the sense of being a minority nation within Canada.

The problem with that conception is that Anglo-Quebeckers become part of the Quebec nation. Indeed, according to that view, Anglo-Quebeckers are described as full active members and as equal citizens within the Quebec nation. Some Anglo-Quebeckers might be shocked by such an inclusive account, but I believe that this is largely due to misunderstandings.

Let me try to remove some of these misunderstandings. The view of an inclusive Quebec nation in which Anglo-Quebeckers would participate does not entail that they should subscribe to the sovereignty of Quebec. Of course, one must not ignore the fact that the self-exclusion of many English Quebeckers can be motivated partly by such political reasons. They do not want to recognise the existence of a Quebec nation including all Quebec citizens because this would, according to them, give fuel to the sovereignist option. If this is their worry, then it should not have a bearing on the main issue we are now raising. Questions of national identity must be disentangled from political questions. One need not be a sovereignist in order to be part of the Quebec sociopolitical nation.

Another reason is that they might wrongly be led to think that they have to choose between being part of the Quebec nation and being part of the Canadian nation. But under the present approach, it is perfectly coherent to be part of a nation within a nation. And so Anglo-Quebeckers can be part of a Quebec nation within the Canadian nation understood in the civic sense, just like all French Quebeckers. It is also compatible with the fact that their most important allegiance would be to the Canadian nation. There is no reason to object to having simultaneously different national affiliations.

Moreover, the inclusion of Anglo-Quebeckers within the Quebec sociopolitical nation is compatible with having the status of a national minority within the Quebec nation. As a minority extension on the territory of Quebec of a national majority of English Canadians, English Quebeckers form a national minority. Quebeckers as a whole should respect these special ties that Anglo-Quebeckers entertain towards the language and culture of English Canada.

Sovereignists, by the way, are now even willing to move a step further. They propose a political partnership with Canada so that, among other things, English Quebeckers could keep a strong political link with Canada, even if Quebec becomes sovereign. We could also imagine the possibility of keeping a dual citizenship after sovereignty. This would be possible, since Canada already accepts dual citizenship. If Quebec adopts the same policy, then nothing prevents Quebeckers from asking for dual citizenship. We could finally also imagine the creation of a citizenship of the union in the event of sovereignty. So whether Quebec becomes sovereign or not, Anglo-Quebeckers would not lose their identity within Quebec.

But what do we require from Anglo-Quebeckers when we are suggesting that they are part of the Quebec nation? We ask them to accept the fact that they belong to a political community containing a national majority of individuals having a specific language, history and culture. It means also that they should accept French as a common public language and accept the institutions of Quebec as providing the common public culture for all Quebeckers. But these requirements must be accepted whether Quebec becomes sovereign or not.

So why should some Anglo-Quebeckers object to being included in the Quebec nation? It could be because they wrongly perceive Quebec nationalism as ethnic. If so, their self-exclusion cannot be accepted as such, because it violates the principle of tolerance. It is certainly crucial to respect the self-representations of English Quebeckers, but not if their own self-representation presupposes a view of the Quebec nation which violates the self-representation entertained by the majority of the population. Indeed, why should we be tolerant toward a self-representation that offends the self-representation of the majority by describing the Quebec nation as ethnolinguistic? If they apply a principle of tolerance, those English Quebeckers should respect the self-representations of the majority of Quebeckers. Most Quebeckers happen to perceive themselves as members of a sociopolitical nation. If English Quebeckers respect that, then they should perhaps modify their initial judgement. So even if I said that we should in general be tolerant towards different self-representations, I feel unable to accept the claim held by some English Quebeckers that they do not belong to the *ethnic or cultural nation* of Quebec, and the reason, to repeat, is that this judgement already reflects a failure to apply a principle of tolerance towards the self-representation of Quebeckers in general.

But does it mean that I am ignoring the self-representation of English Quebeckers? On the contrary, we must be respectful of their self-representation, but this self-representation can only be measured by objective criteria. Those members of the Quebec political community who are Canadian citizens and who have decided to reside in Quebec have become citizens of Quebec in the juridical sense. In addition to that, if they all participate within the political community and want to be recognised as full Quebec citizens, this serves as an objective criterion for determining that they represent themselves as part of the Quebec nation. As full participants in Quebec society, they become full 'citizens' in the political sense of the word, and this is all we need in order to be able to treat them as members of the Quebec nation. If someone enters into various associations, pays her taxes, expresses her views, votes during elections and referendums, conforms to the rules and regulations governing Quebec institutions, and asks to be treated as a full Quebec citizen, then that person represents herself as part of the Quebec nation.

Some might object that many Quebeckers see their own nation as including francophones only.[7] It is true that there are still some Quebeckers describing themselves as French Canadians, but all the polls confirm that these are a very small minority within the population. Recent polls have confirmed that the vast majority of Quebeckers (77 per cent) admit the existence of a Quebec people.[8] Of course, there are also French Quebeckers who are tempted to endorse a cultural view of the Quebec nation, but this is because they are rightly reluctant to accept a civic account based only on citizenship. This by the way reveals more than anything else the adequacy of the sociopolitical account for the Quebec people. Quebeckers wish to embrace an inclusive conception of their nation, but they also believe that there would not be a Quebec nation if it were not for the French national majority. But it is precisely this twofold dimension which is captured by the sociopolitical account of the nation.

Other French Quebeckers are reluctant to include English Quebeckers, but it is because they believe that English Quebeckers want to exclude themselves from the nation. In other words, many French and English Quebeckers express their desire for inclusion into a single society, but both believe that this desire is not shared by the other group. We need not avoid facing these mutual exclusions, for they do not constitute a counter-example to the claims that I am making. On the contrary, they reveal that there is a desire for inclusion on both sides. Since the self-representation of Quebeckers not only involves a description of what they are but also an expression of what they want to be, and since their desire is to remain an open society, the national consciousness of Quebeckers is thus slowly turning the Quebec people into a sociopolitical nation.

Some argue that Quebeckers are committed to a form of cultural nationalism because the main arguments of nationalists have been based upon the protection of language and culture and based upon a particular historical argument concerning the existence of two founding peoples. Now it is true that Quebec nationalism has always involved the defence of French language, the promotion of Quebec culture and the use of such an historical argument. But this should not be seen as favouring one particular group over the others within Quebec society, for French is now the common public language of all Quebeckers and the Quebec culture is nothing over and above common public institutions (government, laws, system of education, libraries, museums, television, newspapers, radios, etc.) belonging to all Quebeckers. To use Will Kymlicka's happy phrase, it is a 'societal culture' understood as a 'structure of culture in a context of choice' and it should not be confined to the particular 'character of culture' held by a certain group during a certain period of time.[9] Finally, the history of Francophones must be at the heart of the common public history shared by all Quebec citizens.

Some English Quebeckers reject an allegiance to the Quebec nation because they cannot imagine having multiple identities. But why not be part of a Quebec nation (in my sociopolitical sense) within a Canadian nation (in the civic sense)? French Quebeckers have accepted that idea since the very beginning of the federation. If they are now increasingly favourable to sovereignty, it is because Canadians do not accept to recognise one of their two national identities, namely their allegiance to the Quebec nation.

A NATION WITHIN A NATION

So we have, on the one hand, a civic conception of the Canadian nation, held by most Canadians, and a sociopolitical conception of the Quebec nation, held by most Quebeckers. As I said, I have ignored for the sake of simplicity the Acadian nation, which is more like a purely cultural nation, and the sixty or eighty Aboriginal nations, which can sometimes be identified as ethnic nations, sometimes as diaspora nations, and sometimes as sociopolitical nations.

We must try to find a way of coping with this complex reality and show how these two different nations (the Quebec nation and the Canadian nation) could live in harmony. In my view, the only way is to defend a basic principle of tolerance. We must respect the self-representations of others. For the minority nation of Quebeckers, this could mean that they have to accept in principle to be part of a civic Canadian nation. They must, in principle, accept their plural identity as Quebeckers and Canadians. And for Canadians, it could mean that they should accept the existence of a Quebec sociopolitical nation within the Canadian nation. In other words, we should accept an idea similar to the one that was once put forward by Lester B. Pearson and according to which Quebec constitutes a nation within a nation.[10]

Some will argue that it is not possible for a civic Canadian nationalist to recognise the existence of many different nations within Canada. The reason is apparently that a civic nationalist sees the nation from an individualistic perspective. The civic nation is nothing more than a community of individual citizens, and therefore it looks as though the civic nationalist must be an ethical individualist. Consequently, for anyone who holds such a conception, there appears to be no room for the recognition of collective rights for minority groups, and so no room for accommodating a Quebec nation within Canada. However, I do not think that this objection is sound. One must not confuse the civic account with ethical individualism. It is possible to be a civic nationalist and to recognise at the same time the existence of a nation within the civic nation. It is true that when the perspective is that of the civic account, the components of the nation are the individual citizens and nothing else. This remains true under the proposed account. But even if the civic account is one in which the main participants are individuals, it need not be committed to ethical individualism, and the reason is that the civic perspective is not the only unique perspective available. If we reject ethical individualism, i.e. the view that the individual must under all circumstances have an absolute priority over the group, and if we no longer believe that the civic perspective about the nation is the only good perspective, it then becomes possible to recognise the collective rights of a nation within the civic nation.

By requiring the political recognition of the Quebec sociopolitical nation within the civic nation, I am thus not asking Canadians to abandon their civic account. I am simply asking them to apply a principle of tolerance. Of course, if civic Canadian nationalists were to accept the existence of a Quebec nation within their nation, they would have to recognise collective rights for that nation. The Quebec nation would enter the public space and this seems, first, to be contradicting the very essence of the civic account. But the recognition of the Quebec nation is not meant to be interpreted as an amendment to their civic account, but rather as an application of a principle of tolerance. When we correctly understand and apply a principle of tolerance in these matters, we come to realise that there is nothing preventing the civic nationalists from recognising different nations within the civic nation. The tolerant civic Canadian nationalist may accommodate the Quebec nation, because she need not be an ethical individualist.

A RENEWED SOCIAL CONTRACT BETWEEN NATIONS

I now turn to more concrete matters. I shall wonder what it would mean for Canadians to accept a Quebec nation. I shall list what is often described as the main traditional demands of Quebeckers. All of these demands presuppose that there is a Quebec people. What would it mean for Canada to recognise the existence of a Quebec people?

(i)   It would mean, first, accepting formally to recognise its existence in the constitution. The Aboriginal peoples are recognised in provisions 25 and 35 of the 1982 constitution, and there is no reason why Canadians should resist amending the constitution in a way that would allow for a formal recognition of the Quebec people.[11]

(ii) Canadians would also have to accept that the principle of equality of status between the provinces cannot be applied to Quebec. If national recognition is to mean anything, there should be a special status given to the province of Quebec within the federation.

(iii) This would in turn entail an acceptance of a general principle of asymmetry in the distribution of powers. Some powers could be offered to the Quebec government without having to offer them to the nine other provinces. In practice, there is already a certain asymmetry involved. Quebec is the only province that has its own income tax, its own civil code, its linguistic laws, and a certain control over immigration policies. The idea is now to accept such kind of asymmetry as a matter of principle and to increase it in order to meet Quebec's traditional demands.

(iv) There should also be a formal recognition that the Quebec government has the responsibility to protect and promote the French language in Quebec, as long as it is done in harmony with the requirement to protect the individual rights of all citizens and the collective rights of the anglophone community within Quebec. The linguistic laws of the Quebec government have constantly been under attack, and a formal recognition of Quebec's distinctly French society should for that reason be entrenched in the constitution.

(v) The Quebec government should be the only government responsible for matters related to culture and telecommunications on Quebec's territory. In other words, Quebec should be sovereign in matters related to culture. There should be a recognition of the fact that there is a common public culture in Quebec that is very different from the common public culture in the rest of Canada. The multiculturalism policy of the federal government should be amended so that it becomes clear that the protection and promotion of the language and culture of immigrants has to go hand-in-hand with their linguistic and cultural integration into one of the two welcoming national communities.

(vi) There should also be a limitation in the federal government's spending power, which has constantly been a way to intrude in provincial jurisdictions such as education and health programmes. Even if, according to the constitution of 1867, some jurisdictions entirely belong to the provinces, the federal government has always used its spending power in order to increase its presence in provincial affairs. It is only natural for a people to be able to conduct its own policies in matters related to education, health and social welfare, and this is why Quebeckers have always required that the federal government should not use its spending power in order to intervene in those jurisdictions.

(vii) Quebec should have a veto over any modification to the constitution that concerns it. There should also be a formal opting out clause allowing financial compensation on any new programme implemented by the federal government if the Quebec government wants to be the one applying such a policy.

(viii) A political recognition of Quebec as a nation must also go hand-in-hand with the recognition that Quebec has a special responsibility towards its national economy. Therefore, Quebec should be afforded all the powers related to unemployment insurance in addition to those of manpower training.

(ix) Quebec should have the power to appoint three of the nine judges in the Supreme Court. A true political recognition of the existence of a Quebec people should go hand-in-hand with an appropriate representation. By allowing appointments to be made by Quebec at the level of the Supreme Court, Canada would be showing that it is taking very seriously the fair representation of Quebec within the Canadian constitutional order.

(x) Quebec should be allowed to increase its presence on the international scene.

These are ten principles that would reflect the multinational character of Canada within Canadian institutions, as far as Quebec is concerned. In order to do the same for the Aboriginal populations of Canada, the federal government should apply the main recommendations contained in the final report of the Royal Commission on Aboriginal peoples. Canada would then not only be a *de facto* multination state. By applying these measures, it would truly become a *de jure* multination state. And there is no reason to think that a true multinational Canada is impossible.

NOTES

1. See Benedict Anderson, *Imagined Communities: Reflections on the Origin and Spread of Nationalism* (New York: Verso, 1983).

2. Kymlicka espouses such a subjective account. Nations must be protected because they are primary goods. See, for instance, Will Kymlicka, *Multicultural Citizenship* (Oxford: Clarendon Press, 1995), p. 86.

3. For a critical examination, see Kymlicka, *Multicultural Citizenship*, pp. 121–123.

4. See Jeremy Webber, *Reimagining Canada* (Montreal & Kingston: McGill-Queen's, 1994).

5. See Philip Resnick, *Thinking English Canada* (Toronto: Stoddart, 1994).

6. See, for instance, the *Common Declaration* initiated by the group Dialogue Quebec–Canada and signed by one hundred Canadian intellectuals. In that document, Canada as a whole is described as a nation. Philip Resnick himself is among those who signed the document. It is available on the web site of the Intellectuals for Sovereignty. See http://www.cam.org/~ipso/Textes/common_declaration.htm

7. There is vast literature in English describing Quebeckers with the French word 'Québécois'. This reveals the natural inclination of many to describe Quebec in cultural terms and not as a sociopolitical nation. See for instance, Kymlicka, *Multicultural Citizenship*, pp. 12, 19, 28–29, etc.

8. This poll was conducted in April 1999 by Angus Reid for the 'Citizens of the nation', a group led by Quebec lawyer Guy Bertrand.

9. Kymlicka, *Multicultural Citizenship*, pp. 76–9, 101–105.

10. For an account centred on Pearson's idea of a nation within a nation and which denounces the policies of Pierre Elliott Trudeau, see Kenneth McRoberts, *Misconceiving Canada* (Oxford, Oxford University Press, 1997).

11. There are many authors arguing for a reform based on a multinational federation, as opposed to a territorial federation. See Philip Resnick, *Toward a Canada-Quebec Union* (Montreal & Kingston: McGill-Queen's University Press, 1991); Resnick, *Thinking English Canada*; Will Kymlicka, *Finding our Way* (Oxford: Oxford University Press, 1998); Will Kymlicka, "Multinational Federalism in Canada: Rethinking Partnership" in Guy Laforest and Roger Gibbins (eds.), *Beyond the Impasse* (Montreal: Institute of Research on Public Policies, 1997); McRoberts, *Misconceiving Canada*; Charles Taylor, *Reconciling Two Solitudes: Essays on Canadian Federalism and Nationalism* (Montreal & Kingston: McGill-Queen's University Press, 1993); and John F. Conway, *Debts to Pay: English Canada and Quebec from the Conquest to the Referendum* (Toronto: Lorimer, 1992).

✗ NO
Canada as One Nation
MICHAEL CHONG

Two main views of Canada—*deux nations* versus one nation—have competed for paramountcy in our political discourse for decades. To provide the historical context, we will first undertake an overview of these two competing views and variations thereof. Then we will attempt to clarify the issue by examining the two broad uses of the word *nation* and analyze the interplay between these two uses. Finally, we will place our findings into the Canadian context, where the conclusion obtained is that the only cogent resolution is to recognize Canada as one nation.

COMPETING VIEWS

The first view can be summarized in the following way. Canada is a state consisting of two founding peoples (*deux nations*) or two founding nations: one French, one English. Each founding nation has a set of unique collective rights to ensure its preservation. This dualist dream—held by many Quebec nationalists and certain anglophones—was championed by Robert Stanfield's Progressive Conservative Party in the 1968 federal election campaign. One version of this view defines the two nations by language: one francophone, one anglophone. Another version defines the two nations by ethnicity, one French, one British. Yet another variation proposes both a French Canadian and an English Canadian nation, each scattered across the territory of Canada. Still yet another version sees the Québécois as a nation, whose territory is the province of Quebec. In that version, the province of Quebec is the primary protector of the Québécois nation and therefore should be accorded special status and powers commensurate to the protection and survival of that nation. Then there is the twist that sees Canada made up of three founding peoples: French, English, and Aboriginal. Finally, another variation proposes Canada as a nation of nations, consisting of Aboriginal nations, the Quebec nation, etc., all under the umbrella of the Canadian nation.

The second view regards Canadian citizenship as the central idea of the nation and state. It can be summarized in the following way: Canada is a state consisting of one nation of 33 million citizens with equal rights and responsibilities, ten equal provinces, and a strong central government. In this view, the government of Canada is the primary protector of all citizens through means such as the Canadian Charter of Rights and Freedoms. Therefore, a strong central government is essential to the continuing protection and survival of the Canadian nation. This view is strongly associated with Pierre Elliot Trudeau, who argued in favour of it during the 1968 federal election campaign against Robert Stanfield and who later introduced the Canadian Charter of Rights and Freedoms. However, its roots can be traced back earlier to people like John G. Diefenbaker, who argued for "one nation" in his address to the 1967 Conservative leadership convention and who, in 1960, similarly introduced the Canadian Bill of Rights. These two competing views—*deux nations* versus one nation—were at the heart of the Meech Lake and Charlottetown battles.

Further confusing the debate within Canada are the various ways in which states and nations interact elsewhere. In some states, the nation—whether ethnic, civic, sociological, etc.—corresponds directly to the state. Such is arguably the case for European states like the Netherlands, Germany, and France, and for some New World states, like the United States. This correspondence gives rise to the term *nation-state*. In other states, multiple nations are to be found within, each inhabiting unique territories. Such is arguably the case for the United Kingdom (which contains the English, Welsh, Scottish and Northern Irish nations) and for the Swiss Confederation (which contains the German, French, and Italian nations). Finally, still other states contain multiple nations whose members are scattered across the territory of the state and who do not inhabit a clearly defined territory. Arguably, such was the case in the former state of Yugoslavia.

THE WORD *NATION*

In the broadest sense, there are two very different uses of the word *nation*. These two uses often are conflated, resulting in much confusion in political discourse. By examining these two different uses, we can begin to clear up some of the confusion surrounding the word.

The first use of the word *nation* refers to a sovereign state—for example, the 192 member states of the United Nations. In this usage, it refers to the legal entity that has sovereignty over a territory and the people that inhabit that territory. This usage is not controversial nor in dispute. In this usage, the nation of Canada is a sovereign state with a territory stretching from sea to sea to sea, inhabited by some 33 million citizens. Over the years, this nation has not been static but has evolved. As Confederation has progressed, both land and people have been added to this nation, most recently with the addition of Newfoundland in 1949. As the era of empire faded, additional sovereignty was granted to this nation through the Statute of Westminster in 1931 and by the elimination of the Judicial Committee of the Privy Council as the court of last appeal in 1949. For the purposes of this discussion, and to avoid confusion, we will use the term *state* to refer to this legal entity.

The second use of the word *nation* refers to a group of people. This is not any random grouping of people but a grouping of people distinguished by certain features. Much has been written about what constitutes a nation in this second use of the word, but it has been difficult to arrive at a commonly accepted definition. It will be argued here that a nation can be distinguished by two essential features.

The first feature consists of objective characteristics commonly held by individuals in the group. These characteristics, which can be objectively delineated and described, can include a common history, language, culture, territory, religion, or even ethnicity.

The second feature consists of a collective will that binds the individuals in the group together. This feature is subjective, as it involves an active desire on the part of individuals to come together as a group of people. This collective will is what George Grant called the "thrust of intention into the future."[1] A nation cannot remain a nation because of its "roots in the past,"[2] he said, but rather remains one because of its thrust of intention into the future. A nation's memory and roots are important features but do not unto themselves constitute a nation. This idea of a collective will is similar to Benedict Andersen's definition of nation as an "imagined political community,"[3] where a common set of imaginations form the core around which individuals can coalesce and commune to form a nation.

As has been previously stated, a nation is distinguished by these two essential features—objective characteristics and a collective will. Both features must be present in any particular nation. Otherwise, anglophone Canadians and Americans together would constitute a nation, for as a group of people, they have certain objective characteristics in common, such as language, culture, and history. (In fact, Americans living in the U.S. northeast have more history in common with Canadians living in central Canada than with their fellow citizens living in Texas. These two groups split during the American Revolution to form two different nations precisely because they had no collective will in common.) Clearly, however, anglophone Canadians and Americans do not constitute a nation. Conversely, a group of people cannot constitute a nation simply by willing it, without having a language, culture, history, territory, religion, or anything else in common. For if that were the case, nations could be figments solely of our imaginations with no correspondence to reality. This is too arbitrary to be meaningful.

There exists a tension between these two essential features of a nation, a tension between objective fact and the collective will, echoing the classical conundrum between necessity and free will. Both essential features are constantly evolving, but their effect on each other is not reciprocal. Over time, the collective will of a group of people *effects* the objective characteristics of the group. Witness the *Révolution tranquille*, in which the collective will of francophone Quebecers effected the removal of the Catholic Church as the primary influence in daily life. The converse of this, however, is not true. The objective characteristics common to a group—such as language, history, culture—cannot *effect* the collective will of the group. They simply provide the static historical context for the group. For if objective characteristics like language, history, or culture *effect* the collective will of a group, then the collective will is a euphemism for necessity and there is no room for free agency. In this sense, the collective will of a nation has primacy over its objective characteristics.

In addition, the objective characteristics of a nation are somewhat arbitrary in two respects. First, the objective characteristics of history, language, culture, territory, religion, or ethnicity can be broadly or narrowly delineated, resulting in a larger or smaller definition of a nation. For example, one can broadly define the territory of a Quebec nation so that it includes the whole of the province of Quebec, as well as the contiguous francophone regions in Ontario and New Brunswick bordering Quebec. Alternatively, one can more narrowly define the territory of a Quebec nation so that it corresponds exactly to the province of Quebec. Thus, how broadly or narrowly these objective characteristics are delineated determines the various combinations in which a group of people can be distinguished as a nation. Second, the number of objective characteristics ascribed to a group of people will also have the effect of determining the various combinations in which any group of people can be distinguished. For example, the Quebec nation could consist of both francophone and anglophone Quebecers, united by the *two* characteristics of a common history and territory. Alternatively, the Quebec nation could exclude anglophones and include only francophone Quebecers, united by the *three* characteristics of a common history, territory, and language. Therefore, the objective characteristics of a nation are somewhat arbitrary and give rise to various ways in which a group of people can be distinguished as a nation. In part, this explains why there is a plethora of ways to describe what constitutes a nation—sociological, sociopolitical, civic, ethnic, diasporic, etc. Due to multiple identities and allegiances inherent to an individual or group, distinguishing the collective will of a group can also be somewhat arbitrary. However, the *primary* identity to which an individual or group shows allegiance is fairly easy to distinguish. In this sense, the collective will of a nation is less arbitrary than are its objective characteristics.

We have demonstrated that, over time, the collective will of a group of people effects the objective characteristics of the group. We have also demonstrated that distinguishing the collective will of a group is less arbitrary than distinguishing its objective characteristics. It then follows that the collective will of a group of people is the decisive factor in determining what constitutes a nation. The decisiveness that the collective will plays in distinguishing a nation gives rise to the doctrine of self-determination.

RELATIONSHIP BETWEEN STATES AND NATIONS

States continue to be the primary international actors and carriers of sovereignty. States also continue to be the primary political vehicles through which citizens express their collective will. Therefore, the ultimate expression of the collective will of a nation can be realized only through the state. Since there are so many ways in which a group of people can be distinguished as a nation, there are many permutations of nations that could be realized through the state. What limits should there be on the realization of a nation through the state?

In my view, the limits should preclude any nation whose objective characteristics—either in full or in part—are based on immutable qualities such as ethnic origin. Basing objective characteristics on immutable qualities denies other citizens not party to those qualities the ability to effect their participation in that nation by the execution of their free will. In this sense, this type of nation is deeply amoral.

The limits should also preclude any nation whose two essential features are not strong enough to warrant this realization, either because of a weak collective will or because of insufficient objective characteristics. Otherwise, pretty much any group of people could form a nation, resulting in so many nations as to make the concept meaningless.

CANADA AS ONE NATION

The discussion of the relationship between nations and states leads us back to a fundamental question: Under what conditions should the realization of a nation through a state take place? In other words, in the Canadian context, what is the principal political community around which Canadians should be organized?

In my view, Canada should be constituted as a state consisting of one nation of 33 million citizens. I believe that the following reasons strongly support my position.

As for the essential features that distinguish a nation, there are both sufficient objective characteristics and a strong enough collective will to distinguish the population of Canada as one nation. Among other characteristics, we have a common history, geography, culture, civil society, and two shared official languages. We also have a sufficiently strong collective will, evidenced by the facts that, despite our differences, we are one of the oldest continual democracies in the world and we continue to stay together.

If, as we have argued, the collective will of a group of people is the decisive factor in determining what constitutes a nation, then there are a number of other convincing reasons that we would want to come together as one nation.

In an age of globalization in which the world is increasingly interconnected and interdependent, nations with small populations will not easily survive—economically, culturally, or otherwise. A nation of three, four, or seven million people has little chance in the era of globalization. This is why the states of the European Union have come together. They have concluded that it is necessary to give up some economic and political sovereignty in order to survive. In the Canadian context, I believe that we are one of the smallest political communities to have a chance of survival in a world of seven billion people. Even then, survival is by no means assured.

In addition, the rapidly changing demographic composition of Canada presents challenges to Canadian society that only a national government can meet. Statistics Canada noted the existence of more than two hundred different ethnic origins in Canada in the 2006 census. In contrast, only about twenty-five different ethnic origins were noted in the 1901 census. In 1901, people who reported Aboriginal, British, or French origins comprised the largest share of the population. In contrast, the 2006 census noted that eleven ethnic origins had passed the one million population mark and an estimated five million individuals now belong to the visible minority population, making up one in six Canadians.[4] In a couple of decades, the changes will be even more pronounced. If the real challenges in Canada are no longer differences between the two founding groups, French and English, but rather the challenges of integrating and unifying an increasingly diverse population, then the rapidly changing composition of Canadian society makes recognition of any sub-national group increasingly problematic. We cannot build an increasingly diverse society on exclusionary grounds.

Regarding the recognition of Quebec as a distinct society (one step away from the recognition of Quebec as a nation) as proposed in the Meech Lake Accord, John Whyte, then dean of the Faculty of Law at Queen's University, noted in 1987 that

the first point to be observed is that the Meech Lake agreement does not embrace ethnic pluralism. If, as has been suggested earlier, the real ethnic tensions to be faced in Canada are no longer the tensions between French and English but, rather, the tensions of multiculturalism and multiracialism, then the special regard for Quebec as the protector of French is at best non-responsive and, at worst, illiberal.[5]

Over twenty years later, this comment is even more apt. Meech Lake proved that English-speaking Canada's side of dualism is dead because of what Alan Cairns calls the "galloping ethnic heterogeneity of English-speaking Canada."[6] While Quebec (Montreal) has proportionally lagged behind much of the rest of Canada in the number of immigrant arrivals, compared with Ontario (Toronto) and British Columbia (Vancouver), there is no doubt about the general trend in Quebec: If English-speaking Canada's side of dualism is dead because of this galloping heterogeneity, then it is only a matter of time before French-speaking Canada's dualism is subjected to the same pressure. If current trends persist, in a few short years almost one in four Canadians will be not only a minority (i.e., of non-French and non-British descent) but a visible minority. There will be not only more visible minorities in Canada than there are francophones but also, among the visible minorities, sizable populations of Canadians of Chinese and South Asian descent (there are already more than one million Canadians of Chinese descent and more than 1.2 million Canadians of South Asian descent). These changing demographics highlight the difficulties in postulating any sub-national group. More important, if an encounter with another person enriches both parties concerned, then retreating into our solitudes gains us little. If our lives as citizens are broadened by encountering other people and ideas, then we get little by isolation and exclusion.

The case for Canada as a nation is based not only on a defensive rationale. Organizing Canadians around the idea of a Canadian nation serves a good political end. We have created something truly unique. Improbably, out of a vast and inchoate land and with a disjointed group of people, we have created one of the oldest continuing liberal democracies in the world, achieved without revolution and largely without violence. So for all these reasons, I believe that Canada should be constituted as a state consisting of one nation of 33 million citizens. Canada is good and unique and a dream worth fighting for.

Some might propose Canada as a nation of nations, where Canada as one nation envelops multiple nations and identities. This is at best complicated and at worst incomprehensible. It also harks back to an imperial age in which an elite caste of colonial administrators acted as the bridge between various nations. This would restrict the social mobility of the vast majority of citizens and runs contrary to the principles of a liberal and democratic society. Furthermore, as has been argued previously, any nation smaller than that of the population of Canada will have difficulty surviving in the era of globalization.

Others might propose to eliminate all concepts of *nation* in Canada and to create a Canadian state in which individual citizens assume the identities they want, without any attempt to formally recognize and realize any nations within the state. In other words, why not Canada as the first post-national state? I reject this view because this would favour the individual over the community to such an extent that there would be little or no room for collective action and expression.

Some will argue that the inability to recognize a sub-national group like the Québécois risks increasing support for Quebec nationalism, which in turn could lead to secession. However, this argument does not hold up upon closer examination. As previously argued, the rapidly changing heterogeneity that English-speaking Canada has experienced is just beginning its impact on Quebec, an impact that will grow more significant with time. This will dilute and diminish support for secession, since new Canadians overwhelmingly place their primary allegiance with the Canadian state. The Clarity Act also makes secession more difficult. In the aftermath of the 1995 referendum results, an alarmed Chrétien government submitted a reference to the Supreme Court on the question of secession. The Supreme Court of Canada declared that a unilateral secession would be contrary to both Canadian and international law. This provided the Chrétien government the argument it needed, and in the year 2000, it passed the Clarity Act. This piece of legislation requires a "clear question" approved by a "clear majority" for any future referendum result to be legitimate, and also makes the Canadian House of Commons the arbiter as to what constitutes a clear question and a clear majority.[7] This higher standard, both in terms of the question and the majority required, diminishes the chance of secession.

If one believes, as I do, in the concept of a single nation within the Canadian state as a force for political good, then let us imagine what nation-building projects could be accomplished together as a Canadian people.

The federal government could implement a policy of official trilingualism to fuse both the linguistic duality and the increasing diversity of Canada. This policy would entail the use of federal spending power to ensure all provinces require that their secondary school graduates be fluent in three languages, two of which would be the official languages of Canada and the third the choice of the student. The goal of this policy would be to create a new generation of Canadians who are perfectly at home in *all* parts of Canada. This policy would achieve a number of different goals. First, it would leverage our position as a trading nation. If we are to be the Phoenicians of the modern world, then knowledge of additional languages is critical to success. Second, it would build on the cultural diversity of the country, building on the many languages that new Canadians have brought with them. Third, it would provide an opportunity to sustain vanishing languages such as Aboriginal languages, as well as ancient Greek and Latin. Fourth, it would address the concerns of francophones about the threats to their language by ensuring greater ubiquity and usage of French. Fifth, it would be a way to preserve our French and English cultural inheritances, since language is the carrier of culture. Finally, this policy of trilingualism would also lead to a more educated and enlightened society, for knowledge of another language is enriching. Many European states already require secondary school students to know three languages as a requirement for graduation, so we would not be doing anything new or impossible. In addition, most western European and Asian states have a degree of multilingualism in their populations much higher than ours, even though they are not officially bilingual.

The federal government could also take a much more expansive interpretation of the trade and commerce power in section 91 of the Constitution to eliminate interprovincial trade and labour mobility barriers. This would allow for the greater east–west mobility of citizens and goods within Canada. In many instances, there are more trade and labour mobility barriers between the provinces within Canada than there are between the sovereign nation–states of the European Union.

These are but a few examples of how Canadians coming together as a single nation can forge a better future than could be done by going our separate ways. In the past, strong central governments have shown leadership and created many of the programs and institutions that mark Canadian society and have made it admired around the world. More than twenty-five years after its introduction, the Canadian Charter of Rights and Freedoms has united Canadians with a set of common rights and responsibilities, making citizenship the touchstone of Canadian society. The creation of the Canada and Quebec pension plans, the introduction of universal health care, the expansion of postsecondary education and training, the establishment of employment insurance (which was *intra vires* provincial jurisdiction but arguably became *intra vires* federal jurisdiction via a constitution amendment because of the fiscal capacity of the federal government)—all in provincial areas of jurisdiction—were effected by past federal governments with the federal spending power and with federal leadership. More important, these programs were created because of the idea that we are one nation of citizens, and, as the realization of that political community, the federal government must engage in nation building.

I believe that the principal political community around which Canadians should be organized is one nation of 33 million citizens. The challenge is to replace the old cleavages of race and region with a new pluralism, for the Canada of tomorrow will be increasingly diverse. This will require an active dialogue among Canadians—whether their ancestors have been here for four or four hundred years. The challenge is to imagine our common future and to undertake the kind of nation-building projects that will ensure a continued thrust of intention into that future.

NOTES

1. George Grant, *Lament for a Nation* (Ottawa: Carleton University Press, 1991), p. 12.

2. Ibid.

3. Benedict Anderson, *Imagined Communities: Reflections on the Origin and Spread of Nationalism,* Revised Edition (London and New York: Verso, 2000), p. 6.

4. Statistics Canada, *The Daily, 2006 Census: Ethnic Origin, Visible Minorities, Place of Work and Mode of Transportation,* available at http://www.statcan.ca/Daily/English/080402/d080402a.htm.

5. Katherine Swinton and Carol Rogerson, eds., *Competing Constitutional Visions: The Meech Lake Accord* (Toronto: Carswell, 1988), p. 268.

6. Alan Cairns, Disruptions: Constitutional Struggles, from the Charter to Meech Lake (Toronto: McClelland & Stewart Inc., 1991), p. 208.

7. Department of Justice, Canada. Clarity Act, 2000, available at http://laws.justice.gc.ca/en/C-31.8/text.html.

POSTSCRIPT

Although Prime Minister Harper initially dismissed the debate over the recognition of Quebec as a nation as mere semantics, it is clear from the above readings that how one conceives of the idea of a nation has important policy and political implications.

One interesting dimension of this debate is the question of whether a nation is primarily an objective concept or a subjective one. Those who think that it is primarily objective will tend to focus on criteria such as shared history, culture, language, religion, or ethnic identity as a measure of nationhood. An example of this approach can be found in Anthony Smith, *The Ethnic Origins of Nations* (Oxford: Blackwell, 1986). Those who conceive of the nation as being primarily subjective see it as a product of the collective imagination and will. Benedict Anderson, in his book *Imagined Communities: Reflections on the Spread of Nationalism* (New York: Verso, 1983), provides an excellent overview of this approach. He sees the modern concept of the nation as being a product of modern forms of mass communication that enables the development of a collective sense of identity on a large scale.

The debate over the recognition of Quebec elicited considerable press coverage. For a sampling of these discussions, see Bill Curry, "PM Dodges 'Semantic Debate' on Quebec," *The Globe and Mail,* June 24, 2006, p. A7; Herbert Bauch, "Quebec Is a Nation within Canada" *Montreal Gazette,* June 28, 2006, p. A9; Stéphane Dion, "What, Exactly, Do We Mean by 'Nation'?," *National Post,* October 26, 2006, p. A14; Bob Rae, "Careless Rhetoric Is Not What Quebec Needs," *National Post,* November 7, 2006, p. A18; Lysiane Gagnon, "Reopening a Constitutional Can of Worms," *The Globe and Mail,* September 25, 2006, p. A15; Tom Axworthy, Serge Joyal, and Jerry Grafstein, "It's a Mistake to Abandon the Idea of One Canada," *The Globe and Mail,* November 27, 2006, p. A15; Norman Spector, "The Québécois Are Part of the Canadian Nation, Too," *The Globe and Mail,* November 27, 2006, p. A15; and Roy Romanow and John Whyte, "Stephen Harper Traded the Peaceable Kingdom for a Trojan Horse," December 8, 2006, *The Globe and Mail,* p. A25.

Michael Ignatieff's proposal can be found in *Agenda for Nation Building: Liberal Leadership for the 21st Century* (2006), pp. 27 and 29. The resolution adopted by the Liberal Party on October 21, 2006, can be found online at http://www.cbc.ca/news/background/liberals/quebecnationalunity.html# resolution.

PART THREE

POLITICAL INSTITUTIONS AND PROCESSES

Is the Prime Minister Too Powerful?

Should Parliament Review Supreme Court Appointments?

Should Party Discipline Be Relaxed?

Is a Mixed-Member Proportional Electoral System in Canada's Interest?

Should Women Focus on Small-p Politics?

Is the Prime Minister Too Powerful?

✔ **YES**
HUGH MELLON, "Coming to Terms with Political Realities: Exploring the Breadth of Prime-Ministerial Power"

✘ **NO**
PAUL BARKER, "Limits on the Power of the Prime Minister"

Students of Canadian politics appreciate that the prime minister is at the centre of political life in Canada. As leader of the national government, the prime minister determines the priorities that set the public agenda. The prime minister is also able to make appointments to important positions, and acts to represent Canada on the world stage. Perhaps the greatest indicator of the power and influence of the first minister is his or her sheer prominence. Canadians might be hard-pressed to name the provincial premiers or the chief justice of the Supreme Court of Canada, but few, if any, would experience the same problem with the prime minister.

There is thus little debate about the significance of the prime minister in Canadian politics. What might be debatable, however, is whether the prime minister dominates to the point that he threatens the healthy functioning of democracy in Canada. There are some who believe, strongly, that such is the case. Canada does not really have parliamentary government, they say, but in fact has what might be called "prime-ministerial" government. According to this perspective, the prime minister encounters few constraints on the exercise of his powers. All the typical powers associated with the prime minister—determining appointments, setting the overall direction of the country, representing Canada's interests in foreign dealings—are exercised with very little opposition. The Latin phrase *primus inter pares* ("first among equals") was once used to describe the prime minister's status: the prime minister was powerful (*primus*), but he faced individuals or challengers who were not merely his subordinates but his equals (*pares*) in some respects. Now, it is argued, the prime minister has no equals—he is *primus*, without any qualification.

Any proposition is only as strong as the supporting evidence. A look at Canadian political life does suggest some backing for the thesis of prime-ministerial government. The prime minister appears able to pass bills into law with little difficulty. He or she also decides who shall sit in cabinet and who shall hold the senior positions in the judiciary and the public service. The prime minister is front-and-centre in the media's coverage of Canadian politics; indeed, he or she might be considered a celebrity or a superstar. The fact that Canadians look instantly to the prime minister in times of trouble also speaks to the primacy of the prime minister. When the terrorist attacks of September 11, 2001, struck the United States, most Canadians turned to the prime minister for guidance on how this country should respond.

The question, however, is whether all this is enough to confirm the prime-ministerial government thesis. The corroborating evidence, to be sure, is impressive, but is it sufficiently impressive to allow us to conclude that Canada is a country with a leader who faces few limits to his or her power? Some answer in the negative. How, for example, can one ignore the influence of provincial premiers? Canadians may find it difficult to name political leaders in the provinces, but there is little doubt that premiers can frustrate prime-ministerial ambitions. Similarly, members of the prime minister's own government, the cabinet ministers, can make matters difficult for the prime minister—just look at the tussle between former prime minister Jean Chrétien and his finance minister Paul Martin. And, of course, the media present a challenge for the leader of the national government. One day the prime minister may appear invincible, the next day quite vulnerable. Such is the life of any celebrity.

In the readings, Hugh Mellon, a professor at King's University College at the University of Western Ontario, contends that the prime minister has an undue degree of power. Paul Barker, one of the editors of *Crosscurrents*, argues that supporters of the thesis of prime-ministerial government exaggerate the power open to the prime minister.

✔ **YES**

Coming to Terms with Political Realities: Exploring the Breadth of Prime-Ministerial Power
HUGH MELLON

From Confederation in 1867 until 2007, a period of one hundred and forty years, only twenty-two individuals have ever served as Canada's prime minister. In one of the world's longest consistently democratic political systems, fewer than two dozen individuals have held this position. The small number becomes even more striking when you realize that numerous occupants held the office for only a short time and that a handful of skilled politicians occupied this esteemed position for significant periods of time. John A. Macdonald served from 1867 until 1873 and then from 1878 until his death in 1891, while Laurier was prime minister from 1896 to 1911. Diefenbaker (1957–1963) won two minority governments plus a huge majority in 1958. Borden (1911–1920), St. Laurent (1948–1957), and Mulroney (1984–1993) each won two national elections while Pierre Trudeau held the post from 1968 to 1979 and then from 1980 to 1984, and Jean Chrétien (1993–2003) won three successive majorities. Yet even these achievements are humbled by William Lyon Mackenzie King, who endured over two decades as prime minister (1921–1926, 1926–1930, and 1935–1948). In short, these nine individuals held the position for over 80 percent of the time Canada has existed as a self-governing nation. This is a remarkable statistic, one that should give rise to reflection upon the position of prime minister and the autonomy and authority that accompany it.

Even if we are prepared to accept that these individuals were superior political candidates and/or leaders (admittedly a contentious hypothesis), it is sobering to contemplate the limited number of occupants of this powerful position. What happens when so much power is confined for substantial periods to a limited number of individuals? Can we hold governments accountable when we have so few individuals with firsthand experience? Do prime ministers truly represent a popular mandate or are they the political beneficiaries of an elite system marked by declining public participation in voting? Bear in mind that voter turnout in the last four Canadian federal elections has ranged between 60 and 70 percent and in the 2007 Ontario provincial election was below 53%, hardly evidence of mass public participation. Are there institutional and political limits sufficient to regulate the behaviour and occasional excesses of Canada's prime ministers? Taken together, these questions and concerns lead to fears that prime ministers are able to consolidate an excess of power, a situation fraught with significant potential dangers. The argument to be made here is that the limitations provided by the political system upon their power are woefully inadequate, and that this reality should concern all those interested in the state of Canada's democratic experience.

When preparing this argument, it was fascinating to take a moment to glance at the Government of Canada website devoted to the prime minister. Readers are urged to do the same, for the self-presentation of the office is enlightening. On October 16, 2007, the day of a Throne Speech and the convening of Parliament, the site was replete with assertions that the prime minister was taking dramatic action on major issues. The prime minister, Stephen Harper, was accorded credit for commissioning a panel to report on Canada's participation in the Afghanistan conflict, announcing a crackdown on drug crimes, promoting a "bolstering" of Arctic sovereignty, and sorting out matters relating to the Atlantic Accord with the premier of Nova Scotia. The accompanying visuals that supplemented the written content also accentuated the prime minister's visibility. Browsers were given the impression of a powerful, overarching prime minister directing action on issues across the board. The combined message is one of assertive action and central direction.

This impressionistic approach to the topic is intriguing but not conclusive, so therefore let us move to making the case for the excesses of prime-ministerial power. Those looking to test the extent of this power have different avenues available to them. What will be attempted here is to examine in turn those sources often cited as offering countervailing influences or checks upon that power in order to show their individual and collective weaknesses as sources of restraint. If each of these sources of control are found wanting, then this consolidates the argument of overreaching prime-ministerial ambition and power. Each of the presumed checks is not without some influence, but as a control upon prime-ministerial determination, they have noteworthy limitations, and while they may on occasion serve as a major check, this is likely more the exception; their ongoing strength should not always be assumed. The sources of restraint to be considered are (a) cabinet and the leading members of the prime minister's political party; (b) public opinion and the constitutional requirement of periodic elections; (c) Parliament and its institutionalized opposition and features like Question Period; (d) the media; and (e) the workings of Canadian federalism. But first a few words upon the role and constitutional authority of the prime minister are in order.

Those wishing to engage in the debate over prime-ministerial power will find a significant and growing literature on the role and authority of the Canadian prime minister. Notable works include Donald J. Savoie's *Governing from the Centre*[1], Jeffrey Simpson's *The Friendly Dictatorship*[2], and the various prime-ministerial memoirs and autobiographies. In fact, as this article goes to print, there are two new memoirs hot off the press: Brian Mulroney's *Memoirs 1939–1993*[3] and Jean Chrétien's *My Years as Prime Minister*[4]. Those looking for a biographical treatment, on the other hand, might try Lawrence Martin's two-volume life of Chrétien, with the prime-ministerial portion covered in volume two, *Iron Man: The Defiant Reign of Jean Chrétien*[5]. These and other related works merit examination in light of the debate presented here.

PRIME MINISTERS AND THEIR AUTHORITY

Prime ministers govern formally upon the basis of their ability to lead a ministry capable of retaining majority support in the elected House of Commons. This role is the product of British traditions and constitutional conventions, for, as Peter Hogg reminds us, the *British North America Act*, which ushered in Confederation in 1867, makes no formal reference to the position. Hogg states, "[T]here is no mention of the Prime Minister, or of the cabinet, or of the dependence of the cabinet on the support of a majority in the House of Commons: the composition of the actual executive authority and its relationship to the legislative authority were left in the form of unwritten conventions—as in the United Kingdom."[6] From these beginnings has sprung an office possessing wide-ranging and influential political tools. Parliamentary arrangements fuse power while disciplined political parties make control easier. As a result, the prime minister can oversee both executive authority and legislative deliberations. Today the office wields tremendous control, leading Jeffrey Simpson, a senior Ottawa observer, to conclude, "The Canadian prime minister is more powerful within this system than any democratically elected leader in other advanced industrial countries."[7] American separation of powers and the lesser degree of discipline among British political parties offer stronger restraints than those encountered by a Canadian prime minister.

Prime ministers possess an impressive political arsenal. One highly significant tool is the power to make a multitude of senior governmental and public service appointments both at home and abroad. Among the many prime-ministerial appointees are cabinet members, ambassadors, parliamentary secretaries, the Governor General, senators, and Crown corporation executives. Earlier reference was made to Prime Minister Harper's website and the announcement of an advisory panel of elite Canadians to advise on the Canadian involvement in Afghanistan. The website makes clear that this is a prime-ministerial announcement, and there is a link to a visual in which Harper is seen announcing the panel's creation. When you take this power in its totality, its potential is obvious. Those wishing to get ahead will soon realize whose opinion will determine their possibilities. Party workers dreaming of a Senate appointment or cabinet advancement likewise know where their appointment will come from. Also note that there are fewer restraints upon the appointment power than are found in the U.S. congressional system, in which various key appointments need ratification by another branch of government.

The prime minister exercises parliamentary leadership and directs the flow of events, aided by cabinet and the whip's office. In practice, attention and clout gravitate to the prime minister and his or her centrality to Question Period, media coverage, and debate. What is more, remember that the upper house in the bicameral legislative arrangement, the Senate, is appointed by the prime minister. The house, crafted to offer "sober second thought" coupled with regional representation, is composed of prime-ministerial appointees. Opportunities for conflicts of interest are immediately evident.

Prime ministers have in the past also possessed the power to set the dates for elections, which allows them to capitalize upon the movement of polls or to catch the Opposition unprepared. This power may be constrained by the movement to fixed elections at the federal level proposed by the Harper government. Whatever the case regarding fixed or flexible election dates, there is an imbalance in resources between a calculating prime minister and those in Opposition.

Prime ministers chair cabinet, which may often entail further strategic advantages, such as the authority to alter cabinet membership, the power to set items on or off a particular agenda, and the ability to offer support or roadblocks to particular ministers. Prime ministers have the authority to appoint senior officials and bureaucrats throughout the government. This comes with ongoing authority to monitor their performance should an issue or political pressures warrant. These powers are important for several reasons. One is the obvious asymmetrical relationship born of having chosen an individual for a post, while retaining the ability to elevate or discipline that person over time. A second is the likelihood of a line of communication from the prime minister through the officials allowing the prime minister to bypass a cabinet minister or ministers. In an environment in which knowledge is power, the availability of multiple information sources is a significant asset. A third reason is the use of appointments and job appraisals to solidify the ranks of loyalists and serve the interests of partisanship and the leader. Political office involves the use of teams of advisors and loyalists, and patronage is one of the most often selected lubricants for the inner workings of this dynamic team and coalition-building.

Opposition parties often score points over the presumed excesses of prime-ministerial appointments, but the advantages of the appointment power and back-channels of information are considerable. Jean Chrétien, for example, was one more prime minister who had donned the mantle of outraged defender of the public interest while in Opposition. Appointments made by the Mulroney government were scrutinized and frequently challenged. Yet, upon election to the prime ministership, the self-same Chrétien found himself less interested in reform. In their study of the first Chrétien government (1993–1997) Greenspon and Wilson-Smith offer this description of the Chrétien attitude:

> He intended to exercise the prerogatives of the office. "It is better that I make the appointments and be accountable for them," others remembered him saying, "than someone else makes them and I be accountable.[8]

Advisors and bureaucratic aides for the prime minister are built into the institutional order. In the carrying out of his or her role as national leader and voice of the country on the international and domestic stages, the prime minister is aided by central agencies and the top levels of staff at the national office of his or her respective political party. Two central agencies, the Prime Minister's Office (PMO) and the Privy Council Office (PCO), are well connected to the prime minister's political or bureaucratic needs for information, contacts, supporting documents, and advice. Meanwhile, the link to his or her political party allows control over campaign planning, national opinion polling, and candidate selection. Leaders attempting to recruit high-profile candidates can often assure them of an easy ride to a desirable riding nomination. Taken together, the prime minister has access to tremendous supports and avenues for influence. This facilitates prime-ministerial direction over important issues like national unity and federal–provincial relations. Donald Savoie, a longtime student of government and bureaucracy, reports that with regard to this policy field, "briefing material prepared by the PCO for new ministers makes it clear that 'the Prime Minister has direct responsibility for the conduct of federal–provincial relations.'"[9]

By virtue of their position and the practices of modern communications media, prime ministers both deliver government messages and oversee the crafting of communications planning. Whether it be through appearances at vital symbolic events (e.g., Remembrance Day commemorations), leaders' election campaign debates, government websites, or media settings like the year-end fireside chat, prime ministers are at the centre of coverage. Government media strategies often reinforce the centrality of the prime minister. For example, it was Prime Minister Paul Martin himself who appeared in a highly publicized media address in the spring of 2005 to defend the Liberal Party from allegations arising from corruption within government advertising expenditures. When the government of Brian Mulroney announced its intention to "explore" the possibility of Canada–U.S. free trade, media preparation included a personal call from Mulroney to U.S. President Ronald Reagan and a major prime-ministerial address to the House of Commons.[10]

As with the overtures made to the U.S. leadership about free trade, prime ministers are generally the dominant voice of Canada internationally. They attend highly visible gatherings like meetings of the G7 or G8, the group composed of the leaders of the richest countries. They also publicly identify themselves with major foreign initiatives. Like his predecessors, Stephen Harper has been the primary Canadian figure at senior international events. Take, for example, Harper's visit to Germany in June 2007, where he participated in talks with both the president and the prime minister of France; the Canada–European Union Summit; and the gathering of the G8, which brought Harper into contact with the political leaders of Germany, the U.S., Great Britain, France, Japan, Italy, and Russia, as well as providing him introductions to significant German business leaders. He was thereby able to present skepticism about the Kyoto Accord as the official national position at a time when support for greater environmental protection was strongly urged among the general Canadian populace.[11]

The breadth of the responsibilities and power available to prime ministers gives them a commanding role in the machinery of government and the broad political landscape. They have a paramount influence over major government appointments; parliamentary debate and questioning; major policy directions in key fields like federal–provincial relations, foreign policy, and other government priorities; media coverage and campaign strategizing; and the leadership of their political party. Their judgment is supplemented by the advice and support of two major central agencies, pollsters, and leading strategists in their own political party. They chair cabinet meetings and set its composition and agendas. This is tangible power supported by senior civil servants, cabinet colleagues, and media advisors. If we are serious about controlling or at least constraining prime-ministerial power, we need to devote increased attention to this task, for at the moment, the leading candidates for restraining the political executive are limited, sporadic, and occasionally unpredictable in their impact.

CABINET AND THE LEADING MEMBERS OF THE PRIME MINISTER'S POLITICAL PARTY

Stephen Harper became Canada's prime minister upon his election on January 23, 2006; his new cabinet, which included a high-profile defector from the Opposition Liberals, was subsequently unveiled in early February with great fanfare. Yet this new team and its specific ministerial assignments were not to remain in place for long. Within little more than a year and a half, this heralded cabinet was altered by two ministerial shuffles. In January 2007, a shuffle affecting such major departments as Environment, the Treasury Board, Justice, and Citizenship and Immigration took place. Later, in August 2007, a second major upheaval occurred, and those responsible for the high-priority fields of Foreign Affairs, Indian Affairs and Northern Development, Industry, Defence, Heritage, and Agriculture were shifted into other roles. Learning a new portfolio, with its attendant responsibilities and multimillion-dollar expenditures, is a Herculean task. Once appointed, the new minister is badgered by the press and client groups seeking audiences and signs of policy direction. Periodic shuffles force new responsibilities on those already endeavouring to master other cabinet assignments and their associated policy challenges and weighty briefing books.

Amid the shuffles, Prime Minister Harper, the cabinet designer, remained firmly in place at the centre. Donald Savoie explains the strength of the prime minister's position this way:

> Ministers . . . know full well that they sit in Cabinet only because one person wants them to be there—the prime minister. The prime minister may well be reluctant to swing the axe, but no one knows for certain if or when he will do it.[12]

The power to assign positions permits the elevation of favourites, the demotion of discontents, and the stymieing of the plans of ambitious underlings. Although cabinet selections need to reflect important political cleavages like region, gender, party factions, and language, do not underestimate the clout arising from the authority to design cabinets and to favour the loyal and supportive.

Prime ministers enter the office with the upper hand over fellow party members. Winning a majority is a tonic for party morale—the leader is a champion. Winning a minority is a disappointment but not necessarily a death sentence. Political parties are often patient with leaders who have been reduced to minority status. Pierre Trudeau successfully endured the humiliation of 1972, and Paul Martin was given another chance after the reduced Liberal numbers in 2004. Prime ministers who win only a minority government typically pledge that they have learned a lesson, that the voters have spoken, and that next time their efforts will produce a parliamentary majority. Meanwhile, minority governments are often in a vulnerable position, and efforts are made within the party to mute expressions of disloyalty to the leader. This should not be surprising, since the potential successor to replace the prime minister is likely to be found in cabinet, and thus his or her approval rating is bound up with that of the government he or she serves.

Note, however, that there is no intention here of speaking of a similar relationship between opposition leaders and their internal party rivals. Past experience, as in the relations between Joe Clark and Brian Mulroney (1980–1984) and between John Turner and Jean Chrétien (1984–1990), indicates that without the lubricant of patronage and power, the party leader is far more vulnerable. Hence, the prime minister likely has better job security than the leaders of the opposition parties.

The condition of contemporary Canadian political parties makes them weak as guardians of ongoing accountability. Many of us may have an image rooted in history of mass parties in which there is an integrated organization, with a dedicated membership who form a sort of institutional family with memory and well-worn conventions. This may no longer be a suitable vision. Sid Noel offers an insightful reexamination of parties in his essay "Leaders' Entourages, Parties, and Patronage,"[13] which encourages us to reassess what we expect of parties. In the past, parties were major vehicles for fundraising, member attachment, and campaign preparation. Much has changed, though. Federal campaign reforms have provided public funding for parties. Campaigns are often leader-driven media efforts organized around a centrally set theme and schedule. Citizen attachment to politics appears to be waning, as turnout at the last two federal elections was only in the low- to mid-60 percent level, and a sampling of recent provincial elections in Ontario (2007), Newfoundland (2007), and Nova Scotia (2006) offers little evidence of voter enthusiasm. Even the 2007 Quebec election, which featured debate over sovereignty and national unity, had a turnout percentage only in the low 70s. Party efforts to allow the signing up of new members during leadership selection seem to produce only temporary votes for preferred candidates rather than ongoing lifeblood. There are ample reasons for concern about the vitality of Canadian parties.

Noel suggests that we instead think about parties as vehicles taken over for periods by ambitious and well-heeled individuals backed by professional entourages personally loyal to them. The party label becomes more of a brand than a historic family that has shared a history together.

> Though actual titles may vary, the inner circle of a typical entourage consists of a chief fundraiser, a chief organizer or campaign director, a communications director (media adviser), one or two senior strategists, a personal aide ("gatekeeper"), a chief media spokesperson or "spinner" (if this role is not filled by the communications director), an opinion pollster, an advertising director, and possibly a spouse.[14]

These and other professionals directly linked to the leader sustain the leader and drive the political party's national presentation. Who then has the status within the party to restrain the prime minister? Those who suggest that cabinet and its particular political party will serve as controls on prime-ministerial influence and decisions have a difficult case to make. Meanwhile, the political party organizational trends delineated by Noel show little sign of abating.

Before exploring the impact of public opinion on elections, it is important to confront head-on the case of the intra-party feud within the Chrétien government involving the challenge from Paul Martin. Some might imagine that the resulting upheaval and change in leadership upends the argument made here. The conventional narrative is that Martin served dutifully as finance minister between 1993 and 2002, helping to fight the deficit and control government finances. Over time, he chafed under the wear and tear of subservience to an individual whom he had challenged in the 1990 Liberal leadership race. Chrétien, for his part, grew tired of Martin's ambition and the machinations of his loyalists. Their overt jockeying for position and strategizing for the future replacement of "yesterday's man" with the political and economic wizard whose cabinet work was yielding annual fiscal surpluses was incessant. Especially galling to Chrétien was a meeting in Toronto's Regal Constellation Hotel in 2000 that was explained by Martin allies as a quiet gathering of Liberals interested in renewal, at which only some of the attendees were operatives in the service of Martin's cause. Intense press coverage and speculation nonetheless ensued. Chrétien responded by staying on and calling an election for late November, which produced a third majority government for the prime minister. Pressure for change continued apace, though, and in 2002 Chrétien finally replaced Martin in cabinet while also acknowledging his own upcoming departure from office was limited. A leadership vote was subsequently held in late 2003, and Martin won with over 90 percent of the votes.

But what is the lesson of this fandango of bitterness, intrigue, and media headlines? Is it that the cabinet and the prime minister's political party can, in a timely and effective manner, regularly hold a prime minister accountable for his or her performance? No, it is, rather, that a prime minister, even one who distrusts grand gestures and bold initiatives, can survive for years in office aided by a coterie of loyalists and that change is exhausting, long, and debilitating. Lawrence Martin, the noted biographer of Chrétien, put it this way:

> For those who thought of public service as an altruistic or ennobling pursuit, the endless power struggle between Chrétien and his finance minister was distressingly juvenile. Chrétien had made the public interest such a personal game that he chose to let a meeting of opponents in a hotel room become his ostensible reason for staying in power for four more years.[15]

If there is a moral to this story, perhaps it is that the struggle for leadership within a political party is an awkward, time-consuming, and often embarrassing display of ambition and rivalry. This conclusion is reminiscent in various ways of the struggles during the death throes of the Diefenbaker government during its minority period of 1962–1963.[16] Cabinet members' or other senior party figures' questioning of the party leader is a blunt and cumbersome tool for controlling the prime minister's performance for a number of reasons. One of the most important of these is that the prime minister has to continue to govern while sorting out the party struggle. Many may understandably join the prime minister in labelling the challenge(s) unseemly and counterproductive. The second key reason is that challenging a leader requires a credible alternative party figure willing to engage in the face-off. Announcing such an intention automatically sets the contender apart. Having thrown his or her hat into the ring, it is unlikely that this person could ever regain the trust of many party loyalists. The third major weakness of this check on prime-ministerial power is that it can cause paralysis within the governing party rather than improved accountability and attentiveness.

PUBLIC OPINION AND ELECTIONS

Are elections effective vehicles for the enforcement and maintenance of prime-ministerial accountability? At a basic level, an election offers potential for either changing or maintaining a particular government, but there are practical limits to its use. Power does periodically change hands, as in the federal elections of 1993 (Chrétien Liberals unseat Kim Campbell Progressive Conservatives and win a majority) and 2006 (Harper Conservatives win minority over Martin Liberals). What is more, Canadian elections are generally useful for fulfilling certain other political functions. Pammett regards them as being good at recruiting candidates and potential leaders, and offering political "parties opportunities to revive and re-establish their organizations."[17] Yet there is more to the story. Canadian elections don't securely foster citizen interest and belief in the political system. Voter turnout is mired in a string of sub-par levels. In the five most recent federal elections—1993, 1997, 2000, 2004, and 2006—turnout as a percentage of eligible voters was only in the 60s (Elections Canada website). If a winning party's share of the votes ranges from the high 30s to the low/mid 40s, a common occurrence, and only roughly

65 percent of those eligible actually vote, this is hardly strong democratic control. Little wonder that Pammett points to those who feel it an advantage that elites are given opportunities to fashion plans without mass scrutiny.[18] Not surprisingly, he also points out the purposeful vagueness of party campaign appeals and the ease with which parties jettison inconvenient pledges. Party election platforms have an uncertain shelf life once a government has been elected; hardly an effective constraint upon government action.

Elections are about the making of a government in the sense that, after an election, the Governor General reviews the results and asks the leaders of the party with the most elected members, or most visible support within the legislature, to form a government. This is a fundamentally important task, but let us not exaggerate its impact on the power and influence of a prime minister in the conduct of his or her office. Elections are sporadic and much can happen between them. In the past, prime ministers possessed the power to set the dates for elections, which could allow them to capitalize upon the movement of polls or to capture the Opposition unprepared. There is currently debate within various Canadian jurisdictions about moving to fixed election dates as in the United States. This may help constrain one aspect of prime-ministerial discretion. It remains to be seen whether it will produce increased accountability, though. Fixed dates four or five years apart, for example, still leave a long period between elections.

Election campaigns rely upon citizen participation and involvement, but as already noted there is reason to worry on this front, given the low levels of voter turnout and public interest. Coupled with this lack of popular interest is the resulting opportunity for elites and active interest groups to marshal their resources and influence in support of favoured causes. With regard to the free trade election of 1988, for example, Brian Mulroney's *Memoirs* makes clear his recognition of the value of business support as a counter to the anti-free trade campaign of the Liberals and NDP. "The Canadian business community, led by Tom D'Aquino and the Business Council on National Issues, rallied vigorously in support of free trade. During the election campaign, business leaders spoke out bluntly and purchased ads in favour of the trade agreement. Their support was unprecedented and effective."[19] And in the 1988 election, the Mulroney Progressive Conservatives were returned with a sizable parliamentary contingent of 169 of 295 seats and 43% of the popular vote. More than half of voters marked ballots for parties officially opposed to the primary agenda item of the sitting prime minister, yet free trade became a reality.

PARLIAMENT

Our examination now turns to focus upon the traditional understanding that Parliament serves as a representative forum wherein governments are judged and regularly called to account through vehicles such as the regular Question Period, the rigours of open debate, and the challenge of maintaining confidence among a collection of active and probing legislators. Assumptions of active and probing debate underestimate the disciplined character of Canadian political parties, which almost always stay on script. Question Period and debate are more often about reciting prepared positions and looking for catch phrases suitable for news coverage than about uncovering underlying realities or scrutinizing administrative detail. Votes are overwhelmingly cast upon party lines. Coordinated party strategy is thus more often a defining feature than active restraint upon prime-ministerial behaviour.

Prime ministers choose cabinets and lead the parliamentary charge, but it should also be acknowledged that their power depends upon the skillful handling of caucus. Leaders must maintain support through those periods when their government's fortunes appear to be waning. Styles vary, but good team building allows a prime minister great leeway. According to Lawrence Martin, "Mulroney was known for his soothing strokes, Trudeau was a study in patience, Mackenzie King was famous for his incisive summations."[20] Their attentiveness paid off, as each enjoyed a career of striking duration and achievement.

Those across the aisle from the ruling party suffer from several key limitations in the parliamentary fray. First of all, the single member electoral system used at the federal and provincial levels militates against opposition parties that do not have a major regional base, such as the Bloc Québécois.[21] Take the just mentioned 1988 federal election. The Liberals and NDP together obtained over 51 percent of the votes cast but received only 126 of the 295 seats. For an added example, note the 1997 federal election, in which the Jean Chrétien federal Liberals managed 155 of 301 seats with less than 39 percent of the votes cast.

A second deficiency is the striking imbalance of resources available to a government as compared to the parliamentary opposition. Being in power means having command of the bureaucracy and enjoying the resulting perks. Prime ministers can direct the preparation of briefing material, can strategize about when to release favourable or damaging information, as well as solicit alternative proposals from staff, with the cost being borne out of government revenues. Governments also engage in active public opinion polling, thus offering the prime minister and his or her cabinet up-to-date insights into the public mood. These opportunities are more pronounced in a parliamentary setting where parliamentarians are often relatively inexperienced. In his 1997 book, *Mr. Smith Goes to Ottawa: Life in the House of Commons,* Docherty refers to this situation and laments instances in which government benches featured more veteran talent than their parliamentary rivals or caucus colleagues. "Simply put, it is difficult for both government backbenchers and opposition members to keep cabinet accountable when they lack the experience and parliamentary savvy of members of the executive."[22]

It must be acknowledged that there are features of parliamentary life that serve to highlight government behaviour and raise questions requiring serious responses. A good example of this was the work done by the Auditor General's Office to uncover the details of the sponsorship scandal that plagued the Chrétien and Martin governments.[23] Offices like those of the auditor general, the official languages commissioner, and the privacy commissioner have significant powers. These control mechanisms play a valuable role, yet their impact is more often than not momentary, and parliamentary skirmishing overshadows their reports replete with analysis and administrative concerns.

The tests of stamina and commitment provided by the daily grind of Question Period and debate are not without importance. Prime ministers must have a diverse skill set and be accomplished performers as well as administrators. Yet, the question at issue here is not whether the job is easy but, rather, whether there are sufficient controls upon prime-ministerial power. Party discipline, public inattention, and the imbalance of cabinet and opposition resources provide reasons to doubt that there are adequate restraints given the public money and critical issues at stake.

MEDIA

There is always room to make the argument that the media, armed with their rights of free expression and opportunities for investigation, are a source of restraint upon prime-ministerial ambition. Certainly stories critical of the government can be aired, but the deeper, more complicated questions are (1) How much of a government's actions are going to be scrutinized?; (2) To what degree are Canadians vigilant about following and working to understand news coverage?; and (3) Are politicians becoming more skilled in massaging press coverage and spinning messages favourable to their cause, thereby gaining an advantage over the press? There is reason to speculate that the answers to each of these will lead us to further question the effectiveness of the media's performance as a check on power.

As to the question of breadth of coverage, there is a limit to how much the media, no matter how vigilant, can be aware of. The Canadian government is a multibillion-dollar enterprise with branch offices (embassies, office buildings, and services) spread out nationally and internationally. How much of this can we reasonably expect the media to cover? At what point will budgets, audience ratings, and entertainment pressures outweigh the coverage of all that governments do? Note that what is being argued here is that the media operate under certain kinds of limitations and work to serve an audience that itself has time and attention pressures. Is it realistic to imagine that the media have resources for news coverage sufficient to oversee the full range of prime-ministerial power?

The second fundamental question is about the vigilance of the audience to (a) demand this kind of detailed coverage and (b) to watch and act upon it. If the media are to act as a check on power that can be regularly depended upon, then there is an implied understanding that the citizens will patronize it. Television ratings, best-seller lists, etc. do not suggest that expanded news coverage is necessarily prevailing. Instead, it may be an option more appealing in civics classes than in the real world of media ratings and commercial broadcasting. Open-line shows airing aggressive comments supplied voluntarily by opinionated members of the general public may be entertaining, but how worried about such opinions is a prime minister in far away Ottawa, a couple of years away from an election?

The final question under this heading relates to the balance of power between busy journalists covering a multitude of breaking stories and the expanding ranks of media advisers, spin doctors, and pollsters servicing prime ministers. Political advisers have grown more adroit in defining media strategies and prescribing visuals that charm the eye but perhaps little more. Election campaigns seem to be caught up in image management. In the words of Paul Nesbitt-Larking in his well-known Canadian media text, "Winning elections seems to depend more and more on the control of image and style."[24] Thus, with the influence of media gurus shaping the presentation strategies of political leaders, there may well be reason to be cautious in judging the impact of the press in its implicit struggle between the investigation into, and acceptance of, prime ministerial messages.

THE WORKINGS OF CANADIAN FEDERALISM

A further check upon prime-ministerial ambition may be found in the restraint provided by the division of powers and the existence of assertive and sizable provincial governments. Strong executive power at both the federal and provincial levels has produced a political system in which first ministers' meetings and inter-governmental agreements are important sources of policy decisions. Herman Bakvis, for example, asserts that "while power may be highly centralized in the hands of the prime minister, the same holds true for provincial premiers. In other words, prime ministerial power and ambition can be easily checked by strong resistance from some of the larger provinces."[25] Executive federalism and competing federal and provincial agendas are thus offered as sources of meaningful restraint.

While important as an argument, there is still something troubling about offering the closed and secretive world of intergovernmental bargaining as a constraint upon the actions of prime ministers. Instead of providing comfort that interested citizens might be able to monitor their federal leader's initiatives, this would seem to intensify the concerns that drive the argument provided by this essay. Many governmental access-to-information regulations offer matters of federal–provincial negotiation as an exception. Which Canadians outside of elite circles had access to the high-stakes negotiations that produced the *Constitution Act* of 1982, the Meech Lake Accord, the Charlottetown Accord? The restraint offered by federal–provincial confrontation is at best a minimal sort of constraint. Advocates of this control assume that provinces and their self-interested political agendas offer more than simply the countervailing force of another competing executive or set of executives. Surely this is a limited type of counter to underlying democratic fears of overall executive dominance.

Federal and provincial governments have a complex political relationship wherein competing claims are voiced and debated. Attention to the division of powers and to provincial reactions may on many occasions serve to limit federal government proposals. Yet, it is also true that despite having limited jurisdiction in various social policy fields like health and higher education, the federal government has been able to shape events through the power to spend or to withhold spending, or to reshape patterns of federal–provincial interactions. What recourse was available to Ontario, Alberta, and British Columbia when the Mulroney government limited the growth in their Canada Assistance Plan transfers in the early 1990s? What recourse was available to provinces when the early budgets of the Chrétien government cut back on transfers and added to provincial expenditure burdens? Federalism and strong provincial governments are a restraint, but do not overlook or underestimate the strength of the federal government position.

CONCLUSION

The prime minister has several sources of significant power, and the political system has inadequate safeguards to combat the excesses of this power. Prime ministers have major advantages in interparty competition. Elections meanwhile are sporadic, and parliamentary life is seemingly more defined by party discipline and the divide between ins and outs than by a collective appraisal of detailed policy and budgetary plans. At the same time, the press contributes to improved accountability, but there are noteworthy limitations to its impact. Governments are huge entities, and only a selection of events can be reported since audience and budgetary pressures constrain coverage. Prime ministers, meanwhile, are supported by a growing circle of advisors, pollsters, and spin doctors that help protect their position. Constraining power is not an easy task. Considering ways to improve the actual track record on this front is an important topic for future debate.

Only a narrow band of Canadians has ever achieved the prime-ministerial pinnacle. Perhaps one of the reasons for the limited number is the imbalance between restraints upon power and the reinforcements of that power. There is a struggle between the exercise of real power by a relatively small number of ambitious and skilled politicians and the efforts of other political actors to keep that power in check; a struggle warranting vigilance.

NOTES

1. Donald J. Savoie, Governing from the Centre: The Concentration of Power in Canadian Politics (Toronto, ON: University of Toronto, 1999).

2. Jeffrey Simpson, The Friendly Dictatorship (Toronto, ON: McClelland and Stewart, 2001).

3. Brian Mulroney, Memoirs (Toronto, ON: Douglas Gibson Books, 2007).

4. Jean Chrétien, My Years as Prime Minister (Toronto, ON: Knopf Canada, 2007).

5. Martin, Lawrence, Iron Man: The Defiant Reign of Jean Chrétien (Toronto, ON: Penguin, 2003).

6. Peter Hogg, *Constitutional Law in Canada, Student Edition* (Toronto, ON: Carswell, 2001), p. 1.2.

7. Jeffrey Simpson, *The Friendly Dictatorship*, p. 4.

8. Edward Greenspon and Anthony Wilson-Smith, *Double Vision: The Inside Story of the Liberals in Power* (Toronto, ON: Doubleday Canada, 1996), p. 220.

9. Donald Savoie, "Power at the Apex: Executive Dominance," in *Canadian Politics*, 4th ed., edited by James Bickerton and Alain-G. Gagnon (Peterborough, ON: Broadview, 2004), p. 146.

10. Brian Mulroney, *Memoirs*, pp. 394–7.

11. CBC News, *Harper Lands in Germany as G8 Summit Approaches*, June 4, 2007, available at http://www.cbc.ca/canada/story/2007/06/03/harper-summit.html?ref=rss. Accessed November 9, 2007.

12. Donald J. Savoie, *Governing from the Centre*, p. 91.

13. Sid Noel, "Leaders' Entourages, Parties and Patronage" in Alain-G. Gagnon and Brian Tanguay, eds., *Canadian Parties in Transition*, 3rd ed. (Peterborough, ON: Broadview, 2007), pp. 197–213.

14. Ibid., p. 206.

15. Martin Lawrence, *Iron Man*, p. 431.

16. Denis Smith, *Tory Rogue: The Life and Legend of John Diefenbaker* (Toronto, ON: Macfarlane Walter and Ross, 1995).

17. Jon H. Pammett, "Elections," in Michael and Glen Williams, eds., *Canadian Politics in the 21st Century*, 7th ed. (Toronto, ON: Nelson, 2008), p. 164.

18. Ibid., p. 165.

19. Brian Mulroney, *Memoirs*, p. 633.

20. Martin Lawrence, *Iron Man*, p. 373.

21. David Docherty, *Legislatures* (Vancouver, BC: UBC Press, 2005), pp. 125–6.

22. David Docherty, *Mr. Smith Goes to Ottawa: Life in the House of Commons* (Vancouver, BC: UBC Press, 1997), p. 9.

23. See Report of the Auditor General of Canada (Ottawa, 2003).

24. Paul Nesbitt-Larking, *Politics, Society, and the Media*, 2nd ed. (Peterborough, ON: Broadview, 2007), p. 146.

25. Herman Bakvis, "Prime Minister and Cabinet in Canada. An Autocracy in Need of Reform," *Journal of Canadian Studies* 15:4 (2001), p. 68.

✗ **NO**
Limits on the Power of the Prime Minister
PAUL BARKER

Many close observers of Canadian politics believe that political power in Canada resides largely with the prime minister and his small group of close advisers. Those who make this argument are careful to admit that the prime minister comes up against some limits, but at the same time they describe Canada as "a kind of monarchy" that is "mandated by democracy."[1] The source of the prime minister's great influence, they say, lies in his access to so many "levers of power."[2] He leads the governing party, controls cabinet and its members, commands the attention of the media, sets the overall direction of the country, and much more. Also important, highly qualified officials located in the central agencies—"superbureaucrats"—help the prime minister control all relevant matters.[3] There are some who urge caution in adopting the notion that government in Canada amounts to "prime-ministerial government." Keith Archer and his colleagues, for instance, say that the national government is "too large and too complex to be directed by a single individual."[4] But such sentiments appear to receive little attention. According to a popular text in Canadian politics, "[m]ost observers agree that Cabinet government has been transformed into a system of prime-ministerial government. . . ."[5] And other reputable sources also diligently outline the case that the prime minister's powers of influence dwarf those of others in the political process.[6]

The belief that the prime minister wields a great deal of power has some merit. The nature of parliamentary government is to situate power in the hands of the political executive, so we expect the prime minister to be influential. But to suggest that this forms the basis of a kind of monarchical democracy goes too far. Though many specific criticisms of the thesis of prime-ministerial government may be made, there are basically two problems with it. One is that it fails to note sufficiently that the prime minister faces some formidable players in the political process. The prime minister is simply not that powerful. There are forces both inside and outside government that can challenge the leader of the governing party. The other problem relates to the conception of competition. The theory of prime-ministerial government assumes that competition for power is viable only when it is patently obvious or present. But prime ministers can be challenged simply by the *threat* of a new competitive force. The prime minister operates in a world of "virtual competition," in which the challenges sometimes appear as only potentialities. The lack of a corporeal presence matters little, because the prime minister acts as if the challenges are real. The key implication here is that there is indeed competition in Canadian politics—more so than suggested by a counting of the observable competitors—and that Canada is not nearly as vulnerable to the effects of concentrated power as suggested by those who see the influence of only the prime minister.

INSIDE GOVERNMENT

The idea of an almost domineering prime minister certainly exaggerates the power the prime minister commands outside the formal structures of government, and it can be argued that it is an exaggeration also of the power commanded inside government. Let us begin with the latter. Donald J. Savoie writes that "[it] is hardly possible to overemphasize the fact that the Canadian prime minister has no outer limits defining his political authority within the government."[7] In fact, one *can* overemphasize the influence of the prime minister. Outer limits exist, and one has to look only at the relations between prime ministers and their ministers to see this point. Take, for instance, former prime minister Jean Chrétien and his then-finance minister, Paul Martin. According to Mr. Chrétien himself, the finance minister had a great deal of leeway in the making of fiscal policy. "I am not going to tell my finance minister what to do," said Mr. Chrétien.[8] And this has been the tradition at the federal level: the finance minister runs the budgetary process. Of course, this is not to say that the prime minister is shut out of this important process—the national leader can never ignore the economic health of the nation. The fact remains, however, that the finance minister is a powerful player in Canadian politics.

A well-known incident involving Mr. Martin and Mr. Chrétien is telling. In the mid-1990s, the finance minister wanted to announce major pension reforms in his budget. The reforms were risky politically, for they proposed to take away some pension benefits from well-off seniors. The prime minister balked at the changes and asked the finance minister to desist from making his announcement. Mr. Martin challenged the prime minister's counsel not once but three times. He intimated that he might resign, which the prime minister realized would hurt his government—it could destabilize markets and would make the government look divided. Though there is some disagreement about what happened next, a close reading of the relevant evidence indicates that the two men fashioned a deal: the announcement would be held back until the next year, but the finance minister could mention the principles of pension reform now. The prime minister had been confronted and had been forced to accept a compromise. This seems some distance from a prime minister without limits.[9]

There are instances of other ministers taking actions that reveal the limits of prime-ministerial power. Allan Rock, a federal minister of health in the Chrétien government, wanted to raise the profile of the federal government in the Canadian health care system. In early 2000, the health minister outlined a "new plan for health care."[10] Under the plan, Ottawa would be instrumental in effecting changes to the primary health care system and in setting up a national home care program. Both primary health care and home care fall within the jurisdiction of the provinces; accordingly, the new plan held the possibility of major disruptions in relations between the federal government and the provinces. Many assumed, though, that this would be acceptable because it was thought that the prime minister had given his consent to the initiative. But the prime minister had done no such thing. A minister had announced a major policy initiative with serious implications for federal–provincial relations–without the prime minister's agreement.[11] Eventually, Mr. Chrétien put a stop to Mr. Rock's proposal, but it was clear that cabinet included members who had their own agendas.

The combination of ministerial ambition and backbencher support can also fatally weaken the prime minister. At the turn of the century, many in the Liberal Party expected Mr. Chrétien to leave office soon and open the way for a leadership race; he had already governed for two full terms, and he was getting older. But the prime minister, upset by attempts within his own party to oust him, surprised many with his actions. He contested a third election in late 2000–and won–and suggested at a minimum that he would complete his third term as leader of the country. The prime minister's actions, especially his speculations on his own future, infuriated both party members and Liberal MPs who wished to see Mr. Martin become prime minister, and they began to call for Mr. Chrétien to step down. For a time, the prime minister resisted, but it was all to no avail. Mr. Martin had made great efforts to gain support of Liberal MPs who failed to make it into cabinet or who were ignored by the prime minister and his advisers in the Prime Minister's Office. The finance minister also had in place an impressive organization dedicated to making him the prime minister. In August 2002, Jean Chrétien announced he would leave office in early 2004, and, by late 2003, he was gone.[12]

For some, the demise of Mr. Chrétien was a product of special circumstances and hardly a sign of inherent prime-ministerial weakness. The former prime minister had been confronted by a minister determined to succeed him and a large group of returning MPs who received nothing from a prime minister unable to give them much. Mr. Chrétien also had no real organization in place to confront his competition–he was too busy running the government and uncertain about continuing beyond his third mandate.[13] All this may be true. But it is also true that a prime minister had been *effectively* pushed aside, an unexpected event in the life of an individual who has many levers of power at his behest. A former senior official in the PMO and respected observer of government gives his read of the demise of Mr. Chrétien:

> . . . Savoie's 1999 metaphor of an all powerful love-like prime minister casting bolts of electricity into the system would have to be recast in 2003 as Jean Chrétien has been sent into retirement after losing control first of his party, then of his caucus. The events of the past year prove that Canada does not have a dictatorship, friendly or otherwise.[14]

In the government of Paul Martin, there were also signs of conflict between the first minister and elected members of his party. Initially, Prime Minister Martin appeared to look favourably on a decision that would see Canada work with the United States to develop a ballistic missile defence system for North America. But dissent in the party helped produce a contrary decision. The prime minister also faced resistance from Liberal MPs who disagreed with his government's support of legislation favouring same-sex marriage. The weakness of Mr. Martin was in part made possible because backbenchers realized that the prime minister was, most of the time, in a minority situation and needed their support. A majority situation might, of course, easily quash these differences. But the fact is that minority governments are part of parliamentary government, and they serve to lessen the power of the first minister.

The experience so far of the minority government of Stephen Harper, at first glance, reveals a prime minister more than able to control his ministers. Reports disclose a number of actions that support this perception. Prime Minister Harper prefers a "hub and spoke" management style, which means that Mr. Harper—as the hub—is able to more easily keep track of the ministers, who are the individual spokes.[15] As with all governments, ministers in the Harper government received "mandate" letters outlining their priorities and what was expected of them, but these letters were much more precise and specific than the usual ones.[16] The PMO, an agency tied tightly to the prime minister, has allegedly assumed much more power and used this influence to carefully prescribe and monitor ministerial statements and interactions with the media and other players in the political process. Yet, even with these developments, cabinet members have managed at times to act in ways contrary to the wishes of the first minister. Harper's minister for intergovernmental affairs publicly disassociated himself from the government's important support of Quebec as "a nation within a united Canada." Other ministers have rebelled against the interventions of the PMO and refused to agree to significant government positions on important issues.[17] More generally, it has to be remembered that the precarious position of minority governments sometimes causes the prime minister to assume a much more controlling posture, a position also made necessary in the case of the Harper government by the relative inexperience of the cabinet.

There is another component of the prime-ministerial thesis that weakens under examination. As part of his attempt to ensure his powerful position, the prime minister (with his advisers) aims to keep his ministers out of trouble so that he "can get things done in areas that matter a great deal."[18] But the prime minister fails in this regard; he is not sufficiently powerful to accomplish this purpose. In these situations, ministers are not acting against the prime minister's wishes. Rather, they are merely being ministers, carrying out their mandates, and in so doing they run into difficulties. One has only to look at the Chrétien government in its later years for confirmation of this point. In early 2000, the minister of Human Resources Development Canada (HRDC) announced that an internal audit revealed that her department had effectively lost track of funds designated for job creation (some accounts put the lost amount at nearly $1 billion). The announcement set off a set of accusations and investigations that greatly hindered the operations of government. The prime minister tried to downplay the problem, saying that "[a]dministrative problems of this nature always exist."[19] But the opposition, the media, and some in the interested public remained unconvinced. The low point of the crisis occurred when the prime minister literally pushed aside, in full view of a television audience, his HRDC minister, who was collapsing under the weight of media questioning.

Other members of the Chrétien government also found themselves in trouble. One of the former prime minister's cabinet members jostled over the issue of divorce with a senator and a Liberal backbencher in the letters section of a national newspaper.[20] Ministers are expected to prevail over lesser members of government, but not in full view of Canadians and not to do so in an imperious fashion. Similarly, the actions of his minister of Indian Affairs and Northern Development led the leader of a prominent First Nations organization to accuse the federal government of trying to extinguish the Aboriginal population and their culture.[21] More serious was the "sponsorship scandal," in which the minister of Public Works and Government Services (and his officials) transferred large amounts of money to Liberal advertising agencies for little or no work. The scandal attracted a great deal of attention and played a role in the demise of the government of Paul Martin. Of course, the Chrétien government held no monopoly over ministerial missteps. Gordon O'Connor, the first minister of National Defence in the Harper government, showed that he had a less than firm grasp of the issues, a failing that eventually resulted in a demotion to a less important department.

On balance, it seems that the prime minister cannot really control his individual ministers. At times, they will pursue agendas that are inconsistent with the prime minister's actions. As Herman Bakvis says, "one can . . . find examples of ministers carving out their own sphere of influence and taking initiatives."[22] The odd minister may also try to unseat the prime minister—and succeed. At other times, ministers will seek to please the prime minister, but the nature of the job—the power and responsibilities—will land ministers in trouble no matter what the prime minister and his central-agency officials attempt to do. Moreover, it is not just the individual ministers who can constrain the prime minister. The collective ministerial or cabinet decision-making system operates to disperse power. For proponents of the prime-ministerial government thesis, the cabinet system works largely to the advantage of the prime minister. In cabinet, he purportedly sets the agenda, controls the dissemination of information, and makes the final decision (and sometimes he fails to bring his decision to cabinet's attention). But this, too, overstates the case. Most prime ministers realize, sooner or later, that this is a recipe for prime-ministerial overload and that government functions well only when ministers run their own departments. Consequently, the cabinet system reflects the power of ministers. According to one study of the Chrétien years, the prime minister's "preference [was] to keep out of the hair of his ministers except in the most unusual circumstances."[23] The Privy Council Office (PCO), one of the most important advisory bodies to the prime minister, comes to a similar conclusion. "The tone of government may be set by the Prime Minister and the cabinet," reads a PCO document, "but most of the policies of the government flow from the exercise of the individual responsibilities of ministers."[24] Even in the Harper government, where there are hints of a more centralized cabinet system, official reports insist on a collegial cabinet decision-making system relying on the initiatives of individual ministers.[25]

Government consists of more than just the executive branch. There are the legislature and the judiciary. The functioning of these two branches also contests the notion of an imperial prime minister. Admittedly, the legislature provides less of a challenge for the prime minister than the other two branches. Nevertheless, it can provide a test for the prime minister, and indeed the first minister under pressure can take actions to strengthen this part of government. Former prime minister Paul Martin, for instance, made a commitment to a number of changes that would strengthen the legislature.[26] Under his plan, party discipline in the House of Commons would be loosened and parliamentary standing committees would be granted more influence. Private members' bills would receive closer consideration and the ethics commissioner would report to Parliament (and not to the prime minister). A proposal that has already had some effect allows parliamentary committees some say in the appointment of Supreme Court justices. Not surprisingly, the present prime minister, in his minority situation, has also felt the influence of the House of Commons, so much so that one of his senior advisers has charged that the opposition parties have effectively—and unconstitutionally—become the de facto government.[27]

As for the judiciary, the advent of the Charter of Rights and Freedoms has made the courts a much more important player in Canadian politics. Some downplay the impact of the courts' interpretation of the Charter on other political actors, including the prime minister. But others suggest that the courts, with their interpretation of the Charter, have altered the distribution of power in Canada.[28] Even when decisions that may favour the prime minister are rendered, the transfer of power is taking place because it is the courts that are exercising authority, not the government leader. The prime minister also sometimes fails in an attempt to use the courts to the government's advantage. The Martin government referred its same-sex marriage legislation to the Supreme Court of Canada partly in the hope that the court would find the traditional definition of marriage inconsistent with the Charter of Rights and Freedoms. With this ruling, the prime minister could avoid the politically damaging task of acting against those who still believed in the traditional definition. But the highest court refused to address this issue and simply said that the new legislation outlining a new definition of same-sex marriage was acceptable without saying whether the old definition was unacceptable. The prime minister himself would thus have to apply the death-blow to a definition of marriage still supported by a large part of the electorate. The adjudication of non-Charter issues can also reveal the power of the courts. In 1998, the Supreme Court of Canada laid out the rules that would govern the secession of Quebec from Canada. Though the opinion of the court is non-binding, it has effectively determined how this country might come to an end. Arguably, the most important decision affecting Canada was not made by the most important individual in Canadian politics; it was made by others.

OUTSIDE GOVERNMENT

Proponents of prime-ministerial government claim that their theory applies only to developments *within* government. The fact that the provinces or the media may limit the power of the first minister is irrelevant because the theory of prime-ministerial government does not extend outside the halls of government. Yet, these outside forces are sometimes used to demonstrate the power of the prime minister. The media, for instance, allegedly turn the first minister almost into a celebrity, which adds to the influence of the office of the prime minister. Similarly, globalization—another external force—also seemingly plays into the hands of the prime minister because it increasingly requires national leaders to make important decisions. Accordingly, it appears that these outside forces ought to be considered when attempting to assess the power of the prime minister. When this is done, it can be seen that they represent a double-edged sword for the prime minister. The media can place the prime minister in the spotlight and make the leader of the government appear well beyond others in the political process, but the media can hurt the prime minister in at least two related ways. The media practise what some call "gotcha journalism," which is an attempt to highlight the gaffes and mistakes of political leaders.[29] Mr. Chrétien was often the target of this kind of journalism, and Mr. Martin also experienced at times a rough ride from the media. Prime Minister Harper has endeavoured to anticipate the influence of the media by restricting their access to ministers and forcing reporters to accept an arrangement whereby the PMO can select who shall ask questions at press conferences. These and other actions—which include calling on the RCMP to eject journalists from a hotel in which Conservative MPs were meeting—suggest a prime minister able to get the upper hand on the media.[30] This is a plausible interpretation, but another is that the Harper offensive against the press reveals the power of the media and the sheer desperation governments feel in their interactions with the fourth estate. The media can also use their investigative resources to force an issue onto the political agenda that can hurt the prime minister. The media made much of Mr. Chrétien's attempt to convince a government agency to provide financial assistance to a business concern in the former prime minister's riding. They also played an important role in making the problems with the aforementioned sponsorship program into a scandal. As for the present prime minister, he has so far escaped any full-blown media investigations, but his government's policy on Afghanistan has attracted a great deal of media interest, as has his allegedly Caesar-like style of leading.[31]

Globalization is another external force that may limit the power of the prime minister. *Globalization* has many meanings and definitions, but basically it focuses on how worldwide forces, especially economic ones, are eroding national boundaries. At present, the nation-state is the primary organizing principle of world politics; however, globalization works to supplant this principle and insert a new one that emphasizes the clout of *supra*national institutions (political and otherwise). In these circumstances, leaders of nation-states, including the prime minister of Canada, should see their power reduced. And in fact there is evidence of weakened leaders, as they accept the dictates of international trade agreements and new tax regimes that demand a common playing field upon which the world's multinational corporations can play.

Proponents of the prime-ministerial government thesis are, however, unconvinced by this kind of analysis. Savoie, for one, says that leaders still maintain great power in a global world because "[t]he designers of the new order in many ways will have to be national politicians and national public services."[32] But this participation of national leaders may be short-lived; they might turn out to be their own gravediggers. Also, those believing in leaders' continued preeminence may be guilty of confusing globalization with "internationalization."[33] The latter refers to the heightened interaction between nation-states, a development that strengthens nation-states and their leaders. But globalization is different; its functioning does not really depend on national leaders getting together and making decisions. Globalization seeks to bypass nation-states because it sees them as an obstacle. It is of interest to note that the original proponent of the prime-ministerial government thesis in the Canadian context now admits that the "power that any Canadian prime minister is able to exercise has been leeching away."[34] According to Denis Smith, the prime minister can hardly stand up to the relentless effects of multinational corporations, free trade agreements, and the worldwide financial markets. In plain terms, globalization greatly curbs the influence of the prime minister.

The provinces represent another force outside the national government that reduces the power of the prime minister. In fact, it may be argued that the provinces are more deserving of attention than other forces outside government because they effectively are *within* government at the national level. As many students of Canadian federalism have argued, there are few policy matters that fail to involve both orders of government.[35] One order thus constitutes an extension of the other and vice versa. Another way to see the possible uniqueness of the provinces in the theory of prime-ministerial government is to compare the parliamentary system with the presidential one. Those who see the prime minister as being too powerful point to the separation of powers in the American political system and how this arrangement limits the president. They then note that the absence of such an arrangement in Canada strengthens the prime minister. But the supporters of theory of prime-ministerial government fail to finish the story. Government in Canada may not be divided *within* government, but it is divided *between* governments. The operation of the federal principle in Canada (unlike that in the U.S.) gives Canada its own version of the separation of powers. To exclude the provinces in a consideration of the power of the prime minister is to fail to appreciate the full operation of government in Canada. As Richard Simeon and Elaine Willis suggest, the nature of federalism in Canada almost appears as the natural attempt of any democracy to find ways to ensure that power is never too concentrated:

> In Canada, the closest parallel to divided government is found not in relations between executive and legislative but in federalism itself. Much of the imagery surrounding divided government in the United States is replicated in analyses of federal–provincial relations in Canada. Just as an assertive Congress challenges the president, so do assertive provinces challenge Ottawa.[36]

When one does consider the provinces and their impact on the prime minister, the restraining effect of the provinces can be seen quite clearly. The provinces have constitutional authority over important matters, and they represent strong regional interests that can clash with the overall national interest. The sheer size and wealth of some provinces also play a part in relations between the provinces and the prime minister. Recent developments reveal the difficulties the provinces pose for the first minister. Over the past decade, Mr. Chrétien, Mr. Martin, and even a reluctant Mr. Harper (who respects provincial jurisdiction more than his predecessors) have attempted to establish a role for Ottawa in health care. In these efforts, they have admittedly succeeded in attaching some stipulations to the use of additional financial assistance from the federal government. But the fact remains that the provinces still largely control the shaping and formulating of health policy. Even more recently, Prime Minister Harper sought to make adjustments to a federal–provincial fiscal arrangement that makes available federal financial support to less well-off provinces. Some provinces accepted the change, but one province condemned it and urged all of its residents (and Canadians) to vote against Mr. Harper, while another launched a constitutional challenge. The Harper government had hoped to establish cordial relations with the provinces, a reality that has seemingly been quashed by unwilling provincial governments.

Recent events are not the only relevant pieces of evidence when considering federal–provincial relations and the power of the prime minister. The history of federalism, at least since the end of World War II, is the history of declining federal power. "The prominent characterizing feature of the evolution of the Canadian federation in the postwar period," write Robin Boadway and Frank Flatters, "is the gradual but persistent decentralization of fiscal responsibilities from the federal government to the provinces (and their municipalities)."[37] Recently, as reflected in its efforts to affect health care, the federal government has sought to reverse this trend, to give the national interest—and the prime minister—greater prominence in important areas of public policy.[38] But the trend seems too strong. The money and power have shifted from the federal government to the provinces. The prime minister leads a government that must contend with the reality that it exists in one of the world's most decentralized federal states. The implication of this for the thesis of prime-ministerial government should be clear: the prime minister may not have a United States Congress to deal with, but he or she does have the provinces.

VIRTUAL COMPETITION

In a well-received book on Canadian politics, Donald J. Savoie writes that prime ministers "have in their hands all the important levers of power." But a few paragraphs later, he also writes that "one of the main preoccupations of the most senior officials in government is to protect the prime minister."[39] The power of the prime minister is evidently combined with a rather precarious hold on office, a state of affairs that seems distinctly odd. Surely, a powerful prime minister is free of constant concern for his or her very survival, yet the reality appears otherwise. Even Mr. Chrétien himself admitted his vulnerability: "It's a survival game played under the glare of light. If you don't learn that, you're quickly finished."[40] The prime minister supposedly governs with few checks; nevertheless, he or she participates in a game of survival in which all participants—including him- or herself—risk fatal blows.

Part of the explanation for this puzzling state of affairs has already been provided. There are constraints on the prime minister's power. The prime minister needs to worry about his or her situation because he or she faces challengers. But the near desperate situation of the prime minister suggests that something more is at work. The prime minister does countenance challengers whom all can see—cabinet ministers, the provinces, the media, the Opposition. However, the prime minister also contends with threats to his or her position, which amount to competitive forces that are not so evident—a kind of "virtual competition." Normally, we associate competition with entities that are clearly present, but competition can also come in the form of possibilities and potentialities. The result is an individual or organization that possesses a near-monopoly situation but that feels itself to be under siege. In the world of business, this phenomenon is recognized. Powerful companies dominate sectors of the private market, but their chief executive officers admit themselves to be almost terrified by competition. For example, the former head of Intel, the fabulously successful maker of computer chips, practises "management by paranoia," and warns other similarly situated business leaders to do the same. Officers of Microsoft, another company with a great deal of dominance, utter similar sentiments.[41] The traditional conception of competition demands the existence of clear competitors who force the more powerful actors to adjust their behaviour accordingly, but another conception sees competition in ghostly threats with very imaginable and lethal outcomes.

With this latter notion of competition, the anxiety experienced by the prime minister and his advisers becomes more understandable. The prime minister feels himself to be in a game of survival because he *is* in a game of survival: "The press want to get you. The opposition want to get you. Even some of the bureau-crats want to get you."[42] On the surface, these sentiments of Mr. Chrétien seem mere hyperbole—there are challenges to a prime minister's power, but not to this extent. But perhaps the former prime minister knows better, for he appreciates the possibilities of disaster in his environment. Take, for instance, the opposition. Normally the House of Commons attracts little attention in discussions of the prime minister's power; party discipline reduces the legislature to a bit player in Canadian politics. But a misstep in Parliament, perhaps during Question Period, can damage the prime minister. That is why his senior advisers spend so much time preparing him and cabinet members for their session in the House of Commons. Of course, this is not to say that Parliament rivals the prime minister, but it is to say that members of Parliament have the capacity to ruin a prime min-ister. Much like a company that can be undermined overnight by a new inven-tion, the prime minister can find himself in serious trouble with a careless response to a question or an insensitive appreciation of a parliamentary matter.

Perhaps even more unsettling in politics (and business) are the threats from the truly unforeseen entities. A prime minister can try to defend himself from the dangers posed by the House of Commons and other well-known elements in the political process. More difficult is a defence against something that essentially emerges from nowhere—a new charismatic leader, a past indiscretion coming to light, a debilitating court decision. In such a world, anything does become possible and prime-ministerial vigilance turns into a practical obsession with challenges to the government.

The important consequence of virtual competition is that the Canadian political process is much less susceptible to the evils of concentrated power than com-monly thought. Again, experience in the private sector is instructive. There are well-known companies with positions of incredible influence and wealth who do not act like entities with a near monopoly of the market. Under monopoly condi-tions, the expectation is that prices will rise, quality will decline, and innovation will disappear. However, this fails to transpire with these companies. Instead, prices fall, quality rises, and innovation takes place.[43] With the appropriate adjustments, the same phenomenon can be seen in political life. Under prime-ministerial government, we should experience high costs, bad public policy, insensitive politicians, and few fresh approaches to societal problems. Some may claim that Canada has all of these, but this would be an exaggeration of the true situation. There are a number of indicators of good government in Canada, a reality that clashes with the predictions of prime-ministerial government. Canada has social policies that are admired around the world, it sometimes serves a useful purpose in foreign affairs (for example, peacekeeping), and the United Nations annually places Canada either at the top of or near the top of the list of the world's best nations in which to live. These outcomes hardly seem consistent with the evils of concentrated power.

CONCLUSION

There is no argument with the claim that Canada's prime minister has substantial influence and that he is the most powerful player in Canadian politics. The objections arise when the claim extends to the notion that the first minister has no real challengers. The thesis of prime-ministerial government suggests that the distance between the prime minister and the other players in the Canadian political process in terms of power is great. The reality, however, is that the gap is not substantial and that it can be bridged. Both inside and outside government there are entities that can remind the prime minister that politics is a game of survival for *all* players. Inside government can be found ambitious cabinet ministers, disgruntled backbenchers, and newly empowered judges; outside government are the media, premiers, provinces, and a world that pays less and less attention to national leaders. To be fair to those who subscribe to the theory of prime-ministerial government, the challenges that emanate from within and from without government are not equally forbidding. The proponents of prime-ministerial government focus on power relations inside government, and one is certainly on more solid ground when trying to argue for the presence of a prime minister without equals *inside* government than when endeavouring to do the same in relation to matters *outside* government. But even inside government the prime minister must be on guard. Moreover, there are always the threats inherent in the world of virtual competition. Many survey the Canadian political process and see very little for the prime minister to worry about, but they do not see what the prime minister sees.

Ultimately, the belief in the all-powerful prime minister founders because it is at odds with the reality of Canada. This country has its problems; nevertheless, it is recognized as a functioning democracy with public policies that stand up well against those of other nations. Unless one believes in benevolent dictatorships, good public policy cannot generally be said to coexist with a political system in which much of the political power lies with one person and his advisers.[44] Canada's national leader is powerful, but not to the point where power turns into a corrupting force. Fortunately, the competitive pressures in Canadian politics are simply too great for us to have reached this point.

NOTES

1. Donald J. Savoie, "The King of the Commons," *Time,* May 3, 1999, p. 64.

2. Donald J. Savoie, *Governing from the Centre: The Concentration of Power in Canadian Politics* (Toronto: University of Toronto Press, 1999), p. 72.

3. Colin Campbell and George Szablowski, *The Superbureaucrats* (Toronto: Macmillan, 1979).

4. Keith Archer et al., *Parameters of Power: Canada's Political Institutions,* 3rd ed. (Toronto: ITP Nelson, 2002), p. 241.

5. Rand Dyck, *Canadian Politics: Critical Approaches,* 5th ed. (Scarborough: Thomson Nelson, 2008), pp. 504–532. Bolding has been removed.

6. See, for example, Savoie, *Governing from the Centre*.

7. Savoie, *Governing from the Centre*, p. 108.

8. Edward Greenspon and Anthony Wilson-Smith, *Double Vision: The Inside Story of the Liberals in Power* (Toronto: Doubleday Canada, 1996), p. 163.

9. Greenspon and Wilson-Smith and the federal budget of 1995, Department of Finance, *Budget Plan* 1995 (Ottawa: Her Majesty the Queen in Right of Canada, 1995), pp. 57–58, provide support for this paper's interpretation of the resolution of this difference between the prime minister and his finance minister. For a different view, see Edward Goldenberg, *The Way It Works: Inside Ottawa* (Toronto: McClelland and Stewart, 2006), pp. 145–47.

10. Robert Fife and Giles Gherson, "Rock Proposes New National Health Plan," *National Post*, January 27, 2000, pp. A1, A11.

11. Anne McIlroy, "Rock's Grand Plan Was News to the PM," *The Globe and Mail*, March 4, 2000, p. A3.

12. For more on this, see Susan Delacourt, *Juggernaut: Paul Martin's Campaign for Chrétien's Crown* (Toronto: McClelland and Stewart, 2003).

13. For a picture of the complexity of Chrétien's situation, see Goldenberg, *The Way It Works*, ch. 22, and the former prime minister's memoirs, Jean Chretien, *My Years as Prime Minister* (Toronto: Knopf, 2007), ch. 14.

14. Thomas Axworthy, "Our Public Service Malady: A Diagnosis," *The Globe and Mail*, September 27, 2003, p. D4. (In this article, Axworthy is reviewing a new book by Savoie: Donald J. Savoie, *Breaking the Bargain: Public Servants, Ministers, and Parliament* [Toronto: University of Toronto Press, 2003]).

15. Brian Laghi, "Discipline, Control Mark PM's Management Style," *The Globe and Mail*, April 8, 2006, pp. A1, A4.

16. John Ivison, "With a Fistful of Power," *National Post*, September 1, 2007, p. A6.

17. Ian Brown, "In Harper's Regime, Big Daddy Knows Best," *The Globe and Mail*, May 13, 2006, p. F6; Brian Laghi and Jane Taber, "Offshore Deal a Crucial Test for MacKay," *The Globe and Mail*, June 13, 2007, p. A12. One might also cite the case of Bill Casey, a Conservative backbencher who failed to support his party's budget and was subsequently ejected from the caucus of the Conservative Party.

18. Savoie, *Governing from the Centre*, p. 336.

19. Daniel LeBlanc, "Multibillion-dollar Mess Routine, Chrétien Says," *The Globe and Mail*, February 1, 2000, p. A5.

20. For the exchange of letters, see the letters section of following editions of the *National Post*: July 10, 2000; July 16, 2000; July 20, 2000; and July 26, 2000.

21. Justine Hunter, "Native Leader Alleges Racist Federal Plot," *National Post*, July 18, 2000, p. A1.

22. Herman Bakvis, "Prime Minister and Cabinet in Canada: An Autocracy in Need of Reform?" *Journal of Canadian Studies* 35, no. 4 (Winter 2001), p. 65.

23. Greenspon and Wilson-Smith, *Double Vision*, p. 35.

24. Privy Council Office, *Responsibility in the Constitution* (Ottawa: Minister of Supply and Services, 1993), p. 62.

25. Government of Canada, *Accountable Government: A Guide for Ministers and Secretaries of State, 2007* (Ottawa: Her Majesty the Queen in Right of Canada, 2007), p. 53.

26. For a discussion of these changes, see Peter Aucoin and Lori Turnbull, "The Democratic Deficit: Paul Martin and Parliamentary Government," *Canadian Public Administration* 46, no. 4 (2003).

27. Tom Flanagan, "Liberal Tactics Amount to Constitutional Back-seat Driving," *The Globe and Mail*, February 20, 2007, p. A19.

28. See the debate between Peter H. Russell and F.L. Morton in Mark Charlton and Paul Barker, eds., *Crosscurrents: Contemporary Political Issues*, 3rd ed. (Scarborough: ITP Nelson, 1998), Issue 14.

29. George Bain, *Gotcha! How the Media Distort the News* (Toronto: Key Porter Books, 1994).

30. Christopher Dornan, "The Cool on the Hill," *The Globe and Mail*, October 20, 2007, p. F3.

31. See, for example, John Ivison, "With a Fistful of Power," p. A6, and Lawrence Martin, "A Prime Minister at the Top of His Imperious Game," p. A15.

32. Savoie, *Governing from the Centre*, p. 107.

33. See Jan Aart Scholte, "The Globalization of World Politics," in John Baylis and Steve Smith, eds., *The Globalization of World Politics: An Introduction to International Relations* (New York: Oxford University Press, 1997).

34. Denis Smith, "Is the Prime Minister Too Powerful?–Yes" in Mark Charlton and Paul Barker, eds., *Crosscurrents: Contemporary Political Issues*, 2nd ed. (Scarborough: Nelson Canada, 1994), p. 159.

35. See, for example, Richard Simeon, "The Federal–Provincial Decision Making Process," in *Ontario Economic Council, Issues and Alternatives–1977: Intergovernmental Relations* (Toronto: Ontario Economic Council, 1977), p. 26.

36. Richard Simeon and Elaine Willis, "Democracy and Performance: Governance in Canada and the United States," in Keith Banting, George Hoberg, and Richard Simeon, eds., *Degrees of Freedom: Canada and the United States in a Changing World* (Montreal and Kingston: McGill-Queen's University Press, 1997), p. 171.

37. Robin Boadway and Frank Flatters, "Fiscal Federalism: Is the System in Crisis?" in Keith G. Banting, Douglas M. Brown, and Thomas J. Courchene, eds., *The Future of Fiscal Federalism* (Kingston: School of Policy Studies et al., 1994), p. 137.

38. Gerard Boismenu and Peter Graefe, "The New Federal Tool Belt: Attempts to Rebuild Social Policy Leadership," in *Canadian Public Policy* 30, no. 1 (2004).

39. Savoie, *Governing from the Centre*, pp. 72–73.

40. Savoie, *Governing from the Centre*, p. 313.

41. Robert J. Samuelson, "The Gates of Power," *The New Republic*, April 23, 2001, p. 31.

42. Savoie, *Governing from the Centre*, p. 313.

43. Samuelson, "The Gates of Power."

44. One might also believe in a "friendly dictatorship." See Jeffrey Simpson, *The Friendly Dictatorship* (Toronto: McClelland & Stewart, 2001).

POSTSCRIPT

In his article, Mellon employs a useful approach to making his case. He documents the arsenal of powers available to the prime minister—the powers are truly impressive—and then makes short work of any possible obstacles that might block the path of the first minister. Yet, there are a few openings for those who wish to think differently about the thesis of prime-ministerial government. Take, for example, the case of former prime minister Jean Chrétien. Mellon himself seemingly admits that Chrétien left office in part because the fates were aligned against him—more concretely, his former finance minister, Paul Martin, and much of his party wanted him gone. Surely, this is evidence that weakens claims of an all-powerful prime minister. Mellon might also be guilty of downplaying the capacity of the media to seriously damage any government and its leader. It is true, as Mellon writes, that the press can cover only so much of government; he is also correct when he says that governments spend increasingly more time managing journalists. But the media need not be expansive in its coverage to hurt a prime minister, and, as Barker says, efforts to curtail the press have the quality of desperation and last resort.

In his article, Paul Barker points out additional problems with the thesis of prime-ministerial government. Ministers can challenge the prime minister—without necessarily facing dismissal—and forces outside government aside from the media can reduce the influence of the prime minister. But Barker, too, may be guilty of exaggeration—he may, in other words, underestimate the true power of the prime minister. He is impressed with how ministers are able to challenge the prime minister, but it looks as if he has ignored the fact that most of these challenges end with the prime minister getting his or her way. As for the prime minister failing to keep the ministers out of trouble, this may be seen as amounting to very little. Finally, Barker highlights the case of Jean Chrétien to make his argument. But the memoirs of the former prime minister and one of his closest advisors, Eddie Goldenberg, suggest that this event is *less* telling than many presume. Mr. Chrétien left on his own terms, pure and simple.

To begin an analysis of the power of the prime minister, the interested student first needs to understand the system of parliamentary government and the prime minister's formal role in it. For this, one might consult Peter Aucoin, "Prime Minister and Cabinet," in James Bickerton and Alain-G. Gagnon, eds., *Canadian Politics*, 3rd ed. (Peterborough: Broadview Press, 1999) or Michael Whittington, "The Prime Minister, Cabinet, and the Executive," in Michael Whittington and Glen Williams, eds., *Canadian Politics in the 21st Century,* 6th ed. (Scarborough: Thomson Nelson, 2004). Jeffrey Simpson's book *The Friendly Dictatorship* (Toronto: McClelland & Stewart, 2001) can then be read for an engaging discussion of the thesis of prime-ministerial government. With these readings completed, the student is ready to tackle the work of Donald Savoie, who is most responsible for the focus on prime-ministerial power: Donald J. Savoie, "The Rise of Court Government in Canada," *Canadian Journal of Political Science* 32, no. 4 (December 1999), Donald J. Savoie, *Governing from the Centre: The Concentration of Power in Canadian Politics* (Toronto: University of Toronto Press, 1999), and Donald J. Savoie, *Court Government and the Collapse of Accountability in Canada and the United Kingdom* (Toronto: University of Toronto Press, 2008). For a shorter presentation of Savoie's position, see Donald J. Savoie, "Power at the Apex: Executive Dominance," in James Bickerton and Alain-G. Gagnon, eds., *Canadian Politics*, 4th ed. (Peterborough: Broadview Press, 2004), or Donald J. Savoie, "The Federal Government: Revisiting Court Government in Canada," in Luc Bernier, Keith Brownsey, and Michael Howlett, eds., *Executive Styles in Canada: Cabinet Structures and Leadership Practices in Canadian Government* (Toronto: University of Toronto Press, 2005).

To appreciate the genesis of this discussion in Canada, one should read Thomas A. Hockin, ed., *Apex of Power: The Prime Minister and Political Leadership in Canada*, 2nd ed. (Scarborough: Prentice-Hall, 1977). The belief that the position of prime minister has become almost too powerful is not limited to those who examine Canadian politics. Other parliamentary democracies may also be operating under prime-ministerial government. For more on this, see Patrick Weller, *First among Equals: Prime Ministers in Westminster Systems* (London: George Allen & Irwin, 1985). Weller has also produced a more recent consideration of cabinet government and the prime minister in Patrick Weller, "Cabinet Government: An Elusive Ideal?" *Public Administration* 81, no. 4 (2003).

Proponents of prime-ministerial power are not without their critics. A critical examination of their position can be found in Herman Bakvis, "Prime Minister and Cabinet in Canada: An Autocracy in Need of Reform?" *Journal of Canadian Studies* 35, no. 4 (Winter 2001). The article addresses directly the analysis of Savoie and others who subscribe to the theory of prime-ministerial government, and he provides as well a useful bibliography on the topic of prime-ministerial power. For an account of the fall of former prime minister Jean Chrétien, one might read Susan Delacourt, *Juggernaut: Paul Martin's Campaign for Chrétien's Crown* (Toronto: McClelland and Stewart, 2003). But on this subject students should also consult the relevant chapters of the memoirs of former prime minister Jean Chretien and his close advisor, Eddie Goldenberg: Jean Chretien, *My Years as Prime Minister* (Toronto: Knopf, 2007), and Eddie Goldenberg, *The Way It Works: Inside Ottawa* (Toronto: McClelland and Stewart, 2006). Prime ministers in other countries also experienced difficult times, including former prime minister Tony Blair of Great Britain. See Geoffrey Wheatcroft, "The Tragedy of Tony Blair," *Atlantic Monthly* (June 2004).

Should Parliament Review Supreme Court Appointments?

✔ **YES**
PETER W. HOGG, "Appointment of Justice Marshall Rothstein to the Supreme Court of Canada"

✗ **NO**
H. PATRICK GLENN, "Constitutional Law, Politics, and Supreme Court of Canada Appointments"

A good bet for inclusion in a politics exam is a question on how Supreme Court justices in Canada are appointed. A decent answer to this question used to be fairly straightforward. The selection process would begin with an appreciation of rules and conventions for regional representation, which stipulate that the composition of the court include three justices from both Quebec and Ontario, two from the western provinces, and one from the Maritimes. This usually meant that the prospective nominee had to be from the same area as the justice he or she was replacing. The next step was for the federal minister of justice to draw up a short-list of candidates based on consultations with interested parties, who may have included the Chief Justice of the Supreme Court, relevant provincial officials, members of law societies, and the Canadian Bar Association. The justice minister then evaluated the candidates in light of their professional capacity, personal characteristics, and diversity. With this done, the minister and the prime minister would discuss the candidates and recommend one of them to cabinet for appointment to the Supreme Court of Canada. Reciting all this, traditionally, guaranteed a first-class mark to a question on judicial appointments, but in recent years a few changes have been made to the appointment process. The most prominent of these changes, which was introduced by the Harper government, is that the person chosen by the justice minister and the prime minister appears before an ad hoc committee of parliamentarians, whose members (twelve MPs) may convey their views or advice to the prime minister on the nominee upon completion of the hearing. The prime minister, who is in no way legally constrained by opinions of the committee, then makes the final decision with the formal consent of cabinet. The proceedings of the ad hoc committee are televised and open to the public. Already, one appointee to the Supreme Court, Justice Marshall Rothstein, has gone through this process.

The insertion of parliamentary hearings into the selection process for Supreme Court members arises in part from the perception of the increasing influence of the country's highest court. The Charter of Rights and Freedoms has made the Supreme Court of Canada a more central part of Canadian politics. Its decisions on the Charter amount to important statements of public policy, often touching the lives of everyday Canadians (e.g., Sunday shopping, abortion, and same-sex marriage). Accordingly, it seems that the selection of the justices should provide for public input; members of Parliament, representing their constituents, ought to have an opportunity to ask various questions of the nominee and to make known their views on the nominee to the prime minister. The appearance of the parliamentary hearings also reflects a more general feeling that the processes of government should be more transparent or clear to the people of Canada.

There are some, however, who find problematic the inclusion of hearings in the selection process. Potential nominees to the Supreme Court might refuse to stand for nomination if they think the process provides the possibility of an embarrassing session before a parliamentary committee. There is also the fear that parliamentary hearings may unnecessarily politicize the selection process—for example, opposition members on the committee might see this as an opportunity to criticize the government. As a result, it might be argued that a more acceptable reform of the selection process lies somewhere between the old way of doing things and parliamentary hearings. In the government of Paul Martin, the justice minister consented to appear before a parliamentary committee to explain two appointments to the Supreme Court. Such an adjustment to the present process might be suitable because it gives elected members—and Canadians—greater insights into the selection process without actually placing the nominees before the committee.

It is not clear whether the present form of parliamentary hearings will remain in place. The concerns with this adjustment in the selection process suggest that proposals for a different way of including public input will be entertained. There may also be pressure to move in the other direction, to give the public hearings an even more prominent place. In the United States, the legislative branch of government, the Congress, has the authority to confirm or nullify a presidential nomination to the Supreme Court of the United States. Some feel that members of Parliament should have powers that exceed the provision of advice to the prime minister, though admittedly such a grant of authority would fit uneasily into a parliamentary system. At a minimum, a committee of the House of Commons ought to be employed instead of an informal group of parliamentarians chaired by a minister of the government.

In the readings, Peter W. Hogg presents a discussion of the first experience with the ad hoc committee of the House of Commons, and in so doing makes the argument for the acceptance of hearings on Supreme Court appointments. As will be seen, Hogg himself, who is Canada's preeminent authority on Canadian constitutional law, played an important role in this new process. H. Patrick Glenn, a professor of law at McGill University, claims that we would be ill-advised to continue to support a selection process that includes one type or another of parliamentary hearings. For Professor Glenn, parliamentary hearings and other attempts to include parliamentary representatives into the selection process fail to appreciate the workings of responsible government and the need for judicial independence.

✔ **YES**
Appointment of Justice Marshall Rothstein to the Supreme Court of Canada
PETER W. HOGG

I. INTRODUCTION

The process for the appointment of Justice Marshall Rothstein to the Supreme Court of Canada in 2006 included the innovation of a public hearing by an "Ad Hoc Committee to Review a Nominee for the Supreme Court of Canada." This committee of parliamentarians interviewed the nominee before his appointment. At the invitation of the committee, I addressed the committee on the limits of judicial speech. What follows is a description of the background to the appointment of Justice Rothstein, and a suggestion as to how the process might be adjusted for future appointments. My remarks to the committee are appended to this commentary.

II. THE POWER AND PROCESS OF APPOINTMENT

The appointment of judges to the Supreme Court of Canada is provided for in the *Supreme Court Act*.[1] The convention that has developed for judicial appointments generally is that chief justice appointments are made on the recommendation of the prime minister and puisne judge appointments are made on the recommendation of the minister of justice. In the case of the Supreme Court of Canada, however, it seems likely that the prime minister is involved in the appointments of the puisne judges as well as the chief justice. In the case of the appointment of Justice Rothstein, Prime Minister Harper made it clear that, after the public hearing, he was going to make the final decision, and he did in fact make the final decision.

Until 2004, no part of the appointment process was public. It was understood that the minister of justice would consult with the Chief Justice of Canada, with the attorneys general and chief justices of the provinces from which the appointment was to be made, and with leading members of the legal profession, but this was all informal and confidential.

In 2004, the Honourable Irwin Cotler, who was minister of justice in the Liberal government of Paul Martin, introduced a more transparent process to find replacements to retiring Justices Louise Arbour and Frank Iacobucci. He presented the names of his nominees for the replacements (Justices Louise Charron and Rosalie Abella) to the Standing Committee on Justice of the House of Commons, and he answered questions posed to him by the committee about the search process and the qualifications of the nominees. After that appearance, the two nominees were appointed. The nominees themselves did not appear before the committee.

When the retirement of Justice John Major was announced in 2005, Minister Cotler announced a new and more elaborate process that would be used to fill the vacancy. After the usual informal consultations with the attorneys general, chief justices, and leading members of the legal profession, the minister would submit a short list of five to eight candidates to an advisory committee composed of a member of parliament (or senator) from each recognized party in the House of Commons, a nominee of the provincial attorneys general, a nominee of the provincial law societies, and two prominent Canadians who were neither lawyers nor judges. The committee would provide the minister with a short list of three names from which the appointment would be made. All of this would take place on a confidential basis. However, the final step would be public: the minister of justice (but not the appointee) would appear before the Standing Committee on Justice to explain the selection process and the qualifications of the person selected.

This process was duly commenced to fill the vacancy left by Justice Major. An appointed advisory committee provided the minister with a short list of three names. However, on 29 November 2005, before the final selection was made, the government was defeated in the House of Commons and Parliament was dissolved for the election that took place on 23 January 2006. One of the policies of the newly elected Conservative government was a public, parliamentary interview process for proposed appointees to the Supreme Court of Canada.

The new Conservative minister of justice, the Honourable Vic Toews, decided to work from the short list provided by the advisory committee appointed by the previous government. The prime minister, no doubt in consultation with the minister of justice, chose one candidate from that list. That candidate then had to submit to the new public interview process. With the agreement of all the party leaders, the government established the Ad Hoc Committee to Review a Nominee for the Supreme Court of Canada. The committee consisted of twelve MPs drawn from each party in proportion to their standings in the House of Commons. The minister of justice, who was one of the Conservative members, was the chair of the committee. His predecessor, Irwin Cotler, was one of the Liberal members.

The committee held a televised hearing on Monday, 27 February 2006. The name of the nominee, Justice Marshall Rothstein of the Federal Court of Appeal, had been made public the previous Wednesday,[2] and members of the committee had been supplied with a dossier that included his curriculum vitae, a list of all of his decisions, four sample opinions in full, a list of his publications, and four sample publications in full. The hearing took place from 1:00 p.m. to 4:30 p.m. It opened with a short introduction of the nominee and the process by the chair (the minister), then continued with opening remarks by me, then with opening remarks by Justice Rothstein, then with questions from the members of the committee, then with a closing statement by me and a closing statement by the chair. During the question period, Justice Rothstein was asked approximately sixty questions in two rounds of questioning.[3]

The committee did not prepare a written report. The prime minister watched the proceedings on television, and no doubt the minister of justice reported to him. As well, at the conclusion of the hearing, the minister invited the members of the committee to communicate their views directly to the prime minister. The result was a foregone conclusion in that the nominee's credentials, his statement to the committee, and his answers to questions left no doubt as to his suitability for appointment, and the reaction of the committee members left no doubt that they would advise the prime minister to proceed with the appointment.

Two days after the hearing, the prime minister announced in a written statement that he had selected the nominee and would recommend him for appointment by the governor in council. Justice Rothstein was duly appointed, and was sworn in as a justice of the Supreme Court of Canada on 6 March 2006.

III. CONDUCTING THE PUBLIC HEARING

I was retained by the Commissioner for Federal Judicial Affairs, whose office administers the processes of federal judicial appointments, to provide advice to the ad hoc committee as to its procedures. My initial thought was that I would prepare a protocol that would limit the kinds of questions that committee members could ask the nominee, and that the protocol would be enforced by the committee chair. However, what emerged from deliberations within the government was the view that a binding protocol was not the way to go, and that the MPs on the committee should be free to ask any questions they wanted. This view was adopted by the committee, which decided that the chair would not attempt to impose limits on the questions that could be asked. My role became one of giving guidance to the committee as to the kinds of questions that could or could not be answered by the nominee. At the hearing, I made an opening statement to the committee explaining what its role was and what the appropriate limits of judicial speech were. I then remained with the nominee at the hearing in case any questions arose with which I could assist.[4]

In retrospect, it was the right decision not to impose any limit on questioning by members of the committee. A protocol enforced by the chair would have given the impression of a tightly controlled hearing; this would have annoyed the MPs, to say nothing of the audience; and I think the committee would not have obtained as full a picture of the nominee. As it was, the questions at the hearing were always civil and respectful, and Justice Rothstein's courtesy and good humour kept it all very pleasant. He was adept at handling the questions. Although the committee members understood the limits of judicial speech, they could not resist asking some questions on top-of-mind policy issues such as crime in the cities, gun control, and the elimination of poverty. Each time, Justice Rothstein acknowledged the validity of the concern and responded by saying something such as "that's your issue, not mine," reminding everyone of the boundaries of questioning. I observed that, without exception, the questioners seemed perfectly happy with this response.

IV. FUTURE HEARINGS

For the future, it would be politically difficult for a federal government to revert to a wholly confidential process, and I think it would be a mistake to do so. Certainly, the hearing established that Canadian parliamentarians can conduct a civil hearing that poses no danger of politicizing the judiciary or of embarrassing the nominee. It is true that in 2006 the stars were particularly well aligned for a peaceful hearing, since the nominee had been drawn by a Conservative government from a short list prepared by a committee set up by a Liberal government and on which all parties were represented. Senate confirmation hearings in the United States are typically focused on issues like abortion, and inevitably take on a partisan and rancorous atmosphere.[5] But the political parties in Canada, unlike the Republican and Democratic parties in the United States, have not defined themselves primarily by reference to issues that have been decided by the highest court, such as abortion. Nor have Canadian prime ministers, unlike American presidents, ever made any effort to pack the highest court with their supporters.[6] Canadian hearings are never likely to become like the American confirmation hearings.

Canadian hearings are advisory only, since neither the *Supreme Court Act* nor the constitution provides any formal role for Parliament. This lowers the temperature in Canada, because in the end the government will be able to insist on the appointment of its nominee. In the United States, by contrast, the constitution requires the appointment of a Supreme Court justice to be made by the president, with the advice and consent of the Senate.[7] The Senate can block the appointment, and senators who do not belong to the president's party have a political incentive to strive mightily to do so. Moreover, in the United States, unlike Canada, there does not seem to be an institutionalized process of consultation to ensure that appointments are always of high quality, so that in some cases there really is legitimate concern about the quality of a presidential nominee. When this occurs, senatorial opposition becomes more bipartisan, and this can lead to the defeat or (more usually) the withdrawal of the nomination.

The prospect of a public hearing operates as a deterrent to a government that is considering making a partisan appointment of a poorly qualified person. This does not seem to be necessary in Canada, where the diligence of the Government of Canada's routine informal process of consultation, which has yielded consistently strong appointments in the past, will undoubtedly continue to yield strong nominations. Presumably, Canadian federal governments will continue to believe that it is good politics to make good appointments. Presumably, as well, governments will not care so intensely about the decisions of the Court that they will want to influence future decisions through the appointment process. I have already made the point that the "wedge issues" in Canadian political debate tend not to be decisions of the Supreme Court of Canada. As well, we have a weaker form of judicial review in Canada under the *Charter of Rights and Freedoms* than the strong form of judicial review in the United States. Judicial decisions striking down laws on *Charter* grounds usually leave room for a legislative response and usually get a legislative response that accomplishes the objective of the law that was struck down.[8] Court packing and court bashing are not as necessary in Canada as American politicians perceive them to be in America.

If the impulse to hold public hearings to interview Supreme Court nominees does not stem from any concerns about the quality of the people nominated or the suspicion of court-packing motives on the part of government, what is the basis for it? I think it is really the democratic notion that important decisions should be transparent. Based on comments in the press and many comments made to me personally after the hearing, lay people as well as lawyers were eager to receive some real information about the work that Supreme Court judges do. People were curious about the way in which cases come to the Court, the materials that have to be studied for each case, the hearing at which all parties' arguments are heard and tested, and the way in which judges try to reach decisions that are faithful to the law and the facts. The public interview of Justice Rothstein was surely a useful antidote to the vague charges of judicial activism that float around after unpopular decisions. It was also interesting to see a judge answer questions about his career and his work, which sent a reassuring message about the industry, ability, and integrity of the person who was about to join the Court.[9]

People are interested in appointments to the Court. This is demonstrated by the experience of the existing judges, each of whom on appointment was bombarded with questions and requests for interviews by the media. There is much to be said for dealing with this media interest in the form of a structured public hearing before appointment. The hearing, which is broadcast on television and reported on by the print media, is inevitably more thorough and informative than the story that any one journalist can realistically expect to obtain alone.

In summary, I am in favour of a public hearing by a parliamentary committee as part of the process of appointing judges to the Supreme Court of Canada. I think that public hearings will significantly benefit Canadians by helping them to understand the appointment process and the judicial function and to learn about the qualifications of the person nominated for appointment. The retention of counsel, the development of guidelines as to what can and cannot be answered by the nominee, and the willingness of committee members to respect the guidelines are features of the 2006 process that should be repeated. With these features in place, judicial independence will not be threatened by public hearings.

V. SCREENING BY AN ADVISORY COMMITTEE

I would make one suggestion for future appointments, and that is to eliminate the screening of potential appointees to the Supreme Court of Canada by an advisory committee. In my view, there are two objections to the advisory committee process. The first is that it compromises what I regard as the desirable principle of executive appointment. For a single, occasional, high-profile appointment, I do not think the government should be restricted to a short list developed by an advisory committee. (Considerations are different for appointments to courts that have to be made frequently, and are not going to attract much public notice.) My concern is that the dynamics of deliberation in a diverse committee may eliminate candidates against whom some objection can be made. The tendency, I would fear, is that only the safest and least controversial persons would achieve consensus in the committee. Such persons are often excellent judges, but may not always be the best person for the Court at that particular time. Consider the precedent of Bora Laskin, who was appointed to the Court in 1970 and elevated to chief justice in 1973. His appointment was controversial because he was the first Jew to be appointed and the first full-time academic to be appointed. He would probably have been regarded as an "unsound" candidate by an advisory committee in 1970. And yet, as Prime Minister Trudeau anticipated at the time, and as is now generally recognized, he made a more important contribution to the Court than a person with more conventional credentials might have done. The 1982 appointment of Bertha Wilson, who was the first woman appointed to the Court, provides another example. My point is that the minister of justice and prime minister are better able, after informal consultations, to assess the nature and force of opposition to a candidate and how that candidate would contribute to the Court, than would a diverse committee that is seeking consensus.[10]

A less important objection to the advisory committee screening process is that too many people are engaged in the selection process, leading to the risk of leaks that could be embarrassing to the persons under consideration. This time, the three names that the advisory committee submitted to the minister of justice were apparently[11] leaked to the media. When the name of the nominee was officially announced, it was obvious who had been rejected. To be sure, it is no disgrace to fail to receive a Supreme Court appointment, but it is preferable for the names of the unsuccessful candidates to be kept secret. That is hard to do if the names and their files have been moved outside the professional civil service and distributed to an advisory committee that may include members who are not accustomed to the constraints of confidentiality in the face of intense media interest.

If there is some force in these two objections to the advisory committee process, then it makes little sense to retain the process when the final nominee is going to be subjected to a public interview process by a parliamentary committee. Surely, that by itself is a sufficient guarantee against a poorly qualified or partisan appointment. It seems to me that executive selection of the candidate (after the normal informal consultations), followed by a parliamentary interview, followed by a final executive decision, is the ideal process for those occasional appointments that have to be made to the Supreme Court of Canada.[12]

NOTES

1. R.S.C. 1985, c. S-26, s.4 provides that appointments are to be made by "the Governor in Council."

2. There was an unfortunate leak, duly reported in the media, of the names of the other short-listed, but unsuccessful, candidates. I discuss this later in this commentary.

3. Three questions were asked per member on the first round, and two per member on the second round. The Committee elected not to continue for a third round.

4. In fact, I was asked two questions by members of the committee; one on practices in other Commonwealth countries, the other on the wisdom of a special constitutional court.

5. Even so, one observes that strongly qualified nominees are prepared to come forward, and they handle the difficult proceedings with aplomb.

6. The original court-packing plan was devised by a Democrat, President Franklin D. Roosevelt, to overcome the destruction of his New Deal at the hands of an ultra-conservative Supreme Court, which believed that measures such as minimum wages or limitations on hours of work, let alone the New Deal programs to combat the depression of the 1930s, were contrary to the Bill of Rights. After the swing judge on the nine-man Court changed his mind in 1937, the so-called Lochner era ended without the implementation of the expansion of the Court that had been proposed by the President. A period of judicial restraint ensued, but decisions in the 1960s and 1970s on issues such as abortion, contraception, pornography, desecration of the flag, and rights of criminal defendants raised the ire of conservatives, prompting a new round of hostility to the Court and open demands for the appointment of more conservative judges.

7. U.S. Const. art. II, § 2(2).

8. The Canadian *Charter of Rights and Freedoms* explicitly permits legislatures to enact limits on *Charter* rights (s. 1) and even to use a notwithstanding clause to override *Charter* rights (s. 33). The common phenomenon of *Charter* decisions being followed by legislative sequels is the subject of considerable literature focusing on the idea of "dialogue" between courts and legislatures. For a recent contribution, see P.W. Hogg, A.A. Bushell Thornton & W.K. Wright, "Charter Dialogue Revisited—Or Much Ado About Metaphors" (2007) 45 Osgoode Hall L.J. (forthcoming).

9. It is possible to exaggerate the transparency of a process that culminates in a public hearing. The candidate does not know, and the hearing will not disclose, what considerations moved the government to choose the candidate over other well-qualified persons. However, each appointment will have unique elements, and considerations of practicality and confidentiality probably make it unrealistic for public information to go beyond information about the role of judges on the Court, the search process, and the qualifications of the particular candidate. And these, I suggest, are the truly important matters.

10. If it were determined to keep the advisory committee at the beginning of the process, its list should not be binding on government, so that an unusual appointment would not be precluded.

11. Neither the minister of justice nor anyone else who was privy to the deliberations of the committee ever publicly acknowledged that the leaked names were in fact the ones on the short list.

12. For other courts, where a steady stream of appointments has to be made, and where there is little media scrutiny of the appointments, different considerations apply.

APPENDIX: JUDICIAL INTERVIEW PROCESS

Notes for opening remarks to Ad Hoc Committee to Review a Nominee for the Supreme Court of Canada

INTRODUCTION

This is an historic moment. It is the first time that a Government nominee for appointment to the Supreme Court of Canada has been interviewed in public by a committee composed of Members of Parliament. The purpose of this new process is to make appointments to the Court more open, and to promote public knowledge of the judges of the Court.

The process is not without controversy. Everyone would agree in principle that important public decisions be open and public. But there are those—many of them in the legal profession—who fear that a parliamentary review of judicial appointments carries more risk than benefit. The critics argue that an open process will tend to politicize the judiciary, and publicly embarrass the distinguished people who are nominated for appointment. This committee, today, has the opportunity to show the critics that they are wrong. This Committee has the opportunity to demonstrate that the Canadian virtues of civility and moderation can make an open and public process work.

ROLE OF COMMITTEE

The authority to make appointments to the Supreme Court of Canada is possessed by the Governor in Council. That is prescribed in the *Supreme Court Act,* and that has not been changed. So this appointment will have to be made by the Governor in Council, which will act on the advice of the Prime Minister. This Committee is charged with providing advice to the Prime Minister. He has undertaken to take into account the deliberations and views of the Committee in deciding whether or not to proceed with the appointment of Mr. Justice Rothstein.

This Committee has the task of interviewing Mr. Justice Rothstein to determine whether he is well qualified to serve on the Court. It really is a job interview, and like any other job interview the questions to the candidate should respect both his dignity and his privacy. As well, any questions put to the candidate should proceed from an understanding of the role that is played by a judge of the Supreme Court of Canada. I want to say something about that role.

ROLE OF JUDGES

Judges decide cases by finding the facts that are relevant and applying the law to those facts. In the appeals that reach the Supreme Court of Canada, there is the further complication that the law itself is usually unclear. That is usually why the case has gone all the way to the highest court. In that case, judges have to decide what the law is, as well as how it applies to the facts of the case.

Before each appeal is heard the judges are required to read and digest a massive amount of material. They read the decisions of the lower courts that are being appealed, they read at least some of the transcript of the evidence at trial, they read the decided cases that are arguably precedents for the case, they read the articles by law professors that bear on the issue, and they read the factums–the briefs of argument–that are filed by counsel on both sides of the case. And then, when the appeal is heard, the judges listen to the oral arguments of counsel on both sides, and they test those arguments by asking questions. Only after carefully considering all of this material, and weighing the arguments on both sides, are the judges able to reach a decision. The Supreme Court of Canada decides about a hundred appeals every year. Each one of them involves the reading and research that I have just described. And of course the Court has to reach a decision on each appeal, and then write an opinion. The Court of nine judges is usually unanimous, but in a minority of cases the Court is divided and one or more dissenting opinions have to be written. So it is a heavy workload that we require of our Supreme Court judges.

LIMITS ON QUESTIONS

When you think about the role that Mr. Justice Rothstein will be called upon to play if his nomination is confirmed, it becomes obvious that there are some questions that he cannot be expected to answer.

He cannot express views on cases or issues that could come before the Court. He cannot tell you how he would decide a hypothetical case. He might eventually be faced with that case. For the same reason, he cannot tell you what his views are on controversial issues, such as abortion, same-sex marriage or secession. Those issues could come to the Court for decision in some factual context or other. Any public statements about the issues might give the false impression that he had a settled view on how to decide those cases–without knowing what the facts were, without reviewing all the legal materials, and without listening to and weighing the arguments on both sides.

Another kind of question that is inappropriate for a judge to answer is the question of why he decided a particular case in a particular way. Because Justice Rothstein is a sitting judge, he has written many opinions. These are listed in the dossier that members of the Committee have been given. Several of the opinions have been included in full as samples. His reasons for decision in each of those cases are set out in writing. While he can talk in general terms about his work as a judge, and even about the issues in particular cases, he cannot give an oral explanation of why he decided a particular case. He has done that in his written opinion. That opinion is a precedent that lawyers and other judges will rely upon. They should be able to rely on the written opinion, and not have to hunt down oral explanations by the judges as well. Written opinions are available to all. Oral explanations are limited to those who hear them.

QUALITIES OF THE NOMINEE

What the members of the Committee can and should do is to satisfy yourselves that this person has the right stuff to be a judge of the Supreme Court of Canada. Does he have the professional and personal qualities that will enable him to serve with distinction as a judge on our highest court? Let me suggest six qualities that you might want to explore in your questioning.

1. He must be able to resolve difficult legal issues, not just by virtue of technical legal skills, but also with wisdom, fairness, and compassion;

2. He must have the energy and discipline to diligently study the materials that are filed in every appeal;

3. He must be able to maintain an open mind on every appeal until he has read all the pertinent material and heard from counsel on both sides;

4. He must always treat the counsel and the litigants who appear before him with patience and courtesy;

5. He must be able to write opinions that are well written and well reasoned; and

6. He must be able to work cooperatively with his eight colleagues to help produce agreement on unanimous or majority decisions, and to do his share of the writing.

Ladies and gentlemen of the Committee: If today you find the person with those qualities, the nation will thank you, and the Prime Minister will have an easy choice ahead of him. That concludes my remarks.

✗ NO
Constitutional Law, Politics, and Supreme Court of Canada Appointments
H. PATRICK GLENN

Should there be Parliamentary confirmation hearings, or public hearings of any kind, for Supreme Court of Canada appointments? There has been only limited discussion of the question in Canada, though a number of themes have emerged.[1] Proponents of hearings have said that the Supreme Court, particularly since the enactment of the Canadian Charter of Rights and Freedoms, exercises important political responsibilities, and that a more openly political appointment process is therefore appropriate. The larger role of the Supreme Court is also said to require increased public knowledge of judges and of judicial aspirants. Confirmation hearings are therefore urged as a means of facilitating public awareness and debate. A further argument, more rooted in a particular philosophy of judicial activity, is to the effect that judges are free to decide cases as they wish and that such unlimited discretion requires political surveillance, at least at the stage of appointment.

Since there have never been confirmation hearings of judicial appointments in Canada, few people have tried to explain or justify their absence. Recently, however, in response to arguments in favour of confirmation hearings, it has been said that the existing process has served Canada well, better than the confirmation process has served the U.S. ("if it ain't broke, don't fix it"); that changes to the existing process would be difficult to implement and not likely to yield better results; that confirmation hearings would give rise to unseemly and inappropriate attacks on appointees while provoking no meaningful response from them; and that the public ordeal of hearings would deter good candidates from seeking judicial office.

A contemporary observer of this debate would probably come to the conclusion that confirmation hearings should be held. They accord with democratic theory; it is true that the judges of the Supreme Court of Canada, who are accountable to no one for their decisions, render judgments that have major political importance; the arguments against hearings seem both undemocratic and elitist, in seeking to protect important people from public scrutiny. Shouldn't we just get on with it?

There may be more to be said. In particular, it seems worthwhile to ask some further questions as to the compatibility of confirmation hearings, or public hearings, with existing Canadian institutions, and as to the relations between law and politics.

I. CONFIRMATION HEARINGS, CONSTITUTIONAL LAW, AND CANADIAN INSTITUTIONS

The creation of confirmation hearings for Supreme Court of Canada appointments is related to the existing political institutions of the House of Commons and the Senate, where hearings would take place; to the Supreme Court itself, whose composition might be affected; and more generally to the Canadian judiciary, for the model of judicial appointment procedure that would be created. In each case, it will be suggested, confirmation hearings are incompatible with existing Canadian institutions and the (justifiable) law and philosophy that underlie them. The Chief Justice of Canada has therefore recently, and pointedly, stated that they would be unconstitutional.[2] Why is this so?

What is the significance of confirmation hearings for the House of Commons and the Senate? In the U.S. model, hearings of Supreme Court nominees are conducted by a committee of the Senate. The hearings are part of the system of checks and balances written into the U.S. Constitution. The executive, in the person of the president, cannot abuse the appointment process (notably to the unelected cabinet), and the Senate holds in effect a veto power over presidential nominees to the cabinet, to executive positions generally, and to the Federal judiciary. Moreover, the Senate majority is frequently of a different political allegiance than that of the president. However, neither the Canadian House of Commons nor the Canadian Senate plays the same role as the U.S. Senate. The Canadian parliamentary system is one of responsible government. The government, or the executive, is responsible to the House of Commons in the sense that it can be defeated by it and turned out of office. The result, however, is that the party that obtains the majority of seats (or votes in the House) will form the government and also control the House. Canada does not have a system of checks and balances. One may agree or disagree on types of government, but ours is unlikely to change in the foreseeable future, at least in this respect. There are, moreover, reasons for systems of responsible government. They have to do with entrusting government to those who have democratically won it and requiring them to act ethically and responsibly for the public good, or be voted out. Checks and balances are not seen as useful or efficient devices to ensure this outcome. They are judged to be ineffective and counterproductive, likely to give rise to partisan bickering and disputes over personalities. Canadian governments, with democratic legitimacy, are entitled to govern. Section 96 of the *Constitution Act* thus gives the power of appointment of judges of superior courts to the Governor General (the cabinet, or executive), and there are no constitutional checks or balances that limit this power, as the Chief Justice has pointed out. To limit this power, a constitutional amendment would be required, and such an amendment would fundamentally change the Canadian system of parliamentary or responsible government.

Submitting judicial nominations to a vote of a House of Commons committee will thus usually not result in nongovernmental control of the nomination, since a majority government will control the votes of the committee. If it does not, as may well occur in the case of a minority government, would a contrary vote of the committee bar the government from proceeding with the nomination? The present government recently refused to proceed with one of its nominations (to a newly proposed federal agency) in the face of a negative vote of a House of Commons committee to which it had chosen to submit the nomination.[3] This must be seen, however, as a political decision, since there would have been no constitutional objection to the appointment having been made. Do we wish to see the same political process emerge with respect to judicial appointments, following a public hearing and a nonbinding vote? Parliamentary custom could be made in this way, but it is recognized that enhancing the power of parliamentary committees may "wreck a system based on Responsible Government."[4] Parliamentary democracies are meant to abide by their constitutions, not systematically neglect them.

We are then left with the possibility, recently adopted by the present government, of a simple public hearing or interview of Supreme Court nominees with no ensuing vote by the committee, though it has already been pointed out that there is "no guarantee that MPs will stick to these rules," and motions and votes may turn out to be inevitable.[5] This procedure of pure publicity and no voting would be in a sense a reversal of the U.S. model, which until the twentieth century consisted of a Senate vote with no hearings. It also stands in sharp contrast with recent U.K. reforms, which rejected public hearings in favour of a more extended consultation process. Is it publicity alone that is sought? This may depend ultimately on our concept of the relations between law and politics (more on that below).

Parliamentary confirmation hearings therefore do not sit well with our political institutions. What about the Supreme Court itself? Does its mandate require appointments only after hearings and the exercise of some form of political control? Here the importance of the Charter and the intermittent activism of the U.S. Supreme Court have dominated the discussion. What is the nature, however, of the Supreme Court of Canada? Amongst western jurisdictions, it has become a rather unique type of court, unlike the highest courts of the U.K., the U.S.A., or France. In each of those countries, the jurisdiction of the highest court is more specialized than that of the Supreme Court of Canada. In the U.S., the Supreme Court is a court essentially for federal and constitutional matters only; its constitutional responsibilities dominate its workload. In the U.K., the House of Lords has historically had no constitutional responsibilities similar to those exercised by the Supreme Court of Canada in application of the Charter, and still has no powers to declare enacted law to be inoperative. In France there are three separate high courts: one for constitutional law, one for administrative law, and one for private law.

The Supreme Court of Canada is the only generalist court amongst these courts. A large part of its docket is given over to criminal appeals, and it continues to hear appeals in all other areas of private and public law. There has been a decline in the number of Charter cases, and in 2006 such cases accounted for only 10% of all cases heard (6% in civil matters and 4% in criminal matters[6]). The Supreme Court is very much a court of law in the traditional sense, deciding individual cases involving individual litigants. Its decisions have important precedential value, but this is true of the decisions of all high courts. It is therefore incorrect to treat the Supreme Court as a fundamentally political institution simply because it has begun to decide Charter cases. It certainly does decide Charter cases, and they are important cases. It is not, however, a court dominated by a political workload, a political agenda, and politically motivated judges. This too is related ultimately to our views concerning law and politics. Do we wish to give dominance to the overtly political part of the Court's workload? The present structure and jurisdiction of the Court does not indicate that this need be done.

Finally, what is the relation of confirmation hearings at the level of the Supreme Court to our entire system of judicial appointments? Would hearings be compatible with the system or constitute a useful model for its reform? Canada originally inherited the British system of appointment of judges, which relies on the professional opinion of a very small number of judges, including the Lord Chancellor, to inform the government's choice of members of the judiciary. As well, judges are chosen from a very small and select group of professionals, those barristers who have become Queen's Counsel. This system of appointment was of course appropriate for the British judiciary, which has historically been very small, with much adjudication being left to lay magistrates (the local notables). The Canadian judiciary, however, has become quite unlike the British judiciary. It is much larger; it is composed largely of professional judges; and its members are generally drawn from a very large, unified legal profession (and not from a very small corps of professional pleaders or barristers). In keeping with these changes to the judiciary, the Canadian system of appointment has changed considerably from the British model. At the provincial level, judicial nominating commissions are becoming the rule. These commissions receive applications and nominations for judicial positions, assess qualifications, and make recommendations for appointment (often in the form of shortlists) to provincial authorities. At the federal level, the process of screening and recommending judicial candidates has become a major activity of the Ministry of Justice, involving consultation with a committee of the Canadian Bar Association, which provides formal evaluations of all candidates. The process is neither secretive nor internal to the government. It is simply not conducted in a public forum.

These changes in the process of appointing Canadian judges have been occurring gradually, and the process of change is certainly not complete. One result of change has been a decline in the importance of political patronage in the appointment process. It is reasonable to think that the quality of the Bench has also been reinforced, since the procedures allow much more information to be processed about a larger number of judicial candidates than would otherwise be the case. Appointments to the Supreme Court of Canada go through a similar, though less formal, process of consultation, and, unlike in the U.S. Supreme Court, there is no criticism of the quality of appointments. It is evident that successive governments have taken the task very seriously and that the visibility of the Court has enhanced the likelihood of high-quality appointments.

The underlying political ethic of this appointment process is that of responsible government, i.e., that it is the task of the government to act, as government, in the public interest. The underlying judicial ethic of the process is that of obtaining a judiciary of the highest quality. Quite absent from the process have been the ideas of checks and balances on government action and of democratic approval of the judiciary. Discussion of the existing judicial appointment process in Canada thus provides little or no support for judicial confirmation hearings, given the underlying principles of responsible government and a judiciary of the highest quality. This conclusion can be seen as without prejudice to the development of judicial nominating commissions, which have as their task the searching out of the best candidates, as opposed to merely eliminating allegedly bad governmental nominations. The latest nomination to the Supreme Court, however, followed the work of an advisory committee half of whose members were drawn from the House of Commons and others who were political appointments. What should one make of such a structure, which has no constitutional foundation? This brings us, finally, to the larger question of the relations between law and politics. What more must be briefly said on this large subject?

II. CONFIRMATION HEARINGS, LAW, AND POLITICS

The relations between law and politics have already been mentioned, in discussing whether judicial appointments and activity should receive some form of democratic approval (which could logically extend to election of judges), whether confirmation or some other form of public hearings should be held before a parliamentary committee of some kind, and whether the Supreme Court should be treated as a political institution. Since democracy has been a relatively successful form of government, its extension to the judiciary appears to be a good thing. Democracy is a form of politics, however, and its application to law means politicizing the legal process in an explicit manner. Do we want to do this?

One of the most frequently made criticisms of the legal order is that it is ultimately political. Since it is ultimately political, we should do away with the legal charade and apply to the legal process the same methods and techniques that are used elsewhere in politics. Law should be the object of public and transparent political debate and be subject to democratic institutions. The notion of the "political" is here very large and appears to extend to most forms of human interaction. Such an attitude underlay the adoption of systems of election of judges in both the former U.S.S.R. (implementing socialist legality) and the U.S.A. (implementing Jeffersonian democracy). We have now had substantial modern experience with the notion of democratizing the legal process in such a direct way. The problems are both theoretical and practical.

Ultimately, our view of judicial activity may be driven by our view of law itself. Is there such a thing, for example, as a natural legal order? The Aboriginal population of this country tells us there is. It teaches respect for the natural environment. We should continue to act in traditional ways since these ways do the least violence to the world. If there is such a natural legal order, it does not require elected judges or a democratic legal process. It requires a legal process that will ensure respect for the natural legal order, and in the Aboriginal legal order, this means adherence to the wisdom of people recognized as elders. Nor do religiously inspired legal traditions insist on democratic legitimation; legal authority is derived from religious learning and some form of official recognition of such acquired authority. In the Western, secular world, these ancient traditions have had and continue to have great influence. Western legal traditions are remarkable, however, for their insistence that law is presently *made* by those entrusted with the task. This philosophical attitude emerged with the Enlightenment, but the Enlightenment did not lead to a radical democratization of the legal process. Something else was also at work.

In contemporary liberal societies, people are entitled to different views and different ways of life. Law is used to regulate and conciliate the conflicts that inevitably arise. Since there is no consistently imposed social fabric, law must do more than it does in a society in which common forms of life are accepted by all concerned. In the inevitable turmoil of social relations, the major teaching of the Enlightenment was that law had to be separated out from politics. Politics would, of course, continue to exist and would give the major forms of direction to society. At the level of daily life, however, where decisions that affect the individual are made, it was felt that the political process was too large, too biased, and too crude, given the infinite detail of social conflict. The person charged with social deviance could not be judged, for example, by those who had made the rules. From the seventeenth century, thus emerged the notion of an independent judiciary, one that was not subject to the political process and that was given remarkable institutional liberty to pursue justice in the individual case. This is why Canada has professionalized its judiciary. No one wishes to be judged by those controlled by someone else, or by those fearing sanctions for the decision they reach, or by those biased by social position or attitude. In short, most of our present legal institutions have been developed not because it is felt that law is somehow inevitably different from politics—more scientific, more technical, or more neutral—but because it has been felt that every possible effort should be made to provide institutional protection to individuals, in liberal, democratic states, from the brute forces of politics. The separation of law and politics does not deny the political character of law but assumes it. It then seeks to control and limit the influence of politics through institutional guarantees of fair process, independent decision-makers, and application of established rules.

The notion of an independent judiciary, one that is not democratically elected and not subject to democratic recall, is thus parallel to and consistent with the political ethic of responsible government. Those entrusted with authority are expected to exercise it in the public interest. There can be no guardians of the guardians, at least in any immediate and direct way. The independence of the judiciary takes the ethic a step further, however, in awarding tenure for life (or its statutory equivalent, the seventy-fifth birthday) to those judged best qualified to have it. Since our judiciary is now a large one, judicial councils have been established to discipline judges for nonjudicial conduct, but no political authority can interfere in the judicial decision-making process, and no judge need fear official or popular sanction for unpopular decisions. Most of our legal institutions today thus represent efforts to separate law from politics, because their confusion has been recognized by most people at most times to be highly undesirable. This is particularly so in Canada, where the Charter of Rights essentially protects the individual from majoritarian politics, and where the multicultural character of the society also implies freedom from majority control. We have an independent judiciary not to be democratic but to provide limits on democracy.

Efforts to democratize and politicize the legal process are visible today because they have been so consistently rejected in the past and because our existing institutions translate this rejection. It is not that no one thought of parliamentary confirmation hearings before the Charter. It is rather that institutions were created that would, as much as possible, free the legal process from the political one. Judges *are* free to decide as they wish, and since they are institutionally free, they choose to decide according to their best appreciation of existing law. This freedom is given to them because you would not want *your* case to be decided on majoritarian political grounds. Creating judicial confirmation hearings, or judicial hearings of any other kind, would not change a great deal in the unfolding of history. It would be a small, further step in the politicization of law, however, and as such, there should be a presumption against such hearings, as indeed there is in this country.

The practical difficulties in democratizing the legal process have been more significant than the theoretical ones, however, in the jurisdictions that have attempted the process. In the former U.S.S.R., the process of election of judges was party-controlled, in the name of authoritarian, socialist legitimacy, and the result was the opposite of democratic control. In the United States, a populist, majoritarian, monocultural tradition prevailed at the state level (leading to election of state judges) but not at the federal level, where the Bill of Rights was to be enforced by an independent judiciary.[7] At the state level, the election of judges has been the object of ongoing reforms designed to eliminate party influence and corruption while reinforcing the quality of judges. The democratic control has been largely illusory, and voter influence, never strong, has been declining steadily in favour of various forms of judicial nominating commissions. What should we make of the U.S. experience?

As mentioned above, confirmation hearings are a relatively recent phenomenon in the United States, beginning only in this century, shortly before World War II. Why did they come about? Why was the presumption against politicization (federal

U.S. judges are appointed, not elected) here reversed? It does not appear to have been the role of the U.S. Supreme Court in deciding Bill of Rights cases that caused the change, since this had been going on for a long time prior to the introduction of confirmation hearings. An independent high court free of political influence and free of democratic pressures in the appointment process is thus entirely compatible with a constitutional democracy. It is even the ideal balance between the will of the majority and individual rights. What appears to have brought about the change, according to U.S. writers, was the process by which appointments to the Court became seen as further means of advancing political goals. Politicians have as their function the task of advancing political goals. Today in the United States there is talk of "transformative appointments," in the sense of appointments that would change the course of decisions of the Court in a political sense (though there is no way of predicting this at the time of appointment). The judges are expected to decide according to a broad, personal political philosophy. Very recently, there has thus been surprise at the emergence of a group of "legal conservatives" in the Court, those who refuse to overrule prior decisions with which they disagree because of the need for legal stability. Yet if governments are entitled to use the Supreme Court for political objectives, and its judges are expected to act as majoritarian political appointees, then it is normal that the process of appointment be politicized and even radically so. It is also normal that the process be subject to the full range of political debate and struggle, as unedifying and inefficient as it frequently is, and Canadian politicians are not genetically different from U.S. politicians. There is no practical means of ensuring only serene and enlightened democratic participation in the nomination process.[8] Most importantly, there appears to be no means of politicizing the appointment process without also politicizing the Court itself.

The Supreme Court has not become a political battleground in Canada. If we are to struggle toward a rule of law for individuals, rather than a rule of political power, it is undesirable that it become a political battleground. Its present role as a court of law should remind us of why it is there. Let's leave it alone. One day it may have to decide my case, or yours.

NOTES

1. See a recent symposium of the *Osgoode Hall Law Journal* at *Osgoode Hall Law Journal* 44 (2007), p. 527 ff., for support of various types of hearing by Peter Hogg, Peter McCormick, Jacob Ziegel, and Kate Malleson.

2. "Keep Politics out of Top Court, McLachlin urges," *The Globe and Mail*, February 3, 2006.

3. For the debate and rejection of the candidate, House of Commons Canada, "Standing Committee on Government Operations and Estimates," Tuesday, May 16, 2006, available at http://www.parl.gc.ca; and for government reaction, *The Globe and Mail*,

May 17 and 18, 2006 (prime minister characterizing conduct of opposition MPs as "buffoonish" after questioning of candidate on prior remarks on immigrant populations characterized as "racist").

4. J.B. Steward, *The Canadian House of Commons [:] Procedure and Reform* (Montreal and Kingston: McGill-Queen's University Press, 1977), p. 167; see also p. 132 ("serious technical, procedural, and constitutional problems"), p. 169 (contrasting "congressionalist" view); and for the necessarily subordinate character of House committees, given that they can have no more than delegated power from the House under the Canadian constitution, W.F. Dawson, *Procedure in the Canadian House of Commons* (Toronto: University of Toronto Press, 1962), p. 202. For similar calls for parliamentary hearings for candidates for the position of governor of the Bank of Canada, which have never taken place in Canada, *The Globe and Mail,* October 6, 2007 (opposed by representative of Bloc Québécois in order "to keep the appointment process as autonomous as possible," this position exhibiting a noteworthy sense of the importance of the constitution of Canada).

5. K. Malleson, "Parliamentary Scrutiny of Supreme Court Nominees: A View from the United Kingdom" (2006) *Osgoode Hall Law Journal* 44, p. 562.

6. See http://www.scc-csc.gc.ca/information/statistics/download/ecourt.pdf, Accessed October 23, 2007.

7. For executive judicial appointments at the federal level in the U.S. as the "proper cure for corruption in the Legislature," see G. Wood, *The Creation of the American Republic, 1776–1787* (Williamsburg VA: University of North Carolina Press, 1969), p. 551.

8. For the highly politicized hearing of a Canadian government appointee and the lack of any means of preventing such conduct in any judicial appointment process, see notes 3 and 5 above; and for Canadian politicians who "could not resist asking some questions on top-of-mind policy issues" in the hearing of a Supreme Court nominee in February 2006, see P. Hogg, "Appointment of Justice Marshall Rothstein to the Supreme Court of Canada" (2006) *Osgoode Hall Law Journal* 44, p. 531.

POSTSCRIPT

In his article, Peter Hogg gives the reader a bird's-eye view of the first use of public parliamentary hearings for nominees to the Supreme Court of Canada. As such, the article is an invaluable contribution to the consideration of this particular reform of the selection process. Hogg also makes an elegant case for parliamentary review of Supreme Court nominees, saying that the significance of the Court requires that the appointments of its members be more apparent to Canadians. The hearings grant the Canadian public an opportunity to better grasp the operation of the third branch of government and to learn more about the justices themselves. However, one may wonder whether the civility displayed in the hearings for Justice Rothstein will carry over into the future. Hogg is confident that the parliamentary review will never mirror the raucous nature of some Congressional proceedings on Court nominees in the United States, but the unpredictability of political forces may prove Hogg wrong. Hogg also seems to think that the advisory role of the ad hoc committee is appropriate because it reduces the possibility of tensions, yet the very rationale for hearings—the need for transparency—may call for a larger role for parliamentarians in the selection process for Supreme Court justices.

In his article, Glenn finds little good to say about public hearings—and seemingly for good reason. If one looks to the American experience, the presence of confirmation hearings seems to be a sign of a highly politicized court system, one in which the rule of law takes a backseat to the sway of political power. However, Glenn's arguments, like Hogg's, are not entirely convincing. He contends that the appointment process in Canada is open and nonsecretive; it is simply not carried out in full view of the public. But surely the absence of a public forum turns the process into what Glenn denies it to be: a closed process. Glenn makes the important point that the present appointment practice helps to shield the judicial process from the intrusiveness of politics and majoritarian thinking. But it might be argued that allowing public hearings would not put a large dent in the shield that protects the independence of the judiciary. Glenn concedes as much but nevertheless seems to argue that hearings go against basic principles regarding judicial appointments. There also appears to be here a fear of the slippery slope—that the small steps toward a more politicized system encourage the taking of larger steps.

A final point to ponder—which is not a criticism of either article—is the structuring of any future parliamentary hearings on nominees to the Supreme Court. For Justice Rothstein, the Harper government employed an ad hoc group composed of members of the House of Commons and chaired by the minister of justice. An alternative to this arrangement might be a standing or permanent committee of the House of Commons. This may seem to be a rather unimportant issue—the significant issue is the existence of some kind of parliamentary body—but it is interesting to note that ministers never chair standing committees. The use of a standing committee may thus deprive the government of the kind of control afforded by the presence of a minister of the crown.

To gain a full appreciation of the debate over the selection of Supreme Court justices, one might begin with a general overview of the Court. For this, see the chapter on the Supreme Court in Peter W. Hogg, *Constitutional Law of Canada, 2007 Student Edition* (Toronto: Thomson Carswell, 2007) or the relevant chapter in Rand Dyck, *Canadian Politics,* 4th ed. (Toronto: Thomson Nelson, 2008). Interest in the selection of Supreme Court justices has been precipitated in large part by effect of judicial interpretation of the Charter of Rights and Freedoms. A number of articles and books have been written on this latter topic: Raymond Bazowski, "The Judicialization of Politics," in James Bickerton and Alain-G. Gagnon, eds., *Canadian Politics,* 4th ed. (Peterborough: Broadview Press, 2004); Radha Jhappan, "Charter Politics and the Judiciary," in Michael Whittington and Glen Williams, eds., *Canadian Politics in the 21st Century,* 7th ed. (Toronto: Thomson Nelson, 2008); Janet L. Hiebert, *Charter Conflicts: What Is Parliament's Role?* (Montreal and Kingston: McGill-Queen's University Press, 2002); Christopher Manfredi, *Judicial Power and the Charter: Canada and the Paradox of Liberal Constitutionalism,* 2nd ed. (Toronto: Oxford University Press, 2001); Robert Martin, *The Most Dangerous Branch: How the Supreme Court of Canada Has Undermined Our Law and Our Democracy* (Montreal and Kingston: McGill-Queen's University Press, 2003); and Kent Roach, *The Supreme Court on Trial: Judicial Activism or Democratic Dialogue* (Toronto: Irwin Law, 2001).

With an understanding of the Supreme Court and its growing importance, it is now possible to approach the writings about the selection process. F.L. Morton has collected a series of articles on this issue in his book *Law, Politics and the Judicial Process in Canada,* 3rd ed. (Calgary: University of Calgary Press, 2002). Jacob Ziegel, a respected professor of law at the University of Toronto, has also written on this matter; see Jacob S. Ziegel, "Merit Selection and Democratization of Appointments to the Supreme Court of Canada," in Paul Howe and Peter H. Russell, eds., *Judicial Power and Canadian Democracy* (Montreal and Kingston: McGill-Queen's University Press, 2001) and his review of recent developments affecting the appointment process: Jacob Ziegel, "Choosing Supreme Court Judges," *Literary Review of Canada,* May 2005. The Chief Justice of the Supreme Court of Canada, Beverly McLachlin, gave an important speech in which she conveyed her sentiments about any reform of the appointment process: Beverly McLachlin, "The Judiciary's Distinctive Role in Our Constitutional Democracy," *Policy Options,* September 2003.

In the past few years, a flurry of actions has taken place in relation to the appointment of Supreme Court justices. In March 2004, the Canadian Bar Association (CBA) put forward its views on the appropriate reform of the appointment process in a document entitled "Supreme Court of Canada Appointment

Process" (available at the CBA website). Around the same time, the House of Commons Committee on Justice, Human Rights, Public Safety and Emergency Preparedness held hearings on the matter and released an important report entitled "Improving the Supreme Court of Canada Appointments Process," May 2004 (available at the Parliament of Canada website). The publication provides some good background on the issue of selection and offers arguably the best description of the old appointment process (provided by the minister of justice through testimony before the committee). Following this, the government made changes to the appointment process for the purpose of selecting two justices to the Supreme Court of Canada, and a parliamentary ad hoc committee was struck to participate in this process and to prepare a report on its activities. The report, which is available at the federal Department of Justice website, is entitled "Report of the Interim Ad Hoc Committee on the Appointment of Supreme Court Justices," August 2004. In April 2005, the federal minister of justice released a paper, "Proposal to Reform the Supreme Court of Canada Appointments Process," that sets out the thoughts of changes that should be made to the ways in which appointments are made to the country's highest court. Finally, in February 2006, the Harper government set up public hearings for Supreme Court of Canada nominees, a discussion of which can be found in an issue of the *Osgoode Hall Law Journal* 44, no. 3 (fall 2006).

The American appointment process is obviously relevant to this debate, so appreciation of this process is in order. Useful are Henry Abraham's two texts, *The Judicial Process: An Introductory Analysis of the Courts of the United States, England, and France,* 6th ed. (New York: Oxford University Press, 1993) and *Justices and Presidents: A Political History of Appointments to the Supreme Court,* 3rd ed. (Toronto: Oxford University Press, 1992); as well as David M. O'Brien's *Storm Center: The Supreme Court in American Politics,* 3rd ed. (New York: W.W. Norton, 1993). The American appointment process is controversial in large part because of Senate hearings on two Supreme Court nominees, Robert Bork (in 1987) and Clarence Thomas (in 1991). For more on these hearings, see Ethan Bronner, *Battle for Justice: How the Bork Nomination Shook America* (New York: W.W. Norton, 1989); and Timothy M. Phelps and Helen Winternitz, *Capitol Games: Clarence Thomas, Anita Hill, and the Story of a Supreme Court Nomination* (New York: Hyperion, 1992). Jeffrey Toobin also speaks to the controversies over appointments to the U.S. Supreme Court in his recently published book *The Nine: Inside the Secret World of the Supreme Court* (New York: Doubleday Publishing, 2007).

Finally, for an international perspective on judicial appointments, see Kate Malleson and Peter Russell, *Appointing Judges in an Age of Judicial Power: Critical Perspectives from Around the World* (Toronto: University of Toronto Press, 2006).

Should Party Discipline Be Relaxed?

✔ **YES**
DAVID KILGOUR, JOHN KIRSNER, AND KENNETH MCCONNELL,
"Discipline versus Democracy: Party Discipline in Canadian Politics"

✘ **NO**
ROBERT J. JACKSON, "The Imperative of Party Discipline in the
Canadian Political System 2007"

David Kilgour, a former member of Parliament from Alberta, had a rocky relationship with the Progressive Conservative Party throughout his career. Elected to Parliament in 1979 as a member of the Conservative Party, Kilgour quit the party caucus in April 1987 in protest over the Conservative government's policies for the West and its failure to develop adequate ethical guidelines for elected representatives. Kilgour rejoined the Tory caucus in February 1988 but soon became critical of his party's proposed Goods and Services Tax (GST). On April 10, 1990, he voted against the government's bill authorizing the GST and, as a consequence, was expelled from the caucus of the Progressive Conservative Party. Kilgour subsequently crossed the floor to sit as a member of the Liberal Party. He has since been reelected four times as a Liberal member of Parliament.

In April 2005, David Kilgour's parliamentary career took yet another twist. Following revelations of the Gomery Commission into misuse of government funds under the sponsorship program in Quebec, Kilgour announced that he could no longer sit in the Liberal caucus in good conscience. Instead, he indicated that he would henceforth sit as an independent in Parliament and would retire from federal politics when the next election was called.

David Kilgour's troubles with his former parties stem from the well-known tradition of party discipline, which requires members of Parliament to vote according to their party's position. Clearly, the member from Alberta has some difficulty with this tradition, and he is not alone. Polls show that only a small percentage of respondents believe that the first priority should be loyalty to his or her party.

Despite this, political leaders have long felt that the principle of party discipline was vital to the functioning of parliamentary government in Canada. When necessary, as in the case of David Kilgour, party officials have shown that they are willing to take strong measures to enforce party discipline—by withholding support for a candidate at election time, by denying parliamentary appointments, or even by expelling a recalcitrant MP from the party caucus.

The rationale for discipline in political parties is a simple one. Canada has a parliamentary system of government that requires that the party in power maintain the support and confidence of the majority of the members of the legislative branch. Without this support, the government would find it difficult to carry out the mandate on which it is elected and, more important, to remain in power. Party discipline is a means of preventing these occurrences.

For many Canadians, as reflected in the following two readings, the debate over party discipline hinges largely on whether or not Canada should move closer to an American model, where members of Congress are seen as being relatively free to vote according to personal conscience and constituency interest. Kilgour, Kirsner, and McConnell argue that relaxed party discipline would advance the cause of democracy and provide better representation for individual constituents. Robert Jackson counters that the weakening of party discipline would give Canada an American-style system in which special interest groups, not elected officials, would control our legislative representatives. He suggests that recent political developments have demonstrated that the traditional model of party discipline continues to well serve the Canadian political system.

✔ **YES**

Discipline versus Democracy: Party Discipline in Canadian Politics
DAVID KILGOUR, JOHN KIRSNER, AND KENNETH MCCONNELL

Parliamentary democracy in Canada is so dominated by political parties that some experts believe the party discipline exerted on most votes in our House of Commons and provincial legislatures is the tightest in the democratic world. Defenders of our model argue that many Canadians prefer it this way because each party's candidates can be presumed at election time to share the party's position on every issue. Others contend our executive democracy, patterned on a system prevailing in Great Britain at least a century and a half ago, requires iron party discipline if our fused legislative and executive branches of government are to function effectively. Another reason, probably the most important, is that our practice makes life easier for leaders of both government and opposition parties.

Unlike the parliamentary systems of nations such as Great Britain and Germany, virtually every vote in Canadian legislatures is considered potentially one of non-confidence in the government. Even a frivolous opposition motion to adjourn for the day, if lost, can be deemed by a cabinet to have been one of non-confidence. The whips of government parties have for decades used the possibility of an early election to persuade their members to vote the party line. The attitude of opposition parties is often so similar that we had several years ago the spectacle of both opposition parties in the House of Commons arguing that a free vote on an abortion resolution would "rip out the heart" of our parliamentary system of government. The constituents of both provincial and federal legislators would be the real winners if party discipline were loosened. Private members from both government and opposition benches could then take positions on government bills and other matters based on assisting constituents instead of their respective party hierarchies.

PARTY DISCIPLINE IN CANADA

W.S. Gilbert put the continuing Canadian political reality succinctly: "I always voted at my party's call, and I never thought of thinking for myself at all." Canadian members of Parliament are essentially passive observers in the formulation and administration of most national policy. Indeed, Sean Moore, editor of the Ottawa lobbyist magazine *The Lobby Digest*, told a committee of MPs in 1993 that they are rarely lobbied by the almost three thousand reported lobbyists then in the capital because "elected officials play a very minor role in governing."

MPs from all parties vote in solid blocs on almost every issue. Government members do so from a fear that a lost vote on a measure will be deemed by their prime minister as a loss of confidence. This stems from the early- to mid-nineteenth-century British responsible government concept that a government falls if it loses the support of a majority in the Commons.

Besides the threat of parliamentary dissolution, private members are also subject to rewards and punishments from party leadership, depending on how they vote. A "loyal" MP who votes the party line will be a candidate for promotion (if in the government party, perhaps to cabinet) or other benefits from the party, such as interesting trips or appointment to an interesting House committee. A "disloyal" MP who votes against the party leadership may be prevented from ascending the political ladder and could ultimately be thrown out of the party caucus. In light of this, "caucus solidarity and my constituents be damned" might be the real oath of office for most honourable members in all political parties.

Reg Stackhouse, a former Tory MP for Scarborough West, in a submission to the Task Force on Reform of the House of Commons in 1985, commented on the discipline imposed on private members of the government party:

> Not only is it demanded that [the member] vote with the government on crucial matters such as the Speech from the Throne or the budget, but also that he vote, speak or remain silent according to the dictate of the government. Even though a government may be at no risk of falling, it requires this all but unconditional commitment, and renders the member a seeming robot, at least imaginatively replaceable by a voting machine.

This is the major defect in Canadian parliamentary democracy: most MPs are essentially brute voters who submit to any demand from their respective party whips. In Canada's current political culture, a prime minister or premier could in practice on all confidence votes cast proxy votes on behalf of all government members. The same practice prevails in the opposition parties because they think themselves obliged to vote in uniform party blocs virtually always. If not, some of our media, seemingly unaware that parliamentary democracy has evolved elsewhere, report that the opposition leaders cannot control their caucuses. This *status quo* has persisted for so long primarily because party leaders and policy mandarins in the executive branch obviously prefer it. A policy advisor in Ottawa reminded a meeting of the Study of Parliament Group that there are about 270,000 federal government employees who work for the executive and perhaps 1,700 who work for Parliament. Measures going into the House of Commons where one party has a majority usually emerge essentially unscathed. Everything follows a highly predictable script: obedient government members praise it; opposition parties rail against it; and plenty of bad measures become law essentially unamended.

The present regional differences and priorities require much better public expression in Parliament, at least if one central institution of our national government is to reflect adequately all parts of a diverse and vast country. Regional voices are frequently suffocated by rigid party discipline and the entrenched habit of the national caucuses to maintain a close eye on what opinion leaders, particularly columnists in Toronto–Ottawa–Montreal, regard as the national interest on any issue. Reforming the role of MPs is not only essential for parliamentary legitimacy in postmodern Canada but vital to "nationalizing Ottawa."

ELIMINATING EXCESSES

A report by the late Eugene Forsey and Graham Eglington (*The Question of Confidence in Responsible Government*) lists a large number of measures defeated in the Westminster Parliament. On most, the cabinet of the day simply carried on, presumably either dropping the failed proposal or seeking majority support for a different measure. For tax bills, the list of such defeats begins in 1834. During 1975, for example, a financial bill of the Harold Wilson cabinet dealing with its value-added tax rate was defeated, but the ministry carried on in office, treating it as other than a confidence vote.

The Forsey–Eglington Report also emphasizes that in earlier years, government MPs in Canada were permitted to vote against cabinet measures. For example, between 1867 and 1872, their study lists fully eighteen pages of cases in which Conservative MPs voted against measures of John A. Macdonald's government. The sky did not fall; Macdonald's government was able to function effectively; government MPs could keep both their self-respect and their membership in the government caucus.

The study also provides interesting data about voting in our House of Commons during other periods: in 1896, fully sixteen Conservative MPs voted with Laurier's Liberals to adjourn a Conservative measure intended to restore Catholic schools in Manitoba; in 1981, sixteen Conservative MPs, including three who later became ministers, voted against the final resolution patriating our Constitution.

The all-party McGrath Report on parliamentary reform came to the conclusion that the role of the individual member must be enhanced. As James McGrath himself said in 1985, "I wanted to put into place a system where being a member of Parliament would be seen to be an end to itself and not a means to an end." On the question of non-confidence, McGrath recommended the following:

- A government should be careful before it designates a vote as one of confidence. It should confine such declarations to measures central to its administration.

- While a defeat on supply is a serious matter, elimination or reduction of an estimate can be accepted.

- In a parliament with a government in command of a majority, the matter of confidence has really been settled by the electorate.

- Government should therefore have the wisdom to permit members to decide many matters in their own personal judgments.

Reg Stackhouse agrees that party discipline must have limits: "Tight party lines need be drawn only when the government's confidence is at stake, that is, when the government decides the fate of a bill is absolutely essential to its objectives."

One way to reduce party discipline in the interest of greater fairness for every province would be to write into our Constitution, as the West Germans did in their Basic Law, that MPs and senators shall "not [be] bound by orders and instructions and shall be subject only to their conscience." Party discipline has certainly diluted this wholesome principle in West Germany, but when combined with another feature of their Constitution—that no chancellor can be defeated in their equivalent of our House of Commons unless a majority of members simultaneously agree on a new person to become chancellor—there now appears to be a more independent role for members of the Bundestag than for Canadian members of Parliament. For example, in the case of the defeat of the minority Clark government in 1979 on its budget, the West German rule would have kept Clark in office unless the Liberals, New Democrats, and Social Credit MPs could have agreed simultaneously on a new prime minister who could hold the confidence of a majority of MPs. A similar rule, if adopted by the House of Commons, would inevitably weaken our party discipline significantly because MPs from all parties could vote on the merits of issues, knowing that defeat would bring down only the measure and not the government.

Another approach would be for each new federal or provincial cabinet to specify at the start of its mandate which matters at the heart of its program will be confidence issues. The Mulroney government, for example, might have spelled out in late 1988 that the Canada–U.S. Free Trade Agreement would be a confidence issue. In those situations, party discipline would be justifiable. Otherwise, its backbenchers would be free to vote for their constituents' interests at all times. This restored independence for legislators would lead to better representation for all regions of Canada and more occupational credibility for Canadian legislators.

A study of the 32nd Legislative Assembly of Ontario (1981–85) indicated that its members voted in uniform party blocs about 95 percent of the time. The same pattern has applied in recent Parliaments in Ottawa. As mentioned above, the Canadian practice suggests that all of the various party leaders could cast a proxy vote on behalf of all their followers without even bothering to have them physically present. It also overlooks that a majority or even a minority government can function effectively without our present stratospheric levels of party solidarity.

THE AMERICAN WAY

In the United States Congress, where admittedly there is a strict separation of powers between the executive and the legislative branches of government, legislation does get passed with far less party loyalty. The constitutional separation of powers and the weakness of party discipline in congressional voting behaviour greatly facilitate effective regional representation in Washington. Unlike the situation in Canada, where a government falls if it loses the support of a majority in the House of Commons on a confidence vote, United States presidents and Congress are elected for fixed terms. Neither resigns if a particular measure is voted down in either the Senate or the House of Representatives.

The practices in our two countries are so different that *The Congressional Quarterly* defines party unity votes there as those in which at least 51 percent of members of one party vote against 51 percent of the other party. Under this definition, itself astonishing to Canadian legislators, the *Quarterly* notes that for the years 1975 to 1982, party unity votes occurred in only 44.2 percent of the 4,417 recorded Senate votes and in only 39.8 percent of those in the House of Representatives. This sample, moreover, includes the years 1977 to 1980, the last period before 1994 when Democrats controlled the White House and both branches of Congress.

Another feature of the congressional system that fosters effective regional input in national policymaking is territorial bloc voting—something quite unknown in Canada's House of Commons. Representatives from the two political parties of the Mountain states, Sun Belt states, New England states, and others vote *en bloc* or work together in committees to advance common interests.

A good example of how effective regional representatives can influence the geographic location of federal government procurement, which affects the geographic distribution of the manufacturing sector, is the Southern congressional influence. It played a major role in the postwar concentration of federal military and space expenditures in the South and in the general economic revival and growth of the Sun Belt. And during 1981–82, the height of the "boll-weevil era," the longtime legislative coalition of Southern Democrats and Republicans was successful more than 85 percent of the time, due to mutual areas of agreement and interest.

The point of this comparison is only to emphasize that, unlike the American Congress, Canadian bloc voting makes bipartisan or tripartisan agreement on anything in our legislatures exceedingly rare. In our current political culture, if a government or opposition MP's loyalty to his or her province clashes with the instruction of the party whip, putting constituents' or regional considerations first in his or her way of voting subjects the MP's prospects for party advancement to considerable risk. Backbench MPs in Canada are thus far less able to represent regional interests effectively than are their counterparts in Washington, where the congressional system provides the freedom for effective regional representation when an issue has clear regional implications. This, of course, is not to suggest that Canada should duplicate the American congressional style of government. Rather, it is to point out that the best solution to ongoing problems of representative democracy in Canada might be to adopt attractive features from various systems, including the American one.

PUTTING CONSTITUENTS FIRST

Canada is a federal state and federalism means that on some issues the will of the popular majority will be frustrated. If the biggest battalions of voters are to prevail over smaller ones under any circumstances, we should drop the charade that we have a federal system of government that respects minorities in times of stress. The notion that the largest group of Canadians, that is, southern Ontarians and metropolitan Quebecers, must be accommodated always has resulted in varying degrees of discontent outside those areas and accompanying feelings of regional irrelevancy.

In an increasingly interdependent world, many Canadians in our outer eight provinces and the territories want new or altered institutions that will represent the interest of both "inner Canadians" (those who live in the Toronto–Ottawa–Montreal corridor) and "outer Canadians" effectively. Unless we move away from the notion that "the national interest" is merely a code phrase for the interests of the most populous regions in the country, frictions between inner and outer Canada are likely to worsen.

If party discipline in Canada were relaxed, representation for all areas of Canada would be improved. It would be easier for, say, Western or Atlantic MPs to defy their party establishments, if need be, in support of regional issues. Coalitions composed of members of all parties could exist for the purpose of working together on issues of common regional or other concern. The present adversarial attitudes and structures of Parliament or legislatures, in which opposition parties oppose virtually anything a government proposes, might well change in the direction of parties working together for the common good.

Members of Parliament today represent an average of about 100,000 residents per riding. Few government and opposition MPs have any real opportunity to put their constituents first in votes in the House of Commons. Real power is concentrated in the hands of the party leaderships. Canadian democracy itself would benefit if we put our present mind-numbing party discipline where it belongs—in the history books.

✗ NO

The Imperative of Party Discipline in the Canadian Political System 2007
ROBERT J. JACKSON

The fact that Canada has been successful as a state leaves some observers perplexed. The Canadian border encases the second-largest geographic land mass in the world under the authority of one Constitution. At the same time, the country is sparsely populated by a narrow ribbon of inhabitants stretched along the forty-ninth parallel. This widely dispersed population is subject to the pull of global economics dominated by its American neighbour to the south. From its genesis, Canada has been a linguistically and culturally heterogeneous society, and is becoming more so with each successive year. Despite the existence of all these centrifugal pressures, what we know today as Canada has existed and thrived for over a century and a quarter.

It is not by historical accident that Canada occupies the position it does today. On the contrary, the fact that Canada exists is the result of deliberate measures taken by Canadian leaders to establish policies and institutions that transcend diversity and bind the country together. Examples include national economic, health, and social policies, a responsible cabinet/parliamentary system of government, and in particular, the establishment of broadly based and national political parties. Institutional structures, such as political parties, can transcend Canadian diversity and provide poles of allegiance against the ever-present centrifugal influences. In order to fulfill this function effectively, the parties themselves must act as cohesive units and strive for party solidarity. Strong parties, based on a broad consensus, are thus vital to the effective functioning of responsible government and the Canadian state. Party solidarity, the apex of which is party discipline, is the guiding principle of the party system in Canada.[1]

Party discipline refers to the ability of the leader in a democratic state to enforce obedience on his or her followers in the legislature and in the party organization. The argument for relaxing party discipline is that MPs should not be "trained sheep" but should, rather, be free to represent the views of their constituents. Members are, after all, elected by their constituents and should be responsible to them. But the issue is not that simple; the Canadian form of government relies on cohesive political parties. In the responsible government model, the party in power is awarded an electoral mandate to enact a legislative program, and its members must support the cabinet and prime minister in order to accomplish this. An MP is not primarily a delegate of his or her constituents. Rather, an MP is elected to serve as a member of a particular party. Within that party, the MP is called upon to deliberate and participate in formulating policies, and then to accept and support the majority decision. The government will not be made more responsive if its members make it more difficult to pass legislation. The prime minister and government must have the means of achieving their objectives.

The Canadian system is premised on the idea that the reason and judgment of politicians are to be respected in the field of policymaking. Parties must be entrusted to deliberate, decide, and then be judged by the electorate. Otherwise, MPs would be elected to deliberate, but constituents, who have not participated in the deliberations, would retain the right to decide. Such a procedure would be ludicrous. MPs do not and should not directly represent their individual constituencies, provinces, or even regions, polling on every issue to see how they should vote. Rather, they are members of a particular party that provides broad perspectives on national issues. They run under the banner of that particular party and seek the privileges offered by it because they are in general agreement with its broad base of national policy directions, directions that can be influenced and adjusted in caucus.

As a British politician pointed out more than a century ago, "Combinations there must be—the only question is, whether they shall be broad parties, based on comprehensive ideas, and guided by men who have a name to stake on the wisdom of their course, or obscure cliques, with some narrow crotchet for a policy, and some paltry yelping shibboleth for a cry." After all, if MPs do not accept the decision arrived at by their executives and party, which groups will they represent? The special pleading of a particular pressure group that has a narrower conception of the national interest?

Party discipline is a feature inherent in the Canadian model of Parliament, and is inextricably linked to the concept of responsible government and the confidence convention. The *Constitution Act, 1867*, established that Canada would have a responsible cabinet/parliamentary system of government. This is the basis of our current system, whereby the cabinet, as selected by the prime minister, is composed of members of the legislature and must keep the confidence of the House of Commons. The system also presupposes an opposition party or parties that are ready and willing to attack the government in an attempt to alter or reject its legislation. The government must therefore enforce party discipline not only to enact its legislative program, but also for the sake of its own self-preservation.

The United States congressional system of government differs from the parliamentary system in several key areas. Rather than fusing the executive and legislative branches of government, the American system is based on the separation of powers. The president and all of his or her cabinet members are prohibited by the Constitution from simultaneously sitting in the executive and legislative branches. The absence of responsible government and the corresponding absence of confidence convention allow the congressional system to function without party discipline.[2]

Calls for the relaxation of party discipline in Canada are not a recent phenomenon. Like the perennial cure for the common cold, the topic of parliamentary reform provides exaggerated hopes for optimists, then later gives way to despair when it fails. As early as 1923, for example, the MP from Calgary, William Irving, introduced a motion in the House of Commons that would have allowed for the relaxation of party discipline by reducing the number of votes considered to be votes of confidence. The motion was defeated, but to this day "reformers" still look to the United States and see the relaxation of party discipline as the panacea for perceived parliamentary inadequacies. Simplistic prescriptions such as the relaxation of party discipline, while seductive, fail to take into account the complexity of the parliamentary system. It is fallacious to assume that certain selected features of the congressional system can be appended to the parliamentary system without seriously affecting the functioning of the entire system.

Imagine a scenario in which party discipline in Canada was significantly relaxed. Issues formerly resolved along party lines, based on consensual lines and accommodation in caucus, would be decided on much narrower grounds. Regionalism and special interests would dominate decision making in the House of Commons, and political parties would cease to serve their function as institutions that bind the country together. The decision-making model now in place, which requires political parties to produce nationally acceptable compromises, would be replaced by an increase in confrontation. MPs liberated from the yoke of party discipline would be saddled by the demands of lobbyists and others representing narrow special interests and regional interests. This scenario is especially disquieting when taken in conjunction with the fact that there are now four parties legitimately competing for seats in the House of Commons, instead of only two or three.

The prospect of minority governments was greatly enhanced following the growth of the western Reform Party and the Bloc Québécois. Since then there has been about as many minority governments as majority governments. In the context of this development, the importance of party discipline increases exponentially. A lack of party discipline during a minority government would result in a chaotic situation where no prime minister could maintain the confidence of the House. Eight of the seventeen elections held since 1957 have resulted in minority governments.

Many of the arguments against party discipline are founded on misconceptions about the practice. The very term "whip," the name given to the party member charged with the task of enforcing party discipline, conjures up images of a menacing disciplinarian imposing the will of the party on recalcitrant MPs. This is not the case, however. While there are instances in which MPs have been coerced or even threatened with sanctions if they do not conform, party discipline is largely self-imposed. Because the majority of MPs enjoy relatively little job security, they do not relish the prospect of facing reelection. Consequently, never in Canadian history has a government been toppled by a breach in party discipline. Furthermore, recent studies indicate that since 1940, no MP from the governing party has ever broken party ranks during a minority government. Nor has any MP ever left the government side with a majority of fewer than nine seats.[3] This indicates that MPs, at least for the sake of their own self-preservation, are willing to tolerate party discipline.

Another misconception is based on the belief that constituents do not want their MPs to toe the party line. This is a somewhat complex issue, owing to the fact that the vote for the executive and legislative representative is fused into the same ballot in parliamentary systems. While it is impossible to determine the exact weight voters give to the individual candidate and the party label, several studies indicate that parties are more important than individual candidates. One report found that shortly after an election, fewer than two-thirds of respondents could correctly give the name of their recently elected MP.[4] More specifically, from 1940 to 1988, thirty-one MPs ran for reelection in the general election following the parliamentary session in which they revolted against their parliamentary caucus and crossed the floor; only twelve of them were successful in the election, and three were forced to run under their former party banner. Only one independent candidate was elected in each of the 2004 and 2006 elections. These figures contrast sharply with the argument that the voters will reward an MP for acting independently and want independents in the House.

The most recent substantive recommendations for reforming party discipline are embodied in the so-called McGrath Report, released in June 1985. The report had three basic conclusions:

1. There should be attitudinal changes.

2. The parties should relax their discipline.

3. There should be organizational reform.

The committee reported, "We believe the country would be better served if members had more freedom to play an active role in the debate on public policy, even if it meant disagreeing with their parties from time to time." The report then called for an "attitudinal change" by backbenchers and asked the prime minister to accept more dissension and defeat of government measures without recourse to the threat or use of dissolution of the House.

Unfortunately, this part of the report is romantic nonsense for the following reasons:

1. Calls for an attitudinal change are unlikely to be effective. The only practicable reform is one that changes the organization around members.

2. There never was a Golden Age of Parliament, as the report implies. In the period before parties, when Canadian MPs were "loose fish," MPs were not free of financial and other social ties that constrained their voting behaviour.

3. The question should not be whether MPs are free to vote against their parties, but rather, whose interests or groups are they adopting when they do so? Free voting does not mean that MPs are free of pressures to conform with other groups' positions.[5] Is it better to have MPs' behaviour determined by widely based cohesive political parties or narrower interest groups?

The facts also belie such utopian assumptions. There has been no relaxation of party discipline in the House of Commons. The urging cries of "reformers" have had no effect. The reality is that MPs are already free to vote as they wish. The point is that they do not choose to exercise their liberty by taking stands against their parties. They will always be subject to constituents, interest groups, and financial pressures: the only question is whether they will follow the dictates of a broadly based party or those of another group with a narrower conception of the national interest. Those who choose wisely stand solidly with their parties, helping to protect the system of government and providing a counterpoint to the centrifugal influences of our geography and society. The increasing number of minority governments strengthens this argument.

NOTES

1. Robert J. Jackson and Doreen Jackson, *Politics in Canada,* 7th ed. (Scarborough: Prentice-Hall, 2008).

2. Robert J. Jackson and Doreen Jackson, *Contemporary Government and Politics: Democracy and Authoritarianism,* 5th ed. (Scarborough: Prentice-Hall, 2007).

3. Paul Conlin, "Floor Crossing in the Canadian House of Commons, 1940–1992" (Carleton University: Unpublished B.A. (Hons.) research paper, 1993).

4. William Irvine, "Does the Candidate Make a Difference? The Macro-politics and Micro-politics of Getting Elected," *Canadian Journal of Political Science* 15, no. 4 (December 1982).

5. Robert J. Jackson, "Executive–Legislative Relations in Canada," in Jackson et al., *Contemporary Canadian Politics* (Scarborough: Prentice-Hall, 1987), pp. 111–125.

POSTSCRIPT

One's stance on the issue of party discipline depends in part on how one interprets the experience of other countries, particularly the United States. David Kilgour likes the freedom that the relaxed party discipline of the American system gives members of Congress to represent their constituents, especially their regional concerns. But Robert Jackson is skeptical—he fears that an American-style system of lax discipline leaves the door open to the excessive influence of special interests on members' voting decisions.

But is there another model that could be followed? As Kilgour notes, in Great Britain, members of the House of Commons may vote against their party without fear of recrimination on issues that are understood by all not to constitute a vote of confidence. Accordingly, a government may be defeated on a particular bill and still survive. It is suggested that such a practice allows MPs some independence in the legislature without putting at risk the life of a government.

Those wishing to understand how Britain has dealt with the issue of party discipline should read John Schwarz, "Exploring a New Role in Policymaking: The British House of Commons in the 1970s," *American Political Science Review* 74, no. 1 (March 1980), p. 23–37. Schwarz examines the changes made to British parliamentary traditions to permit a greater amount of "cross-voting." He argues that these changes have greatly strengthened the role of the House of Commons in the legislative process.

Not everyone is convinced that the British experience can be readily adapted to Canada. C.E.S. Franks, in *The Parliament of Canada* (Toronto: University of Toronto Press, 1987), notes that there are a number of factors that make the British experience unique. Because of the much larger number of members in the British House of Commons, party discipline is much harder to enforce. A large number of safe seats, in which MPs are confident that they will win reelection, make them less dependent on party patronage for their postparliamentary livelihood. The cabinet in Britain is much smaller. Long-serving MPs from safe seats, who are not obsessed with promotion to the cabinet, are much less likely to succumb to the brandishing of their leader, as both Margaret Thatcher and John Major have learned to their chagrin. In contrast, there is a much higher turnover among Canadian MPs, who generally do not feel secure enough to challenge a leader they feel is necessary to their own reelection chances.

The applicability of the British experience to Canada is also explored in Peter Dobell, "Some Comments on Party Reform," in Peter Aucoin, ed., *Institutional Reforms for Representative Government* (Toronto: University of Toronto Press, 1985). Dobell is not optimistic about the prospect of Canadian party leaders relinquishing their strong control over party discipline in the near future. However, he does propose some minor modifications that would give some flexibility to individual MPs.

During his tenure in office, Jean Chrétien tended to take a tough stance on party discipline, not infrequently removing backbenchers for committee assignments or threatening to not sign their nomination papers either for voting against the government or even for absenting themselves from votes. Before succeeding Jean Chrétien as prime minister, Paul Martin, in a speech in October 2002, outlined the ways in which he would bring about parliamentary reforms to enhance the voice of MPs, strengthen accountability, and relax party discipline. His announced plan would introduce a system of identifying three types of parliamentary votes. Only a limited number of votes on "fundamental issues" would require full party support. A second level of votes would require members of cabinet to support the government but allow other party members to vote free from party discipline. And the third category of votes would allow all MPs to vote as they wished, without the pressure of party discipline. Martin noted that this would make up the majority of parliamentary votes in the future. For an analysis of Martin's proposals, see Peter Aucoin and Lori Turnbull, "The Democratic Deficit: Paul Martin and Parliamentary Reform," *Canadian Public Administration* 46, no. 4 (Winter 2003).

On becoming prime minister, Martin kept his promise and implemented the new way of classifying votes. During his time in office, the majority of bills fell into the second category. Two bills were defeated during Martin's minority government, both relating to government organizational issues relating to the division of foreign affairs from international trade. But since the government did not consider these confidence measures, their defeat did not bring down the government. Martin's government fell on a straightforward non-confidence motion in November 2005. Despite Martin's professed flexibility, he did expel Carolyn Parish from the caucus when her outspoken criticism of the United States had become an embarrassment to the government, and two other Liberal MPs, including David Kilgour, left the caucus over disagreements with policy. Since coming to office, the government of Stephen Harper, facing a minority situation, has tended to take a more reassertive approach to party discipline, dismissing Garth Turner from the caucus for his criticism of some Conservative policies. And, in March 2007, Harper expelled Nova Scotia MP Bill Casey from the caucus for voting against the government's budget, arguing that the equalization formula that it contained amounted to gutting of the 2005 Atlantic Accord negotiated between the provinces and the federal government.

Is a Mixed-Member Proportional Electoral System in Canada's Interest?

✔ **YES**
JOHN L. HIEMSTRA AND HAROLD J. JANSEN, "Getting What You Vote For"

✘ **NO**
NELSON WISEMAN, "Not Knowing What You'll Get"

Canadian elections produce curious results. In the 2000 federal election, the victorious Liberal Party won the majority of seats with less than a majority of the popular vote. In the national election of 2004, the same Liberal Party failed to get the majority of the seats, but the percentage of seats it won was greater than the percentage of voters it attracted. In the 2001 B.C. election, the winning party won nearly all of the seats while securing only 58 percent of vote; in the 1997 New Brunswick election, the provincial Liberals did win *all* the seats—with only 60 percent of the vote. Clearly, in all these elections, the winners got more than they deserved. Just as clearly, it meant that the losers received less than they deserved. In the 2004 federal election, the NDP received almost 16 percent of the vote but managed to win only 6 percent of the seats (and in the federal election of 2006 the percentages were eighteen and nine); in the two aforementioned provincial elections, the losing parties attracted 40 percent of the vote while winning almost no seats.

On viewing these outcomes, one might be tempted to conclude that the Canadian electoral process had simply got the math wrong. Surely, the percentage of seats won should roughly reflect the percentage of votes won. But that is not how elections work in Canada. Instead, the electoral system divides the country into constituencies or ridings and then declares the winner in each constituency to be the one who receives the most votes. With these rules, a party may win many seats by small margins, with the result that the disjunction between the distribution of seats and votes emerges. In the Canadian electoral system, there is no reward for coming second, third, or any place other than first. Only the candidate with the greatest number of votes gets to sit in legislative assemblies. It is this quality that leads to the curious results.

Of course, an explanation is not a defence. For some, the single-member plurality system, the name commonly given to Canada's election system, is unacceptable. The system plainly distorts the preferences of voters; it gives some parties too many seats and others too few. In a democracy, it might be argued that an electoral system should strive to represent the true wishes of the people. But this fails to occur in Canada. Accordingly, various types of proportional representation (PR) electoral systems have been proposed to establish a greater equality between the percentage of votes and percentage of seats won. One type of PR system has become especially popular: this is the mixed-member proportional (MMP) system. Under MMP, some seats are still selected through the old system, but others are allocated in such a way to ensure that in the end the percentage of seats is proportional to the percentage of votes. One of the attractions of MMP is that it soothes the concerns of those who feel that we are moving too fast with electoral reform. MMP manages to mix the old with the new, a seemingly acceptable arrangement.

But many still remain uncomfortable with MMP and PR in general. Some feel this way because they fear that the reforms inevitably lead to weak coalition governments, while others believe that proportional representation produces elected officials without any constituency responsibilities. Arguably, a more important concern is the inability of PR systems to work well with the possibility of the cycling of majorities in government. Research has shown that voting can lead to one majority being easily trumped by another. PR proponents claim that their system will more accurately reflect the will of the people, but the fact is that there is no one majority that registers the wishes of the electorate—there are many. In light of the inherent instability of government actions, it might be preferable to have an electoral system that allows voters to more easily identify elected officials responsible for the offerings of government. If so, MMP and other versions of PR become unattractive because of their tendency to produce multiparty coalitions. Alternatively, the single-member plurality system (SMP) looks ideal because it usually elects single-party majority governments. In coalition governments, the existence of many policy-makers makes it easier to escape responsibility; in majority governments, the presence of only one party enhances efforts directed at ensuring accountability.

At various times, the reform of the electoral system has been an important issue. Now seems to be such a time. The results of recent elections have led to serious questioning of the plurality system (though, admittedly, the general public evinces little concern). In the past few years, three provinces have held referenda on electoral change, two of which asked the citizenry whether MMP should be introduced. However, the fact that in two of the referendums a majority of the voters rejected change while the third failed to meet the required level of support suggests that the questioning has not been enough to cause electoral reform. But it is unlikely this issue will disappear soon, for perceptions of the failings of the single-member system are too widespread.

In the debate, John Hiemstra, Harold Jansen, and Nelson Wiseman wrangle over the merits of introducing a system of MMP in Canada. Hiemstra is a professor of political science at King's University College in Edmonton, while Jansen teaches at the University of Lethbridge. Nelson Wiseman is a professor of political science at the University of Toronto. A point of clarification: as evident from Wiseman's essay, the Canadian system is sometimes called 'first-past-the-post.'

✔ YES
Getting What You Vote For
JOHN L. HIEMSTRA AND HAROLD J. JANSEN

In the past few years, we have seen citizens in many Canadian provinces take a close look at the way they elect representatives to their provincial legislatures. Although none of these proposed reforms has yet to be implemented (even though almost 60% of British Columbians voted for change in 2005), the activity shows that more and more Canadians have become aware of and concerned about the way they elect their representatives: the single-member plurality electoral system. Their concerns are well-founded. An almost universally accepted principle of democracy is that governments should make decisions by majority rule. The plurality system rarely produces conditions in which this happens and thereby fails to reflect Canadians' political opinions in the House of Commons. In fact, using the plurality electoral system to elect members of Parliament (MPs) to the House deepens divisions within Canada, weakens the accountability of MPs to electors, and undermines representative democracy. In short, it is time for the federal government to join those provinces that have taken a close look at their electoral systems.[1]

This essay argues that the plurality method for electing MPs to the House of Commons should be replaced with a system of proportional representation (PR). There are many variants of PR in use around the world, but the one we advocate for Canada is a mixed-member proportional (MMP) electoral system. MMP would make every vote count, enhance national unity, give an accurate reflection of the political opinions of Canadians in the House, and strengthen MPs' sense of obligation to the voters. This essay draws on national and provincial examples to make this case, since both levels currently use the plurality electoral system.

A MODEST REFORM

In Canadian federal elections, we use the current single-member plurality electoral system to decide who will be our representatives in the House of Commons. The country is divided into 308 single-member districts, each of which elects one MP to the House. The winner in each district is decided by the plurality formula. Simply put, the candidate in a riding who wins more votes than the other candidates—even if less than 50 percent—is the winner and takes the seat as MP in the House of Commons.[2]

Adopting MMP would require only modest reforms to our current system; it could be implemented by a simple act of Parliament and without a constitutional amendment. The number of federal MPs per province is determined by several factors, of which population is the most important. Under the plurality system, the provinces are carved into geographical electoral districts, with one MP elected in each district. Under MMP, this would continue to happen, but only half of the

MPs allocated to each province would represent single-member districts as they do now. The other half would be chosen from party lists provided by the parties and would be awarded to each party in such a way as to ensure that each party's representation in Parliament matches its share of the popular vote in that province.

For example, under the plurality formula in 2006, the Conservative Party won every single one of Alberta's 28 seats. If the election had been held under MMP,[3] fourteen MPs would have been elected in single-member districts. The Conservatives would likely have won all of those. The remaining fourteen MPs would not represent specific districts but would be divided between the parties to make sure that their overall share of Alberta's representation in Parliament reflected their share of the vote. These MPs would be elected off of party lists provided by each party. The Conservatives' 65 percent of the vote would have entitled them to nineteen of the overall 28 Alberta MPs, so five list MPs would have been added to the fourteen MPs elected in single-member districts, bringing their total to nineteen. None of the other parties would have won any seats in single-member districts, but their share of the overall vote would have entitled them to seats—the Liberals would have been awarded four list seats, the NDP three, and the Green Party two seats. In this way, MMP would ensure each party earned the number of seats to which it was entitled.[4]

Although calculating the number of seats each party would receive is more complicated than under the plurality system, voting in a federal election under MMP would be straightforward. Voters would vote twice: once for the candidate they would like to represent their particular district in the House of Commons and a second vote for the party list they prefer. The local candidate they support may even be from a different party. Voters in countries around the world seem to have no trouble using MMP; there is no reason to expect that Canadians would either.

There are many variations in how MMP systems have been implemented throughout the world. But the increased popularity of MMP reflects an emerging consensus that MMP systems offer the "best of both worlds."[5] Voters continue to have an individual MP who is "theirs" and can deal with problems they are having with government, one of the advantages of the plurality system. At the same time, voters benefit from having their ideas reflected accurately in our national deliberative chamber, the House of Commons. Clearly, this is the major advantage of proportional representation; an MMP system would ensure that voters consistently get what they actually voted for.

MAKING EVERY VOTE COUNT

As a democratic state, all Canadians should have a say in composing the House of Commons, since it deliberates on and approves the laws that govern us all. Sadly, Canada's plurality electoral system repeatedly fails to deliver just and equitable representation when it allows the "winner to take all."

An electoral system is unjust when it fails to give each vote its due. This is frequently the case with the plurality system. In the 1997 federal election, for example, more than 60 percent of voters supported parties other than the Liberal Party, yet they were represented in the House of Commons by less than half of the members of Parliament. In 1984, the Progressive Conservatives won half the vote but won three-quarters of the seats in the House of Commons. Seen another way, the other half of the electorate had their views represented by only a quarter of the MPs. In 2006, 51.2 percent of voters cast votes for candidates who did not get elected. Thus, they ended up being represented by MPs they did not vote for and a party they did not support. The plurality system effectively disenfranchised a majority of the voters in the 2006 election.[6]

The injustice done by the plurality electoral formula is illustrated even better by the results of two recent provincial elections. In the 2001 British Columbia provincial election, Gordon Campbell's Liberal Party won 97 percent of the seats (77 out of 79) with only 58 percent of the vote. That left the 21 percent of voters who supported the NDP with only two seats, and the 21 percent who supported other parties with none. In the 2007 election, Newfoundland and Labrador's popular premier was reelected with almost 70% of the vote, but he took 92 percent of the seats. Even more dramatically, the plurality system can give every seat to one party, as happened in the 1987 New Brunswick election, when Frank McKenna's Liberal Party won 100 percent of the seats with 60 percent of the popular vote. This left the other 40 percent of the voters unrepresented by the parties they supported. Besides misrepresenting the views of voters, the single-member plurality system in these cases returned very small oppositions, making it difficult for legislatures to hold the government accountable, the traditional function of oppositions in our British-style parliamentary system. These are not isolated cases, either. In the words of one of Canada's leading scholars of political parties and elections, lopsided provincial election results are the "dirty little secret" of provincial politics.[7]

The other serious defect in the plurality electoral system is its inequity; that is, it often makes your vote count for less than others. For example, in the 2000 federal election, 1,051,209 voters in Ontario supported the Canadian Alliance party, but the plurality system gave it only two seats in that province. In British Columbia, the plurality system rewarded the 797,518 Canadian Alliance voters with twenty-seven seats. In other words, it took fewer than 30,000 B.C. Alliance voters to elect an MP, while in Ontario, it took over half a million to do so. Clearly, the vote of an Alliance supporter in British Columbia was worth a lot more than a vote in Ontario.

Plurality is a "winner takes all" system that almost always overrewards the winning party. In contrast, MMP is widely recognized as more just and equitable, in that it accurately translates the percentage of the vote each party wins into a proportionate percentage of seats in the House of Commons. MMP would greatly reduce the injustice and inequity experienced by voters under the plurality system. In short, MMP would give you what you vote for, which is reason enough to adopt it in Canada.

MMP AND GOVERNMENT EFFECTIVENESS

Proportional representation systems such as MMP are almost always acknowledged as the fairest electoral systems.[8] Yet some still reject any kind of PR for Canada because they fear it would make the government ineffective. They argue that the plurality method produces stable and effective majority governments out of minority electoral returns, while MMP would produce unstable and ineffective minority governments. Canadians should not have to choose between effective government and a just and equitable electoral system. Fortunately, the experiences of other countries show that PR electoral systems offer both improved representation and effective government. It is easy to selectively present specific examples of other countries where either a proportional or plurality electoral system has worked well or not well, but the most valuable evidence comes from studies that systematically incorporate the experience of several countries. Arend Lijphart, a noted expert on electoral systems, did just this in a comparative study of established democracies and found that countries using PR maintain public order and manage the economy as well as countries that use majoritarian electoral systems, such as plurality.[9]

Besides this comparative evidence, we can look at Canada's experience with minority governments. Canada has had effective government since well before Confederation. Yet there does not seem to be any connection between this effectiveness and the plurality electoral system's ability to produce majority governments. In the fifteen elections since 1962, Canada's plurality system produced seven minority governments, which is not exactly a stellar record.[10] In spite of these minority governments, Canada's governments have generally been effective. In his seminal study of Canada's Parliament, C.E.S. Franks concludes that "there is no evidence that minority parliaments are less efficient than majorities."[11]

It is true that minority governments have tended to fall more quickly than majority governments in Canada. However, this is less due to the inherent instability of minority governments than to the incentive the plurality system gives to some parties to collapse minority governments. The large parties know that a small shift in the vote toward their party will often be magnified into a large increase in seats and into a majority government for them. The Liberal Party lost the 1979 election, for example, but, after bringing down a minority Conservative government, recaptured a majority government in 1980 with only a 4 percent shift in the popular vote! This incentive to collapse a minority government would be neutralized by PR.

If Canada adopted MMP, minority and coalition governments would undoubtedly be more common. But we have already seen that the frequent minority governments under the plurality system do not render the government ineffective. Nor is it the case that coalition governments are automatically weak or unstable. In PR systems like MMP, political parties normally win a steady percentage of the vote in each election. Since forcing an election under MMP would likely not dramatically alter party strengths, parties are encouraged to work for just policy compromises within Parliament. Thus, coalition governments will be able to "get things done" for Canada. The improvement is that coalitions get things done while involving a majority of the MPs who truly represent a majority of Canadians. PR gets rid of artificial majority governments that make decisions on important issues such as health care reform or climate change with the support of less than half of the voters.

Critics also suggest that PR causes unstable governments by promoting too many small parties. Under plurality, however, Canada has already produced many small parties, a contradiction of "Duverger's law," which asserts that a plurality electoral system tends to produce a two-party system. This diversity of smaller parties should not be denied, since it reflects the real political views of Canadians. Moreover, except for Ontario and Quebec, the provincewide lists required by MMP would have relatively few MPs. Thus, parties would still require a significant proportion of the vote to earn a seat in the House of Commons from these party lists, in turn discouraging splinter parties.

Canada has remained stable even though the plurality system has produced repeated minority governments and has encouraged destabilizing regional parties. The reason for this is Canada's strong, democratic, and tolerant political culture. Adopting MMP would not suddenly change this. Nor would MMP transform Canada into an unstable regime like pre–World War II Weimar Germany.[12] Canada's strong, democratic political culture has kept and will continue to keep our system stable. Canada with MMP would more likely resemble modern Germany, which has used MMP for over five decades and remains eminently stable and unified.[13]

MMP CAN INCREASE NATIONAL UNITY

Some critics also argue that MMP would weaken national unity. They charge that it would magnify divisions between regions and between English and French cultures. They claim that, although the plurality electoral system has treated this diversity unfairly, at least this system has kept our country stable and united. The facts show, however, that quirks in plurality actually serve to worsen these divisions in Canada.

One way the plurality system undermines national unity is by "rewarding" small, regionally concentrated parties. Canadian history is full of examples of small, regional parties that have won substantial representation in Parliament. Parties like the Progressives, Social Credit, the Creditistes, and the Reform Party have flourished under a plurality electoral system by being able to translate a relatively small number of votes into a relatively large share of the seats. Particularly troublesome is the tendency of plurality to reward regionally concentrated parties that, in some cases, have promoted separatism or a sectional view of Canada. The plurality system has multiplied their negative impact by rewarding them with far more seats than their electoral support warrants. In the 2006 federal election, for example, the separatist Bloc Québécois (BQ) won 68 percent of the seats in Quebec with the support of only 42 percent of Quebec voters. In 1997 and 2000, fewer than 40 percent of Quebec's voters supported the Bloc, but both times it still won a majority of the province's seats in the House of Commons. This also occurred in Quebec provincial elections, where the plurality system has allowed the separatist Parti Québécois to form four majority governments even though the party has *never* won a majority of the votes. In 1998, the PQ won a majority government (76 out of 125 seats) with 42.9 percent of the vote, but the provincial Liberal Party won the support of more Quebec voters, with 43.6 percent of the vote! Because of this, Quebec is one of the provinces seriously debating the merits of adopting PR.[14]

Another way the plurality electoral system weakens national unity is by robbing seats from small, nationally oriented parties with supporters dispersed across the country. For example, the NDP is a national party with a social democratic vision that has some support in all regions of the country. Yet, under the plurality system, it always receives fewer seats in the House of Commons than its support would justify. In the 2006 federal election, for example, the NDP earned only 29 seats (9.4 percent) in the House of Commons, even though the party earned 17.5 percent of the vote, spread across the country. Even more shocking is that a million more Canadians voted for the NDP than supported the BQ, but the NDP won 22 fewer seats! Under MMP, the NDP would have won 55 seats (from every province in Canada except P.E.I.), a fair reflection of its national support. Unfortunately, the plurality system hurts small parties with support dispersed across the regions, even when they try to appeal to all Canadians, wherever they might live.

The plurality system also weakens national unity by overrewarding large parties in regions where they have strong support while underrewarding them where their support is weak. Thus, Canada often lacks truly national parties in the House. When large parties win the majority of the seats in one region but none in another region, they have the incentive to cater to one region, so divisions in Canada are perpetuated and worsened. For example, in the 1980 federal election, the Liberal Party formed the government but did not win a single seat in British Columbia, Alberta, or Saskatchewan, although it won over 20 percent of the vote in these provinces. Meanwhile, it won 74 of 75 seats, or 99 percent of the seats, in Quebec with 68 percent of the popular vote. In 2004, over one and a half times as many people voted for the Conservative Party in Quebec than in Saskatchewan, but the plurality system's distortions gave the Conservatives thirteen seats in Saskatchewan, and none in Quebec. While the Conservatives are undoubtedly strongest in the West, the electoral system does not reflect the depth of their support in Central and Eastern Canada. Even the Liberal Party, when it enjoyed relatively widespread national support, was a victim of this distortion. Only 46 percent of the total votes received by the Liberals in 2004 were cast in Ontario, but 56 percent of Liberal MPs came from that province, exacerbating the perception that the Liberals are only an "Ontario party." This flaw leads voters to develop a regionally skewed perception of the parties' support. It also handicaps the governing and opposition parties' ability to include regional viewpoints in their caucus discussions. In fact, plurality gives parties an incentive to favour regions where they might receive large electoral payoffs, while ignoring other regions.

The weaknesses of the plurality system, Alan Cairns concludes, make Canada's electoral system "divisive and detrimental to national unity."[15] MMP is a better way to handle Canada's regional divisions, since it gives seats to national parties in direct proportion to the percentage of popular vote they win in the election. Since every vote counts in MMP, parties have a strong incentive to take a national viewpoint on issues and to search for votes in all regions. While MMP allows voters to develop and support regional parties, it does not unfairly reward these parties. It also encourages the growth of parties that will integrate the regions of Canada.[16]

THE PLURALITY SYSTEM PRODUCES FALSE MAJORITY GOVERNMENTS

Another claim for the plurality electoral system is that it allows voters to select a government at the same time as they elect their representatives. Indeed, forming a cabinet is largely routine in Canada's parliamentary system, where the party winning the most seats usually forms the government. But it is an illusion to suggest that voters purposefully or automatically select a government. In fact, the majority of Canadians have not been involved in selecting most of Canada's governments. Since World War II, only two of our national governments have been formed by a party that won a majority of the popular vote in an election (1958 and 1984).[17] Over time, the plurality system is producing governments with a majority of seats but resting on the support of an increasingly small proportion of the electorate.[18]

In practice, the plurality system routinely allows a minority of voters to select the majority of the seats, and thus determine the government. This problem with plurality is closely related to Canada's multiparty system. In the 1997 federal election, when five major parties contested the election, the plurality system translated the Liberals' 38.5 percent of the vote into a majority government. These results were not an anomaly; such distortions occur repeatedly in federal and provincial elections. The fact that there are four parties in Parliament reflects the diversity of political visions in Canada's political culture, a reality that ought to be reflected in our foremost representative and debating legislative chamber.

The plurality electoral system also allows a small shift in the vote to determine who will form the next government. In the 1979 election, Joe Clark's Conservatives were supported by 36 percent of Canadians and took 48 percent of the seats to form a minority government. The Liberals gathered 40 percent of the vote and took 40 percent of the seats. In the 1980 election, the Liberals increased their share of the vote by only 4 percent but won a clear majority government with 52 percent of the seats. And in the following election of 1984, a shift of 17 percent of the vote to the Mulroney-led Tories allowed the Progressive Conservatives to increase their seats by 38 percent, from 37 percent to 75 percent of the seats!

Defenders of the plurality electoral system often cite this property of the plurality system as a desirable feature. They argue that the sensitivity of the plurality system to small shifts in the popular vote allow voters to defeat governments. Besides the question of whether it is appropriate for a tiny minority of voters to determine who will or will not form a government, the problem is that this mechanism works very inconsistently under plurality. While a shift in the popular vote may cause a change of government, just as often, it does not! The actual seat totals depend on a number of factors, including the regional distribution of the vote, the number of political parties, and the division of the vote between these parties. The relationship between seats and votes under the plurality system is not a smooth line on a graph; it is far more random than that. This type of chancy outcome in the formation of governments under plurality is illustrated pointedly in two provincial elections in British Columbia. The NDP failed to form the government in 1986 when its 42.6 percent of the vote translated into 31.9 percent of the seats. In the 1991 election, however, NDP popular support dropped to 41 percent of the vote, yet it took 68 percent of the seats and formed the new government. Sometimes, plurality allows a party to win more seats and form the government with fewer votes than the main opposition party. In the 1979 federal election, for example, the Conservatives formed a minority government when they won 36 percent of the vote and 136 seats while the Liberals won 40 percent of the vote and only 114 seats. This "wrong winner" phenomenon is even more common in provincial elections, most recently in the 2006 New Brunswick election, when the Liberals won a majority government despite the fact that more voters supported the Progressive Conservative party. Had then PC premier Bernard Lord followed the recommendation of his Commission on Legislative Democracy and implemented an MMP system, he might still have been premier!

Selecting a government through the plurality electoral system has the further side effect of distorting the public's perception of the parties' strengths. A month after the 1988 federal election, nobody remembered that the Tories won 57 percent of the seats with only 43 percent of the vote. The public is constantly reminded of the percentage of seats a party won, but not the percentage of the vote it won. This fake majority of seats is then leveraged into a rhetorical "popular mandate" to adopt their policy platform! For example, Prime Minister Mulroney used his minority electoral support to pass the highly unpopular Goods and Service Tax, as well as the controversial Free Trade Agreement with the U.S.A. In a democracy, majorities ought to consult minorities in making policy; the plurality system allows minorities to determine policy without necessarily having to consult the majority.

The plurality system is often associated with a party system with only two political parties. The diversity and complexity of Canadian society, however, has meant that Canada has developed many political parties. It is a mistake to think that we can solve the problems created by the plurality system by wishing the country had a two-party system rather than reforming the electoral system itself to reflect the realities of Canadian society. We must accept that Canadians have deeply held political views and choose different parties to express these views. Political parties ought to play the critical role of providing an integrated set of principles around which they harmonize the many diverse and sometimes conflicting policies into a coherent platform. This would give voters a real choice. The democratic answer to voter differences is to amend our electoral system so that it responds to the diversity of beliefs and actions of Canadians, and not to force the current system to produce the result the critics want. The real challenge is to allow the deeply held political views of Canadians to be properly, safely, and fairly expressed and accommodated in politics. People with different ethnic, religious, or ideological views often arrive at, or endorse, a particular policy for their own distinct reasons. An MMP system will give no viewpoint a hegemonic grip on the system, instead forcing all parties to discuss their real differences as a means of arriving at mutually acceptable policies. The end result is that governments elected by proportional representation tend to reflect the preferred policies of citizens much better than do those elected by the plurality system.[19]

Since MMP would make the House of Commons accurately reflect the opinions and views of Canadians, it would be better to shift the duty of forming governments away from "chance" and to our MPs. This would give the majority of voters a stronger say in the creation of government. It would place the task of forming governments in the hands of our MPs who currently hold the power of dissolving governments. This conforms with and develops Canada's parliamentary theory.

THE PLURALITY SYSTEM WEAKENS REPRESENTATIVE DEMOCRACY

Indeed, voters would have a greater say over all aspects of their MPs' actions if MPs were obliged to represent their supporting voters. What we see in Canada today is that the plurality electoral system is weakening representative democracy. Representative democracy was created in response to the increasing number of citizens entitled to be involved in politics but who lack the time or energy to study political issues and devise fitting solutions. Most Canadians expect their representatives to engage actively in policymaking for them. Even so, plurality fails to give representatives a clear mandate from the voters and does not allow voters to hold MPs responsible for their actions.

Instead, the plurality system is increasingly encouraging Canadians to weaken or even bypass representative democracy. The weakening of the relationship between voters and representatives occurs because plurality requires politicians and parties to compromise too early in the process. Before an election, politicians are forced to develop lowest common denominator policies that will appeal to a plurality of voters in each riding. For example, some voters believe the state should strongly intervene to protect the environment, while others believe market forces will correct environmental problems. In response to this spectrum of opinions, most political parties develop a compromised platform that homogenizes the environmental views of Canadians. While this is done to attract the wide range of voters necessary to win a plurality of votes in a single district, it undermines wide-ranging debate about environmental policy in the House of Commons.

Early compromises on policy produce pragmatic, look-alike parties. Election campaigns increasingly focus on party leaders and image and downplay principles, policy platforms, and the teams of politicians behind the leaders. Pragmatic parties make principled discussion rare in the House of Commons and foreclose the opportunity for accommodation between principled party platforms. Consequently, voters seldom know what their MPs and parties stand for and find it difficult to hold them accountable. At the same time, MPs do not receive clear mandates from voters. In these and other respects, plurality weakens the relationship between voters and representatives.

Increasingly, voters are turning away from these indistinct parties. Many are abandoning the electoral process altogether, as Canada's decreasing levels of voter turnout indicate.[20] Some are turning to interest groups for better representation. Political parties are responding to this challenge to their representative role by merely becoming brokers for interest groups. Other voters are pushing reforms such as recall, referenda, and initiative, which bypass representative democracy.[21] Thus, the dynamic set in motion by plurality actually encourages voters to bypass their representatives, a process that is undermining the very essence of representative democracy.

IMPROVING THE QUALITY OF REPRESENTATION

In opposition to plurality, an MMP electoral system would strengthen Canada's political system by encouraging a new dynamic. MMP encourages strong political parties, but would also encourage them to define how they are distinct from the others in order to attract votes. In order to compete effectively, parties would need to develop clearer principles and to define their policy platforms. This would allow political parties to become vehicles for voters to give mandates to MPs and to hold them accountable between elections. MPs would clearly be obliged to act in accordance with the principles and policies that they agreed to with supporters. This would include serving the individual voters according to these principles, if the parties want to maintain electoral support. MPs with a sense of obligation to voters would be a clear advance over the plurality system that limits voters to rubber-stamping or jettisoning representatives at election time.

One common criticism of MMP systems is that they create "two classes" of MPs, namely, those elected in single-member districts and party list MPs. The argument is that those MPs who represent single-member districts have different responsibilities than those who are elected from party lists. The evidence from Germany, the country with the longest experience with MMP, suggests that such concerns are misplaced. The German experience has been that party list MPs do get involved in constituency work, often focusing on single-member districts where their party lost. There is also little evidence in the German case to suggest that party list MPs are more likely to be cabinet ministers than MPs elected by plurality.[22]

Again, although we can point to specific exceptions in both proportional and plurality electoral systems, the overall evidence from other countries shows that PR has been superior to the plurality electoral system in bringing minority parties into legislatures, thereby improving the quality of representation. It has also increased the parliamentary representation of women, ethnic groups, and cultural minorities.[23] Significantly, PR has done so without extensive affirmative action programs. PR has also allowed parties to improve the overall quality of individual MPs on their lists. PR also allows citizens to be free to join the political party of their choice and to decide whether their party's MPs will be "trustees" who will independently deliberate on issues; "delegates" who mechanically reflect their views; "mirrors" that reflect their gender, age, ethnic, or other characteristics; or defenders of their party's interests and positions.[24] If "party bosses" dominate under MMP, it will be the fault of those who create parties that tolerate them and of the voters who support them. When this has proven to be a significant problem, many countries have developed systems that allow voters to change the order of the names on the list, thus removing some of the control party officials have over who gets elected.

MMP allows parties and governments to be as good or as flawed as the people they represent. It leaves the public free to decide which groups or principles or approaches it wants represented, by creating parties to reflect these concerns. MMP ultimately leaves the voters to decide which parties they want to be represented by in the House of Commons. For example, if 7 percent of Canadians support the Green Party's approach to environmental issues, MMP will give it 7 percent of the seats, no more and no less.

CONCLUSION

Democratic principles are the foundation upon which political life in Canada rests. The plurality and MMP electoral systems are structures through which Canadians can exercise their democratic choices. But structures are not neutral. They reflect values that the people in a society want the system to advance and thus encourage citizens to act in a certain way. The dominant value of our current plurality system is stability—which it is supposed to achieve by translating a minority of votes into a majority government. In spite of the plurality electoral system, however, Canada has frequently produced minority governments. The plurality system also produces electoral outcomes that aggravate and intensify Canada's regional divisions. Too many outcomes of the plurality electoral system have been chancy, unfair, and inequitable. Also, plurality has encouraged the growth of pragmatic and brokerage parties that weaken the incentives of MPs to represent their voters. In spite of these problems, Canada remains a stable, democratic political system.

Since Canada is stable in spite of the plurality system, it has ample room to add the values of justice and equity to stability by adopting an MMP electoral system. MMP makes every vote count and produces results that are proportionate to what voters desire. MMP would also best serve Canada's distinctive needs. It would increase Canada's stability by improving regional representation in major parties, while reducing the unjustified strength of small, divisive parties that happen to have regionally concentrated support.

The biggest asset of MMP, however, is that it enhances representative democracy by encouraging MPs and parties to develop a clearer profile on principles and policies. Voters will have a better idea of the mandate they are giving to MPs and thus be able to hold MPs accountable for their principles, policies, and political actions. An MMP electoral system should be adopted in Canada since it is the fairest and most effective way to fix Canada's real democratic deficit.

NOTES

1. In October 2004, when British Columbia's Citizens Assembly on Electoral Reform recommended that B.C. adopt the single transferable vote form of proportional representation, 57.7 percent of British Columbians voted to accept the recommendation, just short of the 60% threshold the government had set for the change. B.C. voters will vote again on the proposal in 2009. Quebec introduced a draft bill that would replace its single-member plurality electoral system with a form of MMP. Sixty-three percent of Prince Edward Islanders voted to retain the single-member plurality system in a plebiscite in 2005. New Brunswick's Commission on Legislative Democracy recommended that New Brunswick adopt a mixed-member proportional electoral system, but the recommendations have not been acted on. In a referendum in 2007, Ontario electors voted to keep their single-member plurality system over the mixed-member proportional system proposed by its Citizens' Assembly. See the essays in Henry Milner, ed., *Steps toward Making Every Vote Count: Electoral System Reform in Canada and Its Provinces* (Peterborough: Broadview, 2004), and Harold J. Jansen, "Making the Impossible Possible: Electoral Reform and Canada's Provinces," in Thomas M.J. Bateman and Rick Myers, eds., *Braving the New World: Readings in Contemporary Politics*, 4th. ed. (Scarborough: Nelson, 2008).

2. Only 40 percent of MPs elected in 2006 won their seats with a majority of the vote in their constituencies. In fact, one MP won a seat with the support of fewer than a third of the voters in his constituency! This is not unusual: in 2004, only 44% of MPs won their seats with a majority of the vote.

3. We are assuming that half of the seats would be allocated in single-member districts, and the other half would be allocated from party lists for the entire province. We are also assuming that voters would support the same party with their list vote as they supported in single-member districts.

4. See David M. Farrell, *Electoral Systems: A Comparative Introduction* (New York: Palgrave, 2001), pp. 97–111, for more details on how MMP works in Germany. See the Law Commission of Canada, *Voting Counts: Electoral Reform in Canada* (Ottawa: Law Commission of Canada, 2004), pp. 83–125, for a detailed discussion on how MMP might be implemented in Canada.

5. Matthew Soberg Shugart, "'Extreme' Electoral Systems and the Appeal of the Mixed-Member Alternative," in Matthew Soberg Shugart and Martin P. Wattenberg, eds., *Mixed-Member Electoral Systems: The Best of Both Worlds* (Oxford: Oxford University Press, 2001), pp. 25–51.

6. This is not an unusual result; in 2004, a majority of Canadian voters (50.2%) voted for a candidate in their riding who did not win.

7. R. Ken Carty, "Doing Democracy Differently: Has Electoral Reform Finally Arrived?" Timlin Lecture, March 1, 2004, University of Saskatchewan.

8. Andrew Reynolds and Ben Reilly, *The International IDEA Handbook of Electoral System Design* (Stockholm: International Institute for Democracy and Electoral Assistance, 1997), p. 62.

9. Arend Lijphart, "Democracies: Forms, Performance, and Constitutional Engineering," *European Journal of Political Research* 25 (1994), pp. 1–17; see also Arend Lijphart, *Patterns of Democracy: Government Forms and Performance in Thirty-Six Countries* (New Haven: Yale University Press, 1999), chs. 15 and 16.

10. The plurality system not only fails to produce regular majority governments but frequently fails to produce the strong oppositions needed to effectively run a parliamentary system. See Alan C. Cairns, "The Electoral System and Party System in Canada, 1921–1965," *Canadian Journal of Political Science* 1 (1968), pp. 55–80.

11. C.E.S. Franks, *The Parliament of Canada* (Toronto: University of Toronto Press, 1987), p. 50.

12. Enid Lakeman reports that if Weimar Germany had used plurality, the Nazis would likely have won *all* the seats, cited in Michael Lind, "A Radical Plan to Change American Politics," *The Atlantic Monthly* 270, no. 2 (August 1992), pp. 73–83.

13. In a review of the research on this question, Louis Massicotte, "Changing the Canadian Electoral System," *Choices* 7, no. 1 (February 2001), p. 21, states that claims of PR undermining democracy have been "discredited." Massicotte's study is updated in Paul Howe, Richard Johnston, and Andre Blais, eds., Strengthening Canadian Democracy (Montreal IRPP, 2005).

14. Quebec has introduced a draft bill to replace its electoral system with a form of MMP. See also Milner, "First Past the Post?" pp. 24–29.

15. Cairns, 92.

16. Harold J. Jansen and Alan Siaroff, "Regionalism and Party Systems: Evaluating Proposals to Reform Canada's Electoral System," in Henry Milner, ed., *Steps toward Making Every Vote Count* (Peterborough: Broadview, 2004), conclude that MMP would be among the best choices to prevent exacerbating regional conflicts.

17. Richard Katz, "Electoral Reform Is Not as Simple as It Appears," in Henry Milner, ed., *Making Every Vote Count* (Peterborough: Broadview, 1999), p. 101, points out that if rejected ballots are included in the vote totals for the 1984 election, then even the Mulroney government did not have the support of a majority of voters, leaving only one government that had the support of a majority of the electorate.

18. Richard Johnston, "Canadian Elections at the Millennium," *Choices* 6, no. 6 (September 2000). Updated version of article can be found in Howe, Johnston, and Blais eds., Strengthening Canadian Democracy.

19. G. Bingham Powell, Jr., *Elections as Instruments of Democracy: Majoritarian and Proportional Visions* (New Haven: Yale University Press, 2000), ch. 9.

20. Although there are certainly multiple causes for voter turnout levels, most comparative analyses of turnout find that proportional representation systems are associated with higher turnout. See Pippa Norris, *Electoral Engineering: Voting Rules and Political Behaviour* (Cambridge: Cambridge University Press, 2004), ch. 7.

21. See Nick Loenen, *Citizenship and Democracy: A Case for Proportional Representation* (Toronto: Dundurn, 1997), ch. 5, for a comparison of PR with these other reforms.

22. Louis Massicotte, Á *la recherche d'un mode de scrutin mixte compensatoire.* Document de travail, Québec, Secrétariat à la réforme des institutions démocratiques, Décembre 2004, ch. 8. Available online at http://www.institutions-democratiques. gouv.qc.ca/publications/mode_scrutin_rapport.pdf.

23. Norris, chapter 8, demonstrates that PR enhances the representation of women. The effect for ethnic minorities is more complex. The plurality system represents minorities well if they are geographically concentrated, but has a harder time when minorities are dispersed. See Norris, ch. 9.

24. Several conflicting definitions of representation confuse this debate; see Hanna Fenichel Pitkin, *The Concept of Representation* (Los Angeles: University of California Press, 1967).

✗ NO

Not Knowing What You'll Get
NELSON WISEMAN

One can only be a skeptical agonistic in predicting the consequences of adopting proportional representation. Once implemented, however, it will difficult to undo. The Burkean dictum "If it is not necessary to change, it is necessary not to change" is the philosophic conservatives' argument against embracing PR. For them, opposition to PR is based on the wisdom of historical experience. Some defenders of the status quo consider the devil they know preferable to the one they do not. Cynics intone that PR will not change much. Power, they claim, will be even more concentrated in the hands of party leaders and their coterie of apparatchiks because the commonly proposed variant of PR, mixed-member proportional (MMP), will likely leave the designation of the candidates elected by PR to party elites.

Stable countries seldom make radical institutional changes. They do not jump on bandwagons that cater willy-nilly to their era's temperament. Canada's fundamental political principles have been shaped without the use of PR. This means that such a change ought to be approached thoughtfully and cautiously. PR may have deleterious implications for the operation of other elements of Canada's institutional infrastructure. PR proponents generally ignore or gloss over them.

SIGNIFICANCE OF ELECTORAL SYSTEMS

The success or failure of polities has relatively little to do with their electoral systems. Canada, in a comparative international perspective, has not fared poorly with its first-past-the-post (FPTP) electoral system (another name for the Canadian system). It belongs to an elite group of states, making up only 13 percent of the world's population, categorized as "full democracies."[1] Some states that sport PR are flawed or flailing democracies. Some are authoritarian. They suffer a "democratic deficit"—the appealing but trite term Paul Martin pinned on Canada's political condition. Canada's policy outputs and quality of life are the envy of many in states with PR.

Immigrants are not deterred from coming to Canada because of its allegedly democratically deficient electoral system. Canadians, in turn, are not drawn to relocate to states such as Latvia, Bolivia, and Iraq because their PR systems represent irresistible democratic beacons. People in those states "know" less about what they are going to get in government policy and performance with their PR electoral systems than Canadians do with FPTP.

Political scientists are in the vanguard of PR's boosters. They consider themselves experts in institutional design. Most political scientists who weighed in on the Meech Lake and Charlottetown accords favoured those debacles too.[2] The accords, products of a hyperventilated constitutional reform industry, depleted the capital of the politicians who sponsored them and proved disintegrative for the polity. This has not, however, chastened many of the same political scientists from pursuing the reengineering of the electoral system via PR. Historians have been less sanguine about both mega-constitutional revisions and sweeping reforms of the electoral system. They have, perhaps, a better appreciation of the established institutions and traditions that have served Canadians well.

FPTP ought not to be judged solely by how precisely votes are converted into party seats. This is too narrow a gauge. What must also be weighed are the geographical, sociological, and historical contexts. Certainly, many states have fared well with PR. They have stable governments, progressive public policies, and honest public administration. PR's partisans are quick to cite states such as Germany and New Zealand. Other states, however, have done poorly with PR.

The United Kingdom and the United States are vibrant democracies that informed the adoption of Canada's FPTP system. India went from being a British colony, like Canada, to becoming the world's largest democracy, and it managed to do so with FPTP. FPTP is a very old institution, but that is an insufficient rationale for its dispatch. Marriage, the family, monarchy, and the church are old institutions, too, yet they are not dismissed as outmoded or obsolete. More vital to a state's welfare than its electoral system are its political cultural underpinnings. This refers to the health and vigour of its civil society, the independence and probity of its judiciary, its media freedoms, transparency and accountability in its public administration, informed dialogue and debate in the formulation of public policies, and the unfettered competition of political ideas. On these scores, any democratic audit of Canada must regard its electoral system as a sidebar. The term "democracy" is too readily bandied about in debates about the electoral system. Democracy has a kaleidoscopic quality that includes but profoundly transcends its electoral rules.

There are complex ramifications to any change in an electoral system. Change does not occur in an institutional vacuum. With PR, Canadians will still have their parliamentary system, their federal–provincial fandangos, and their beloved Charter of Rights. Canadians may be unhappy with their parliamentarians, but they want to keep their parliamentary system. That system arose in the context of two loosely knit parties, government and a "loyal" opposition ready to take the reins of office if the government falters. Canadian parliamentary practice evolved with new parties being accommodated within the FPTP system. Party discipline has increased dramatically and many lament this, but PR will reinforce and not reverse it. PR elections, if international experience is any guide, will also lead to the further proliferation of parliamentary parties.[3] This will likely accentuate popular frustration with Parliament.

Most Canadians are unaware that alternatives to the single-member plurality system are not alien to Canada's history. Public appetite for electoral reform was greater a century ago than it is today. In the 1920s, when the Progressives were in full flight as the second largest federal party, they agitated for PR. Parliament debated its merits and rejected it in a free vote.[4] As the Progressives and their causes quickly lost altitude, nothing came of the PR idea federally. Manitoba and Alberta adopted new electoral regimes that produced more proportionality, but that did not render them more democratic in terms of converting public opinion into public policy.

Manitoba used the Hare system of partial PR—with its single transferable ballot—between the early 1920s and late 1950s to elect MLAs in Winnipeg, which formed one large multi-member constituency.[5] In Manitoba's rural single-member ridings, the alternative or transferable ballot was used. In both cases, voters marked their ballots preferentially (1, 2, 3, and so on if they wished). The victor in rural ridings was declared only after securing 50 percent of the first and subsequently transferred ballots, while Winnipeg candidates required a vote total determined by a formula that divided the number of votes cast by the number of seats. Most of the elections led to coalition governments, but the CCF leader who joined one of them came to call it a "fool arrangement,"[6] a nightmare for his party. Most provinces have had multi-member constituencies at some time in their histories, and some adopted a religious denominational basis of representation. These were sometimes legally mandated (as in Newfoundland) and other times (as in Prince Edward Island and New Brunswick) they were governed by customs— unwritten but well understood and respected rules. British Columbia used the alternative vote in the 1950s. It also used dual-member constituencies that only disappeared in 1991.

Proponents of PR argue that the appearance of more parliamentary parties may be neutral because PR eliminates strategic voting. Voters can opt for their true preference rather than feeling they ought to plump for the lesser of evils, which is what many do under FPTP when they calculate that their preferred party has little chance of success in their riding. A proliferation of parties, however, may also have drawbacks. It may lead to governmental deadlock or produce a government whose agenda results in voters not getting what they thought they had voted for. PR will also further weaken an MP's discretion. Those elected on party lists, as in the MMP system, will be beholden to their party and not to riding constituents, since they will not be representing any constituency beyond their party.

DISAPPOINTMENTS OF PR

PR proponents often talk of it as a tonic for citizen alienation, cynicism, low voter turnout, and overbearing, unresponsive government. Such claims linking the electoral system to pathologies of citizen disengagement—low voter turnout and low levels of citizen efficacy and trust in government—are dubious. Governments produced by PR are not necessarily more sensitive and responsive to public opinion or adaptable to changing circumstances and public needs than those produced by FPTP. Notwithstanding their MMP system, German political analysts are no less preoccupied with *verdrossenheit,* or voter disillusionment, than their Canadian peers. In the past few decades, voter turnout has decreased across the western industrialized world.[7] Canada is no exception. In New Zealand, which had a voter turnout of 89 percent using FPTP in 1984, voter turnout in the first election with MMP in 1996 declined to "probably the lowest voting turnout of any twentieth-century" election in the country's history.[8]

There are better indicators of a citizenry's contentment with its electoral system than voter turnout. Italy has PR and, like two dozen other states, has compulsory voting. The efficaciousness of its electoral system therefore cannot be measured by voter turnout. Other indicators, however, point to the Italian public's discontent with PR. In 1991, Italians voted in a referendum to modify their electoral system so that 75 percent of MPs would be elected by FPTP. They wanted more of what PR proponents allege is the undemocratic, unfair FPTP system. Their referendum victory did not bear fruit, as politicians finessed it and, in Italy's 2006 election, 18 parties elected MPs. Seven parties won 30 or more seats each. In a 2007 reprise of public discontent with PR, more than 800,000 Italians signed a petition to try to force another referendum that would reduce the number of smaller parties by greater use of FPTP. They wanted "to move Italy away from decades of political instability."[9]

Paradoxically, low voter turnout may signify satisfaction or justifiable apathy with the state of political affairs. It may reflect the public's sense that it does not much matter who gets elected, that the ship of state is stable or that its trajectory is impervious to change and that the quality of one's life and material well-being are secure or, in any case, unaffected by whomever holds government's reins. High voter turnout may reflect societal angst, as it did in Quebec's emotionally charged and divisive sovereignty referendum in 1995. Turnout was an astronomical 94 percent, but families, coworkers, and others with longstanding cordial relations found that the passions unleashed by the referendum tore asunder their amicable bonds. That is one reason there has been little appetite for another referendum.

Expecting that PR would produce a more consensual, accountable, and transparent politics, New Zealanders voted in favour of an MMP system in a referendum. They saw PR as a way of holding politicians to their promises. They realized that there would be more proportionality in their parliament's composition, but they did not appreciate the critical importance of the party vote, rather than the constituency vote, in determining the government's ultimate complexion. After New Zealand's first MMP election, party leaders disappeared behind closed doors for eight weeks, hammered out party alignments, and horse-traded cabinet portfolios. The small New Zealand First Party, which had campaigned on getting rid of the National Party government and its fiscally conservative policies, turned around and threw its lot in with it. This is not what those voting for the upstart party expected. Public opinion judged the new style of politics reprehensible. In the aftermath of the first MMP election, politicians—who had been cool to PR—embraced it while the public turned against it. Polls showed that voters would have overwhelmingly rejected MMP in another referendum.[10] New Zealanders' hopes for a less adversarial, more cooperative politics were dashed. They expected that the denial of a majority for any one party would be positive, but they found to their chagrin that coalition cabinets behaved like the old single-party majority ones did. The same is likely to happen in Canada.

One rationale for PR is that it will make parliament more of a social mirror of society. Proponents foresee more women and minorities placed high on the party lists used in the MMP system so that parliamentary faces will be more diverse. That did occur in New Zealand, where women's representation rose from 21 to 29 percent. There is no guarantee, however, that it will happen: Israel's 2006 election returned only 17 women (or 14 percent) to its Knesset, a lower percentage than that in Canada's 2006 election (21 percent) and Ontario's 2007 election (27 percent). Furthermore, the rationale for greater representation of politically disadvantaged groups overlooks where power actually resides in a parliamentary system—with the cabinet and not with the more representative party caucuses. Again, the New Zealand case is instructive: more women than ever appeared in parliament after the first MMP election, but fewer women, only one, appeared in a cabinet of twenty, a "power reversal" for New Zealand's female MPs.[11] In contrast, women constituted 21 percent of Canada's 1997 post-election cabinet.

There is something troubling about engineering group representation by using PR. It is divisive of a common citizenship. The notion that only a woman, an Aboriginal, or a member of a visible minority can represent members of those groups is pernicious because it categorizes citizens in ways that may not be their primary or preferred political identification. It tells men or non-Aboriginals, for example, that a woman or an Aboriginal may be an unworthy representative of their interests. This view of representation detracts from a cardinal democratic principle: respect for an individual's unmediated choice of who ought to represent him or her. It tells a woman that her womanhood or the colour of her skin or her Aboriginal status is more important than who she wants to represent her.

The Latvian and Belgian experiences are also instructive for Canadians pondering the alleged virtues of MMP. Latvia's population is less than the City of Toronto's, and its size is roughly comparable to the Greater Toronto Area. Latvia's president until recently was a Cold War émigré to Canada. A distinguished graduate of the University of Toronto and McGill University, she served as vice-president of the Science Council of Canada and was admitted as an Officer of the National Order of Quebec. Immensely popular in her native land, Vaira Vīķe-Freiberga was drafted to become its president in the post-Soviet era and was twice elected to the post. During her tenure, she wistfully recalled the simplicity of Canada's electoral system and compared it to the daunting challenge she faced in trying to get the leaders of Latvia's 11 (now 12) parties in the Saeima (parliament) to construct a stable government.[12] Latvia's experience is a reminder of the potential proliferation of parties and its consequences even in small states. In

Belgium, one of the western nations pointed to positively by PR's proponents, negotiations over forming a government were still ongoing more than four months after the country's 2007 election.

The proposed MMP system that Ontarians rejected in 2007 by a margin of 63 percent to 37 percent set a bar of 3 percent for a party to gain representation. In Israel's 2006 election, with the bar set at 2 percent, 31 parties competed, and 12 won seats. When one considers Canada's vastness, its regional and cultural fault lines, and the uneven distribution of its natural resource endowments and economic wealth, compared to small states like Latvia and Israel, the chances are heightened for more parties and for more regionally and culturally divisive ones. In small states, regional parties are not a concern. In Canada—as the Progressives in the 1920s and the Reform Party and the Bloc Québécois in the 1990s demonstrated—an appetite for regional parties exists, and they have, by definition, voraciously narrow agendas. These are not broad-based national parties representing a cross-section of socioeconomic interests and groups.

A virtue of FPTP is that it encourages "big tent" or brokerage parties. A party hoping to gain power must strive to incorporate, accommodate, cater to, and express the interests of a medley of groups and regions. Such parties—a mélange of people from different regions and strata of society—fulfill a nationally integrative role. They endeavour to be the representational social mirrors that many MMP proponents eagerly demand of the electoral system. Perversely, MMP could contribute to ghettoizing and dividing groups in the cause of representing them. Senior citizens, for example, concerned that their issues are overlooked, would have an incentive to withdraw from a large inclusive party like the Liberals, Conservatives, or the NDP and could be encouraged to form, for example, their own Pensioners Party. This occurred in Israel, and when the 2006 election dust settled, the Pensioners Party played a major role in the cabinet's construction and in the discussion of the issue of war and peace, something about which its election platform said nothing. Similarly, Aboriginals, women, or religious minorities may be dissuaded from participation in parties that are broad-based nationally and programmatically. MMP encourages them to hive themselves off and use a new party, constructed on the limited identities of its supporters, to extract concessions for narrow self-serving interests with less pressure to compromise than exists under the present system. The creation of a Toronto Party, insistent on full-blown provincial status for the city, would not contribute to national or provincial unity. If successful, it would be devastating for Ontario's hinterlands, which are dependent on fiscal transfers for social programs and infrastructure made possible by their being part of a larger, wealthier, provincial state.

In constructing coalition governments in a multi-party context, the smallest party to the coalition may exert disproportionate influence in determining the fate and policy thrust of the government. Conversely, a party that consistently wins a significant plurality of votes in elections could be kept from participating in government indefinitely. Small single-issue parties could consistently wield more power than the largest, but sidelined, party. Another possibility is a grand coalition of the two largest parties, as occurred in Germany after its 2005 election. Whatever configuration of parties forms the government, it will not be what voters voted for or thought they were going to get. Proportionality in the legislature will likely not translate into proportional influence in government. Coalition governments constructed under MMP—such as one where the largest party teams up with a fourth place finisher—will give that small party disproportional influence compared to the second and third largest parties.

A threshold of 5 percent of votes as a condition for parliamentary representation, as in New Zealand and Germany, may be thought of as an effective rampart against regional and other culturally divisive parties. The representational bar in Canada, however, whatever the percentage threshold, will be set provincially rather than for the country as a whole.[13] That is, if a party wins 30 percent of Albertans' votes, it will get 30 percent (or at least 9) of the province's current 28 seats in parliament. The three most westerly and resource-rich provinces could throw up a Western Rights Party even more potent than the Reform Party. A British Columbia First Party dedicated to pursuing nothing but B.C.'s interests is conceivable. Such parties will not contribute to national unity and coherent national policymaking. Some in the east will be sure to make a case for an Atlantic Party. Although the four Atlantic provinces account for only 10 percent of the seats in the House of Commons, just a few seats—10 or 11, which is a third of the Atlantic seats—could propel such a narrowly focused party into a king-maker role in a fragmented parliament. Imagine a proliferation of provincial and other parties—the Family Coalition Party, the Marijuana Party, the Libertarian Party, the Party of People with Disabilities, etc.—and consider their influence in the making and breaking of coalition governments. With MMP providing incentives for the formation of such parties, the effect on Canadian unity of the current somewhat unbalanced regional caucuses will appear piddling in comparison.

PUSH FOR PR

The drive for PR appears inexorable even while public opinion appears disconnected from the issue. In the past decade, five provinces and Parliament have toyed, at different levels of engagement and commitment, with electoral reform. Prince Edward Island's voters, like Ontario's, given a chance to weigh in on MMP, turned it down decisively (64% said "no") in a 2005 referendum. When one considers that turnouts in FPTP elections in P.E.I. have consistently been over 80 percent, public detachment from the electoral reform issue is revealed in the turnout for the referendum: a paltry 35 percent. In Ontario, a poll conducted before its 2007 referendum found that only 28 percent were familiar with the MMP proposal, and the Conservative leader reported that, in all his travelling around the province, only three people raised the issue.[14] In the Ontario referendum, 138,000 fewer valid votes were cast than in the FPTP election that took place concurrently.[15]

Like the constitutional reform misadventures of earlier days, the pursuit of PR is an elite pleasure industry of political scientists, political junkies, and smaller parties like the Greens and the NDP that have an interest in it. The Ontario referendum won majority backing in only five of the province's 107 constituencies, and four of those were won by the NDP. Paradoxically, the NDP, which has never secured a percentage of federal parliamentary seats commensurate with its share of the popular vote, may ultimately be a casualty of the MMP system it seeks. Its self-styled coalition of unionists, feminists, environmentalists, gays and lesbians, people of colour, and others may well fracture.

A majority of British Columbia's voters, 58 percent, opted for the single transferable vote (STV) in their 2005 referendum on electoral reform, but that proved insufficient because the B.C. government had set a bar of 60 percent approval for its adoption when it originally promised the referendum. One reason support for electoral system change was greater in B.C. than in Ontario—where it was rejected by a vote of 63 to 37 percent—was that the potential quirkiness of the FPTP system was actually displayed in three consecutive B.C. elections. In 1991, the NDP won power even while its popularity dipped below levels it had attained when it lost in the 1970s and 1980s. Then, in 1996, the NDP was reelected to another majority although the Liberals won more votes. In 2001, when the Liberals swept to power on an impressive 57 percent of the vote, they won a lopsided 77 (or 97 percent) of the 79 seats. In Ontario's 2003 election, in contrast, the Liberals formed a government with a healthy but more modest majority after capturing a decisive 46.5 percent of the vote. The Ontario result was historically consistent with past results, and the election of a Liberal majority government was not publicly perceived as "stolen," which is admittedly a potentially unseemly upshot of FPTP. Ontario produced a mix of governments—three parties won majority governments over the course of three elections in the span of eight years between 1987 and 1995. While no party captured a majority of voters—none has since 1937—the results reflected in each case a popular consensus for change in favour of the party that prevailed.

The three provincial governments conducting the referenda did not tell voters that they would set a 60 percent bar when they promised a referendum. We may only speculate why they set it so high. Most politicians, particularly those from the large parties, prefer the status quo. FPTP holds out a better prospect for them to wield majority power. In Manitoba and Saskatchewan, where the NDP is a major party, it has never pursued PR, in contrast to the federal and Ontario NDP, which are minor parties. Politicians from large parties tend not to publicize their preference, for that could alienate some voters. Nevertheless, they may promise a referendum on the issue because they perceive that the public will appreciate the idea that its will could actually count and may reward the party that gives it a direct voice in the matter. That is what happened in New Zealand. To capitalize on this belief, in both the B.C. and Ontario cases, the referenda were held by the governing party at the same time as the general election. In Ontario, the Conservatives declared that they were opposed to MMP only on the eve of the referendum, after polls made it clear that it would fail.[16]

Both the B.C. and Ontario governments encouraged those favouring PR by opening the issue of electoral reform. The governments themselves, however, would not speak in favour of it. They insisted that they were neutral. Both provinces used a Citizens' Assembly to consider and propose, if the Assembly so decided, an alternative electoral system. The Citizens' Assemblies were exercises in deliberative democracy, a supplement to representative democracy. Political scientists and others expert in electoral systems educated the Citizens' Assemblies in the various forms and outcomes of PR and FPTP systems. Then, the CA members, meeting on weekends in small groups and plenary, opted for PR over the FPTP status quo. In Ontario's case, they chose the MMP form of PR by a vote of 94–8. The ultimate upshot, the referendum's results, demonstrated that the assembly's members were whistling in the wind: barely more than a third of their fellow citizens embraced their proposal at the ballot box.

The Citizens' Assemblies' members did not reflect their citizen peers' views. Nor was the CA as representative of the public as was claimed by the government. Only citizens interested in serving on the assembly could be chosen. Unlike a legal jury, randomly selected with service mandatory, the CA was neither. In B.C. and Ontario, the CAs were constructed, consistent with the view of democratic representation as a social mirror, to reflect gender balance. With each constituency permitted one representative, this meant that no men were eligible to represent half of the constituencies and no women the other half. Notwithstanding the gender balance, the Ontario assembly was not a representative demographic mirror of the public. One member of the assembly observed that a third of the members were retirees. As for those who appeared at the 29 meetings in 17 cities, they were unrepresentative of their communities. "In some cases the public were homogeneous—e.g., a large group from an old age home."[17] Attendance ranged from seven in Dryden to about two hundred in Toronto, a city of well over two million.

The CAs' recommendation to jettison FPTP in B.C. and Ontario was predictable. Those making oral and written submissions to Ontario's CA were not representative of Ontarians' public opinion. Self-selected, they were overwhelmingly in favour of PR with 692 of the 986 offering "pro" comments and only 78 (or 8 percent) tendering "con" comments. A repeated theme in the submissions was that PR would produce a more demographically representative legislature. Women and visible minorities' underrepresentation in Canadian political institutions was depicted as systemic discrimination. It is noteworthy then that of all the comments submitted to the CA, only 21 percent were by women, a lower percentage than the percentage of women in Ontario's legislature. This suggested that women were less interested than men in the assembly's work, but the assembly, given its gender composition, could not be accused of systemic discrimination.

CONFRONTING THE OTHER SIDE

John Hiemstra and Harold Jansen offer a number of rationales for why FPTP ought to be discarded and PR adopted. They project positive scenarios with MMP. They note that one of the main arguments for FPTP is that it offers good prospects for stable government because a plurality of votes for a party usually translates into a majority of seats. As they accurately observe, Canada has nonetheless frequently had minority governments. Indeed, an oddity of the Jean Chrétien years was that—with five parties elected to produce a pizza parliament in 1993, 1997, and 2000—a majority government emerged at all. The 2004 and 2006 elections, with only four parties, yielded the more logical outcome of a multi-party parliament—a minority government. If the current four parliamentary parties survive, and even if new parliamentary parties do not appear, FPTP majority governments composed exclusively of members from a single party caucus are less likely in the future. Canada's minority as well as its majority governments have provided relative political stability by international standards. The greatest threats to Canadian unity, paradoxically, have come during periods of majority government, as during the Meech Lake imbroglio, the Charlottetown Accord, and Quebec's sovereignty referenda and when all the parties sided with the government.

Hiemstra and Jansen contend that FPTP aggravates and intensifies regional divisions because it has produced regionally lopsided caucuses. Certainly, the success of the Chrétien Liberals in capturing 98 of Ontario's 99 seats in 1993 and then 101 and 100 of the province's 103 seats in the 1997 and 2000 elections respectively demonstrated lopsidedness. The Liberals won those contests with bare majorities of between 51 and 53 percent of Ontarians' votes. The dramatic over-representation of Liberals in Ontario was twinned with their substantial under-representation in the west. Conversely, the Reform/Alliance Party, with the support of between 24 and 26 percent of Ontario's voters in that same trio of elections, did not win more than two seats in 2000 and was shut out in 1997. Such outcomes are unusual and were produced by what proved to be but a temporary fissure on the political right, with Reform and the Progressives Conservatives competing for the same pool of voters to the Liberals' benefit. The 2004 and 2006 elections produced more typical and less severe distortions once the right reunited. In Ontario in 2006, the Liberals won 51 percent of the seats with 40 percent of the votes, the Conservatives won 38 percent of the seats with 35 percent of the votes, and the NDP won 11 percent of the seats with their 19 percent of votes. Neither the lopsided results of the 1990s' elections nor the more balanced results of the more recent ones affected national unity. It is the premiers and the provinces, rather than the federal caucuses that vote along predictable party lines, that are the pivotal players in national unity debates.

The impact on national unity of the mathematical asymmetry between seats and votes produced by FPTP pales in comparison to the impact on unity that would result if unabashedly selfish regional parties were to emerge and take root. MMP would likely unleash them. Hiemstra and Jansen blithely and naïvely assume that, with MMP, the existing parties would continue to secure levels of popular support across the country similar to those of the past. What would change positively, from their perspective, is that the existing party caucuses would more accurately reflect those parties' differing levels of regional support. This, however, would almost certainly not occur, because the existing party system would most likely fracture, given the incentive MMP provides for regional and narrow single-issue parties. Such parties would likely fracture one or more of the established broadly based parties. By definition, single-issue parties lack an overarching policy agenda and a "big tent" mentality that strives to incorporate people from different backgrounds, interests, and regions. Canada's diversities and social heterogeneity would fuel these new parties. Such parties would not foster what Canadians share in common. They would highlight non-ideological divisions among Canadians rather than economic class divisions such as the gaps between rich and poor Canadians wherever they live. Broadly based parties and platforms will compete with and give way to narrow special interest parties. The virtue of the existing system is that it encourages parties to broker, within themselves, Canada's regional and social diversities.

CONCLUSION

FPTP has served Canada well in comparative perspective. To replace it with MMP would contribute to endangering Canadian unity. It could produce governments with policies tailored to single-interest parties that capture very low percentages of the vote. Their handfuls of seats would disproportionately determine government's complexion and direction. The MMP solution to the shortcomings of FPTP may prove worse than the problem. Adopting MMP is akin to buying a pig-in-a-poke.

NOTES

1. Laza Kekic, "The Economist Intelligence Unit's Index of Democracy," pp. 3, 6, available at http://www.economist.com/media/pdf/DEMOCRACY_INDEX_2007_v3.pdf.

2. Alan C. Cairns, "Political Science, Ethnicity and the Canadian Constitution," in David P. Shugarman and Reg Whitaker, eds., *Federalism and Political Community: Essays in Honour of Donald Smiley* (Peterborough: Broadview, 1989), p. 117.

3. André Blais and Ken Carty, "The Psychological Impact of Electoral Laws: Measuring Duverger's Elusive Factor," *British Journal of Political Science* 21 (1991), pp. 79–93.

4. Denis Pilon, "Explaining Voting System Reform in Canada, 1874 to 1960," *Journal of Canadian Studies* 40, no. 3 (Fall 2006), p. 147.

5. *Revised Statutes of Manitoba, 1940,* I, ch. 57. For analysis of the results, see Nelson Wiseman and K. W. Taylor, "Ethnic vs. Class Voting: The Case of Winnipeg, 1945," *Canadian Journal of Political Science* 7, no. 2 (June 1974), pp. 314–28.

6. *Winnipeg Free Press,* Sept. 17, 1949.

7. S. Pharr, R. Putman, and R. Dalton, "Trouble in the Advanced Democracies," *Journal of Democracy* 11, no. 2 (2000), pp. 5–25.

8. Jack Vowles, "Offsetting the PR Effect? Party Mobilization and Turnout Decline in New Zealand, 1996–99," *Party Politics* 8, no. 5 (2002), p. 587.

9. "Italian Election Petition Earns 800,000 Signatures," *The Globe and Mail,* July 25, 2007.

10. Thérèse Arsenau, CBC radio program, "Ideas," February 9, 1998.

11. Thérèse Arsenau, "Electing Representative Legislatures: Lessons from New Zealand," in Henry Milner, ed., *Making Every Vote Count: Reassessing Canada's Electoral System* (Peterborough: Broadview, 1999), p. 140.

12. Interview with Joe Schlesinger, CBC TV program "Foreign Assignment," February 21, 2004 http://www.cbc.ca/foreignassignment/20040221.html.

13. *Constitution Act, 1985 (Representation),* Statutes of Canada, 1986, c. 8, Part I.

14. Robert Benzie, "Reform's on the Ballot: Now If They Only Cared," *Toronto Star,* September 1, 2007.

15. Elections Ontario, "Referendum Results," available at http://www3.elections.on.ca/ internetapp/realtimereferendum.aspx?lang=en-ca&gf73=0&contestid=2&channel_id ={923146e7-4d81-42a8-99f0-e61f5ab50387}&lang=en, and Elections Ontario, "2008 By-Election," available at http://www3.elections.on.ca/internetapp/realtimehome .aspx?lang=en&channel_id={923146e7-4d81-42a8-99f0-e61f5ab50387}&lang=en. Accessed on October 21, 2007.

16. Robert Benzie, "Reject MMP, Conservatives Tell Voters," *Toronto Star,* October 9, 2007.

17. "Update on the Consultation Phase of the Ontario Citizens' Assembly," March 3, 2007, available at http://snider.blogs.com/citizensassembly.

POSTSCRIPT

The two articles present some good arguments, but they also leave some questions unanswered. John Hiemstra and Harold Jansen nicely reveal the benefits of mixed-member proportional (MMP) system, but one wonders whether they understate the possible costs of such a system. Coalition governments, an inevitable result of MMP in Canada, may produce policies whose coherence is lacking. The benefit of single-member plurality (SMP) is that a single voice typically determines policy, but the multiple voices in MMP may produce government outputs that endeavour to satisfy the demands of the varied parties in government. Hiemstra and Jansen are little worried with the prospect of two types of MPs under MMP. But it seems possible that those unattached to a constituency may find themselves a little lost, especially in light of the fact that constituency work makes up the bulk of the work of most elected representatives. The two authors also applaud MMP because of its ability to ensure appropriate representation in government. But again one wonders. The presence of coalition governments will produce power arrangements in government that fail to reflect the distribution of the vote in the legislature. A minor party, with little of the popular vote, may team up with a more powerful party to secure its aims in exchange for support. In other words, there is no guarantee that the distribution of the popular vote will be recorded in the actions of government. MMP addresses concerns of representation in the legislative branch, but may have little effect on the distribution of support in the most powerful branch in parliamentary government—namely the executive branch.

Wiseman makes a number of good points, the most important of these arguably being the failure of some to realize that a rough equating of the quality of democracy with a nation's electoral system is foolish. But it is also true that Wiseman's effort is not invulnerable to criticism. Canada may indeed be more attractive than other countries with PR, but this does not mean that Canada should eschew any serious consideration of electoral reform—successful nations can always become more successful. Wiseman is critical of the attempt of MMP to make formal political life more representative of society, but the fact that women, for instance, typically represent about one-fifth of elected representatives can be unsettling. Finally, Wiseman may also be charged with failing to assuage or ease feelings that the existing electoral system in Canada is simply unfair. There may indeed be problems with MMP—nothing is ever perfect—but at least it seeks to ensure that the parties and their supporters get what they deserve.

Students wishing to pursue the subject of electoral reform might begin with Heather MacIvor's short overview of electoral reform in Heather MacIvor, "A Brief Introduction to Electoral Reform," in Henry Milner, ed., *Making Every Vote Count: Reassessing Canada's Electoral* System (Peterborough: Broadview Press, 1999). Other useful introductions to elections and electoral reforms are Eric Mintz, David Close, and Osvaldo Croci, *Politics, Power and the Common Good: An Introduction* to *Political Science* (Toronto: Pearson Education Canada, 2006), chapter 10; John Courtney, *Elections* (Vancouver: UBC Press, 2004), chapter 6; and Roger Gibbins and Loleen Youngman, "The Institutional Expression of Multiple Identities: The Electoral Reform Debate," in Thomas M.J. Bateman and Thomas Epp, eds., *Braving the New World: Readings in Contemporary Politics*, 3rd ed. (Toronto: Thomson Nelson, 2004). The next step is to dive into the detailed analyses of the first-past-the-post system and its main competitors. Here, students might start with J. Paul Johnston and Harvey E. Pasis, eds., *Representation and Electoral Systems: Canadian Perspectives* (Scarborough: Prentice-Hall, 1990). This text contains many of the classic articles on electoral reform in Canada, including the seminal article by Alan C. Cairns and the response to his article by J.A.A. Lovink. Most recent examinations of electoral reform (such as MMP) include Henry Milner, ed., *Making Every Vote Count: Reassessing Canada's Electoral System* (Peterborough: Broadview Press, 1999); Henry Milner, "The Case for Proportional Representation," in Hugh Thorburn and Alan Whitehorn, eds., *Party Politics in Canada,* 8th ed. (Scarborough: Prentice-Hall, 2001); Louis Massicotte, *Changing the Canadian Electoral System* (Montreal: Institute for Research on Public Policy, February 2001); and the entire July–August 2001 issue of *Policy Options*. A rigorous analysis of electoral reform and MMP can also be found in Law Commission of Canada, *Voting Counts: Electoral Reform in Canada* (Ottawa: Law Reform Commission, 2004).

The issue of electoral reform is not merely a matter of concern for academics. Provincial governments in Canada have been looking long and hard at this issue, and some seen poised to make some changes. For more on developments in the provinces, students should see Henry Milner, ed., *Steps toward Making Every Step Count: Electoral Reform in Canada and Its Provinces* (Peterborough: Broadview Press, 2004). This text also offers good general articles on electoral reform, which makes it a book that must be read by all interested in this debate topic. Another more recent publication on the same matter is Harold J. Jansen, "Making the Impossible Possible: Electoral Reform and Canada's Provinces," in Thomas M.J. Bateman and Rick Myers, eds., *Braving the New World: Readings in Contemporary Politics*, 4th ed. (Scarborough: Nelson, 2008). As mentioned, three provinces have held referenda on electoral reform, two of which asked whether MMP should be adopted. For more on the Ontario referendum, students should consult Ontario Citizens' Assembly on Electoral Reform, *One Ballot, Two Votes: A New Way to Vote in Ontario* (Toronto: Queen's Printer for Ontario, 2007).

The experience of other countries with the plurality system and proportional representation is relevant to the discussion of electoral reform in Canada. On this topic, the following might be consulted: Arend Lijphart and Bernard Grofman, eds., *Choosing an Electoral System: Issues and Alternatives* (New York: Praeger, 1984); Vernon Bogdanor and David Butler, eds., *Democracy and Elections: Electoral Systems and Their Political Consequences* (Cambridge: Cambridge University Press, 1983); and Michael Dummett, *Principles of Electoral Reform* (Oxford: Oxford

University Press, 1997). Especially relevant are Matthew Soberg Shugart and Martin P. Wattenberg, ed., *Mixed-Member Electoral Systems: The Best of Both Worlds?* (Oxford: Oxford University Press, 2001), and the aforementioned *Steps toward Making Every Vote Count: Electoral Reform in Canada and Its Provinces*. Both contain pieces on the operation of MMP in other countries. Also, special attention may be given to Arend Lijphart, "Democracies: Forms, Performance, and Constitutional Engineering," *European Journal of Political Research* 25 (1994), pp. 1–17. What makes this article so central to the debate is that it denies that one must concede a decline in the effectiveness of government in order to introduce PR. For more on Lijphart's work, students might want to consult Arend Lijphart, *Patterns of Democracy: Government Forms and Performance in Thirty-Six Countries* (New Haven and London: Yale University Press, 1999), chapters 15–16.

Should Women Focus on Small-p Politics?

✔ **YES**
JACQUETTA NEWMAN, "Small-p Politics: Women Working Outside Formal Political Structures"

✗ **NO**
JACQUETTA NEWMAN, "Say It Five Times Fast: The Pitfalls of Small-p Politics and a Plea for Large-P Politics"

One of the more salient issues for women in Canadian political life—if not the most salient—is their failure to achieve greater representation in formal political structures. Women typically constitute only about one-fifth of the members of legislative assemblies, and the percentages are not much better in other institutional parts of government. A great deal of work and thinking on the part of the women's movement and others has been directed toward fixing this problem. Women have been urged to participate more actively in political parties and to consider more aggressively occupations that increase the chances of gaining entrance into government. Feminist groups have also supported the candidacies of women and provided political muscle to parties that champion the cause of more equal representation in politics. Even political leaders, normally absorbed with electoral victory, have intervened in various ways for the purpose of securing more women for a career in political life.

All of these efforts and more assume that entrance into the world of "large-P politics"—a term to describe the formal structures and processes of government—generate substantial benefits for women. Policies directed at women will become more effective, the value of equality in society will be strengthened, and the manner of doing politics itself may change for the better. Few, if any, question the focus on large-P politics because the return on this type of politics is seemingly so apparent. However, there is some concern that the energies of those pressing for these ends may be misdirected. History reveals that important advances for women have not necessarily been achieved through activities in the world of formal politics; rather, it has been the efforts of women in charities, community groups, advocacy groups, and other informal structures that have paved the way for women. These bodies form the world of "small-p politics," and it is this world that has been central to successes in securing greater equality in politics and elsewhere. Accordingly, it is argued that women should rethink their strategy of political activity and pay more attention to those institutions that have worked so well in the past, concentrating less on political parties and legislative assemblies and more on the structures of society outside of government.

Integral to small-p politics and its successes is the notion of "social capital," which refers to the trust and networking abilities people build up by associating with each other through the informal processes and structures of society. Women meet in their neighbourhoods, for example, when looking after young children, and in so doing become aware of their common needs and subsequently enter into discussions about how to meet these needs. Volunteer organizations or community groups also become settings in which women can talk about important issues and make plans for action. Out of these and other types of interactions emerges the social capital that enables the world of small-p politics to become a powerful and influential actor in political politics. Just because some societal structures and processes fail to receive the publicity and attention of formal politics, this hardly means they are insignificant.

The claim for small-p political activity is attractive, partly because it suggests that political power can reside in our everyday activities. Women only have to be themselves, to live their normal lives, in order to secure political gains. Yet, there is the uneasy feeling that this seems almost too good to be true. Surely, some of the activities associated with small-p politics can actually get in the way of political activity. Looking after children may indeed lead to collective action but can just as easily produce exhausted mothers wishing only refuge in their homes. Researchers also suggest that the type of social capital produced by women can for one reason or another be difficult to translate into political advancement. Interestingly, men also create social capital, and theirs is seemingly more transferable into political capital. More generally, leaders of women's movements and organizations may cringe at the idea of giving up the fight in the arena of large-P politics. They sense that to make gains in formal politics one has to *be* in formal politics. To not be involved in political parties and legislative assemblies is to engage in pure folly.

In the readings, Jacquetta Newman, the co-author of *Women, Politics, and Public Policy* and a professor of political science at King's University College at the University of Western Ontario, makes the case for *and* against shifting the focus of women's political activity away from large-P politics and toward small-p politics.

✔ YES

Small-p Politics: Women Working Outside Formal Political Structures
JACQUETTA NEWMAN

In democracies there is a tendency to assess a group's political power and influence by measuring its success in attaining positions within the structures of political representation as members of elected government and, more generally, as participants in national and regional assemblies. Our understanding of democratic citizenship is often predicated on the notion of representation and the formal rights to vote and participate in electoral politics, which as Young and Everitt point out reflects the centrality to democratic governance of the "representative institutions that achieve their mandates through popular election."[1] Not surprisingly then, the struggle for suffrage in the early twentieth century by the first wave of the women's movement and their achievement of formal political rights for women is a significant benchmark in the struggle for women's equality.

However, two features should be noted here; first, that since 1918 and 1929, recognition of women's political citizenship has had only limited success in Canada. Nearly a century later, Canadian women still have not achieved equal representation in Canadian institutions of democratic governance. As of the January 2006 federal election, women make up only 20.8 percent of the Canadian House of Commons—64 women in a 308-member house—ranking forty-eighth in the world and tied with the Principality of Monaco.[2] In the provincial legislatures, supposedly closer to the politicians' homes and more likely to appeal to those who prefer not to have to travel constantly to and from the national capital, the average for women's representation was 19.7 percent of the seats, from a high in Manitoba of 31.5 percent to a low of 11.1 percent in the Yukon and Nunavut Territories and 14.5 percent in Alberta and New Brunswick.[3] Looking at national elections since 1968, we can see that women, who make up half of the population, have found it difficult to break out of the low 20 percent region in terms of their representation in the House. Women interested in political representation have a better chance to enter Parliament as an appointed senator than as an elected MP. Women make up 35 percent of the Canadian Senate.

Second, the political action of women to push for the vote and achieve formal political rights did not occur within the representative and electoral structures, but found its power and expression in communities of women that formed within civil society, outside the formal structures of politics. The example of the first wave of the women's movement illustrates that politics can occur informally in community networks that focus on the day-to-day problems faced by people and can also have influence on public policy. To get the full story regarding women's political activism in Canada, we have to turn our attention from the formal structures of legislatures and political parties to the political work women undertake through and in civil society. It is the intention of this article to address this world of small-p politics.

In *Habits of the Heart*, Bellah et al., make a distinction between three conceptions of politics: (1) the politics of consensual community, (2) the pluralist politics of interest competition, and (3) the politics of nation. The first conception, which Bellah referred to as the politics of community, concerns the activity of putting into effect "the moral consensus of the community, reached through free face-to-face discussion, where, "citizenship is virtually coextensive with getting involved with one's neighbours for the good of the community."[4] It is an activity that participants do not see "as politics at all."[5] The second conception refers to the world of party and electoral politics, "the complicated, professional yet highly personal, business of adversarial struggles, alliance building, and interest bargaining. . . . For most people, it lacks the immediacy of everyday involvement. . . . Supporting candidates by voting is the typical expression of this understanding for most people, keeping politics at arm's length."[6] Finally, the third conception, the politics of nation, refers to the high affairs of state that transcend local everyday concerns. It is the first conception of community politics that represents small-p politics; the second and third forms, associated with the structures of the state and the formalized activities of parties, elections, and legislatures, represent the large-P politics that is conventionally defined as politics proper. Birte Siim makes a similar distinction between "'small democracies' of everyday life and the 'big democracy' of political parties and organized government."[7]

Consequently, when we refer to small-p politics, we are envisioning the political nature of local, grassroots-focused (although it may be termed "thinking globally, acting locally"), face-to-face, and day-to-day activities that are often framed in terms of things that have to get done for the good of the community. As such, it comprises charity work, volunteerism, and work with nongovernmental and/or social movement activities. It is a useful distinction because it forces us to broaden our understanding of politics and helps us explain how the activities of women over the last century have had a far greater impact on Canadian politics and society than their numbers in legislative assemblies reflect. It also opens up the possibility that politics can occur outside the formal structures of the state and that activities within civil society influence, sometimes profoundly, both the state and society.

Simply conceived, civil society is composed of voluntary civic and social organizations that are distinct from the institutions of the state, family, and the economy. This includes organizations such as charities, nongovernmental organizations, community groups, women's organizations, faith-based organizations, professional associations, unions, self-help groups, social movements and social movement organizations, business associations, coalitions, and advocacy groups, which as the list suggests come in many forms and with varying levels of formal organization and power.[8] While in the past the activities undertaken in civil society were considered unconnected to the political sphere, or "pre-political," recent work in political science and sociology has come to take more seriously the connection between community life and political life.

This has definitely been evidenced in the popularity of the term *social capital* and the proliferation of studies regarding the requirement of social capital for healthy democracy. The most popular definition of social capital is that of Robert Putnam, who defines *social capital*,

> By analogy with notions of physical capital and human capital—tools and training that enhance individual productivity—"social capital" refers to features of social organization such as networks, norms, and social trust that facilitate coordination and cooperation for mutual benefit. . . . In the first place, networks of civic engagement foster sturdy norms of generalized reciprocity and encourage the emergence of social trust. Such networks facilitate coordination and communication, amplify reputations, and thus allow dilemmas of collective action to be resolved.[9]

In his work on Italy and the United States, Putnam examines how membership in community organizations enhances democratic participation and decision-making and how in the U.S. decline in group membership has consequences for democratic engagement. Social capital has significance for political activity because the experiences, skills, networks, and "capital" developed through these networks of trust and reciprocity bring people into political engagement. "[P]atterns of formal and informal sociability build up relations of trust and reciprocity. The resultant social capital enhances individuals' capacity to join together in collective action to resolve common problems (or ensure that governments address such problems)—it capitalizes political engagement."[10] Other authors conceive social capital more broadly or narrowly[11] with more or less attention to the issue of politicization and conflict. Consequently, there are debates as to what social capital actually entails, and accusations are made that the term suffers from "definitional diversity" and "over-versatility." As Edwards and Foley complain, "the concept seems to take on the property of a gas expanding or contracting to fit the analytical space afforded by each historical or sociopolitical setting."[12] However, for our purposes, we identify the common thread that runs through the various conceptions of social capital: that experience and participation in social networks facilitate the building of values of trust and reciprocity, which provide resources and training to enhance political engagement, participation, and influence.

Why does the idea of social capital have significance for women's politics? The simple answer is that social capital approaches appear to fit well with the social and political activities undertaken by women. Putnam argued that one of the reasons for the decline of social capital in the U.S. is the move of women into paid employment during the 1970s, which gave them less time to commit to social involvement. For Putnam, this indicates that much traditional social capital was built and supported by women,[13] although in later work he qualifies this argument, attributing the decline to factors such as increased physical mobility, changing demographics, and the technological transformation of leisure. However, apart from this suggestion of Putnam's, "social capital studies in political science have tended to focus upon male-dominated activities. They have selected men's social capital–related activities, while often neglecting entire spheres of relevant activity where women's efforts are concentrated."[14] It is only recently that feminist scholars have undertaken to examine social capital and its relevance to women's politics.[15]

As Lowndes argues, "empirically, the concept seems attractive for the attention it directs toward the intersection between community life and politics, and toward informal as well as formal domains of political activity."[16] It fits well because women's activities are assumed to be more involved in community volunteer work and concerned with looking after the local needs of family and neighbours. Social capital addresses the dichotomy between the public and private that feminists argue is at the heart of patriarchy, where *the public* refers to the arena where public decisions are taken, the public interest and good are determined, and public policy is made—the world of large-P politics—and *the private* is removed from formal politics and embedded in the nurturing and domestic duties of the home, small-p politics. This division of society into public and private spheres is nonsense, and social capital helps illustrate this nonsense. It is "important in the reconsideration of the role that women play within our political system as social capital focuses attention on the implications of the private sphere and private relationships for public life."[17] It is the so-called private sphere where many relationships of reciprocity and trust are built and the skills and capacity for political engagement are developed.

This is borne out historically; as suggested earlier, one of the notable features of the first wave of feminism was that the campaign for suffrage found its power and expression in the community groups and clubs that brought women together to undertake good works, some associated with churches and others more secular. For example, in Canada, the Canadian branch of the Women's Christian Temperance Union (WCTU) at the turn of the century campaigned to change drinking habits, but it was also concerned with the promotion of family moral values through religious evangelism, voluntary social activism, and education programs. Like the Women's Institutes for farming women, it was significant because it provided "a forum for middle-class women to become active participants in their own communities long before they were accorded the perquisites of full citizenship through the right to vote."[18] Women's associations, clubs, and groups functioned to bring together and create networks of women barred from public political and economic work. They also provided space for women to work for social reform, which sometimes resulted in policy changes, particularly in the regulation of alcohol and prostitution. Clearly, they asserted that women had a role in determining the public good. This impulse brought women into formal politics because, as their campaigns for social reform expanded, they found that more political leverage was required to achieve action from national and provincial legislatures. An obvious way to create political pressure was the vote.[19]

Arneil, Sapiro, Clemens, and Skocpol[20] tell similar stories regarding the first wave of the women's movement in the U.S. At the turn of the century, women's clubs and charitable organizations channelled social concerns and desire for social reform in a way that blurred any distinction between social and political activity.

> Fraternalism created the singular option of political organization for women under the rubric of women's clubs ... What is striking is how these groups sought to change public policy almost from the beginning. The three major women's groups formed at the end of the nineteenth century were the Women's Christian Temperance Union in 1874, the General Federation of Women's Clubs in 1890, and National Congress of Mothers (later the PTA) in 1897. These women's associations, if seen through a gendered lens, were not simply about building communities and social trust but forums within which women could channel their misgivings about the way politics was being run, particularly in the area of social policy."[21]

These authors also point out that there is an inevitability to the formation of these groups, as they were one of the few ways that women denied formal political power could influence and access political change. As Sapiro argues, "social capital may be an especially potent resource for people who lack political standing or human or financial capital either to compensate for this deficit or to leverage an increase in standing."[22] As a result, we need to recognize these groups as *political*, not just social, actors. Their social networks and activism do not just "lead to" politics but expand its definition.

This ethos is carried through into the second wave of the women's movement. For the second wave, formal access to rights was clearly not enough to guarantee women's equality, as women's subordination appeared to be maintained in all spheres of their lives: in political institutions, the workplace, schools, churches, clubs, and the family. For example, the practice of consciousness-raising, a hallmark of second wave feminism that brought small groups of women together to share their experiences of men, work, sex and sexuality, and so on, does not immediately strike one as political. However, in fostering a sense of shared experience, anger, and ultimately empowerment, women came to understand that their personal grievances were political. As Adamson, Briskin, and McPhail argue, consciousness-raising was "instrumental in actually mobilizing [women] as active participants in their own struggle for liberation."[23] Women's anger was transformed into political action and women were brought to formal organizations through these informal groups.

Throughout the second wave period, women established women-centred services—rape crisis centres, health centres, abortion and contraceptive services, safe houses for battered and homeless women, centres for single mothers, magazines, journals, art galleries, cultural centres, and publishing companies. These grassroots efforts came to illustrate the second wave's feminist character of "women doing it for themselves." As Roberta Hamilton points out, these endeavours influenced the way that mainstream structures thought about and dealt with women.[24] All of these activities were connected to public policy—by making transparent the services women required, providing models for service provision, and in some cases becoming the structures through which policy was applied by state funding.

Current studies of social capital by feminist scholars examine the broadened definition of politics and its consequence for women as political actors. Of particular interest is the role of child and elder care in political activity and engagement. As Herd and Harrington Meyer ask,

> A woman spending hours at her mother-in-law's bedside is a dutiful daughter-in-law, while a stranger or neighbor sitting beside the same bed is a hospice volunteer. Hospice and respite care providers often provide the care work that some families do not have the time, money, or other resources to provide. How can we argue that a hospice volunteer caring for a neighbor is engaged in a civic activity, while a woman caring for her elderly aunt is not?[25]

Is there a distinction between the two, and if so what is the distinction? Herd and Harrington Meyer argue that of course such care is a form of civic engagement, "as voluntary or as altruistic as other forms of civic engagement."[26] While there is a great deal of pressure for women to perform such work, they "can and do walk away from it—they decide not to care." This work intrinsically involves the development of networks of reciprocity and trust between not just family members but neighbours and friends. "A mother picks up her neighbor's children, along with her own, from school or sports practices, knowing that in exchange she can count on her neighbor to oversee both of their children playing in the driveway a couple of afternoons per week. A neighbor takes out an older woman's garbage every Thursday morning so that her daughter does not have to make a special trip."[27] Examining the case of child care, Lowndes concurs: "we know that school runs, child care swaps and baby-sitting circles all involve relationships of reciprocity and mutuality. Child care networks clearly fit with common definitions of social capital forming activities: 'regular contact with others beyond the sphere of the family or the market ... the kind of face-to-face relations of relative equality associated with participation in common endeavours.'"[28]

Feminist scholars and activists have discussed and campaigned vehemently on issues regarding the position of women's caring roles in our society, demanding recognition of the value of this unpaid work. "[C]are is work and that care work should be both a right and an obligation of social citizenship."[29] It is private and unpaid and consequently is seen as unproductive, both economically and societally. The study of care work and social capital encourages us to consider that this work not only has value economically but also is intrinsically valuable for democracy and democratic engagement.

In turn, social care work brings women into politics. As Herd and Harrington Meyer report, caring is an oft cited reason for women's involvement in environmental movements: "[g]ood moms want good air and good water."[30] They go on to list a series of studies where networks based on family care were translated into political campaigns. As Lowndes points out, "shared concerns" developed through the informal relationships around child care "serve to mobilize self-help and campaigning activity, which in turn 'spill over' into the formal political arena as activists' competence grows."[31] It appears fairly clear cut, for example, that a group of mothers chatting while watching their children play road hockey in the neighbourhood gets involved with the municipal government to work on plans for traffic dampening, or a woman caring for an elderly parent becomes involved in efforts to have funding increased for in-home nursing visits. Put this way, the avenues for translating social action into political action appear almost limitless.

The emphasis on small-p politics, or the politics of social capital, has become even more significant as the Canadian state (along with other Western industrial states) has devolved its social welfare responsibilities to the level of community and voluntary organizations.[32] Consequently, voluntary organizations have become much more active and influential in the policymaking process. As Rachel Laforest identifies, the federal government in Canada has come to recognize "the voluntary sector as an important pillar of Canadian society along with the private and public sectors.... More than ever before, voluntary organizations are implicated in the process of governance and the voluntary sector has emerged as an important actor and partner in both policy-making and service delivery."[33] This has the advantage of bringing to light the work undertaken in local communities by women. However, it also has disadvantages, because much of this social work falls to women, who often remain unrecognized and unpaid and now find themselves facing three work shifts: paid employment, family work, and community work. In addition, this volunteer–state partnership can work against political involvement. While Laforest identifies, that "forms of political representation are evolving as voluntary sector organizations gain influence in the policy process" and "new opportunities for engagement in policy are transforming the terms of access to policy-making," she also points out that, this has changed the "structure of the voluntary sector, its identity, and its pattern of relationship.... [It] signaled to voluntary organizations that advocacy was no longer an appropriate strategy for making one's claims to the state. Increasingly, volunteer organizations engage in political advocacy and campaigning at the risk of losing funding and their claims to legitimacy within policy networks."[34] Therefore, while social capital is developed, its convertibility into political capital may be seriously limited.

This gives us some indications that, as we shall see in the other side of this debate, we cannot be too sanguine about the social capital concept as a "magic bullet" for finding forms of women's political power. However, notwithstanding concerns about the possible limitations of small-p politics, the argument of this paper is that this form of political activity has great potential for women and their participation in politics. Social capital offers a great deal to the study of women's politics primarily because it encourages us to cast our definitional net more widely to include ostensibly social activities as intrinsically political. It allows us to link informal community-based activity with broadly political phenomena, which helps us make visible significant forms of political power. In addition, gender approaches help us develop a better understanding of social capital and small-p politics. For example, as Lowndes suggests, we need to know "how in different contexts, do relationships of trust and mutual reciprocity 'capitalize' political engagement? Here the social capital debate has much to learn from the existing literature on women's unorthodox routes to political engagement and from feminist perspectives on citizenship."[35]

We also need to more fully examine the complex links between civil society action and public policy.[36] We have to keep in mind that it is difficult to establish clear causality between civil society action and progressive political results for women without factoring in the role of women in formal political structures, the willingness of formal structures to work with women outside the structures, the party composition and associated ideological disposition of government, and the general views on the issue in larger society. As discussed above, more attention needs to be paid to the nature of voluntary work, and because much of this work takes place unattached to organizational and membership structures, methods have to be found to ensure that it is included along with more formal work. Significantly, greater attention needs to be paid to how these social activities are translated into political resources and how social relationships are drawn upon for and in political engagement. One way to approach these concerns is to expand studies of social capital from statistical studies of values, voting behaviour, and organizational membership (but this is not to say this is unimportant) to qualitative case studies, ethnographic studies of informal volunteer networks, and individual life histories. This will help illustrate more fully the mechanisms of social capital development and use.

If politics is the process by which we organize ourselves into collective communities, the conceptions of social capital have the potential to further not only our understandings of women's politics and small-p politics, but all politics in general.

NOTES

1. Lisa Young and Joanne Everitt, *Advocacy Groups* (Vancouver: UBC Press, 2004), p. 22.

2. "Inter-Parliamentary Union," October 11, 2007, available at http://www.ipu.or/wmn-e/classif.htm.

3. "Women's Representation in Canada—Provincial," available at http://jnewman.ca. Accessed on October 16, 2007.

4. Robert Bellah et al., *Habits of the Heart: Individualism and Commitment in American Life* (Berkeley, CA: University of California Press, 1985), p. 200.

5. This is an interesting feature given the literature examining women volunteers where the term *politics* is rejected by participants as a description of their actions. As Vivien Lowndes stated in "It's Not What You've Got, But What You Do With It: Women, Social Capital, and Political Participation," in Elisabeth Gidengil and Brenda O'Neill, eds., *Gender and Social Capital* (New York: Routledge, 2006), "female activists often do not identify themselves as being 'active in the community' because they regard their activities (such as after-school clubs or tenants' groups) as an extension of their domestic caring roles" (p. 224). See also Amy Blackstone, "It's Just about Being Fair: Activism and Politics of Volunteering in the Breast Cancer Movement," *Gender and Society* 18, no. 3 (2004), pp. 350–368, for an interesting discussion of attitudes toward politics, feminism, and activism in the Koman Breast Cancer Foundation, which organizes the "Run for the Cure" in the U.S., and Nina Eliasoph, *Avoiding Politics: How Americans Produce Apathy in Everyday Life* (Cambridge, UK: Cambridge University Press, 1998), for a more general discussion.

6. Bellah et al., *Habits of the Heart*, p. 200.

7. Birte Siim, "Engendering Democracy: Social Citizenship and Political Participation for Women in Scandanavia," in *Social Politics* 1 (1994), pp. 286–305.

8. Centre for Civil Society, London School of Economics, "What Is Civil Society?" available at http://www.lse.ac.uk/collections/CCS/what_is_civil_society.htm. March 1, 2004. Accessed October 29, 2007.

9. Robert Putnam, "Bowling Alone: America's Declining Social Capital," *Journal of Democracy* 6.1 (1995), p. 67.

10. Lowndes, "It's Not What You've Got," p. 213.

11. Pierre Bourdieu and James Coleman, along with Putnam, are most often recognized as having published the seminal work on social capital. For good reviews and critiques of the literature, see Stephen Baron, John Field and Tom Schuller, *Social Capital Critical Perspective.* (Oxford, UK: Oxford University Press, 2000); Michael W. Foley and Bob Edwards, "The Paradox of Civil Society," *Journal of Democracy* 7.3, pp. 38–52; and Bob Edwards, Michael W. Foley, and Mario Diani, *Beyond Tocqueville: Civil Society and the Social Capital Debate in Comparative Perspective* (Hanover: Tufts University/University Press of New England, 2001).

12. Foley and Edwards, "The Paradox of Civil Society," p. 42.

13. Putnam, "Bowling Alone," pp. 65–78.

14. Lowndes, "It's Not What You've Got," p. 223.

15. See, for example, Barbara Arneil, "Just Communities: Social Capital, Gender, and Culture," in Elisabeth Gidengil and Brenda O'Neill, eds., *Gender and Social Capital*

(New York: Routledge, 2006), pp. 15–43; Barbara Arneil, *Diverse Communities: The Problem with Social Capital* (Cambridge, UK: Cambridge University Press, 2006); Elisabeth Gidengil and Brenda O'Neill, "Removing Rose Colored Glasses: Examining Theories of Social Capital through a Gendered Lens," in Elisabeth Gidengil and Brenda O'Neill, eds., *Gender and Social Capital* (New York: Routledge, 2006), pp. 1–14; Pamela Herd and Madonna Harrington Meyer, "Care Work: Invisible Civic Engagement," *Gender and Society* 16, no. 5 (October 2002), pp. 665–688; Vivien Lowndes, "Women and Social Capital: A Comment on Hall's 'Social Capital in Britain,'" *British Journal of Political Science* 30 (2000), pp. 533–540; Lowndes, "It's Not What You've Got" (above); and Theda Skocpol and Morris P. Fiorina, *Civic Engagement in American Democracy* (Washington, DC: Brooking Institution, 1999).

16. Lowndes, "It's Not What You've Got," p. 215.

17. Joanna Everitt, "Gender Role Orientations and the Conversion of Social Capital into Political Engagement," in Elisabeth Gidengil and Brenda O'Neill, eds., *Gender and Social Capital* (New York: Routledge, 2006), p. 276.

18. Nancy Sheehan, "The WCTU and Education Strategies on the Canadian Prairie," *History of Education Quarterly* 24, no. 1 (1984), pp. 103 & 107.

19. Jacquetta Newman and Linda White, *Women, Politics, and Public Policy: The Political Struggles of Canadian Women* (Don Mills, ON: Oxford University Press, 2006), p. 69.

20. Arneil, "Just Communities"; Arneil, *Diverse Communities;* Virginia Sapiro, "Gender, Social Capital, and Politics," in Elisabeth Gidengil and Brenda O'Neill, eds., *Gender and Social Capital,* (New York: Routledge, 2006); Elizabeth S. Clemens, "Organizational Repertoires and Institutional Change: Women's Groups and Transformation of American Politics, 1890-1920," in Theda Skocpol and Morris P. Fiorina, eds., *Civic Engagement in American Democracy* (Washington, DC: Brooking Institution, 1999), pp. 81–110; Theda Skocpol, *Protecting Soldiers and Mothers: The Politics of Social Provision in the United States 1870s to 1920s* (Cambridge: Harvard University Press, 1992).

21. Arneil, "Just Communities," p. 20.

22. Sapiro, "Gender, Social Capital, and Politics," p. 172.

23. Nancy Adamson, Linda Briskin, and Margaret McPhail, *Feminist Organizing for Change: The Contemporary Women's Movement in Canada* (Don Mills, ON: Oxford University Press, 1988).

24. Roberta Hamilton, *Gendering the Vertical Mosaic: Feminist Perspectives on Canadian Society* (Toronto: Copp Clark, Ltd., 1996), pp. 57–60).

25. Herd and Harrington Meyer, "Care Work," p. 674.

26. Ibid., p. 675.

27. Ibid., p. 675.

28. Lowndes, "It's Not What You've Got," p. 223–24. (An endnote number (50) has been removed from the quotation.)

29. Herd and Harrington Meyer, "Care Work," p. 666.

30. Ibid, p. 673.

31. Lowndes, "Women and Social Capital," p. 537.

32. See Rachel Laforest, "Governance and the Voluntary Sector: Rethinking the Contours of Advocacy," *International Journal of Canadian Studies* 30 (2004), pp. 185–203, and Janine Brodie, *Politics on the Margins: Restructuring and the Canadian Women's Movement* (Halifax: Fernwood Publishing, 1995).

33. Laforest, "Governance and the Voluntary Sector," p. 187.

34. Ibid, pp. 186 & 193.

35. Lowndes, "Women and Social Capital," p. 536.

36. For example, see Cheryl Collier, "Do Strong Women's Movements Get Results? Measuring the Impact of the Child Care and Anti-Violence Movement in Ontario 1970–2000," Paper presented to the annual meeting of the Canadian Political Science Association, London ON, June 2–4, 2005, and Cheryl Collier, "How Party Matters: A Comparative Assessment of the Openness of Left- and Right-Wing Governments to Women's Issues in Ontario and British Columbia," Paper presented to the annual meeting of the Canadian Political Science Association, Saskatoon, SK, May 30–June 1, 2007.

✗ NO

Say It Five Times Fast: The Pitfalls of Small-p Politics and a Plea for Large-P Politics

JACQUETTA NEWMAN

Men alone cannot make just laws for men and women, just as any class of people cannot legislate justly for another class. To deny women the right of lawmaking is to deny the principle of democracy. The workingman knows what he wants better than the capitalist can tell him,—the wearer of the shoe knows where it pinches. . . . The women's point of view has been ignored in the making of our laws, and that is why we have such gross injustice in laws relating to women. Do you think if women had been consulted in framing the laws that a woman's virtue would be held at the same value as a tree or shrub growing in a public park or garden, and valued at five dollars? Yet in our laws of Manitoba today it is so regarded. The abduction of a young girl is punishable by five years' imprisonment but the stealing of a cow is punished by a fourteen year sentence. Property has ever been held dearer than flesh and blood when the flesh and blood are woman's. In March of last year a drunken man turned out into the storm his wife and two children, one an infant, who later died from this exposure. The evidence showed that the poor woman's life had been a perpetual hell of abuse and mortal fear,—the man was given six months, afterwards commuted to two. In Brandon, last September, a farm laborer stole fifteen dollars and a blue silk handkerchief from a companion, and he was sent down for one year with hard labor. . . .

But the day is breaking, and the darkness is fleeing away. Four million women in the United States now enjoy full parliamentary franchise. Women vote in New Zealand, Australia, Iceland, Finland, Norway and China, and have some measure of franchise in many other countries.[1]

—Nellie McClung

The above words were part of a speech made in 1914 by Canadian suffragette Nellie McClung. For the suffragettes, the focus was on formal political rights like the right to vote, because they understood that the way to significantly affect public policy was through electoral influence and ultimately the right to run for and hold elected office. McClung said as much in the same 1914 speech:

For centuries [women] have been acting the good Samaritan by their philanthropies, their private and public charities, their homes for the friendless, for orphan children, free kindergartens, day nurseries; they have been picking up the robbed, wounded and beaten. Now they are wondering if they cannot do something to clear up the road. Investigation is now taking the place of Resignation. . . . This is the meaning of the woman's movement, and we need not apologize for it.[2]

Charitable work was not enough, for while it would alleviate suffering in the short term, it could not solve the causes of suffering. This required a form of social and political reform that was the preview of the provincial and national legislatures. For Nellie McClung and the first-wave feminists, the formal structures of large-P politics mattered, and they still do.

SMALL-p POLITICS IS NOT THE "MAGIC BULLET" TO THE PROBLEM OF WOMEN'S POLITICAL POWER

While a focus on small-p politics illustrates the intrinsically political nature of social activities often undertaken by women and sheds light on the division of society into public and private spheres, it also raises a significant question: if women are such successful social capitalists, why is this not reflected in their political capital? Given the understood propensity for women to engage in the volunteerism associated with community care, it seems surprising that women still continue to be largely absent from formal political activity. One reason is the "luxury of time." Approaches to social capital need to recognize that, along with enhancing political engagement, care work can interfere with civic activity. Herd and Harrington Meyer point to the burden of being both a social and political actor:

> [W]e suggest that participation in these traditional forms of civic engagement interferes with the provision of care work such as cleaning, cooking and bathing. After all someone has to take care of the children while mothers attend protests and rallies. In fact there is evidence that some women use their activism to escape domestic responsibilities.[3]

In acknowledging that child care, cleaning, cooking, and bathing are active forms of participatory citizenship with far-reaching civil benefits, "we recognize not only that they have civic and political value, but that women's inaction is not due to a lack of or decline in their moral values, but rather because of the gender dynamics of care work."[4] Often volunteer community care and social work is not social capital but just unpaid and unrecognized work that just needs to get done. If the individual does not have the time or energy to convert work into a form of social capital, work is just that—work.

The social capital developed by men and women may not translate into the same sort of political capital. In her reservations regarding the concept of social capital, Vivien Lowndes points out that because men and women undertake different types of activities, there are significant differences in the types of social capital developed.[5] In a study of social capital in Great Britain in the 1990s, Lowndes found important differences in the involvement of women compared to men:

> More than twice as many men as women undertook voluntary work related to sports and recreation (29 per cent compared with 13 per cent). Women, by contrast, were more active in voluntary work in the fields of health, education and social services. As for the specific roles undertaken, men were more likely to occupy committee posts, while women dominated in visiting and befriending activities.[6]

This corresponds to research that sees women as more strongly connected to neighbourhood networks than men, having more robust patterns of social exchange, and having more ready access to social support. However, it also illustrates that social capital itself is gendered and, as Lowndes argues, the social capital developed by men may be better suited to "getting ahead" in politics while that developed by women is better for "getting along" in everyday life.[7]

Social capital may get women into politics, but it may also hold them back. We know that women are most active in what could be called the "lower," or more informal, reaches of politics. The more formal the political process becomes, the less likely women are to be active. It seems that women often cross the boundary between community activity and political action in pursuit of particular issues or causes. Having got there, however, they are less likely than men to progress up the political ladder or to move into more formal political arenas.

To crudely follow the economistic analogy at the centre of social capital studies, in making the conversion of social capital to political capital, women find that because their social capital is different, it is of less value. Virginia Sapiro picks up this point when she discusses the fungibility (the ability to exchange or replace a good with one of comparable worth) of social capital.[8]

Not all organizational or interpersonal ties create social capital that is useful for the same purposes, regardless of who is involved. If women's clubs and organizations are generally considered irrelevant to politics, or are not directly interconnected enough with the networks in which political leaders are embedded, there is relatively less politically relevant social capital to be gained from these organizations. If the types of relationships that serve as resources for local political leadership are found among the people who hold elite professional and business positions, and these are male-dominated fields, or among the members of particular clubs and organizations, and these are restricted to men, women's social capital will have little value in politics. Viewed from this perspective, social capital does not really dissolve the division between the public and private. In fact, it perpetuates the division, because women develop private social capital while men develop public social capital.

Ultimately, when we review the reservations voiced by Herd and Harrington Meyer, Sapiro, and Lowndes, the old model of the public man and private woman reappears.

> The argument here is a familiar one in the political, business, and artistic spheres: as the saying goes, behind every great man, there is a great woman.... Women's social capital provides many male politicians with practical support (freeing them from domestic and neighbourhood responsibilities) and also with political support, in the sense of community-based information, knowledge and contacts.[9]

The social capital developed by women actually operates as a resource for men but not for women—in other words, women produce social capital while men spend it. The informal small-p politics of consensual community may actually be a disadvantage for women.

Finally, we need to look hard at the assumption that women undertake the lion's share of voluntary community activism. In Young and Everitt's discussion of advocacy groups, the finding was that "the gender differences among interest group activists are not statistically significant."[10] When we look at formal categorized voluntary participation, the distinction between women and men disappears. For example, a recent report from Statistics Canada on charitable donations claimed by Canadian taxpayers showed that of the 5,752,630 charitable donors in 2006, 44 percent were women while men accounted for 56 percent.[11] The National Survey on Giving and Volunteer Participation (NSGVP), undertaken by Statistics Canada as part of the government's Voluntary Sector Initiative, also found little difference in the participation of women and men as volunteers and donors. The 2004 Canadian Survey of Giving, Volunteering and Participating (Statistics Canada, 2004) reports that 11.8 million Canadians, or 45 percent of the population, volunteered their time to charities and other nonprofit organizations.[12] The most common activities were organizing, supervising, or coordinating activities or events and fundraising, followed by serving as unpaid members of committees or boards and engaging in teaching, educating, or mentoring, which were undertaken in sports and recreation, social services, education and research, and religious organizations.[13] When volunteerism was broken down by sex for rates of volunteerism and hours, the difference was not great, nor was there a great difference between top volunteers (defined as individuals giving 180 hours or more annually).

The NSGVP presents itself as being a "barometer of voluntary and civic action," and the 2004 survey does note that volunteerism does take place outside state-defined "charitable organizations" and traditional community groups.

> Many Canadians also help others directly on their own without working through a charitable or voluntary organization.... [T]he most commonly reported activities were providing help at an individual's home such as

TABLE 11.1

VOLUNTEER RATES AND DISTRIBUTION OF VOLUNTEER HOURS BY PERSONAL CHARACTERISTICS

Sex	Volunteer rate %	Average annual hours	Median volunteer hours	Population distribution	% of volunteer hours
Male	44	168	60	49	48
Female	47	168	64	51	52

Source: Statistics Canada 2004, p. 33.

TABLE 11.2

% OF POPULATION WHO ARE TOP VOLUNTEERS AND % OF VOLUNTEER HOURS

Sex	% of volunteers who are top volunteers	top volunteers as a % of total population	% of total annual volunteer hours
Male	11	5	37
Female	12	6	40

Source: Statistics Canada 2004, p. 38.

cooking, cleaning, gardening, maintenance, painting, shoveling snow or repairs (reported by 60%), providing health related or personal care, such as emotional support, counseling, providing advice, visiting the elderly, and unpaid babysitting (50%), and helping by shopping, driving someone to the store or to other appointments (46%).[14]

This clearly speaks to the informal civic engagement identified as primarily the purview of women, but it is not as clear if this volunteerism is included in the numbers given above for rates of volunteerism and hours. If it does, then we must seriously research or reconsider our assumptions of the work undertaken by women. We may have put too much stock in the focus on small-p politics as a way for women to build political power and influence. As the above statistics indicate, women may not hold a special or dominant place in the networks of small-p politics. Men would appear to be equally involved, and when we combine this observation with the previous argument regarding the importance of the "type of social capital" developed, it would appear that men are equally involved in the types of small-p politics that are best for developing political advantage. The focus on women's social capital may have exaggerated the amount and nature of the work undertaken. As a result, we must be very careful in accepting that small-p politics is a magic bullet for women building political power and influence.

There is a need for much further research on the activities of women in our society and more detailed examination of small-p politics and its relationship to the large-P politics of the state. As the "yes" article admits, the links between small-p politics and public policy are very complex, and the role of women in formal political structures, the willingness of formal structures to work with women outside the structures, and the party composition and associated ideological disposition of governments are very significant factors. In short, large-P politics matters, and it matters a lot.

IT IS CRITICAL THAT WOMEN CONTINUE TO ENGAGE IN LARGE-P POLITICS

If the goal is to influence public policy for the good of women, then it is important for women activists to be involved in forums where public policy is decided. As Alexa McDonough, former leader of the Nova Scotia and federal NDP and member of Parliament, states, "[T]hat is where the power lies; that is where decisions are made."[15] Since governments are powerful decision-making bodies, it is important to be where the action is. Therefore, large-P politics and engagement in electoral and legislative politics are critical. This position is reflected in the tendency for the literature on women in politics to focus on the lack of women representatives in political parties and parliaments. The understanding is that the more women are involved in large-P politics and the more success they have in getting elected as representatives, the more power and influence they will have in getting women's concerns onto the political agenda.[16]

Granted, there is no guarantee that women members will act or speak on behalf of other women. The electoral system is based on the conception that the member is representative of a territorial constituency, not a social constituency, and even if it were the case, not all women share the same interests. It is the debate between descriptive or mirror representation—that is, representation based on the proportion to population (women constitute 51 percent of Canadian society; therefore, they should have 51 percent of the seats in the legislature)—and substantive representation, where the ideas put forward by both women and men representatives are in line with the needs and interests of women. However, while it is debatable that complete substantive representation results from closer approximations of descriptive representation,[17] either way, substantive or descriptive, requires a continued engagement in the formal structures of large-P politics. As Bashevkin points out, "although considerable debate has focused on how to define a meaningful presence or 'critical mass' of women in politics, this procedural perspective suggests numbers of women can matter for the climate as well as the content of group debate."[18]

Lisa Young speaks to the risks of focusing on small-p politics and rejecting engagement in large-P politics: "[A]s autonomous political action has gradually supplanted efforts to engage with political parties ... Canadian political parties have become less responsive to the policy concerns of the women's movement and have focused less attention on including women in political elites."[19] Without pressure from women engaging with the political parties, parties have not seen it necessary to respond to women's issues and demands. This is unfortunate, because when we look at examples of governments that have included larger numbers of women or that have been ideologically disposed to listen to women's concerns, the public policy environment has been much more amenable to women.

In 1990, the New Democratic Party of Ontario under Bob Rae won the provincial election, taking 38 percent of the popular vote and 74 of the 130 seats in the province. Significantly, women made up 26 percent of the party's elected members compared to 13 percent for the Liberal opposition, and 15 percent of the Progressive Conservative MPPs. The number of women in the NDP caucus, combined with Rae's stated commitments to women's issues and the women's movement, resulted in a record number of women appointed to the NDP cabinet. Eleven women sat in the twenty-five-member cabinet, a whopping 44 percent, including a number of avowed feminists such as Marion Boyd (Minister of Education 1990, Women's Issues, Community and Social Services 1991, and Attorney General 1993), Evelyn Gigantes (Health 1990 and Housing 1991), and Frances Lankin (Government Services 1990, Health 1992, Economic Development and Trade 1993). In British Columbia, the election of the New Democratic Party in 1991 also saw a significant rise in the number of women in the government caucus and cabinet. British Columbia NDP leader Mike Harcourt "appointed seven women to his cabinet (27 per cent)—at that point the highest percentage of women ever appointed to a BC cabinet—many of them feminists."[20]

As Cheryl Collier and Lesley Byrne relate in their examinations of the success of women MMPs and the women's movement during this time (Collier for Ontario and B.C., Byrne for Ontario), the numbers of women in government and particularly high-profile cabinet positions did have an impact on women's policy. By comparing Ontario policy regarding child care and violence against women from 1980 to 2002, Collier found that "seven positive policy responses (the most by any government in Ontario) and only one mixed response"[21] occurred when the Rae

TABLE 11.3
WOMEN IN THE ONTARIO LEGISLATURE AND CABINET

Election year	Progressive Conservatives caucus %	NDP caucus %	Liberals caucus %	Government party	Cabinet numbers Women/Total	Cabinet %
1981	6*	5	3	PC	2/28	7
1985	6	12	6*	Lib	2/23	9
1987	6	16	17*	Lib	4/26	15
1990	15	26*	13	NDP	11/25	44
1995	13*	24	13	PC	4/20	20
1999	15*	44	20	PC	5/25	20

* Years when 100% of women elected were promoted to cabinet.

Source: Collier, 2007.

TABLE 11.4
WOMEN IN THE BRITISH COLUMBIA LEGISLATURE AND CABINET

Election year	Social Credit caucus %	NDP caucus %	Liberal caucus %	Government party	Cabinet numbers Women/Total	Cabinet %
1979	6	15	n/a	SC	1/19	5
1983	6	18	n/a	SC	1/19	5
1986	8	23	n/a	SC	2/19	10.5
1991	0	31	18	NDP	7/19	37
1996	n/a	31	24	NDP	5/15	33
2001	n/a	100	22	Lib	8/28	28.5

Source: Collier, 2007.

NDP government held power between 1990 and 1995. Byrne, in her work interviewing women cabinet members and MPPs in Ontario during the Rae years, observes

> Clearly, one of the most important tests of substantive representation is the extent to which women cabinet ministers affected feminist public policy. While their impact was less profound than many Ontario women's groups had hoped and expected, the Rae government did enact important milestones in this area. They included a job creation program with specified child care provisions, increases to the provincial minimum wage, extended parental leave provisions, protection for home workers, employment equity legislation that required employers to ensure their workforces reflected the diversity of the larger community, pay equity laws that raised the pay of more than a million women, enhanced funding for violence against women (in areas of prevention, treatment and education) and child care initiatives, the legalization of midwifery and full public health insurance coverage for clinic abortions.[22]

This was, according to the cabinet ministers interviewed by Byrne, the result of the women in cabinet working together on behalf of women's concerns and voting as a block. Similarly, the Harcourt era in British Columbia represented a high point for women's issues: "Harcourt created the Ministry of Women's Equality (MWE) that considerably improved policy for women. According to Gawthrop, from 1991–93, 'the NDP managed to achieve more for women's equality in two years than the Socred did in the previous fifteen.'"[23] On issues of child care and violence against women, Harcourt's NDP government recorded thirteen positive policy responses, the most of any single government in British Columbia.[24]

These studies and others[25] indicate that party ideology is a key element in a government's openness to women's issues, with centre and left-of-centre parties more responsive to women's claims and more amenable to women's participation. They also indicate that having numbers of women in formal politics affects the policies for women. "Parties in power generally are most likely to view women's movement claims as legitimate if they share the same ideological goals and feminists form one of their key constituencies."[26] However, this is not without some qualifications. Both Byrne and Collier point out that while links between the government and the women's movement were more open during the periods of NDP governments, those links were not as open as movement activists and feminist cabinet ministers would have wanted. According to Byrne, in Ontario, "many of the [women's organizations] believed the government had not accomplished enough particularly during the final two years of its mandates when the overwhelming focus was on fiscal restraint rather than social justice issues. Several ministers I interviewed referred to this slowing of progressive policy change as a disappointing part of their cabinet experience that they would not want to repeat."[27] Similarly, in B.C. as the economic climate changed and the commitment to women's issues declined, activists and party insiders interviewed by Collier noted that the rhetoric of fiscal conservatism became more prevalent in the NDP in 1994, threatening women's policy issues. "Over time, Harcourt found it difficult to 'walk the tightrope' between appeasing the core constituencies of the NDP and allaying the fears of business groups that were uncomfortable with a social democratic government."[28] With a change in provincial NDP leadership to Glen Clark, women's issues were less visible in the 1996 election, and while the number of women in cabinet remained stable, only one woman was appointed to a high-profile portfolio.[29]

These qualifications return us to the debate over whether women's political power and influence is best derived from descriptive/mirror representation or substantive representation, but the numbers still appear to matter. It is clearly not a question of either–or; the situation is a complex mix of numbers of women, party ideology, feminist consciousness, political opportunity, and women's movement strength and the strategies it adopts. Nonetheless, it is undeniable that formal political structures, large-P politics, and the willingness and ability of women to engage in them are a critical part of this complex puzzle. "If a party comes to power with feminist principles, and the leader appoints significant numbers of women to cabinet, then we conclude that regime can exert a major impact on public policy."[30]

WHAT DOES IT MEAN TO BE A CITIZEN IN A DEMOCRACY?

Finally, we must view any debate between committing to small-p politics and large-P politics from the perspective of what citizenship entails in our democratic system. As Young and Everitt point out, "at the heart of modern democracy lie representative institutions that gain their mandates through popular election. The location of popular sovereignty in these institutions is the hallmark of modern democracy."[31] Our notions of citizenship are bound up in our understanding of the formal structures of democracy and large-P politics being the centre of political power. Citizenship itself refers to one's membership in a political community and its accompanying rights, particularly access to participate in the political and legal institutions that design and determine that power and how it is used.

Democratic self-government means that people should be able to make decisions about their community and about themselves, by themselves. As Nellie McClung pointed out in the speech opening this article, "men alone cannot make just laws for men and women, just as any class of people cannot legislate justly for another class." Arscott and Trimble pick up this sentiment, arguing that while it might be true that men are quite capable of representing women's interests, they "cannot claim power for women and they cannot hold power in women's stead."[32] It is not good enough for only men to make policy for women, as it is not good enough for only white women to make policy for women of colour, as it is not good enough for only able-bodied persons to make policy for disabled persons, and so on. Democracy requires some level of participation in voting, in political parties, in elected office and so on, from all the various groups and interests in a society for a community to be considered self-governing.

By removing oneself from the world of large-P politics, one runs the risk of losing one's place and legitimacy in the community's negotiation or discourse of how power should be distributed and wielded. It undermines the conception of democratic citizenship. "From the perspective of democratic representation women's presence as public actors confirms, while their absence disconfirms, the legitimacy of democratic practices."[33] Therefore, while we should not throw the proverbial baby out with the bathwater and reject small-p politics outright, we must recognize the perils inherent in women taking an either–or approach in how they deal with politics. And to that end, we certainly cannot reject engagement in large-P politics.

NOTES

1. Candace Savage, *Our Nell: A Scrapbook Biography of Nellie L. McClung*. (Halifax: Goodread Biographies, James Lorimer, 1979), pp. 83–84.

2. Ibid., p. 82.

3. Pamela Herd and Madonna Harrington Meyer, "Care Work: Invisible Civic Engagement," *Gender and Society* 16, no. 5 (October 2002), pp. 669–670.

4. Ibid., p. 671.

5. Vivien Lowndes, "Women and Social Capital: A Comment on Hall's 'Social Capital in Britain,'" *British Journal of Political Science* 30 (2000), pp. 533–540, and Vivien Lowndes, "It's Not What You've Got, But What You Do With It: Women, Social Capital, and Political Participation," in Elisabeth Gidengil and Brenda O'Neill (eds.), *Gender and Social Capital* (New York: Routledge, 2006), pp. 213–240.

6. Lowndes, "Women and Social Capital," p. 534.

7. Lowndes, "It's Not What You've Got," p. 228.

8. Virginia Sapiro, "Gender, Social Capital, and Politics," in Elisabeth Gidengil and Brenda O'Neill, eds., *Gender and Social Capital* (New York: Routledge, 2006), p. 175.

9. Lowndes, "It's Not What You've Got," pp. 230–231.

10. Lisa Young and Joanne Everitt, *Advocacy Groups* (Vancouver: UBC Press, 2004), p. 30.

11. This may be partially explained by the fact that for couples, donations would be applied against the larger income for tax purposes and for the most part that is the male wage-earner. See Dawn Walton, Paul Waldie, and Tavia Grant, "More Donations, Fewer Donors," *The Globe and Mail*, November 2, 2007, p. A1.

12. Statistics Canada, *Highlights from the 2004 Canadian Survey of Giving, Volunteering and Participating* (Ottawa: Minister of Industry, June 2006), catalogue no. 71-542-XIE, p. 33.

13. Ibid., p. 12.

14. Ibid., p. 12.

15. Meredith Ralston, *Why Women Run* (Montreal: National Film Board, 1999).

16. For example, see Joni Lovenduski and Pippa Norris, eds., *Gender and Party Politics* (London: Sage Publications, 1993); Jane Arscott and Linda Trimble, eds., *In the Presence of Women: Representation in Canadian Governments* (Toronto: Harcourt Brace, 1997); Jill Vickers, "Towards a Feminist Understanding of Representation," in Jane Arscott and Linda Trimble, eds., *In the Presence of Women: Representation in Canadian Governments* (Toronto: Harcourt Brace, 1997), pp. 20–46; Manon Tremblay and Linda Trimble, eds., *Women and Electoral Politics in Canada* (Don Mills: Oxford University Press Canada, 2003); Jacquetta Newman and Linda White, *Women, Politics, and Public Policy: The Political Struggles of Canadian Women* (Don Mills, ON: Oxford University Press, 2006), p. 69; Marian Sawer, Manon Tremblay, and Linda Trimble, eds., *Representing Women in Parliament: A Comparative Study* (New York: Routledge, 2006); Sylvia Bashevkin, ed., *Are Doors Opening Wider? Studies of Women's Political Engagement in Canada* (Vancouver: UBC Press, forthcoming).

17. See Lesley Hyland Byrne, "Feminists in Power: Women Cabinet Ministers in the New Democratic Party (NDP) Government of Ontario 1990–1995," *Policy Studies Journal* 5, no. 4 (1997), pp. 601–612; Virginia Sapiro, "When Are Interests Interesting? The Problem of Political Representation of Women," *The American Political Science Review* 75, no. 3 (1981), pp. 701–21; Vickers, "Towards a Feminist Understanding of Representation"; Sawer, Tremblay, and Trimble, *Representing Women in Parliament;* and Bashevkin, *Are Doors Opening Wider?*

18. Sylvia Bashevkin, "Introduction," in Bashevkin, ed., *Are Doors Opening Wider? Studies of Women's Political Engagement in Canada* (Vancouver: UBC Press, forthcoming).

19. Lisa Young, "Can Feminists Transform Party Politics? The Canadian Experience," in Manon Tremblay and Linda Trimble, eds., *Women and Electoral Politics in Canada* (Don Mills, ON: Oxford University Press, 2003), p. 77.

20. Cheryl N. Collier, "How Party Matters: A Comparative Assessment of the Openness of Left- and Right-Wing Governments to Women's Issues in Ontario and British Columbia 1980–2002.," Paper presented at the annual meeting of the Canadian Political Science Association, University of Saskatchewan, Saskatoon, May 30–June 1, 2007, p. 15. Used with permission and thanks.

21. Ibid., p. 19.

22. Byrne, "Feminists in Power," and Lesley Hyland Byrne, "Can Changing Nomination Rules Change Public Policy? The Ontario Experience, 1990–1995," in Bashevkin, ed., *Are Doors Opening Wider? Studies of Women's Political Engagement in Canada* (Vancouver: UBC Press, forthcoming).

23. Cited in Collier, "How Party Matters."

24. Ibid., p. 21.

25. See Arscott and Trimble, *In the Presence of Women;* Collier, "How Party Matters"; and Sawer, Tremblay, and Trimble, *Representing Women in Parliament.*

26. Cheryl N. Collier, "Do Strong Women's Movements Get Results? Measuring the Impact of Child Care and Anti-Violence Movements in Ontario 1970–2000," Paper presented at the annual meeting of the Canadian Political Science Association, London, Ontario, June 2–4, 2005, p. 3.

27. Byrne, "Can Changing Nomination Rules Change Public Policy?"

28. Collier, "How Party Matters," p. 15.

29. Ibid., p. 15.

30. Byrne, "Can Changing Nomination Rules Change Public Policy?"

31. Young and Everitt, *Advocacy Groups*, p. 22.

32. Arscott and Trimble, *In the Presence of Women*, p. 4.

33. Bashevkin, "Introduction."

POSTSCRIPT

In her first article, Newman makes the convincing case that the activities of everyday life have the potential to enhance the participation of women in political life and to achieve policy outcomes essential to the equality of the sexes. In a way, this argument is an extension of one of the insights of feminist thinking, namely that the attempt to separate the public and private dimensions of society is ill-advised and may actually be harmful. When women congregate to watch their children play hockey or run into each other at school events, they are developing the networks—the social capital—that can be used to achieve larger political ends. For Newman, women need not look only at formal political structures for advancement. It may be enough to examine more carefully the promise inherent in the routines of their daily lives.

Accordingly, the case for small-p politics is strong, yet it is not totally convincing. At times, it seems too good to be true, and usually phenomena that evoke this quality are indeed just too good to be true. It is nice to think that mothers watching a game of road hockey can lead to better traffic conditions or that a daughter providing comfort to an elderly mother may be transformed into a reformer of long-term care, but one has to wonder whether this is realistic. As well, it seems where social capital may be capitalized is in the formation of powerful women's interest groups, which may be seen more properly as an element of large-P politics. Finally, the opportunity cost of the small-p politics seems high because it means the neglect of the effort to achieve greater women's representation in the offices of government. It is true that success for women lately in large-P politics has been disappointing, but it seems rather premature to give up on this endeavour. Patience is a virtue.

In her second article, Newman furthers the argument against a reliance on small-p politics. Sometimes caring for children or looking after sick ones is exactly what it appears to be: hard work. Such activities have little or nothing to do with politics, and to argue otherwise is to engage in a cruel hoax. It is also true, as Newman claims, that participation in formal politics can precipitate major changes in public policy, something that will likely elude most activities in the world of small-p politics. However, it may be that the Newman of large-P politics slights the insights of the Newman of small-p politics. In the second piece, Newman quotes a former NDP leader who claims that it is in the formal political institutions "where the power lies" and "decisions are made." Now, it is certainly the case that formal decisions are arrived at in the legislature, but this outcome is not necessarily—and often is not—a result of power within this same body. Rather, power, as Newman reveals in her first effort, can arise out of the activities of women in the vast array of activities found outside of formal politics. Also, the Newman of large-P politics founds her case partly on the claim that the social capital of small-p politics has provided little. But surely we have seen some important advances that have contributed to the greater well-being of women.

This debate arises largely out of the disappointments with the representation of women in formal political institutions and processes. For an examination of this situation in Canada, students should read the following: Linda Trimble and Jane Arscott, *Still Counting: Women in Politics across Canada* (Peterborough: Broadview Press, 2003), Jacquetta Newman and Linda A. White, *Women, Politics, and Public Policy: The Political Struggles of Canadian Women* (Toronto: Oxford University Press, 2006), Manon Tremblay and Linda Trimble, eds., *Women and Electoral Politics in Canada* (Toronto: Oxford University Press, 2003), and Lisa Young, *Feminists and Party Politics* (Vancouver: UBC, 2000). Some additional readings might be consulted to acquire an appreciation of women and political representation in the United States and elsewhere: Jennifer L. Lawless and Richard L. Fox, *It Takes a Candidate: Why Women Don't Run for Office* (New York: Cambridge University Press, 2005), and Marian Sawer, Manon Tremblay, and Linda Trimble, eds., *Representing Women in Parliament: A Comparative Study* (New York: Routledge, 2006).

As for sources on the world of small-p politics and social capital, students might start with Robert Putnam, *Bowling Alone: The Collapse and Revival of American Community* (New York: Simon & Schuster, 2000), the text that gave widespread currency to a particular conception of social capital. The next task is to consider readings on social capital and women in politics, and for this the interested reader should examine the various contributions in Brenda O'Neill and Elisabeth Gidengil, eds., *Gender and Social Capital* (New York: Routledge, 2006). Additional readings include those listed in the references found at the end of the two Newman papers.

PART FOUR

POLITICAL ISSUES

Are Prohibitions on Private Health Care
Inconsistent with the Charter of Rights?

Should Religious Beliefs Be Excluded
from Consideration of Public Policy?

Should Representation in Parliament
Mirror Canada's Social Diversity?

Should the Court Challenges Program
Be Reinstated?

Are Prohibitions on Private Health Care Inconsistent with the Charter of Rights?

✔ **YES**
CHIEF JUSTICE BEVERLEY MCLACHLIN AND JUSTICE JOHN MAJOR
(WITH JUSTICE BASTARACHE IN AGREEMENT),
"Opinion in *Chaoulli v. Quebec*"

✗ **NO**
JUSTICE IAN BINNIE AND JUSTICE LOUIS LEBEL (WITH JUSTICE
MORRIS FISH IN AGREEMENT), "Opinion in *Chaoulli v. Quebec*"

In June of 2005, the Supreme Court of Canada released an eagerly awaited decision addressing the question of whether prohibitions on the use of private insurance for medically required care in Quebec were in violation of the Quebec Charter of Human Rights and Freedoms and the Canadian Charter of Rights and Freedoms. Two private citizens of Quebec, one a doctor and the other a patient, had averred that the lack of access to private insurance was inconsistent with provisions in the two charters that protected the life and security of a person. The absence of private insurance to pay for medical and hospital care allegedly put at grave risk patients facing long wait times in the public health-care system. In a split decision, a slim majority of the court—four of the seven justices involved in the decision—said that the Quebec Charter had indeed been violated. As for the Canadian Charter, only six of the justices decided on this question, with three on each side.

For Quebec, the implication of the decision was clear: the Quebec Charter had not been respected and access to private insurance would have to be granted. A year later, the government of Quebec introduced new legislation allowing use of private insurance for selected procedures with provision to add additional ones. However, for the rest of Canada, or at least those provinces other than Quebec with similar prohibitions on private insurance (a few provinces had none), the significance of the Supreme Court's decision was more complicated. In these provinces, the Quebec Charter was not applicable, so the majority decision had no effect; as for the Canadian Charter, it *was* applicable and people in these provinces—and arguably Canadians in general—had an interest in knowing which set of judges in the deadlocked decision was the more convincing. The fact that a couple of court challenges contesting comparable insurance provisions in provinces outside Quebec also underlined the importance of the conflicting opinions of the court.

For the justices who saw a violation of the Canadian Charter, the combination of the prohibitions and the long waiting times translated into a clear abrogation of a citizen's right to security of life. However, the Charter provision containing this right, section 7, states that a deprivation of a person's right to life and security might be acceptable if done in accordance with rules of fundamental justice. The judges identified a failure to respect fundamental justice as situations in which the laws that violate rights are arbitrary or unrelated to the purpose of the legislation in which the offending laws are contained. The government of Quebec had argued that the prohibitions were necessary to protect the viability of the Quebec public health care system; the fear was that easier access to private insurance might lead to a two-tiered system—higher-quality private care for the well-off and lower-quality public care for the less well-off. But the judges found no evidence to support this concern. The experience of other countries revealed that private insurance arrangements and public health care systems could coexist quite well. Accordingly, the laws underlying the prohibitions were labelled arbitrary. The Canadian Charter allows for violations of rights on the grounds that the offending law constitutes a reasonable limit, but here too the justices ruled against the prohibitions.

The remaining three justices disagreed with the reasoning of their colleagues and provided a scathing critique of the other side's use of evidence to support their claim of arbitrariness. They argued that a more prudent examination of the facts of the case led to a more generous assessment of the prohibitions on private insurance. The justices were convinced that one could argue that the prohibitions and the preservation of a single-tier system—in which all Canadians receive the same access to the same type of care—followed one from the other. Without the prohibitions, Canada's public health system would be in difficulty. With this reasoning, the justices supported the restrictions on private insurance and found no violation of the Charter.

As mentioned, legal challenges similar to the one in Quebec have been launched in a few provinces (Ontario and Alberta) with prohibitions on private insurance and other elements of private medicine. Eventually, these two cases may find their way to the Supreme Court of Canada, at which time the most senior justices in Canada will have an opportunity once again to make important decisions affecting the operation of Canada's health care system.

The readings are the two opinions addressing the question of whether bans on private insurance for medically required care violate the Canadian Charter of Rights and Freedoms (a third opinion involves only the Quebec Charter). The editors have inserted comments (bracketed by ~) into the two opinions either to clarify points or to summarize parts of the opinions that are omitted.

✔ **YES**

Opinion in *Chaoulli v. Quebec*

CHIEF JUSTICE BEVERLEY MCLACHLIN AND JUSTICE JOHN MAJOR (WITH JUSTICE BASTARACHE IN AGREEMENT)

~ Both opinions refer to the opinion of Deschamps J., who is the only one of the seven justices participating in the case who limited her decision to a consideration of the prohibitions and their relation to the Quebec Charter of Human Rights and Freedoms. McLachlin and Major refer to the appellants in the case, Jacques Chaoulli and Geroge Zeliotis. The two men, the one a doctor and the other a patient, first brought the case to the attention of the courts. ~

[102] THE CHIEF JUSTICE AND MAJOR J. – We concur in the conclusion of our colleague Deschamps J. that the prohibition against contracting for private health insurance violates s. 1 of the Quebec Charter of Human Rights and Freedoms, and is not justifiable under s. 9.1. On the argument that the anti-insurance provision also violates s. 7 of the Canadian Charter of Rights and Freedoms ('Charter'), we conclude that the provision impermissibly limits the right to life, liberty and security of the person protected by s. 7 of the Charter and has not been shown to be justified as a reasonable limit under s. 1 of the Charter.

[103] The appellants do not seek an order that the government spend more money on health care, nor do they seek an order that waiting times for treatment under the public health care scheme be reduced. They only seek a ruling that because delays in the public system place their health and security at risk, they should be allowed to take out insurance to permit them to access private services.

[104] The Charter does not confer a freestanding constitutional right to health care. However, where the government puts in place a scheme to provide health care, that scheme must comply with the Charter. We are of the view that the prohibition on medical insurance in s. 15 of the Health Insurance Act, and s. 11 of the Hospital Insurance Act, violates s. 7 of the Charter because it impinges on the right to life, liberty and security of the person in an arbitrary fashion that fails to conform to the principles of fundamental justice.

[105] The primary objective of the Canada Health Act, R.S.C. 1985, c. C-6, is 'to protect, promote and restore the physical and mental well-being of residents of Canada and to facilitate reasonable access to health services without financial or other barriers' (s. 3). By imposing exclusivity and then failing to provide public health care of a reasonable standard within a reasonable time, the government creates circumstances that trigger the application of s. 7 of the Charter.

[106] The Canada Health Act, the Health Insurance Act, and the Hospital Insurance Act do not expressly prohibit private health services. However, they limit access to private health services by removing the ability to contract for private

health care insurance to cover the same services covered by public insurance. The result is a virtual monopoly for the public health scheme. The state has effectively limited access to private health care except for the very rich, who can afford private care without need of insurance. This virtual monopoly, on the evidence, results in delays in treatment that adversely affect the citizen's security of the person. Where a law adversely affects life, liberty or security of the person, it must conform to the principles of fundamental justice. This law, in our view, fails to do so.

[107] While the decision about the type of health care system Quebec should adopt falls to the Legislature of that province, the resulting legislation, like all laws, is subject to constitutional limits, including those imposed by s. 7 of the Charter. The fact that the matter is complex, contentious or laden with social values does not mean that the courts can abdicate the responsibility vested in them by our Constitution to review legislation for Charter compliance when citizens challenge it. . . .

[108] The government defends the prohibition on medical insurance on the ground that the existing system is the only approach to adequate health care for all Canadians. The question in this case, however, is not whether single-tier health care is preferable to two-tier health care. Even if one accepts the government's goal, the legal question raised by the appellants must be addressed: is it a violation of s. 7 of the Charter to prohibit private insurance for health care, when the result is to subject Canadians to long delays with resultant risk of physical and psychological harm? The mere fact that this question may have policy ramifications does not permit us to avoid answering it.

SECTION 7 OF THE CHARTER

[109] Section 7 of the Charter guarantees that 'everyone has the right to life, liberty and security of the person and the right not to be deprived thereof except in accordance with the principles of fundamental justice.' The disposition of this appeal therefore requires us to consider (1) whether the impugned provisions deprive individuals of their life, liberty or security of the person; and (2) if so, whether this deprivation is in accordance with the principles of fundamental justice. . . .

DEPRIVATION OF LIFE, LIBERTY OR SECURITY OF THE PERSON

[110] The issue at this stage is whether the prohibition on insurance for private medical care deprives individuals of their life, liberty or security of the person protected by s. 7 of the Charter.

[111] The appellants established that many Quebec residents face delays in treatment that adversely affect their security of the person and that they would not sustain but for the prohibition on medical insurance. It is common ground that the effect of the prohibition on insurance is to allow only the very rich, who do

not need insurance, to secure private health care in order to avoid the delays in the public system. Given the ban on insurance, most Quebeckers have no choice but to accept delays in the medical system and their adverse physical and psychological consequences.

[112] Delays in the public system are widespread and have serious, sometimes grave, consequences. There was no dispute that there is a waiting list for cardiovascular surgery for life-threatening problems. Dr. Daniel Doyle, a cardiovascular surgeon who teaches and practises in Quebec City, testified that a person with coronary disease is 'sitting on a bomb' and can die at any moment. He confirmed, without challenge, that patients die while on waiting lists: Inevitably, where patients have life-threatening conditions, some will die because of undue delay in awaiting surgery. . . .

[114] Dr. Eric Lenczner, an orthopaedic surgeon, testified that the one-year delay commonly incurred by patients requiring ligament reconstruction surgery increases the risk that their injuries will become irreparable. Dr. Lenczner also testified that 95 per cent of patients in Canada wait well over a year, and many two years, for knee replacements. While a knee replacement may seem trivial compared to the risk of death for wait-listed coronary surgery patients, which increases by 0.5 per cent per month, the harm suffered by patients awaiting replacement knees and hips is significant. Even though death may not be an issue for them, these patients 'are in pain,' 'would not go a day without discomfort' and are 'limited in their ability to get around,' some being confined to wheelchairs or house bound.

[115] Both the individual members of the Standing Senate Committee on Social Affairs, Science and Technology who intervened in this appeal and the Canadian Medical Association cited a Statistics Canada study demonstrating that over one in five Canadians who needed health care for themselves or a family member in 2001 encountered some form of difficulty, from getting an appointment to experiencing lengthy waiting times. . . . Thirty-seven per cent of those patients reported pain. . . .

[118] The jurisprudence of this Court holds that delays in obtaining medical treatment which affect patients physically and psychologically trigger the protection of s. 7 of the Charter. In R. v. Morgentaler, [1988] 1 S.C.R. 30, Dickson C.J. concluded that the delay in obtaining therapeutic abortions, which increased the risk of complications and mortality due to mandatory procedures imposed by the state, was sufficient to trigger the physical aspect of the woman's right to security of the person. He found that the psychological impact on women awaiting abortions constituted an infringement of security of the person. Beetz J. agreed with Dickson C.J. that '[t]he delays mean therefore that the state has intervened in such a manner as to create an additional risk to health, and consequently this intervention constitutes a violation of the woman's security of the person.'

[119] In this appeal, delays in treatment giving rise to psychological and physical suffering engage the s. 7 protection of security of the person just as they did in Morgentaler. In Morgentaler, as in this case, the problem arises from a legislative scheme that offers health services. In Morgentaler the problem arises from a legislative scheme that offers health services. In Morgentaler, as in this case, the legislative scheme denies people the right to access alternative health care. (That the sanction in Morgentaler was criminal prosecution while the sanction here is administrative prohibition and penalties is irrelevant. The important point is that in both cases, care outside the legislatively provided system is effectively prohibited.) In Morgentaler the result of the monopolistic scheme was delay in treatment with attendant physical risk and psychological suffering. In Morgentaler, as here, people in urgent need of care face the same prospect: unless they fall within the wealthy few who can pay for private care, typically outside the country, they have no choice but to accept the delays imposed by the legislative scheme and the adverse physical and psychological consequences this entails. As in Morgentaler, the result is interference with security of the person under s. 7 of the Charter. . . .

[121] . . . In Morgentaler, as here, the system left the individual facing a lack of critical care with no choice but to travel outside the country to obtain the required medical care at her own expense. . . .

[123] Not every difficulty rises to the level of adverse impact on security of the person under s. 7. The impact, whether psychological or physical, must be serious. However, because patients may be denied timely health care for a condition that is clinically significant to their current and future health, s. 7 protection of security of the person is engaged. Access to a waiting list is not access to health care. As we noted above, there is unchallenged evidence that in some serious cases, patients die as a result of waiting lists for public health care. Where lack of timely health care can result in death, s. 7 protection of life itself is engaged. The evidence here demonstrates that the prohibition on health insurance results in physical and psychological suffering that meets this threshold requirement of seriousness.

[124] We conclude, based on the evidence, that prohibiting health insurance that would permit ordinary Canadians to access health care, in circumstances where the government is failing to deliver health care in a reasonable manner, thereby increasing the risk of complications and death, interferes with life and security of the person as protected by s. 7 of the Charter. . . .

DEPRIVATION IN ACCORDANCE WITH THE PRINCIPLES OF FUNDAMENTAL JUSTICE

[126] Having concluded that the ban on private medical insurance constitutes a deprivation of life and security of the person, we now consider whether that deprivation is in accordance with the principles of fundamental justice. Our

colleagues Binnie and LeBel JJ. argue that the record here provides no ground for finding that the deprivation violates the principles of fundamental justice. With respect, we cannot agree. . . .

[128] The principle of fundamental justice implicated in this case is that laws that affect the life, liberty or security of the person shall not be arbitrary. We are of the opinion that the evidence before the trial judge supports a finding that the impugned provisions are arbitrary and that the deprivation of life and security of the person that flows from them cannot therefore be said to accord with the principles of fundamental justice. . . .

[130] A law is arbitrary where 'it bears no relation to, or is consistent with, the objective that lies behind [it].' To determine whether this is the case, it is necessary to consider the state interest and societal concerns that the provision is meant to reflect. . . .

WHETHER THE PROHIBITION ON PRIVATE MEDICAL INSURANCE IS ARBITRARY

[135] The government argues that the interference with security of the person caused by denying people the right to purchase private health insurance is necessary to providing effective health care under the public health system. It argues that if people can purchase private health insurance, they will seek treatment from private doctors and hospitals, which are not banned under the Act. According to the government's argument, this will divert resources from the public health system into private health facilities, ultimately reducing the quality of public care.

[136] In support of this contention, the government called experts in health administration and policy. Their conclusions were based on the 'common sense' proposition that the improvement of health services depends on exclusivity. They did not profess expertise in waiting times for treatment. Nor did they present economic studies or rely on the experience of other countries. They simply assumed, as a matter of apparent logic, that insurance would make private health services more accessible and that this in turn would undermine the quality of services provided by the public health care system.

[137] The appellants, relying on other health experts, disagreed and offered their own conflicting 'common sense' argument for the proposition that prohibiting private health insurance is neither necessary nor related to maintaining high quality in the public health care system. Quality public care, they argue, depends not on a monopoly, but on money and management. They testified that permitting people to buy private insurance would make alternative medical care more accessible and reduce the burden on the public system. The result, they assert, would be better care for all. The appellants reinforce this argument by

pointing out that disallowing private insurance precludes the vast majority of Canadians (middle-income and low-income earners) from accessing additional care, while permitting it for the wealthy who can afford to travel abroad or pay for private care in Canada.

[138] To this point, we are confronted with competing but unproven 'common sense' arguments, amounting to little more than assertions of belief. We are in the realm of theory. But as discussed above, a theoretically defensible limitation may be arbitrary if in fact the limit lacks a connection to the goal.

~ The paragraph immediately below talks about the experience of the "appellants at trial." As with nearly all cases, this one began at the lower court level—the trial level—and then moved to a court of appeal before making it to the Supreme Court of Canada. Both the trial and appellate courts decided against Chaoulli and Zeliotis. ~

[139] This brings us to the evidence called by the appellants at trial on the experience of other developed countries with public health care systems which permit access to private health care. The experience of these countries suggests that there is no real connection in fact between prohibition of health insurance and the goal of a quality public health system.

[140] The evidence adduced at trial establishes that many western democracies that do not impose a monopoly on the delivery of health care have successfully delivered to their citizens medical services that are superior to and more affordable than the services that are presently available in Canada. This demonstrates that a monopoly is not necessary or even related to the provision of quality public health care.

[141] In its report The Health of Canadians—The Federal Role, the Standing Senate Committee on Social Affairs, Science and Technology discussed in detail the situations in several countries, including Sweden, Germany, and the United Kingdom. The following discussion of the health care systems in these three countries is drawn directly from the findings in volume 3 of the report The Health of Canadians—The Federal Role, vol. 3, Health Care Systems in Other Countries, Interim report (2002) ('Kirby Report').

[142] In Sweden, as in Canada, access to public health care is universal. The public health care system is financed predominantly by the public sector through a combination of general taxation and social insurance (i.e., employer/employee contributions) and employs a user fee mechanism. Unlike in Canada, private health care insurance that covers the same benefits as public insurance is 'legal' in Sweden. However, only a small minority of the population purchase private insurance. The result is a system of public health care coverage that provides quality care on a broader basis than in Canada and encompasses physicians, hospital services, drugs and dental care. In Sweden, the availability of private health care insurance appears not to have harmed the public health care system.

[143] In Germany, public health care insurance is administered by 453 Sickness Funds—private non-profit organizations structured on a regional task or occupational basis. Sickness Fund membership is compulsory for employees with gross incomes lower than approximately $63,000 Canadian, and voluntary for those with gross incomes above that level. Although all Sickness Funds are regulated at the federal level through what is known as the 'Social Code Book,' they are essentially run by representatives of employees and employers. As in Sweden, public health care coverage is broader in Germany than in Canada, including physician services, hospitals, prescription drugs, diagnostic services, dental care, rehabilitative care, medical devices, psychotherapists, nursing care at home, medical services by non-physicians (physiotherapists, speech therapists, occupational therapists, etc.) and income support during sick leave.

[144] In Germany, as in Sweden, private health insurance is available to individuals at a certain income level who may voluntarily opt out of the Sickness Funds. Private coverage is currently offered by 52 private insurance companies that are obliged to offer an insurance policy with the same benefits as the Sickness Funds at a premium that is no higher than the average maximum contribution to the Sickness Funds. Private health care coverage is also available to self-employed people who are excluded from the Sickness Funds and public servants who are de facto excluded from participating in Sickness Funds as their health care bills are reimbursed at the rate of 50 per cent by the federal government. Private insurance covers the remainder.

[145] Despite the availability of alternatives, 88 per cent of the German population are covered by the public Sickness Funds: this includes 14 per cent to whom private insurance is available. Of the remaining 12 per cent, only 9 per cent are covered by private insurance and less than 1 per cent have no health insurance at all. The remaining 2 per cent are covered by government insurance for military and other personnel.

[146] The United Kingdom offers a comprehensive public health care system—the National Health Service (NHS)—while also allowing for private insurance. Unlike Canada, the United Kingdom allows people to purchase private health care insurance that covers the same benefits as the NHS if these services are supplied by providers working outside of the NHS. Despite the existence of private insurance, only 11.5 per cent of the population have purchased it. Again, it appears that the public system has not suffered as a result of the existence of private alternatives.

[147] After reviewing a number of public health care systems, the Standing Senate Committee on Social Affairs, Science and Technology concluded in the Kirby Report that far from undermining public health care, private contributions and insurance improve the breadth and quality of health care for all citizens, and it ultimately concluded, at p. 66:

The evidence suggests that a contribution of direct payments by patients, allowing private insurance to cover some services, even in publicly funded hospitals, and an expanded role for the private sector in the delivery of health services are the factors which have enabled countries to achieve broader coverage of health services for all their citizens. Some countries like Australia and Singapore openly encourage private sector participation as a means to ensure affordable and sustainable health services.

[148] Nor does it appear that private participation leads to the eventual demise of public health care. It is compelling to note that not one of the countries referred to relies exclusively on either private insurance or the public system to provide health care coverage to its citizens. Even in the United States, where the private sector is a dominant participant in the field of health care insurance, public funding accounts for 45% of total health care spending.

[149] In summary, the evidence on the experience of other western democracies refutes the government's theoretical contention that a prohibition on private insurance is linked to maintaining quality public health care.

[150] Binnie and LeBel JJ. suggest that the experience of other countries is of little assistance. With respect, we cannot agree. This evidence was properly placed before the trial judge and, unless discredited, stands as the best guide with respect to the question of whether a ban on private insurance is necessary and relevant to the goal of providing quality public health care. The task of the courts, on s. 7 issues as on others, is to evaluate the issue in the light, not just of common sense or theory, but of the evidence. ...

[151] Binnie and LeBel JJ. also suggest that the government's continued commitment to a monopoly on the provision of health insurance cannot be arbitrary because it is rooted in reliance on 'a series of authoritative reports [that analysed] health care in this country and in other countries' (para. 258); they are referring here to the reports of Commissioner Romanow (Building on Values: The Future of Health Care in Canada: Final Report (2002)), and Senator Kirby. We observe in passing that the import of these reports, which differ in many of their conclusions, is a matter of some debate, as attested by our earlier reference to the Kirby Report. But the conclusions of other bodies on other material cannot be determinative of this litigation. They cannot relieve the courts of their obligation to review government action for consistency with the Charter on the evidence before them.

[152] When we look to the evidence rather than to assumptions, the connection between prohibiting private insurance and maintaining quality public health care vanishes. The evidence before us establishes that where the public system fails to deliver adequate care, the denial of private insurance subjects people to long

waiting lists and negatively affects their health and security of the person. The government contends that this is necessary in order to preserve the public health system. The evidence, however, belies that contention.

[153] We conclude that on the evidence adduced in this case, the appellants have established that in the face of delays in treatment that cause psychological and physical suffering, the prohibition on private insurance jeopardizes the right to life, liberty and security of the person of Canadians in an arbitrary manner, and is therefore not in accordance with the principles of fundamental justice.

SECTION 1 OF THE CHARTER

~ Past decisions of the Supreme Court of Canada have led to a legal test for determining whether a Charter violation rises to a reasonable limit on a right or freedom. The brunt of the test, which is employed by McLachlin and Major below, requires three things: namely, that the means and end of the legislation at issue are related to each other; that the right is restricted or limited as little as reasonably possible; and that the salutary effects of the limitation exceed the detrimental effects. ~

[154] Having concluded that the prohibition on private health insurance constitutes a breach of s. 7, we must now consider whether that breach can be justified under s. 1 of the Charter as a reasonable limit demonstrably justified in a free and democratic society. The evidence called in this case falls short of demonstrating such justification.

[155] The government undeniably has an interest in protecting the public health regime. However, given the absence of evidence that the prohibition on the purchase and sale of private health insurance protects the health care system, the rational connection between the prohibition and the objective is not made out. Indeed, we question whether an arbitrary provision, which by reason of its arbitrariness cannot further its stated objective, will ever meet the rational connection test under R. v. Oakes, [1986] 1 S.C.R. 103.

[156] In addition, the resulting denial of access to timely and effective medical care to those who need it is not proportionate to the beneficial effects of the prohibition on private insurance to the health system as a whole. On the evidence here and for the reasons discussed above, the prohibition goes further than necessary to protect the public system: it is not minimally impairing.

[157] Finally, the benefits of the prohibition do not outweigh the deleterious effects. Prohibiting citizens from obtaining private health care insurance may, as discussed, leave people no choice but to accept excessive delays in the public health system. The physical and psychological suffering and risk of death that may result outweigh whatever benefit (and none has been demonstrated to us here) there may be to the system as a whole.

[158] In sum, the prohibition on obtaining private health insurance, while it might be constitutional in circumstances where health care services are reasonable as to both quality and timeliness, is not constitutional where the public system fails to deliver reasonable services. Life, liberty and security of the person must prevail . . . if the government chooses to act, it must do so properly.

[159] We agree with Deschamps J.'s conclusion that the prohibition against contracting for private health insurance violates s. 1 of the Quebec Charter of Human Rights and Freedoms and is not justifiable under s. 9.1. We also conclude that this prohibition violates s. 7 of the Canadian Charter of Rights and Freedoms and cannot be saved under s. 1.

✗ NO

Opinion in *Chaoulli v. Quebec*
JUSTICE IAN BINNIE AND JUSTICE LOUIS LEBEL (WITH JUSTICE MORRIS FISH IN AGREEMENT)

INTRODUCTION

[161] The question in this appeal is whether the province of Quebec not only has the constitutional authority to establish a comprehensive single-tier health plan, but to discourage a second (private) tier health sector by prohibiting the purchase and sale of private health insurance. The appellants argue that timely access to needed medical service is not being provided in the publicly funded system and that the province cannot therefore deny to those Quebeckers (who can qualify) the right to purchase private insurance to pay for medical services whenever and wherever such services can be obtained for a fee, i.e. in the private sector. This issue has been the subject of protracted debate across Canada through several provincial and federal elections. We are unable to agree with our four colleagues who would allow the appeal that such a debate can or should be resolved as a matter of law by judges. We find that, on the legal issues raised, the appeal should be dismissed.

[162] Our colleagues the Chief Justice and Major J. state at para. 105:

> By imposing exclusivity and then failing to provide public health care of a reasonable standard within a reasonable time, the government creates circumstances that trigger the application of s. 7 of the Charter.

[163] The Court recently held in Auton (Guardian ad litem of) v. British Columbia (Attorney General), [2004] 3 S.C.R. 657 that the government was not required to fund the treatment of autistic children. It did not on that occasion address in constitutional terms the scope and nature of 'reasonable' health services. Courts will now have to make that determination. What, then, are constitutionally required 'reasonable health services'? What is treatment 'within a reasonable time'? What are the benchmarks? How short a waiting list is short enough? How many MRIs does the Constitution require? The majority does not tell us. The majority lays down no manageable constitutional standard. The public cannot know, nor can judges or governments know, how much health care is 'reasonable' enough to satisfy s. 7 of the Canadian Charter of Rights and Freedoms ('Canadian Charter') and s. 1 of the Charter of Human Rights and Freedoms, R.S.Q. c. C-12 ('Quebec Charter'). It is to be hoped that we will know it when we see it.

[164] The policy of the Canada Health Act, R.S.C. 1985, c. C-6, and its provincial counterparts is to provide health care based on need rather than on wealth or status. The evidence certainly established that the public health care system put in

place to implement the policy has serious and persistent problems. This does not mean that the courts are well placed to perform the required surgery. The resolution of such a complex fact-laden policy debate does not fit easily within the institutional competence or procedures of courts of law. The courts can use s. 7 of the Canadian Charter to pre-empt the ongoing public debate only if the current health plan violates an established 'principle of fundamental justice.' Our colleagues McLachlin C.J. and Major J. argue that Quebec's enforcement of a single-tier health plan meets this legal test because it is 'arbitrary.' In our view, with respect, the prohibition against private health insurance is a rational consequence of Quebec's commitment to the goals and objectives of the Canada Health Act.

[165] Our colleague Deschamps J. states at para. 4:

> In essence, the question is whether Quebeckers who are prepared to spend money to get access to health care that is, in practice, not accessible in the public sector because of waiting lists may be validly prevented from doing so by the state.

This is so, but of course it must be recognized that the liberty and security of Quebeckers who do not have the money to afford private health insurance, or who cannot qualify for it, or who are not employed by establishments that provide it, are not put at risk by the absence of 'upper tier' health care. It is Quebeckers who have the money to afford private medical insurance and can qualify for it who will be the beneficiaries of the appellants' constitutional challenge.

[166] The Quebec government views the prohibition against private insurance as essential to preventing the current single-tier health system from disintegrating into a de facto two-tier system. The trial judge found, and the evidence demonstrated, that there is good reason for this fear. The trial judge concluded that a private health sector fuelled by private insurance would frustrate achievement of the objectives of the Canada Health Act. She thus found no legal basis to intervene, and declined to do so. This raises the issue of who it is that should resolve these important and contentious issues. Commissioner Roy Romanow makes the following observation in his Report:

> Some have described it as a perversion of Canadian values that they cannot use their money to purchase faster treatment from a private provider for their loved ones. I believe it is a far greater perversion of Canadian values to accept a system where money, rather than need, determines who gets access to care.
>
> (Building on Values: The Future of Health Care in Canada: Final Report (2002), at p. xx ('Romanow Report'))

Whether or not one endorses this assessment, his premise is that the debate is about social values. It is not about constitutional law. We agree. . . .

[175] The argument for a 'two-tier system' is that it will enable 'ordinary' Canadians to access private health care. Indeed, this is the view taken by our colleagues the Chief Justice and Major J. who quote the appellants' argument that 'disallowing private insurance precludes the vast majority of Canadians (middle-income and low-income earners) from accessing' private health care (para. 137). This way of putting the argument suggests that the Court has a mandate to save middle-income and low-income Quebeckers from themselves, because both the Romanow Report and the Kirby Report found that the vast majority of 'ordinary' Canadians want a publicly financed single-tier (more or less) health plan to which access is governed by need rather than wealth and where the availability of coverage is not contingent on personal insurability. Our colleagues rely in part on the experience in the United States (para. 148) and the fact that public funding in that country accounts for only 45 per cent of total health care spending. But if we look at the practical reality of the U.S. system, the fact is that 15.6 per cent of the American population (i.e. about 45 million people) had no health insurance coverage at all in 2003, including about 8.4 million children. As to making health care available to medium and low-income families, the effect of 'two-tier' health coverage in the U.S. is much worse for minority groups than for the majority. Hispanics had an uninsured rate of 32.7 per cent, and African Americans had an uninsured rate of 19.4 per cent. For 45 million Americans, as for those 'ordinary' Quebeckers who cannot afford private medical insurance or cannot obtain it because they are deemed to be 'bad risks,' it is a matter of public health care or no care at all.

[176] It would be open to Quebec to adopt a U.S.-style health care system. No one suggests that there is anything in our Constitution to prevent it. But to do so would be contrary to the policy of the Quebec National Assembly, and its policy in that respect is shared by the other provinces and the federal Parliament. As stated, Quebec further takes the view that significant growth in the private health care system (which the appellants advocate) would inevitably damage the public system. Our colleagues the Chief Justice and Major J. disagree with this assessment, but governments are entitled to act on a reasonable apprehension of risk of such damage.... While the existence of waiting times is undoubted, and their management a matter of serious public concern, the proposed constitutional right to a two-tier health system for those who can afford private medical insurance would precipitate a seismic shift in health policy for Quebec. We do not believe that such a seismic shift is compelled by either the Quebec Charter or the Canadian Charter....

THE CANADIAN CHARTER OF RIGHTS AND FREEDOMS [THE RIGHT TO LIFE, LIBERTY AND SECURITY OF THE PERSON UNDER S. 7 OF THE CHARTER]

[191] Like our colleagues McLachlin C.J. and Major J., we accept the trial judge's conclusion that in some circumstances some Quebeckers may have their life or 'security of the person' put at risk by the prohibition against private health insurance....

~ The two justices go on to argue that "liberty," a further aspect of s. 7 in addition to life and security of the person, has not been violated. This contention narrows the extent of the violation but does not contradict the earlier admission in paragraph 191 that aspects of s. 7—life and security of the person—have not been respected. ~

[207] As stated, the principal legal hurdle to the appellants' Charter challenge is not the preliminary step of identifying a s. 7 interest potentially affected in the case of some Quebeckers in some circumstances. The hurdle lies in their failure to find a fundamental principle of justice that is violated by the Quebec health plan so as to justify the Court in striking down the prohibition against private insurance for what the government has identified as 'insured services.'

PRINCIPLES OF FUNDAMENTAL JUSTICE (UNDER SECTION 7 OF THE CANADIAN CHARTER)

[209] ... the formal requirements for a principle of fundamental justice are threefold. First, it must be a legal principle. Second, the reasonable person must regard it as vital to our societal notion of justice, which implies a significant societal consensus. Third, it must be capable of being identified with precision and applied in a manner that yields predictable results. These requirements present insurmountable hurdles to the appellants. The aim of 'health care to a reasonable standard within reasonable time' is not a legal principle. There is no 'societal consensus' about what it means or how to achieve it. It cannot be 'identified with precision.' As the testimony in this case showed, a level of care that is considered perfectly reasonable by some doctors is denounced by others. Finally, we think it will be very difficult for those designing and implementing a health plan to predict when its provisions cross the line from what is 'reasonable' into the forbidden territory of what is 'unreasonable,' and how the one is to be distinguished from the other. . . .

[220] Much of the argument pursued by the Chief Justice and Major J., as well as by Deschamps J. in her reasons relating to the Quebec Charter, revolves around the vexing issue of waiting lists, which have notoriously fuelled major public debates and controversies. . . .

[221] Waiting times are not only found in public systems. They are found in all health care systems, be they single-tier private, single-tier public, or the various forms of two-tier public/private. Waiting times in Canada are not exceptional. The consequence of a quasi-unlimited demand for health care coupled with limited resources, be they public or private, is to ration services. . . .

[222] The expert witnesses at trial agreed that waiting lists are inevitable. . . . The only alternative is to have a substantially overbuilt health care system with

idle capacity. This is not a financially feasible option, in the public or private sector.

WHO SHOULD BE ALLOWED TO JUMP THE QUEUE?

[223] In a public system founded on the values of equity, solidarity and collective responsibility, rationing occurs on the basis of clinical need rather than wealth and social status. . . . In general, the evidence suggests that patients who need immediate medical care receive it. There are of course exceptions, and these exceptions are properly the focus of controversy, but in our view they can and should be addressed on a case-by-case basis.

Availability of Public Funding for Out-of-Province Medical Care

[224] Section 10 of the Health Insurance Act provides that in certain circumstances Quebeckers will be reimbursed for the cost of 'insured services' rendered outside Quebec but in Canada (Regulation respecting the application of the Health Insurance Act, R.R.Q. 1981, s. 23.1), or outside Canada altogether (s. 23.2). There is no doubt that the power of reimbursement is exercised sparingly, and on occasion unlawfully; see for example Stein v. Tribunal administratif du Québec, [1999] R.J.Q. 2416 (S.C.). One of the difficulties in assessing the effectiveness of this individual remedy is that neither Dr. Chaoulli nor Mr. Zeliotis is before the Court with an actual medical problem. (The trial judge, as stated, dismissed Mr. Zeliotis' personal health complaints as unsubstantiated.) The reimbursement scheme for out-of-province services exists as a form of safety valve for situations in which Quebec facilities are unable to respond. As Stein shows, there are lapses of judgment, as there will be in the administration of any government plan. The existence of the individual remedy, however, introduces an important element of flexibility, if administered properly. . . .

[264] The safety valve (however imperfectly administered) of allowing Quebec residents to obtain essential health care outside the province when they are unable to receive the care in question at home in a timely way is of importance. If, as the appellants claim, this safety valve is opened too sparingly, the courts are available to supervise enforcement of the rights of those patients who are directly affected by the decision on a case-by-case basis. Judicial intervention at this level on a case-by-case basis is preferable to acceptance of the appellants' global challenge to the entire single-tier health plan. It is important to emphasize that rejection of the appellants' global challenge to Quebec's health plan would not foreclose individual patients from seeking individual relief tailored to their individual circumstances.

THE EVIDENCE RELIED ON BY THE CHIEF JUSTICE AND MAJOR J. DID NOT SATISFY THE TRIAL JUDGE AND IS NOT, IN OUR VIEW, PERSUASIVE

[225] The Chief Justice and Major J. cite Dr. Lenczner as an authority at para. 114 but the trial judge pointed out that Dr. Lenczner had not been qualified as an expert witness, and counsel for Mr. Zeliotis agreed. Dr. Lenczner's comments were largely anecdotal and of little general application. He described a patient who was a golfer, and thus lost his access to his golf membership for that season. He also stated that a tear can increase over time and get to the point of being irreparable, but no studies or general evidence was adduced to show the incidence of such cases in Quebec. Our colleagues comment at para. 112 that 'a person with coronary disease is 'sitting on a bomb' and can die at any moment.' This is true, of course. He or she can die at home, or in an ambulance on the way to the hospital. Again, our colleagues write, 'patients die while on waiting lists' (para. 112). This, too, is true. But our colleagues are not advocating an overbuilt system with enough idle capacity to eliminate waiting lists, and such generalized comments provided no guidance for what in practical terms would constitute an appropriate level of resources to meet their suggested standard of 'public health care of a reasonable standard within reasonable time' (para. 105).

[226] We have similar concerns about the use made by the appellants of various reports in connection with other OECD countries. These 'country' reports were included in an Interim Kirby Report but not in its final version. The Final Kirby Report's recommendation was to stick with a single-tier system. We think the Court is sufficiently burdened with conflicting evidence about our own health system without attempting a detailed investigation of the merits or trade-offs made in other countries, for their own purposes. A glance at the evidence shows why.

[227] Our colleagues the Chief Justice and Major J. state, at para. 142, that in Sweden only a very small minority of the population actually utilize public insurance. Yet, the Interim Kirby Report goes on to take note of more recent trends:

> The growing rate of the number of insured, or people on private health care insurance, is some 80% or something like that now. It is growing very fast due to the normal waiting lists and the problems within the system today....

[229] We are not to be taken as disputing the undoubted fact that there are serious problems with the single-tier health plan in Canada. Our point is simply that bits of evidence must be put in context. With respect, it is particularly dangerous to venture selectively into aspects of foreign health care systems with which we, as Canadians, have little familiarity. At the very least such information should be filtered and analysed at trial through an expert witness.

[230] ... We thus conclude that our colleagues' extracts of some of the tour d'horizon data published in the Interim Kirby Report do not displace the conclusion of the trial judge, let alone the conclusion of the Kirby Report itself. Apart from everything else, it leaves out of consideration the commitment in principle in this country to health care based on need, not wealth or status, as set out in the Canada Health Act....

ARBITRARINESS

[233] We agree with our colleagues the Chief Justice and Major J. that a law is arbitrary if 'it bears no relation to, or is inconsistent with, the objective that lies behind [the legislation]' (para. 130). We do not agree with the Chief Justice and Major J. that the prohibition against private health insurance 'bears no relation to, or is inconsistent with' the preservation of access to a health system based on need rather than wealth in accordance with the Canada Health Act. We also do not agree with our colleagues' expansion of the Morgentaler principle to invalidate a prohibition simply because a court believes it to be 'unnecessary' for the government's purpose. There must be more than that to sustain a valid objection....

[235] Rejecting the findings in the courts below based on their own reading of the evidence, our colleagues the Chief Justice and Major J. state (at para. 128):

> We are of the opinion that the evidence before the trial judge supports a finding that the impugned provisions are arbitrary and that the deprivation of life and security of the person that flows from them cannot therefore be said to accord with the principles of fundamental justice.

We note that our colleagues refer to the evidence before the trial judge rather than the view taken of that evidence by the trial judge. The trial judge reached a contrary conclusion on the facts, and deference is due to her view of that evidence....

[243] The appellants' argument in favour of a parallel private regime is one of a 'win/win' prediction; i.e. that waiting times in the public regime will be reduced if those who can afford private insurance leave the public waiting lists in order to receive private health care. However, the Kirby Report states flatly that 'allowing a private parallel system will ... make the public waiting lines worse' (vol. 4, at p. 42). This conclusion is supported by the Romanow Report (p. 139: '[P]rivate facilities may improve waiting times for the select few ... but ... worse[n them for the many]')....

[245] The Australian experience, as reported by Dr. Wright, is that at present delays in the Australian public system are caused largely by surgeons' reluctance to work in public hospitals and by their encouragement of patients to use the private system on a preferential basis....

[246] The same is true for the United Kingdom, which has a two-tier health system where physicians who want to practise privately are required to practise a minimum number of hours in the public system. There, an Audit Commission of the National Health Service reported that surgeons do on average a third to half again as many operations for private fees as they do in the public system, and that they spend less time than they are contracted for working in the public system in order to conduct private practice. . . .

[247] Both the Romanow Report and the Kirby Report examine the current shortage of health care professionals in Canada . . . and in rural parts of Canada in particular . . . Dr. Wright testified that the experience in all jurisdictions with two-tier health care systems (e.g., the United Kingdom, Australia, New Zealand and Israel) demonstrates a diversion of energy and commitment by physicians and surgeons from the public system to the more lucrative private option. . . .

[249] The evidence suggests that parallel private insurers prefer to siphon off high income patients while shying away from patient populations that constitute a higher financial risk, a phenomenon known as 'cream skimming' . . . The public system would therefore carry a disproportionate burden of patients who are considered 'bad risks' by the private market by reason of age, socio-economic conditions, or geographic location. . . .

[252] The expert witnesses at trial (other than the appellants' witness Dr. Coffey) and the Romanow Report and the Kirby Report all agree that the most cost-effective method of providing health care is through public single-tier financing. Dr. Wright testified at trial that the 'public administration criterion [of the Canada Health Act] renders the Canadian health care system one of the most efficient in terms of the ratio of productivity to administrative costs in the world'. . . .

[255] With respect to the impact on the financial resources of the public system, the experts testified that the introduction of a parallel private health regime would likely increase the overall cost of health care to Canadians. . . .

CONCLUSION ON 'ARBITRARINESS'

[256] For all these reasons, we agree with the conclusion of the trial judge and the Quebec Court of Appeal that in light of the legislative objectives of the Canada Health Act it is not 'arbitrary' for Quebec to discourage the growth of private sector health care. Prohibition of private health insurance is directly related to Quebec's interest in promoting a need-based system and in ensuring its viability and efficiency. Prohibition of private insurance is not 'inconsistent' with the state interest; still less is it 'unrelated' to it.

[257] In short, it cannot be said that the prohibition against private health insurance 'bears no relation to, or is inconsistent with' preservation of a health system predominantly based on need rather than wealth or status. . . .

[258] As to our colleagues' dismissal of the factual basis for Quebec's legislative choice, the public has invested very large sums of money in a series of authoritative reports to analyse health care in this country and in other countries. The reports uniformly recommend the retention of single-tier medicine. People are free to challenge (as do the appellants) the government's reliance on these reports but such reliance cannot be dismissed as 'arbitrary.' People are also free to dispute Quebec's strategy, but in our view it cannot be said that a single-tier health system, and the prohibition on private health insurance designed to protect it, is a legislative choice that has been adopted 'arbitrarily' by the Quebec National Assembly as that term has been understood to date in the Canadian Charter jurisprudence.

~ The two justices then deny the Morgentaler case as supportive of the appellants because it dealt with criminal law and not matters of health policy. This claim is important because it rejects another aspect of the reasoning put forward by McLachlin and Major in support of Chaoulli and Zeliotis. ~

CONCLUSION UNDER SECTION 7 OF THE CANADIAN CHARTER

[265] For the foregoing reasons, even accepting (as we do) the trial judge's conclusion that the claimants have established a deprivation of the life and security of some Quebec residents occasioned in some circumstances by waiting list delays, the deprivation would not violate any legal principle of fundamental justice within the meaning of s. 7 of the Canadian Charter.

[279] We would dismiss the appeal.

POSTSCRIPT

In their opinion, Chief Justice McLachlin and Justice Major make a good case for believing that the prohibitions on the purchase of private insurance violate s. 7 of the Charter. The justices show that there is reason to think that the prohibitions can threaten the life and security of the person and that the reasonable limits clause provides no protection for government in establishing these bans. It also has to be appreciated that the justices make a nuanced case: they are careful to conclude that the violation takes place only when access to publicly funded care is limited through unreasonable wait times. However, there are grounds for a less than complete acceptance of the decision. The evidence supporting the claim of risk to life and security seems curiously anecdotal, relying largely on the testimony of a few doctors. The justices' claim of arbitrariness also appears to rely on flimsy evidence, this time on a cursory review of the health outcomes in a few selected countries with a parallel private health care system.

The opposing opinion is also persuasive, which helps to make this issue appealing. McLachlin and Major claim that prohibitions are unacceptable when wait times are unreasonable; yet, as Binnie and his fellow justice claim, nowhere is there an attempt to offer a definition of a reasonable waiting time. Thus, the aforementioned nuance may in fact be a vague and unworkable statement that provides little help to legislators willing to satisfy the courts. This second opinion admits that the right of security might be put in peril at times, but it rejects the claim that the prohibitions and the preservation of a sound, publicly funded health care system are unrelated. For the justices, there is nothing arbitrary at all about the actions of the Quebec government in relation to the ban on private insurance for medically required care. Notwithstanding these strengths of the opinion, it has the same quality that afflicts other statements of support for Canada's health care system: it paints a picture of relative calm when in fact many Canadians appear to feel let down or even betrayed by the system.

To investigate this debate, students should acquire a good understanding of the actual decision of the Supreme Court and the history of the case. For this, one ought to consult the following: Peter H. Russell, "*Chaoulli*: The Political versus the Legal Life of a Judicial Decision," in Colleen M. Flood, Kent Roach, and Lorne Sossin, eds., *Access to Care, Access to Justice: The Legal Debate over Private Health Insurance in Canada* (Toronto: University of Toronto Press, 2005), Christopher Mandredi and Antonio Maioni, "'The Last Line of Defence for Citizens': Litigating Private Health Insurance in *Chaoulli v. Quebec*," *Osgoode Hall Law Journal* 44 (2006), Patrick J. Monahan, *Chaoulli v. Quebec and the Future of Canadian Healthcare: Patient Accountability as the 'Sixth Principle' of the Canada Health Act* (Toronto: C.D. Howe Institute, 2006), and Peter W. Hogg, Constitutional Law of Canada, Student Edition 2007 (Thomson Carswell, 2007), 668–673 and 1084–1086. The complete decision itself can be found at the website of the Supreme Court of

Canada, and edited versions of the decisions of the lower courts are provided in Flood, Roach, and Sossin, eds., *Access to Care, Access to Justice*.

The opinions of the Supreme Court in *Chaoulli v. Quebec* have been the object of a great deal of analysis. The following represent only a few of the attempts to assess the case and its implications: Colleen Flood, "Chaoulli's Legacy for the Future of Canadian Health Care Policy," *Osgoode Hall Law Review* 44, no. 2 (2006), Colleen M. Flood, Mark Stabile, and Sasha Kontic, "Finding Health Policy 'Arbitrary': The Evidence of Waiting, Dying, and Two-Tier Systems," in Flood, Roach, and Sossin, eds., *Access to Care, Access to Justice*, the aforementioned Monahan, *Chaoulli v. Quebec and the Future of Canadian Healthcare*, and Tom McIntosh, *Don't Panic: The Hitchhiker's Guide to Chaoulli, Wait Times and the Politics of Private Insurance* (Ottawa: CPRN, 2006).

The aftermath of the *Chaoulli* decision is important. On release of the decision, some feared it meant the end of medicare in Quebec and perhaps Canada; others felt its implications to be much less. For an appreciation of the actual impact, the following can be considered: Government of Quebec, *Guaranteeing Access: Meeting the Challenges of Equity, Efficiency and Quality, Consultation Document*, February 2006, Gerard W. Boychuk, "Patience!... Wait Time Guarantees and Conservative Health Care Policy," in G. Bruce Doern, ed., *How Ottawa Spends 2007–2008: The Harper Conservatives–Climate of Change* (Montreal and Kingston: McGill-Queen's University Press, 2007), and Michael Kirby, "The Only Two Options for Funding the Wait-Time Guarantees," *Policy Options* (July–August 2006).

The issue of wait times is central to the *Chaoulli* case. For a primer on wait times, see Health Council of Canada, *Wait Times and Access*, January 2005.

Should Religious Beliefs Be Excluded from Consideration of Public Policy?

✔ **YES**
JUSTICE MARY SAUNDERS, "Opinion in *Chamberlain v. Surrey School District #36*"

✘ **NO**
JOHN VON HEYKING, "Against the Edwardians: Why Religion Has a Place in Public Debate"

What role, if any, should religious beliefs play in the making of public policy? While this issue has often been contested in the United States, it has generated less debate in Canada. However, this has begun to change in recent years. During the 2000 federal election, the political opponents of Stockwell Day tried to focus attention on his religious beliefs, suggesting not too subtly to voters that such beliefs could make him dangerous if his party won the election. In the run-up to the 2005 federal election, a *Globe and Mail* article entitled "Christian Activists Capturing Tory Races" noted that the fact that a number of well-known evangelical Christians had won Conservative nominations raised concerns about a "hidden agenda" and the fear that, if elected, they would try to "hijack" the party's policy agenda. In the 2007 Ontario election, when the Conservative leader John Tory suggested that public funding should be extended to all faith-based schools, opponents of the measure focused particularly on the detrimental impact that religion frequently has on public life. And, in Quebec, the government convened a special commission to examine what constitutes a "reasonable accommodation" of religious beliefs and practices in a modern, secular, multicultural society.

From these examples, it is clear that the relationship between religious beliefs and public policy continues to be a contentious issue in Canadian politics. This issue has probably received some of its most intense scrutiny in the courtrooms of the province of British Columbia. Bringing much public attention to this issue was the debate surrounding the selection of approved books for primary school children in provincial public schools. In British Columbia, the provincial *School Act* grants school boards responsibility for approving the educational resource materials that teachers use in classrooms. In 1995, the Ministry of Education implemented a new Personal Planning curriculum for kindergarten to grade seven, which included a family life component.

In 1996, the Surrey school board passed a resolution that apparently prohibited the use of educational materials that were not on a prescribed list. The Gay and Lesbian Educators of B.C. (GALE)—an organization that advocates for change in the school system to create a positive environment for homosexual and bisexual persons—had developed a list of books that portray homosexual relationships positively. A teacher in the Surrey school district requested that three books from the GALE list be approved for use in teaching kindergarten and grade one students in the Surrey school district. The books were reviewed three times by various levels of the school district administrative staff. All agreed that the books dealt with sensitive material and were likely to cause parental concern over the presentation of same-sex parenting to kindergarten and grade one children. The superintendent of schools for the school district declared that the three books were unnecessary for achieving the objectives of the school curriculum. Since use of the books would be controversial among the parents in the community, it was decided that the final verdict should come from the school board, which was elected by that community.

On April 24, 1997, the Surrey school board formally considered the request for approval of the three books. The meeting was widely attended and garnered considerable media coverage. Several submissions were received, including ones from GALE and from the B.C. Civil Liberties Association. At the end of the presentation, the school board, by a vote of 4–2, passed a resolution declining to approve the books. Following this result, the teacher involved applied to the B.C. Supreme Court for a ruling that the school board resolution be declared invalid and that an order be issued requiring the school board to pass a resolution approving the books in question.

In the subsequent court case, Justice Mary Saunders of the B.C. Supreme Court determined that indeed the school board's resolution should be quashed. In explaining her decision, Justice Saunders pointed out that section 76 of the British Columbia *School Act* required that all schools be run on "strictly secular and nonsectarian principles." This she took to mean that not only should schools not show denominational bias, they should also be "independent of religious considerations." In other words, all religious motivations and reasons should be excluded from policy decisions. Interestingly, in a dispute between the parties over evidence, the justice allowed the petitioner's lawyers to introduce information regarding speeches given by the chair of the school board prior to taking that office because they gave some insight into the "state of mind" of the board chair in making her decision. The justice seemed to be saying that even if no explicitly religiously based arguments were used, any evidence that decisions taken might be rooted in religious principles could disqualify them from the public arena. Further, while the B.C. *School Act* states that schools should inculcate the "highest morality" in children, the school board is precluded from making any decisions "based in a significant way on religious considerations." Saunders argued that the principles on which this "highest morality" should be based are to be found in the Charter of Rights and Freedoms.

This case goes to the heart of some critical questions. Is it permissible for public officials to make decisions that are motivated in part by religious belief? Does the Charter of Rights and Freedoms require that moral beliefs that originate from religious belief be excluded from public debate? Does "secular" essentially mean "nonreligious"? What role, if any, should religious convictions play in the public square? In the first reading below, we have an excerpt from Justice Mary Saunders in the Surrey schoolbook case, in which she addresses some of these issues. In response, Professor John von Heyking of the University of Lethbridge makes the case for the role of religion in public debate.

✔ **YES**

Opinion in *Chamberlain v. Surrey School District #36*
JUSTICE MARY SAUNDERS

[...]

THE BOOKS RESOLUTION

[...]

[75] I turn then to the question of whether the School Board, by its Books resolution, acted contrary to s. 76. This is really a question of whether it acted contrary to s. 76(1), whether by its decision it failed to conduct the schools on strictly secular and non-sectarian principles. This is both a question of interpretation of s. 76(1) and a question of fact.

[76] There is no question that the resolution is non-sectarian. The issue is whether it infringes the requirement that the schools "be conducted on strictly secular . . . principles."

[77] The petitioners contend that the School Board made its decision on a religious basis, running afoul of s. 76(1). The School Board contends that it acted in the best interests of the children, with consideration for the parents' rights to teach their children their religious and moral values and beliefs regarding homosexual conduct.

[78] The words "conducted on strictly secular . . . principles" have been part of the requirements of public schools for a very long time, but, to the court's knowledge, have not been judicially considered prior to this case. In the education setting, the term secular excludes religion or religious belief. Combining the word "secular" with the words "strictly" and "principles," and considering the history of schools in British Columbia as being beyond overt church or religious intervention or influence, I conclude that the words "conducted on strictly secular . . . principles" precludes a decision significantly influenced by religious considerations. This interpretation is consistent with the increasingly pluralistic nature of modern British Columbia and accords with the obligation to give statutory provisions a fair, large and liberal interpretation: *Interpretation Act,* R.S.B.C. 1996, c. 238, s. 8.

[79] The School Board submits that the section does not require it to place into the classroom books which are morally contentious. It says that the books in issue here, presenting families with same-sex parents as normal and same-sex parents as not "bad," are morally contentious, may tend to confuse children and may interfere with parental education on religious and moral matters.

[80] These submissions must be viewed in light of all the language in s. 76. Section 76(1) directs a School Board, administrators and teachers to refrain from religious based education or management motivated by religious considerations. At the same time s. 76(2) directs the moral education of children to a high plain by language requiring inculcation of the highest morality. Section 76 has the effect of distinguishing religious influence from issues of morality, precluding the first while requiring the second.

[81] The issue underlying this case illustrates this difference. Affidavits placed before the court by the School Board depose that some religions or churches with adherents in the community hold that homosexual activity is wrong. Yet in considering the highest morality as those words are used in the *School Act,* it is appropriate to consider the values embodied in the *Charter of Rights and Freedoms* and import them into the moral standard that must be applied: *Hills v. A.G. (Canada),* [1988] 1 S.C.R. 512, at 518. Recent cases under s. 15 of the *Charter of Rights and Freedoms* state that s. 15 protects equality rights for those of a homosexual orientation: *Egan v. Canada,* [1995] 2 S.C.R. 513; *Vriend v. Alberta,* [1998], 1 S.C.R. 493.

[82] The School Board says that s. 15 of the Charter protects persons, not conduct, and thus that it protects homosexual persons, not homosexual conduct. On this reasoning, the School Board says that it sought to balance tolerance for homosexual persons with the views of some parents that homosexual conduct is not acceptable. This position is not consistent with the observations at p. 595 in *Egan v. Canada* by Mr. Justice Cory that:

> . . . individuals, because of their uniqueness, are bound to vary in these personal characteristics which may be manifested by their sexual preferences whether heterosexual or homosexual. So long as those preferences do not infringe any laws, they should be tolerated.

The protection of the *Charter* is not intended to be hollow. Where a defining characteristic of a person is his or her conduct and the conduct is not unlawful, s. 15 of the *Charter* protects equality rights for that person complete with his or her conduct. I conclude that s. 76 does not protect a decision based on religious views as to homosexual conduct.

[83] I conclude, therefore, that s. 76(2) requires a school board to adhere to a high moral line which is consistent with the *Charter of Rights and Freedoms,* at the same time that s. 76(1) of the *School Act* precludes a school board from making a decision based in a significant way on religious considerations.

[84] On this reading of s. 76 of the *School Act,* the question is whether the Books resolution was based in a significant way on religious considerations. This is a question of fact.

[85] The primary evidence on the basis of the School Board's decision is from the lone trustee who provided evidence and from the Superintendent of Schools.

[86] The deponent trustee, one of the four trustees who voted in favour of the motion, deposed that prior to the April 24, 1997 School Board meeting she had received hundreds of calls from members of the Surrey community, the vast majority of whom supported the April 10, 1997 GALE resolution. She deposed that in reaching her decision on April 24, 1997 she considered as relevant to the motion the questions of age appropriateness of the books' subject matter, their necessity to teach the curriculum and whether they dealt with the subject matter in a way that reflects the needs and values of the Surrey community including parents. She deposed that another trustee who voted in favour of the motion expressed concern that the books would initiate discussion on a sensitive issue. A third trustee in support of the motion expressed concern that if the Board approved the books kindergarten and grade one students in the School District would be exposed to the issues (same-sex parents) raised by them, and stated that he considered the books to be age inappropriate because they would create confusion and conflict.

[87] In cross-examination on her affidavit, the trustee testified that she did not consider that the books by themselves would have an adverse effect on children. She spoke of the lack of community consensus on introducing the books into the classroom, and said that the lack of consensus was a factor in not approving the books. She agreed that the focus of discussion centred on the fact that the books raised issues of a sensitive nature, and weight was given to the concerns of parents. She confirmed her view that teaching on the subject of same-sex relationships should allow a child to validate beliefs that the relationship would be morally wrong from their religious viewpoint.

[88] In his affidavit, the Superintendent of Schools acknowledged his anticipation that approval of the three books as educational resource material would be a very controversial decision among parents. On cross-examination he testified that he felt parents would feel the decision was "values sensitive" for them. He stated that he had questions concerning the age appropriateness of the concepts in the books, but it is clear from the record that he did not recommend that the books not be approved.

[89] In its submissions the School Board referred to affidavits from parents and members of the community in support of its argument on s. (2) of the *Charter* that it had protected the parents' and children's freedom of religion by passing the Books resolution. This affidavit evidence from parents included the following statements:

(i) "If the Three Books were used in either of our sons' classes, our children would be confused at the challenge to their own faith and family values";

(ii) "...I am opposed to the introduction of the Three Books into Kindergarten and Grade One classrooms for the following reasons:

    (a) the Three Books portray same-sex couples ... in a manner contrary to my personal religious beliefs";

(iii) "The Three Books would introduce to children in Kindergarten and Grade One a particular worldview or brand of morality. The morality or worldview is directly in conflict with deeply held family and religious values";

(iv) "We believe, and would like to teach our children that according to our religious views, the homosexual lifestyle is wrong";

(v) "This is a matter of significant religious importance to me and the views expressed by the Three Books conflict with my religious views and those of my family";

(vi) "My concern is that I and my wife be able to teach our children according to our religious beliefs without having the school teach them something, at an early age, which runs counter to what we believe";

(vii) "I am opposed in accordance with my religious beliefs to my children being taught a redefinition of the traditional family";

(viii) "We are opposed to the introduction of the Three Books ... for the following reasons:

    (a) Surrey Schools should not negate our right as parents to teach our children ... in accordance with our family and religious views;

    (b) it is our strongly held religious belief that homosexual behaviour, including same-sex couples, is contrary to the teaching of the Bible";

(ix) "I wish to teach my children according to my own religious beliefs and oppose lessons at school which contradict what I am attempting to teach my children";

(x) "The Three Books raise issues with respect to homosexuality and same-sex couples that are morally contentious. If used in Kindergarten and Grade One classrooms in Surrey they would create conflict between many families in the District who have religious or moral beliefs opposed to the views presented in the Three Books, and the teacher or school";

[...]

[92] In addition, the School Board filed affidavits from several religious leaders. These affidavits were countered by the petitioners with affidavits from other persons formally associated with churches. The affidavits from religious leaders filed by the School Board in support of its position include the following statements:

(i) from the Steering Committee of the Surrey Evangelical Churches: "Our Churches are extremely concerned that the Three Books present same-sex couples and introduce the issue of homosexuality in a positive light, contrary to the Biblical teachings and doctrine which form the basis of our beliefs";

(ii) from a pastor of a church: "The Three Books would introduce to children at the Kindergarten and Grade One levels a unique board [sic] of morality or worldview. This morality or worldview is directly in conflict with the morality and worldview of most members of the Evangelical Free Church";

(iii) from a priest of a Roman Catholic Church: "I am of the view that the Three Books create an irreconcilable conflict between the views stated in the Three Books regarding the topic of homosexuality, and the doctrine of the Church.

". . . I am opposed to the introduction of issues relating to homosexuality and same-sex couples, which issues [sic] necessarily bring into conflict religious and moral views on the subject";

(iv) from a Muslim who is on the Surrey/Delta Management Committee of the B.C. Muslim Association: "The Three Books present homosexuality and homosexual conduct as acceptable and morally equal to heterosexuality. This contradicts the teachings of the Qur'an and the beliefs of Muslims";

(v) from a leader of the Guru Nanak Sikh Gurdwara Society: "In the Sikh faith, homosexuality is considered a moral and social sin which we are instructed to resist.

"I have read the books. . . . This message directly conflicts with the religious teachings of the Sikh faith";

(vi) from a leader of the Verdic Hindhu Society: " . . . This message [from the books] directly conflicts with the teachings of the Hindhu faith. The Three Books display a lifestyle which we, as Hindhus, believe is immoral. . . ."

[93] On review of all the evidence in this case on the basis of the School Board's decision, I conclude that when the School Board passed the Books resolution, some of the trustees who voted in favour of the resolution were motivated to a

significant degree by concern that parents and others in the School District would consider the books incompatible or inconsistent with their religious views on the subject of same-sex relationships.

[94] In addition to the respondent's affidavit evidence and its submissions in court to the effect that it did consider, and was entitled to consider, the views of parents that use of the books in the classroom would be contrary to their sincerely held religious and moral views, there is evidence that at least one trustee who voted for the motion (who did not provide an affidavit), has campaigned for several years to promote a greater role for religion in governance of the community, including on the issue of homosexuality. The evidence on the views and activities of this trustee, in the absence of an affidavit in explanation, reasonably supports the conclusion that this trustee's decision was significantly influenced by personal religious considerations on the issue of homosexuality.

[95] I conclude that by giving significant weight to personal or parental concern that the books would conflict with religious views, the Board made a decision significantly influenced by religious considerations, contrary to the requirement in s. 76(1) that schools be "conducted on strictly secular... principles."

[. . .]

V. CONCLUSION

[106] This decision is based upon a very old provision of the *School Act* enjoining religion or overt religious influence in the conduct of the schools. Many other issues were raised by the petitioners under the principles of administrative law. The petitioners also relied upon the *Charter of Rights and Freedoms*, s. 2(a) freedom of religion, s. 2(b) freedom of expression and s. 15 equality rights. In doing so the petitioners and the respondent cited many cases expressing great principles of law, including *Roncarelli v. Duplessis* (1959), 16 D.L.R. 689, [1959] S.C.R. 121 and those cases dealing with race and science in the schools. Given my conclusion on s. 76 of the *School Act,* and for the reasons of Mr. Justice Hollinrake in *Russow v. B.C.* (A.G.), *supra,* I do not address those issues.

[107] I conclude that the Books resolution is contrary to s. 76(1) of the *School Act,* and is therefore *ultra vires.*

[108] The Books resolution is hereby quashed. [. . .]

✗ NO

Against the Edwardians: Why Religion Has a Place in Public Debate
JOHN VON HEYKING

Recently in Canada, the claim that religious arguments have no place in public debate has been used to deny the legitimacy of religious arguments to oppose the inclusion of gay-friendly books in elementary school libraries,[1] to suspect religious political candidates of harbouring a "hidden agenda"[2] in opposing abortion, and to prohibit home-school parents from using religious materials as part of their children's education.[3]

In determining whether, or the degree to which, religious arguments have a place in contemporary political debate, it is worthwhile pondering the meaning of the following four statements made by prominent figures in Canadian and U.S. politics:

1. "We have waited more than 340 years for our constitutional and God-given rights."[4]

2. "Human rights has emerged as the new secular religion of our time."[5]

3. "An unjust law is a human law that is not rooted in eternal law and natural law."[6]

4. "Go into any courtroom, police station or welfare office, and you will find real individuals ignoring the different surfaces of each person they deal with and addressing the juridical equal beneath. They are addressing a moral fiction. Yet it is this fiction, and our devotion to it, that enables us to be just. The entire legitimacy of public institutions depends on our being attentive to difference while treating all as equal. This is the gamble, the unique act of the imagination on which our society rests."[7]

As these quotations show, clarifying whether religion has a role to play in political debate requires one to be clear on what one means by religion and what one means by politics.

If one takes the common, but unreflective, meaning of the two terms, religion is frequently said to consist of matters of faith that are indemonstrable, whereas politics usually has to do with matters that are open to discussion, persuasion, and are in some way demonstrable. Thus, it is frequently argued that religion should be private and therefore should not play a role in politics, while politics is about things that can be debated in rational form. This arrangement is frequently called the secular form of liberal politics, as opposed to the pluralistic form, whereby religious perspectives participate with other voices in debating public policy (and which I shall defend).[8]

The secularist view of removing religion from political debate would result in the following conclusions regarding the four statements quoted above:

1. African-Americans living in the American South must be denied civil rights, including full voting and employment rights, because the Reverend Martin Luther King appealed to God as the basis of their rights. That they appeal to the constitution is irrelevant, because the constitution simply abolishes slavery. It is silent on other rights.

2. Former Canadian Justice Minister Irwin Cotler's justification for Bill C-38, which legalized same-sex marriage, is illegitimate because it is based on a religion of human rights.

3. The Reverend Martin Luther King's appeal to the eternal or natural law to overturn legislative acts is irrelevant because such terms are religious in origin. The concepts of eternal law and natural law are a vestige of medieval religious thinking and lack scientific credibility, just as creationism and intelligent design lack scientific credibility.

4. Despite Dr. Michael Ignatieff's desire to treat people equally, his admission that equality is a "moral fiction" and "act of imagination" means the basis of the laws of Canada are null and void, and just as make-believe as arguments stemming from religion, from the perspective of scientific reason.

Claims 1 and 2 seek to establish human rights on the basis of a divine transcendent source. The Reverend Martin Luther King derives his argument for equality and rights from the Hebrew and Christian Bible. From a secularist perspective, his arguments constitute a prima facie violation of church–state separation. The secularist perspective would marginalize the central figure of the civil rights movement in the United States in the twentieth century.

Irwin Cotler derives human rights from what he calls the new "secular" religion. Cotler's statement seems at odds with the general sense of *secular* as it relates to science. However, the concept of secular political religion is in fact consistent with the central thrust of the scientific Enlightenment that purportedly supports church–state separation. According to philosophers including Voltaire, Turgot, and John Stuart Mill, history is moving in a progressive direction, toward ever-increasing enlightenment, freedom, and scientific control over the natural world. Many scholars have shown how these views are a form of belief insofar as they presuppose a view of humanity's historical future that cannot be demonstrated.[9] Secularism makes its own faith claims, one of which is its faith in progress. Just as ancient societies were bound together using myths about their place in the cosmos, modern "secular" societies organize themselves according to myths, or what Plato called "noble lies," to give their citizens meaning. According to Cotler, the myth of human rights and equality is the central myth of Canada. However, it is a myth and a form of belief. It is not predicated on science.

Statement 3 speaks to something called universal and natural laws from which human laws must draw. In his "Letter from a Birmingham Jail," Martin Luther King explicitly draws from the teachings of Saints Augustine and Thomas Aquinas, two medieval theologians of the Christian church. From a secularist perspective, basing equality on medieval theologians is equivalent to explaining the origin of the human species according to the principles of creationism or intelligent design. Whatever the deficiencies of creationism and intelligent design (and there are many), the comparison is incorrect because the subject matters differ. Creationism and intelligent design purport to explain physical reality, while Reverend King drew from Augustine and Aquinas to understand moral and political reality.[10] Moral and political realities differ from physical reality, and one requires different methodologies to examine different types of reality. I agree with the secularist that one would not look to Augustine and Aquinas to understand quantum physics, but neither would I assume that the methods of modern physics or biology are appropriate for fully understanding morality and politics.[11]

According to Augustine and Aquinas, human beings derive their dignity, that which grounds ethical obligations for treating fellow humans justly, on their being in the image of God. While they derived the symbol *imago Dei* from Biblical and classical sources, the idea is prevalent among numerous schools of thought. Just because a concept exists within a religious tradition does not mean it is exclusively a religious concept. *Imago Dei* symbolizes something primordial about our obligations toward another. Before we can say *what* we owe another, we must know *that* we owe another on account of the other being the sort of being that makes moral claims upon us. Aquinas expressed this primal obligation as the right that is prior to the just. Joseph Pieper explains: "The concept of 'being due to,' of 'right,' is such a primordial idea that it cannot be traced back to a prior, subordinating concept. That is to say, it can at best be described, but not defined."[12] It is on this basis that Reverend King appealed to eternal and natural laws to defend equality: equality is predicated on his observation (and those of Augustine and Aquinas) that human beings depend on a transcendent order for their dignity.

Contemporary human rights scholars and activists are more likely to look to Enlightenment thinkers to support their ideas. But the most thoughtful of these thinkers, Immanuel Kant, says something quite similar to our medieval theologians. Compare his summary of human dignity with Pieper's account above: "Humanity itself is a dignity, for man can be used by no one (neither by others nor even by himself) merely as a means, but must always be used at the same time as an end."[13] Kant believed we ought to treat human beings as ends instead of means, not out of self-interest, but because humanity *is* a dignity. His insistence on predicating humanity on dignity compares with Aquinas's claim that right is prior to justice, that there is something primordial about our obligations to others. While Kant wanted to defend dignity and the categorical imperative on the grounds of reason alone, his inspiration and motivation operate within a framework that depends on Christian articulations of transcendence.[14]

Kant maintained religious tonalities while attempting to get away from a religious justification of dignity, which suggests something enduring about religious sensibilities in the way we justify important issues like rights and equality. For this reason, Jeremy Waldron points out that liberal philosophy has yet to develop a successfully nonreligious way of speaking of dignity and equality.[15] Insofar as Canadians use the language of rights, dignity, and equality, and speak of these in reverential terms, they draw upon a deeper well of thinking that they purportedly reject when they insist on a secularism that removes religious arguments from public life. Canadians act as parasites, or "Edwardians," when they use religious terms but do not understand, or purposefully evacuate, the religious meanings of those terms.[16] By doing so, Canadians coast not only on the philosophical and religious traditions that sustain their regime, but also on the deeper inspirations and sources that sustain what they most genuinely cherish.[17]

Michael Ignatieff's statement concerning equality, Statement 4, clearly expresses this Edwardianism. He claims we get our sense of equality and commonality not from the "abstract human identity of nakedness" or "denuded human suffering," but, more likely, from human differences, which are expressed through human agency: "So it is not the naked body we share in common, but the astoundingly different ways in which we decorate, adorn, perfume and costume our bodies in order to proclaim our identities as men, women, members of this tribe or that community."[18] He explains *difference* as the "ceaseless elaboration of disguises, affirmations, identities and claims."[19] Ignatieff does not claim with absolute certainty that difference is the source, but it plays a central role in his "moral fiction." It is a noble lie he wants us to believe. How strange it is that he wants us to believe what he openly admits is a fiction.

In considering human nakedness and human agency as the basis of dignity, Ignatieff echoes a famous statement of Immanuel Kant: "Two things fill the mind with ever new and increasing admiration and awe: the starry heaven above me and the moral law within me."[20] For Kant, the "moral law within me" is the source of human dignity because it "reveals a life independent of all animality and even the whole world of sense." Conversely, the "starry heaven" "annihilates ... my importance as an animal creature, which must give back to the planet (a mere speck in the universe) the matter from which it came, we know not how." Ignatieff rejects "nakedness" as the basis of equality for the same reason Kant thinks the "starry heaven" annihilates our sense of dignity. Identifying our essence in terms of biological species is weak because biology returns to the earth. Ignatieff, who has firsthand experience of war zones, has seen what happens when people regard one another as mere dirt.

Thus, Ignatieff appeals to agency and difference as the basis of dignity or what he calls "supreme value."[21] Yet, differences, especially stated as agency, express inequality, as shown in the debates over the rights of the disabled and the unborn. For example, Sue Rodrigues appealed to the Supreme Court to extend her the right to be euthanized because her body was wracked with ALS.[22] Her body is unequal to a vigorous and healthy body. Such inequality is a major reason that some people support euthanasia for the chronically ill or those who appear to be in a permanent vegetative state: people with vigorous and healthy bodies—those able to "decorate, adorn, perfume and costume" their bodies—judge those without them as lacking in dignity and living a life not worth living. People with vigorous and healthy bodies regard dignity as rooted in the ability of individuals to remain active and to make choices. This is frequently called "extrinsic" or "subjective" dignity, or what Ignatieff terms "agency." People who seem incapable of mental or physical activity, those who lack agency, are thereby deemed lacking in dignity. Those who defend the dignity of the disabled appeal to "objective" or "intrinsic" accounts of dignity, and frequently draw from religious arguments to support their views.[23] If it follows from the position of "extrinsic" or "subjective" dignity that the disabled have no dignity, then defenders of the disabled point out that they, arguably society's most vulnerable members, would have no defense against state-enforced programs of euthanasia, sterilization, and eugenicist projects that have characterized massive breaches to human rights in a place like Nazi Germany, as well as in Canada.

Ignatieff understands such dangers, but his appeal to "difference" is insufficient. He means the "ceaseless elaboration of disguises, affirmations, identities and claims" to express a recognition of the mystery of otherness, and in this sense, it compares with the *imago Dei* symbolisms of Augustine and Aquinas, and the dignity of Kant. However, treating selfhood as a ceaseless construction of disguises—of self-creativity—(1) relies too much on human strength and self-assertion as the basis of dignity and (2) provides an extremely thin sense of the being to whom we owe justice: what kind of notion of selfhood gets articulated by a ceaseless play of disguises? Is there anything behind the disguises? Moreover, disguises are meant to hide and to deceive. Why should we respect one who deceives? Ignatieff hedges on this question because he speaks of "ceaseless elaboration" instead of "ceaseless deception." *Elaboration* implies continuity of a self behind the disguises, but Ignatieff fails to provide an account of what hides behind the masks.

Ignatieff's hedging reveals his Edwardianism because it shows him drawing upon the deeper sources of dignity and equality—*imago Dei*—while at the same time rejecting them. By appealing to this dance of disguises as the human self, Ignatieff appeals to a postmodern dream that human beings are autonomous authors or creators of their identities and their values. His is a genteel version of the Promethean dream that is associated with the likes of Nietzsche (no friend of egalitarianism) and even has its roots in Kant. Even so, what Ignatieff overlooks is that this Promethean dream of self-sufficiency, which rejects the past in the belief in its self-creativity, ironically draws upon the past in Jewish and Christian understandings of divine will, except now it is man who thinks he has divine power of creativity.[24] The irony of this Promethean dream is that postmodern man thinks he creates himself and his values, and he is oblivious of the intellectual and moral sources of his own self-perception. The Promethean dream, which appeals to a large number of Canadians who view themselves as autonomous moral actors who make their own choices, is a self-deception. Ignatieff's Edwardianism, which implicitly draws upon *imago Dei,* allows him to be more sober than Prometheus. His account of difference allows for decency because difference can also be an expression of belonging, which means the source of difference lies beyond sheer human will (by a smidgeon).[25]

Yet, in implicitly drawing from *imago Dei,* Ignatieff also rejects it, as indicated in his rejection of "nakedness." While our nakedness can reveal inequality (e.g., differences of vitality, strength), it also reveals our vulnerability. We are all subject to sickness, disease, hunger, cold, isolation, and other vicissitudes of human existence we suffer in silence. These are expressions of human weakness, which Ignatieff dismisses when he rejects the notion that human rights are based on "instincts of pity for denuded human suffering."[26] While Ignatieff may be correct in questioning the reliability of "instincts," is it any wonder that the inspiration for human rights develops in cultures that have long contemplated the meaning and mystery of human vulnerability in "denuded human suffering"? Does not Ignatieff recognize in this language the figure and suffering of Jesus Christ and the "suffering servant" of the Israelite prophets, not in terms of an abstract species but in the concrete person?[27] Do we not need rights precisely because we are so fragile, because the autonomous agent is in fact a "moral fiction"? Superman does not need human rights. Ignatieff reveals his Prometheanism when he fails to see this mystery in "nakedness" and chooses "agency" and "difference" instead. This turn toward agency, while tentative, might reveal not so much skepticism toward instincts as contempt toward weakness. However, his Prometheanism is genteel, or Edwardian, because it draws upon a culture with some habituation in seeing the mystery of that suffering, which restrains "agency." Relying on the culture while corroding it is an untenable position, and helps explain Ignatieff's appeals to "moral fiction" and "gamble." However, Ignatieff's Edwardian "moral fiction" also confirms Jeremy Waldron's argument that nonreligious ways of speaking of human rights and equality are insufficient, and that religious ways of speaking about them would help us sustain the moral and political principles we cherish.

Increasingly, it has been the strategy of liberal democracies to maintain peace by taking contentious issues like religion off the table of public debate. The drive to make religion private is part of a liberal strategy of finding a common basis on which a diverse population can sustain a common way of life. Extreme sectarianism, Puritanism, and apocalyptic theologies can contribute to what Thomas Hobbes called "the seditious roaring of a troubled nation"[28] because their adherents no longer see themselves as sharing a common world. However, at what point does the liberal strategy end up disenfranchising religious people? At what point does the liberal strategy become an overextended secularist strategy that ends up provoking "seditious roaring"?[29] The modern liberal state has expanded its powers and its role in people's private lives so much that it is easy to see how a call to remove religion from public life implies removing it from private life as well. For example, does government provided health care require all obstetricians to perform abortions? Is there no room for obstetricians to avoid this practice on the grounds of religious conscience? Moreover, as physics, genetics, and reproductive technologies advance our abilities to manipulate genes, biological traits, and matter, it will become increasingly difficult to evaluate or even recognize the ethical implications of these actions if our very views of human nature are reduced to biology and matter.[30] To prohibit religious arguments for human dignity from participating in public debate is to submit ahead of time to the technological imperative of the conquest of nature.

Liberal democracy draws upon religious and philosophical principles of right, dignity, and equality that liberalism has difficulty defending on its own terms. Numerous scholars speak of the crisis of liberalism, which refers to the persistent failures by liberal philosophers (as opposed to partisan liberals or Liberals, though they may be those as well) to provide a comprehensive defence of liberalism.[31] Instead, they, like Ignatieff, speak of "moral fiction" and "gamble." Thus, it is strange that we find rigorous efforts to eliminate religion from liberal public life at the very moment liberal philosophers seem incapable of providing a defence of liberalism. Seen in this light, calls to eliminate religion from public life consist of an illiberal "circle the wagons" strategy: a short-term strategy to consolidate a collective, supposedly secular, identity from the religious "other" when those driving the wagons—our secular liberal intellectuals—know full well that theirs is a losing strategy.[32]

With this in mind, let us return to our four statements with a more nuanced understanding of religion and politics that adheres more adequately than secularism to liberal principles of pluralism and dignity:

1. Rev. King's letter appropriately uses "God talk" by appealing both to America's constitutional tradition of equality and to the language of the "laws of nature and nature's God" in the Declaration of Independence.

2. Human rights arise in a culture with a strong tradition of fighting for and respecting the dignity of all. Whether dignity should be grounded on a secular ideology or religious tradition or on something else can only be decided by a culture of dialogue in the institutions that sustain that dialogue and debate.

3. Unjust laws mistreat the human person, whose dignity transcends the enactments of Parliament, court, or other governmental agent.

4. Appeals to postmodern "moral fictions" or "noble lies" to sustain the political principles we cherish the most are insufficient, and largely the result of a secularist turn away from the religious and philosophical sources of the human person that have sustained those principles over the centuries. As a society, we need to get beyond our complacent acceptance of being lied to with moral fictions, and instead return to a serious reconsideration of the moral, philosophical, and religious debates concerning human dignity, equality, and rights.

Permitting religious arguments in political debate is not simply a matter of throwing a bone to a noisy minority in the hope that, because their viewpoints are outdated, they will soon fall into the silence of irrelevancy. Rather, it is necessary to permit religious arguments in political debate for the basic reason that liberal democracy depends on a plurality of arguments and positions to sustain a healthy regime. Unlike our Edwardian proponents of the noble lie, religion takes seriously the Socratic question of how a human being, and a human society, ought to live. The level of their seriousness depends also on adherents of religious communities' being open to having their traditions questioned and challenged, and having something persuasive about them both in terms of their arguments as well as the model lives they aspire to lead and hold up as shining examples for the world around them. Keeping this pluralism open is especially important at a time when liberals themselves are unsure as to what counts for a healthy liberal regime, and religious arguments can help all of us understand that.

NOTES

1. *Chamberlain v. Surrey School District #36* (1998), 60 B.C.L.R. (3d) 311.

2. Iain T. Benson, "Christian Activists Get Party Nominations: Woo, Scary," *Centre Articles* 82 (May 27, 2005), Centre for Cultural Renewal, available at http://www.culturalrenewal.ca/qry/page.taf?id=37&_function=detail&sbtblct_uid1=102&_nc=3950ab1bd7dc849c4bfd02f17fbcc2ff.

3. Iain T. Benson, "Restricting Parents' Home Teaching of Religion to Their Children: How Democratic," *Centre Articles* 24 (April 16, 2004), Centre for Cultural Renewal, available at http://www.culturalrenewal.ca/qry/page.taf?id=37&_function=detail&sbtblct_uid1=39&_nc=3950ab1bd7dc849c4bfd02f17fbcc2ff.

4. Reverend Martin Luther King, Jr., "Letter from Birmingham Jail," available at http://www.stanford.edu/group/King/frequentdocs/birmingham.pdf. I thank Dr. David Klassen for pointing me to this and a few other sources discussed in this paper. He provides a more sustained argument for religion and human dignity and equality in his paper "Rights Talk and God Talk: Religious Faith and Natural Rights," paper presented to "Pluralism, Politics, and God: An International Symposium on Religion and

Public Reason," Newman Centre, McGill University, September 13–15, 2007, available at http://www.davidklassen.net/files/Conference_paper_–_Rights_Talk_and_God_Talk_David_Klassen.pdf.

5. For example, Irwin Cotler, Speech to Parliament of Canada, *Hansard* (37th Parliament, 2nd session) October 28, 2002, available at http://www2.parl.gc.ca/HousePublications/Publication.aspx?pub=hansard&mee=16&parl=37&ses=2&language=E&x=1#Int-309675.

6. King, "Letter from Birmingham Jail."

7. Michael Ignatieff, *The Rights Revolution* (Toronto: Anansi, 2000), p. 139.

8. For clarification on the difference between monistic secularism, which privatizes religion, and pluralistic secularism, which has a role for public participation by religious voices, see Wilfred McClay, "Two Concepts of Secularism," *Wilson Quarterly* 24, no. 3 (Summer 2000). The British Columbia Court of Appeal used this article in overturning a lower court's decision that ruled religious voices have no role in debating public policy on account of Canada's supposed "secular" character. For further reflections on the problematic character of "secular" in legal and political thinking, see Iain T. Benson, "Notes Towards a (Re)Definition of the 'Secular'" (2000), 33 *U.B.C. L. Rev.* 519; Benson, "Considering Secularism," in Douglas Farrow, ed., *Recognizing Religion in a Secular Society: Essays in Pluralism, Religion, and Public Policy* (Montreal and Kingston: McGill-Queens University Press, 2004), pp. 83–98; Douglas Farrow, "Of Secularity and Civil Religion," ibid., pp. 140–82. See also John von Heyking, "Harmonization of Heaven and Earth?: Religion, Politics, and Law in Canada," (2000), 33 *U.B.C. L. Rev.*, pp. 663–98.

9. This story has been told numerous times, most recently by Michael Burleigh, *Earthly Powers: The Clash of Religion and Politics in Europe from the French Revolution to the Great War* (Toronto: HarperCollins, 2006) and *Sacred Causes: The Clash of Religion and Politics, from the Great War to the War on Terror* (Toronto: HarperCollins, 2007); most in-depth by Eric Voegelin, *Modernity without Restraint: The Political Religions*; *The New Science of Politics*; and *Science, Politics, and Gnosticism, Collected Works of Eric Voegelin*, vol. 5, Manfred Henningsen, ed. (Columbia, MO: University of Missouri Press, 2000); *History of Political Ideas, Collected Works of Eric Voegelin*, vols. 19–26; *Order and History*, vols. 14–18. On secularism and progress in Canada, see the articles by Benson, Farrow, and Heyking cited above.

10. In fact, a strong case can be made that creationism (and less so, intelligent design) are social myths, despite their attempt to explain geology and biology. Creationism in particular is a social myth created in reaction to an implication of Darwinism that human beings, since they descend from animals, lack dignity. Creationism uses a pinched reading of the Bible and of scientific data to support a social view, and in this sense it must be understood as a social myth, perhaps analogous to Michael Ignatieff's desire to make a myth or "moral fiction" out of "difference" (analyzed below). On creationism and Darwinism as social myths, see Lee Harris, "Why 'Theology Is a Simple Muddle,'" *TCS Daily*, August 19, 2005, available at http://www.tcsdaily.com/article.aspx?id=081905B.

11. On what an Augustinian political theory might look like, see John von Heyking, *Augustine and Politics as Longing in the World* (Columbia, MO: University of Missouri Press, 2001).

12. Joseph Pieper, *The Four Cardinal Virtues* (Notre Dame: University of Notre Dame Press, 1966), p. 47.

13. Immanuel Kant, *The Metaphysical Principles of Virtue,* trans., James Ellington (New York: Bobbs-Merrill Company, Inc., 1964), p. 127.

14. David Walsh, *The Growth of the Liberal Soul* (Columbia, MO: University of Missouri Press, 1997), pp. 212–219.

15. Jeremy Waldron, "Religious Contributions in Public Deliberation," *San Diego Law Review* 30 (1993), pp. 846–47.

16. Iain T. Benson applies "Edwardianism," an English, largely post-Romantic, literary genre that infused immanent phenomena with transcendent meaning, to contemporary political and culture discourse. See "The Use of Religious Concepts in a Post-religious Age: Canada's Continuing Edwardianism," *Centre Articles* 125 (September 25, 2006), Centre for Cultural Renewal, available at http://www.culturalrenewal.ca/qry/page.taf?id=37&_function=detail&sbtblct_uid1=159&_nc=3950ab1bd7dc849c4bfd02=f17fbcc2ff.

17. By making this dual claim, I am not arguing Canada is or ought to be a "Christian" nation. The Canadian founders, being good classical liberals, understood that sectarianism could rip apart the regime (see Frederick Vaughan, *The Canadian Federalist Experiment: From Defiant Monarchy to Reluctant Republic* (Montreal and Kingston: McGill-Queens University Press, 2003), pp. 134–51; Janet Ajzenstat, *The Political Thought of Lord Durham* (Montreal and Kingston: McGill-Queens University Press, 1988), pp. 35–41. Even so, they, like contemporary politicians and activists, were practical men (and today, women) who did not always realize or think about the deeper justifications of their own political positions. For an extended analysis for this "compactness" in the liberal tradition, see Walsh, *The Growth of the Liberal Soul.*

18. Ignatieff, *The Rights Revolution,* p. 41.

19. Ibid., p. 53.

20. Kant, *Critique of Practical Reason,* trans., Lewis White Beck (Indianapolis: Bobbs-Merrill, 1956), p. 166.

21. Ignatieff, *The Rights Revolution,* p. 53.

22. *Rodriguez v. British Columbia (Attorney General),* [1993] 3 S.C.R., p. 519.

23. On intrinsic or objective dignity, see Leon Kass, "Defending Human Dignity," Bradley Lecture to American Enterprise Institute, February 5, 2007, available at http://www.aei.org/events/filter.foreign,eventID.1376/event_detail.asp. On extrinsic or subjective dignity, see Peter Singer, *How Are We to Live?: Ethics in an Age of Self-Interest* (New York: Prometheus Books, 1995).

24. See Boris DeWiel, "Athens vs. Jerusalem: A Source of Left–Right Conflict in the History of Ideas," *Journal of Political Ideologies* 9, no. 1 (February 2004), pp. 31–49, and Eric Voegelin, *Science, Politics, and Gnosticism* (Wilmington, DE: ISI Books, 1968).

25. Ignatieff, *Rights Revolution,* p. 54.

26. Ignatieff, *Rights Revolution,* p. 43.

27. See Brian Tierney, *The Idea of Natural Rights: Studies on Natural Rights, Natural Law, and Church Law* (Grand Rapids, MI: Wm. Eerdmans, 2000). Of course, Christian experience presupposes Jewish experience. See David Novak, *Covenantal Rights: A Study in Jewish Political Theory* (Princeton: Princeton University Press, 2000) and Eric Voegelin, *Israel and Revelation, Order and History I, Collected Works of Eric Voegelin,* vol. 14, Maurice Hogan, ed. (Columbia, MO: University of Missouri Press, 2001 [1956]).

28. Thomas Hobbes, *Leviathan*, ch. VIII.

29. Janet Ajzenstat argues that much of the tumults Canada has suffered in the past decades (i.e., lack of confidence in institutions, constitutional wrangling, factionalism) have been the result of a form of political romanticism that expects too much from political life (Janet Ajzenstat, *The Once and Future Canadian Democracy* (Montreal and Kingston: McGill-Queen's University Press, 2003) and *The Canadian Founding* (Montreal and Kingston: McGill-Queen's University Press, 2007)).

30. For an account of what a world where this occurs might look like, see Aldous Huxley, *Brave New World* (New York: HarperCollins, 1994).

31. In addition to Walsh, see J. Judd Owen, *Religion and the Demise of Liberal Rationalism: The Foundational Crisis of the Separation of Church and State* (Chicago: University of Chicago Press, 2001).

32. A particularly brutal but candid admission of this strategy is offered by John Barber, "Tory's Proposal a Call to Arms for Secular Humanism," *The Globe and Mail*, September 6, 2007, p. A12, available at http://www.rbcinvest.theglobeandmail.com/servlet/ArticleNews/ PEstory/LAC/20070906/BARBER06/Columnists/columnists/columnistsNational/3/3/3. A more refined example is found in Mark Lilla's call to retrieve Hobbes in the secularist Kulturkampf against evangelicals and other "messianic" religious figures (*The Stillborn God: Religion, Politics, and the Modern West* (New York: Knopf, 2007)).

POSTSCRIPT

In the Surrey schoolbook case, Saunders's finding was appealed by the Surrey school board to the B.C. Court of Appeal. The ruling of the Court of Appeal reversed the previous decision. The justice noted that the school board's decision to refuse approval of the three books did not violate the *School Act* and was fully consistent with the Charter. In making this decision, the Court of Appeal noted that "a religiously informed conscience should not be accorded any privilege, but neither should it be placed under a disability." The Court of Appeal particularly rejected the suggestion by Justice Saunders that moral decisions influenced by religion are excluded under the *School Act*. To accept such a position, the court ruled, "would negate the right of all citizens to participate democratically in the education of their children in a truly free society" and would make "religious unbelief a condition of participation in the setting of the moral agenda" in schools. Thus, Saunders's narrow interpretation of what it means to be secular was not upheld in this instance.

These court rulings deal directly with the question of the legitimacy of using religiously based arguments in debating and deciding matters of public policy. Contemporary liberal political theorists have often been critical of the use of religiously based arguments in political debates. They frequently argue that the modern liberal democratic polity has to be protected from the potentially divisive and destabilizing impact of public religious conflict. To do this, a twofold strategy must be used: politics must be secularized, and religious beliefs must be kept to the private realm, not the public.

Some contemporary liberal theorists take these assumptions to mean that all religiously based lines of reasoning should be excluded from the public sphere. Instead, citizens should employ only "secular" or "rational" positions that are accessible to all. Richard Rorty, for example, in an article entitled "Religion as Conversation Stopper" argues that in contemporary society it should "seem bad taste to bring religion into discussions of public policy." (*Philosophy and Social Hope*, London: Penguin, 2000, p. 169). In her judgment, Justice Saunders seems to have gone even beyond this position, contending that even if religious arguments are not employed, any proof that public policy decisions could be rooted in religious beliefs could be a basis for excluding such decisions.

Other contemporary liberal theorists take a less exclusionary point of view. Robert Audi and John Rawls both maintain that such a limiting approach is discriminatory and serves only to silence religiously motivated advocates. They assert instead that citizens may use religiously motivated arguments as long as they also advance other arguments in support of their position that do not depend in any way on religious belief. Governments and courts should rely on these broader arguments, which are open to everyone, as the ultimate basis for making their decisions.

Jonathan Chaplin gives a detailed examination and critique of these issues in "Beyond Liberal Restraint: Defending Religiously Based Arguments in Law and Public Policy," *UBC Law Review* 33, Special Issue (2000), pp. 617–46. Chaplin puts forward that there is little real evidence that religiously based arguments will contribute to greater divisiveness in society, and he sets out his own views on the appropriate role for religiously based argumentation in the public sphere. In addition to Chaplin's article, this special issue of the *UBC Law Review* on "Religion, Morality, and Law" contains a useful collection of articles dealing with the relationship between religion and public policy. And John von Heyking's "Harmonization of Heaven and Earth? Religion, Politics, and Law in Canada" (in this same issue) provides helpful background to this debate. See also the useful collection of essays in Douglas Farrow, ed., *Recognizing Religion in a Secular Society: Essays in Pluralism, Religion and Public Policy* (Montreal and Kingston: McGill-Queen's University Press: 2004).

Students will also find instructive the following materials on the interaction between religion and law in Canada: Paul Horwitz, "The Sources and Limits of Freedom of Religion in a Liberal Democracy: Section 2(a) and Beyond," *University of Toronto Faculty Law Review* 54, no. 1 (Winter 1990), pp. 1–64; Timothy Macklem, "Faith as a Secular Value," *McGill Law Journal* 45, no. 1 (2000), pp. 3–63; Albert Menendez, *Church and State in Canada* (Amherst, NY: Prometheus Books, 1996); and Ron A. Skolrood and Young-Jae Kim, "Religion and the State," found at http://lawsonlundell.com/resources/ReligionandtheState.pdf. John von Heyking, who is a professor of political science at the University of Lethbridge, also maintains a useful list of resources covering the relationship between religion and politics; the list can be accessed via his home page at the university's website.

Should Representation in Parliament Mirror Canada's Social Diversity?

✔ **YES**
TIM SCHOULS, "Why Group Representation in Parliament Is Important"

✗ **NO**
JOHN H. REDEKOP, "Group Representation in Parliament Would Be Dysfunctional for Canada"

Canada is a representative democracy in which, every four or five years, we choose certain individuals (members of Parliament) to act on our behalf. We empower them to act as our agents and to represent our interests in the national decision-making process. As long as representative democracy has existed, there has been debate over the exact nature that representation should take.

Much of this debate has focused on how the representative is expected to carry out his or her duties. Traditionally, three different views of representation have been put forward. First, there are those who argue that the representative is to act as a *trustee*. That is, members of Parliament are given a mandate to act as they best see fit on behalf of the interests of the electors. MPs are given considerable leeway to exercise their personal judgment in balancing the interests of their constituents with those of the broader community and in coming up with policies that best serve the common good. While the representatives can exercise wide latitude in making decisions, the voter will hold them accountable by removing them from office at the end of their term if they are perceived to have failed in adequately representing the voter's interests.

Second, there are those who argue that the representative is to act primarily as a *delegate*. According to this view, members of Parliament are to act primarily as they have been instructed to by the voters rather than trusting their own judgment as a guide. Representatives should not stray too far from the explicit wishes of their constituents. A variety of techniques such as constituent surveys, public hall meetings, and even telephone referendums have been used in recent years by MPs, especially those from the former Canadian Alliance party, before voting on a particular issue in an attempt to ascertain what the "instructions" of the electorate were.

Third, representatives have been seen as first and foremost *party members* who act and vote primarily according to the dictates of the party leadership. This perspective assumes that the representatives in a party act as a team and that voters choose which team they feel best represents their interests. Like the trustee model, the electorate must wait until the next election to render a judgment on the success of the representative in representing its interests. The debates that follow in Issues Fourteen and Fifteen address weaknesses of the party model of representation and ways that these deficiencies in representative government can be addressed.

In recent years, the debate over representation has shifted toward a more fundamental question—to what extent do the representatives in Parliament reflect the characteristics of ethnicity, language, and gender that are found in the population at large. On one level, this argument suggests that to be truly "representative," Parliament should be composed of the same proportion of social groups as is Canadian society at large. Parliament, in other words, should be a microcosm of Canadian society. If the population is composed of 51 percent women, 6 percent visible minorities, and 4 percent Aboriginal people, then there should be at least the same proportion of representatives elected to Parliament from each of these groups. A basic premise of this argument is that voters, especially those from minority and marginalized groups within society, will not see the decisions of Parliament as being fully legitimate unless the voters see themselves reflected in the social makeup of the legislature. As the social and cultural makeup of Canada changes, our political institutions could increasingly lose credibility if their composition does not adequately reflect the changing face of the country.

However, this argument goes beyond the question of simply increasing the numerical representation of certain social groups, such as women, in Parliament. It argues that representation is important because, once elected, women will act in the interests of women. They will interpret issues and respond to them differently than a male representative would. Thus, the election of women and minority groups to Parliament would result in substantive changes in the content of public policy, as the views of groups once marginalized and unrepresented in the political system would now be given voice within the corridors of power. Only those who know from experience what it is to be a woman, an Aboriginal person, or a member of a visible minority can truly represent other members of these groups.

In the essays below, we examine in greater depth this view of representation. Tim Schouls sets out the philosophical case for ensuring that the social diversity of Canada is represented in the Canadian legislature. In response, John Redekop examines the implications of this move away from more traditional definitions of representation and questions both the wisdom and practicality of such an approach.

✔ **YES**
Why Group Representation in Parliament Is Important
TIM SCHOULS

An increasing number of Canadians are convinced that the system of parliamentary representation in Canada is unfair because it is seen as unrepresentative of Canada's social diversity as a whole. Parliament has long reflected the regional and linguistic composition of Canada by allocating seats in the House of Commons and Senate in a manner that ensures adequate representation of provincial interests at the national level. But this exclusive concern for provincial and regional representation is now being challenged by nonterritorial groups who demand representation on the basis of characteristics that are not tied to geography. These groups argue that if the full diversity of Canada's population is to be reflected in Parliament, its representative character must be expanded beyond that of territory to include guaranteed seats for disadvantaged groups such as women, Aboriginal peoples, ethnic and visible minorities, and people with disabilities. The belief here is that parliamentary representatives must share central experiences and assumptions with those they represent if those representatives are to understand their constituents' needs and interests. Conversely, these groups believe that they cannot be adequately represented if their needs and interests are not advanced by those who share their gender, Aboriginal status, ethnicity, race, or disability.

The conventional Canadian approach to representative democracy, as represented in the article that follows by John Redekop, is generally hostile to claims for guaranteed group-based representation. According to Redekop's view, effective representation does not depend upon representatives and constituents sharing the same personal attributes. Instead, the effectiveness of representatives is measured by the degree to which they are able to present and advance the concerns and claims of their constituents. According to his line of argument, just as lawyers can represent clients who are very different from them, so too can representatives protect the interests of those whose lives have little in common with their own.

While this article will not take direct issue with this more traditional understanding of democratic representation, it will argue that democracy in Canada can be considerably deepened and enhanced when the composition of the House of Commons substantially reflects the social diversity of the Canadian population.[1] No doubt, MPs can represent constituents who are very different from them, but at the same time, it is not always obvious that this representation has been effective in cases where the constituents in question have been subject to historical disadvantage and marginalization. Of course, not all groups in Canadian society have been marginalized or have suffered disadvantage, but for those that have, their argument that seats in the House of Commons be guaranteed to them is worthy of serious examination. For democracy implies equality, but where conditions of marginalization and disadvantage exist, it necessarily follows that some groups possess greater opportunity, and thus privileges and powers that others do not. In the Canadian parliamentary setting, white males from professional and business backgrounds have historically dominated the House of Commons and Senate, and, as a result, it is they who have traditionally held a monopoly upon the political reigns of power. Conversely, many women, Aboriginal peoples, certain ethnic and visible minorities, and people with disabilities claim that they have been marginalized, which means, among other things, that they have been minimally represented in parliamentary discussions and decision-making processes. This article will argue that where political marginalization of groups has historically existed, active reform to secure these groups seats in the House of Commons is a healthy democratic response. Not only will such reform ensure marginalized groups a greater presence and thus a voice in the parliamentary process, but also such reform may encourage the development of legislation and laws that take more fully into account the views of marginalized groups. In short, an active reform process will counteract the current imbalance in political power and so promote greater democratic equality of opportunity and participation in the House of Commons for Canada's socially diverse groups.

GROUP IDENTITY IN CANADA

It could be argued that to focus exclusively upon demands by marginalized groups for political inclusion within the House of Commons is to largely miss the point of group identity politics in Canada. The range of political differences and objectives represented by Canada's diverse population is extensive, pushing far beyond the kinds of solutions that a politics of inclusion within the House of Commons can offer. To be sure, over the last twenty-five years or so, Canadians have begun to define themselves in new ways, and the politics of parliamentary inclusion is in large part an initiative that attempts to address those changes. For political purposes, Canadians used to identify themselves largely with their provinces of origin, with their use of French or English as their first language, and with their Catholic or Protestant religion. In response, the House of Commons was set up, both in terms of its allocation of seats and in terms of representation within cabinet, to reflect this geographic, linguistic, and religious diversity. In recent years, however, a new set of identity categories has become increasingly salient for many Canadians, categories associated primarily with changing conceptions of ethnicity and with the newfound political relevance of gender. Immigration and demographic trends of the 1970s to the 1990s have made Canada a far more multiethnic and multicultural country, while strong feminist initiatives during this same time frame have elevated the political status of women. New Canadians with origins in the Caribbean, Africa, Middle East, Central and South America, and Asia identify themselves not simply as provincial residents speaking either English or French but, more importantly, as members of ethnic groups with distinctive perspectives and interests to offer to the broader Canadian political agenda. Feminists, meanwhile, point out that the social and political structures of Canada reinforce men's power to the detriment of women. In response, redress of the current structural imbalance of power between men and women constitutes a central component of the feminist political agenda. In short, attachments to geography, language, and religion are receding in their overall political importance. At the same time, attachments to ethnicity and gender are becoming more significant politically. Against these shifting demographic trends, it is therefore not surprising that the conventional geography-based strategy for allocating House of Commons seats is coming under increasing attack.

However, despite the need to address the challenge of representation in the House of Commons for the marginally represented categories of women and ethnic groups, Canadian identity politics is more typically driven by demands for Aboriginal self-government and the recognition of Quebec's "distinct society." Like women and ethnic minorities, Aboriginal peoples and the citizens of Quebec argue that the existing conventions of representation do not grant them standing that is proportional to their numbers in Canada. From the perspectives of their leaders, however, greater representation in Parliament will not guarantee Aboriginal peoples and the citizens of Quebec the kind of legislative power they need to secure their political objectives within Canada. Their numbers are simply too small and their influence too weak to counteract the legislative priorities of the non-Aboriginal, non-Québécois parliamentary majority. Hence, Aboriginal peoples demand an equal partnership with federal and provincial governments based upon the recognition of their inherent right to self-government, while Quebeckers demand at minimum an expansion of their powers within the federal system of government so as to increase their provincial autonomy within Canada. Thus, when Aboriginal peoples and Quebeckers claim that they do not enjoy equal powers within Canada, they typically seek solutions within the realm of intergovernmental affairs rather than parliamentary representation.

When considering the arguments for greater parliamentary representation for disadvantaged or marginalized groups within Canada, it is important to realize from the outset that the demands for political inclusion by Aboriginal peoples, the citizens of Quebec, women, and ethnic and visible minorities are not naturally all of one piece. Aboriginal peoples and Quebeckers demand more autonomy *from* Parliament through self-government and special provincial status (or secession), while women and ethnic and visible minorities demand more autonomy *within* Parliament through elevated levels of representation. In fact in many respects, the demands of the former two groups are mirror images of those of the latter groups. Be that as it may, the demands for equal representation within Parliament remain an important concern for some groups. The intent of this article is to draw attention to only this very small piece of the larger, often poorly interlocking, Canadian identity puzzle.

REPRESENTATIONAL DEFICITS

On the surface, there is an undeniable, indeed, almost irrefutable, logic attached to the demand that the House of Commons reflect the diversity of the Canadian population. At present, for example, electoral mechanisms organize Canadians into geographically bound constituencies. While Redekop is quite right to point out that dividing voters into constituency groups makes sense from a practical point of view, such a division also carries with it the assumption that voters' primary political identity flows from their attachment to territory. MPs are thus linked to their constituents in geographic terms. The geographical division of the electorate encourages voters to think of their varied interests (whether relating to jobs, social security, the environment, etc.) largely in terms of where they live.

Now, while features associated with geography may well shape citizens' identities in some respects, Canadians also possess diverse identities by virtue of their cultural, gender, ethnic, and religious differences, which have very little to do with geography. It therefore stands to reason that along with geographic affiliation, Canadians may want to be represented by those who share their Aboriginal status, gender, ethnicity, or religious identity. There is an intuitive logic attached to the idea, for example, that when legislative initiatives dealing with abortion, childcare, or pay equity are before the House of Commons, female constituents may want to be represented by women who can identify with these issues because they are women. Similarly, when legislative initiatives dealing with reserve-based economic ventures or housing starts are before the House, it makes sense that Aboriginal constituents may want to have Aboriginal people representing their interests. According to this line of reasoning then, there is clearly something amiss when representation within the House is monopolized by a single group (upper- and middle-class males, for example), a group, moreover, that most likely possesses a relatively limited range of perspectives. Indeed, most well-intentioned Canadians would probably readily admit that where underrepresentation of certain groups exists, reforms ought to be encouraged to stimulate a more proportional balance of representation in the House.

While there have been a few improvements, it is undeniably the case that the composition of the House of Commons is only a very pale reflection of the diverse social characteristics of the Canadian population, as can be seen in the following three examples. In the 1988 federal election, thirty-nine, or 13.2 percent, of the MPs elected were women; in the 1993 election, fifty-four, or 18.3 percent, were women; in the 1997 and 2000 elections, sixty-one, or 20.2 percent, were women. This percentage increased only to 21 in the 2004 election. Given that women constitute 51 percent of Canada's population, the severity of their underrepresentation in the House is hard to miss.[2] In the case of Aboriginal peoples and visible minorities, underrepresentation in the House is even more striking.[3] Aboriginal peoples constitute approximately 4 percent of Canada's population, yet they were able to capture only 1 percent of the seats (three of a total 295) in each of the

1988 and 1993 elections.[4] Visible minorities, meanwhile, while constituting 6.3 percent of Canada's population, captured only 2 percent of the seats (six out of 295) in 1988, though they improved their fortunes slightly by increasing their share to 3 percent (nine out of 295) in the election of 1993.[5] Compare these lean numbers to the following scenario. If a proportional share of seats were given to each of the three groups mentioned above, women would be entitled to 153 seats, Aboriginal peoples to twelve seats, and visible minorities to nineteen seats out of the total 301.[6]

The obvious question here is why do women, Aboriginal peoples, and visible minorities persist in being so severely underrepresented in the House of Commons? There is no short answer to this question, for the barriers that inhibit each group from entering electoral politics are numerous and in many respects different from one another. Women, for example, have traditionally avoided political life at the national level because the heavy demands of family life and a political career often strain significantly against one another. Moreover, the challenge associated with securing financing to contest constituency nominations and run campaigns, coupled with the perception that the fierce competition associated with politics is symptomatic of a male domain, has made the political arena at the national level minimally appealing for many women.[7] Aboriginal candidates share with women the structural barrier of limited financing. In addition, as the Committee for Aboriginal Electoral Reform argues, "Canada's history of assimilationist policies has had an adverse impact on Aboriginal perceptions of Parliament and the value of participating within it."[8] The negative feelings Aboriginal peoples hold against Parliament as a colonial instrument of oppression means that many Aboriginal people are inclined not to vote in federal elections. This in turn discourages parties from fielding Aboriginal candidates, as there is little incentive for them to use such Aboriginal candidates in attempts to win a largely apathetic Aboriginal vote. Barriers inhibiting the participation of visible minorities are also readily identifiable. For example, Daiva Stasiulis argues that for many recent immigrants a significant barrier exists in the form of lack of familiarity with Canada's two official languages and with the customs of the British parliamentary tradition.[9] This barrier is compounded in turn by party politics that tend to identify the issues of Canadian politics along a French–English continuum and to engage in the recruitment of candidates by using old, well-established networks that have little, if any, connections to the immigrant community.

Given these structural barriers, it seems but a small step to justify reforms aimed at securing a proportional number of women, Aboriginal peoples, and ethnic and visible minorities in the House of Commons. Moreover, the case for inclusion only gathers strength when we recognize that the primary reason women, Aboriginal peoples, and ethnic and visible minorities are absent from the House of Commons is that they have been ignored and marginalized by the male hierarchy that holds power. Given that men dominate the House of Commons, it only stands to reason that they will have greater opportunity and power to advance their perspectives and legislate their preferences. Conversely, it has been well documented that, relative to men, women suffer greater social and economic disadvantage, a condition that in turn means that women have fewer political resources than men. Aboriginal peoples and ethnic and visible minorities, meanwhile, have long struggled against what Iris Marion Young calls cultural imperialism.[10] In the Canadian setting, cultural imperialism has typically manifested itself in the form of English and French cultures establishing societywide norms. Aboriginal, ethnic, and visible minority cultures, conversely, were traditionally stigmatized as being inferior and in need of transformation to align them more closely with the perspectives and worldviews of the two dominant cultures.

THEORIES OF REPRESENTATION

It is largely in reaction to these structural barriers that numerous calls for reform leading to a more proportional balance of representation in Parliament have been issued over the years. In essence, calls for proportional representation constitute a claim to tip the scales of the currently imbalanced composition of the House of Commons toward a more balanced representation of Canada's social diversity. If the political assumptions associated with white male privilege hamper the capacity of minorities to gain access to the House of Commons, then on democratic grounds surely no effort should be spared to get more minority representatives into the House. Moreover, the urgency that many marginalized groups attach to their claims for inclusion flows directly from the fact that the House of Commons lies at the symbolic heart of representative government in Canada. It is with this state institution more than any other that the primary qualification to become an MP is purely and simply the ability to represent. No doubt, as Redekop points out, many MPs get elected simply because they are better than their opponents in capturing the vote. But in the end, the test of good service is established by the degree to which constituents judge their MP to have been an effective representative on their behalf. This stands in sharp contrast to employment within the judiciary or bureaucracy, for example, where professional expertise and academic qualifications are of first importance. Simply put, legislatures exist to represent the population they serve; this is their central function. It is therefore imperative from the point of view of numerous marginalized groups that, if they are to achieve social and political equality in any meaningful sense, they simply must achieve proportional standing in the parliamentary domain where many of their interests are so regularly considered and debated.

If the case for more proportional inclusion in the House of Commons is so compelling, then why do so many Canadians accept with little trouble the prevailing patterns of white, male-dominated representation? In order to get a handle on this question, it is important that we step back for a moment and examine with some care the conflicting understandings that lie behind the idea of representation itself.

To date, there has been significant agreement in Canada that the practice of parliamentary democracy ought to adhere to a liberal conception of representation. From a liberal point of view, it is the individual who is to be treated as the most important of all political entities. This means that when it comes to representation, each individual is to count equally as one, and no one as more than one. In the context of elections, moreover, this concern for individual equality translates into the well-known slogan One Person, One Vote. What is of principal importance from the liberal point of view, then, is that while group interests can be advanced (given that it is individuals who form groups for the deliberate purpose of promoting common interests), individual interests must not be ignored in the process. Indeed, for liberals, to represent groups exclusively potentially poses two immediate dangers to the individual. First, when MPs represent group interests, they tend to regard those interests as held by all members of the group. However, not all group members may hold the same interests. For example, some women may dissent from a particular daycare strategy, yet if women are treated as a group, MPs may be tempted to regard the endorsement of the strategy by some women as an endorsement by all. Focusing upon the interests of each and every individual gets around this problem of universalizing interests. Second, to focus upon the interests of groups brings with it the possibility that MPs will privilege some groups over others. In this scenario, not only are dissenting individuals within privileged groups left unrepresented, but so too are all members of groups who are not fortunate enough to gain the attention of MPs in the first place.

In the interests of equality of representation, then, representatives are elected to advance the individual interests of their individual constituents. To be sure, the interests of constituents will regularly conflict, and so the MP will be forced to make compromises and secure tradeoffs. The measure of effective representation is determined when, despite being faced by the challenge of conflicting interests, MPs are nevertheless able to take appropriate positions demonstrating that they have taken the interests of all their constituents into account. The issue, then, is not who is in the House of Commons doing the representing, but rather whether the MP, regardless of personal characteristics, is able to get the job done on behalf of his or her constituents. In short, MPs may well possess different social, ethnic, or sexual characteristics from those they represent, but this should not matter if MPs demonstrate a constant readiness to respond in helpful ways to their constituents' needs.

This liberal argument of representation is certainly a very powerful one. But on its own, this liberal theory simply does not do full justice to the political marginalization and exclusion that many women, Aboriginal peoples, and ethnic and visible minorities experience. As Redekop so powerfully argues, men can represent women (much as a male lawyer can represent a female client) if the issue in question is a legislative initiative to which both men and women agree. But what Redekop fails to take seriously is that with respect to many issues, women,

Aboriginal peoples, and visible and ethnic minorities will want to be represented by those who are like them because they believe that their identities carry with them distinctive experiences that white male MPs will be hard-pressed to understand. Women, for example, may possess experiences and consequently perspectives that are distinct from those of men with respect to the issues of childbearing and child care, sexual harassment and violence, the division of paid and unpaid labour, and the matter of women's exclusion from significant portions of the economic and political world.[11] Furthermore, with respect to Aboriginal peoples, Ovide Mercredi and Mary Ellen Turpel argue, "As Peoples with distinct cultures, languages, governments, territories and populations in Canada, we must be recognized as full and equal participants in the Canadian political system. We can speak for ourselves and no one else has the political or spiritual authority to speak for us. Canadians cannot speak for us because Canadians are different."[12] What is at issue here is not so much the capacity of MPs to advocate on behalf of their female, Aboriginal, or ethnic and visible minority constituents per se; minorities would certainly endorse any initiative that sees MPs support and advance their political agendas. More directly, what is at issue is the desire of women, Aboriginal peoples, and ethnic and visible minorities to gain a more proportional balance in the House of Commons on the grounds that they have been marginalized and excluded from representing themselves in the past.

At the same time, it is critical to underscore the point that the leaders of marginalized groups do not generally stake their claim for greater inclusion on the grounds that they share common interests–interests, moreover, that they believe only their own representatives are capable of putting before the House of Commons. Such an argument cannot provide the moral foundation for a claim to greater inclusion, because the experiences of marginalized groups are normally too varied to be contained within a single common interest. Women have different perspectives on abortion, child care, and pay equity, for example, while Aboriginal peoples have different perspectives on economic development, land claims, and self-government. Within their respective communities, women and Aboriginal peoples may thus share common policy concerns, but this does not mean that they will also share the same views on how those concerns ought to be handled. Minority groups are not homogeneous, possessing single, distinct policy perspectives. Such images portray far too simplistic a view of the world. Because minority groups do not by definition possess common policy interests, the strength of the argument for greater inclusion in the House of Commons necessarily lies elsewhere.

The argument for greater inclusion in the House of Commons gathers far more strength when considered within the framework of political marginalization or exclusion. The representational claim of marginalized groups is a forceful one because groups want to overcome the barriers of domination that have excluded them from participating in an equitable way in the House in the past. As the argument goes, if the distinct voices and (internally multiple) perspectives of marginalized social groups are not represented in the House, then it is almost certainly the case that the legislative initiatives and policy outcomes of the dominant white male majority will (continue to) prevail. In essence, what marginalized groups are saying is that they have a right to participate in these parliamentary discussions whatever their opinion may be on the matter under consideration. In this sense, the demands for parliamentary inclusion put forward by women, Aboriginal people, and visible and ethnic minorities flow from their common experiences of exclusion as groups, and from their mutual desire to engage more directly in parliamentary debate and decision making. To be sure, as Redekop points out, inclusion in parliamentary debate is not in and of itself enough to guarantee satisfactory legislative outcomes for marginalized groups. Influence can be effective only to the degree that marginalized groups can make their presence felt where power in parliamentary government is exercised—by the majority party and, more particularly, by the prime minister and cabinet drawn from the majority party. At the same time, however, without presence in the House of Commons, there is little opportunity for marginalized groups to exercise any influence at all.

The larger point that the leaders of marginalized groups seek to establish, however, is that because white males have traditionally monopolized parliamentary power, they cannot at this juncture in history take the place of the very groups they have marginalized by standing in as their representatives. As social groups, women, Aboriginal peoples, and visible and ethnic minorities need to be represented by other women, Aboriginal peoples, and visible and ethnic minorities because they share identities, which goes along with having been historically excluded. Thus, for example, men may be able to advance women's interests, but what men cannot do is stand in for women when women want to have all their diversity *as women* represented in the House of Commons. This is a task that only women can perform for themselves. Against historical patterns of exclusion, the presence of women in the House of Commons ensures that all the diverse and quite possibly conflicting interests of women will actually be heard and debated in Canada's central representative political arena.[13]

In sum, the proportional presence of women, Aboriginal peoples, and visible and ethnic minorities in the House of Commons matters because this presence would have the effect of counteracting the current hierarchy of white male power. A more sustained and numerically balanced presence would help to raise the profile of marginalized groups and thereby possibly place their multiple issues more regularly before the House. In this vein, Young argues, "The principle of group representation calls for some means by which the needs, interests, knowledge, and social perspective of oppressed or disadvantaged groups receive explicit and formal representation in political discussions and decision-making. The primary argument for such group representation is that where there are social group differences and some groups are privileged and others oppressed, group representation is necessary to produce a legitimate communicative forum."[14] Proportional representation of marginalized groups in the House of Commons would ensure that the full range of views represented by Canada's diverse population would have the opportunity for expression on a consistent and ongoing basis. This may in turn encourage a situation in which "those who had previously monopolized positions of power and influence might be equally encouraged to recognize their partiality and bias."[15]

OBJECTIONS

In the article following, Redekop raises a number of objections against the arguments put forward thus far. Let me conclude by addressing the three that are most significant.

First, Redekop argues that a politics of parliamentary inclusion based on gender, ethnic, or other minority identities introduces or possibly intensifies divisions between Canadian citizens–divisions, moreover, that arguably may not be of the first importance in the public eye. He points out that Canada has enough trouble as it is building points of commonality between Canadians in Parliament, so why should Canadians further fuel the fire of divisions by paying attention to gender- and ethnicity-based claims to inclusion? Indeed, would it not be far better to encourage citizens to focus on matters of policy instead and try to build alliances across identity differences in support of policy initiatives that all groups can support? To cede to demands for parliamentary inclusion by marginalized groups, argues Redekop, would seem only to add additional stress to an already severely stretched Canadian unity fabric.

There is no easy answer to this objection, for Redekop is undoubtedly right that the demand for inclusion by women, Aboriginal peoples, and visible and ethnic minorities would add a new and potentially divisive dimension to parliamentary politics. However, one way to partly allay these fears of division is to recognize that what marginalized groups are asking for is not to be separated from the structures of Canadian democracy but, rather, to be more fully included within them. Contrast, for example, the demands of Quebec separatists with the demands of marginalized groups and consider which is the more divisive force within Canadian politics. Quebec separatists threaten political unity within Canada because they question the credentials of the Canadian government to exercise any authority over them. Marginalized groups, on the other hand, have drawn attention to their identities only because they want to be more fully included in the political discussions that shape the political identity of Canada as a whole. Thus, although marginalized groups may focus upon the political importance of their social differences, what they are actually doing, as Will Kymlicka puts it, is trying to find avenues for "full membership in the larger society."[16] From this perspective, the demand for greater inclusion by marginalized groups can be seen as an important endorsement of the Canadian parliamentary system.

Redekop's second objection relates to who potentially qualifies for distinct representation within Parliament. If Parliament is to be considered truly representative of Canada's social diversity, Redekop asks, then does this mean that all sectors of the Canadian population should be represented, including, for example, the aged, teachers, students, factory workers, retail sales workers, parents, athletes, and environmentalists? Once we accept the view that the characteristics of people play a role in determining whether they feel adequately represented in Parliament, then we seem to be in the absurd position of having to consider the claims for inclusion by a potentially endless list of groups. Moreover, even if we can establish which groups might qualify for guaranteed representation, Redekop asks, how do we go about establishing who legitimately belongs to which group? Is the attempt to establish boundaries simply too difficult, given that so many people now have what might be called "hybrid" identities (e.g., a person may be both female and Aboriginal)? In other words, on what basis do we distinguish legitimate claims by groups for parliamentary inclusion from those that are not legitimate?

Again, there is no straightforward answer to Redekop's objection, though Anne Phillips points us in a helpful direction. She argues that the case for greater inclusion of women, ethnic groups, and ethnic and visible minorities rests upon "an analysis of the existing structures of exclusion."[17] That is, a system of fair representation does not mean that any or all groups are entitled to specific representation on the basis of some purported principle of equality or fairness. Instead, what we must do is focus upon those particularly urgent instances where the oppression of groups has led to those same groups experiencing a profound degree of marginalization and exclusion from the political process. Proportional representation of groups is thus never simply required but must be determined on a case-by-case basis in reference to these questions: Has this group been historically oppressed? Will proportional representation in Parliament constitute a significant step in overcoming those conditions of oppression? In other words, what qualifies groups for greater inclusion is the likelihood that without guaranteed access to the arena of policymaking they will be unable to overcome their current experiences of exclusion and marginalization. While this approach does not get around the difficulties associated with defining who is and who is not a member of a disadvantaged group, it at least narrows the field of potential candidates who may be eligible for guaranteed representation. Against these more restrictive criteria, women, Aboriginal peoples, and numerous visible minority and ethnic groups in Canada are able to put forward a very strong case.

Third, Redekop argues that the proposal to move to identity-based representation is condescending toward those groups that would benefit from guaranteed seats because, among other things, such representation would relegate them to the status of second-class MPs. If groups can't make it to the House of Commons on their own, in other words, and are thereby "reduced" to relying upon special governmental facilitation to get them there, they will undoubtedly lack credibility.

No doubt, securing seats through special guarantees does constitute a significant departure from standard electoral practice in Canada. But though a departure, these reform proposals are not in and of themselves condescending to disadvantaged and marginalized groups. Here everything depends on one's perspective. Despite what Redekop says, disadvantaged and marginalized groups are not after guaranteed seats because the dominant male hierarchy has told them that such a course of action would be good for them. To accept the directives of the dominant male hierarchy on these grounds would indeed be condescending. On the contrary, disadvantaged and marginalized groups who make the point are saying that they are after guaranteed seats because this is the only way they will be able to break the stranglehold upon power that the dominant male hierarchy now exercises over them. They would stand for office and get elected through conventional channels, in other words, if they could reasonably expect to be successful in this way. The trouble is that their success is minimized because the dominant male hierarchy (which constitutes a minority in demographic terms) has been very effective at retaining its vast majority of seats in the House since it has at its disposal a disproportional share of the party and electoral machinery needed to win elections. From this perspective, the only way to break this cycle of dominance is to make structural changes that directly challenge the male hierarchy. One way to mount this challenge is through a system of guaranteed seats.

CONCLUSION

Redekop is quite right to point out that the practical complications associated with getting a system of guaranteed seats off the ground are considerable. I have no easy solutions to offer. However, there simply being practical difficulties associated with reform should not lead us to abandon the project. Advocates of reform tell us that a system of guaranteed seats is an integral component of their larger project to overcome the debilitating cycle of political marginalization and exclusion they now experience. The question is, what is the best route to heeding this call for justice? There is, of course, safety to be had in steering the ship of democratic practice in Canada into the tranquil waters of the status quo rather than into the rocky waters of reform. The latter route may well lead to significant structural damage to the parliamentary ship as we know it. However, avoiding rocky waters also means that those who now hold power will continue to pilot the ship. The message that the marginalized and disadvantaged in Canada draw to our attention is that this inclination toward "safety" may be less than desirable.

NOTES

1. I will leave aside the question of representation in the Senate, as this would raise issues that lie beyond the scope of this paper.

2. See Jane Arscott and Linda Trimble, "In the Presence of Women: Representation and Political Power," in Jane Arscott and Linda Trimble, eds., *In the Presence of Women: Representation in Canadian Governments* (Toronto: Harcourt Brace & Company, Canada, 1997), pp. 1–17.

3. Ed. note. As of 2007, Aboriginal MPs in the House of Commons numbered only four.

4. See Committee for Aboriginal Electoral Reform, *The Path to Electoral Equality* (Ottawa: Committee for Aboriginal Electoral Reform, 1991), p. 2.

5. See Daiva Stasiulis, "Deep Diversity: Race and Ethnicity in Canadian Politics," in Michael S. Whittington and Glen Williams, eds., *Canadian Politics in the 1990s* (Toronto: Nelson Canada, 1995), pp. 199–200.

6. In the June 1997 federal election, the number of House of Commons seats contested was raised from 295 to 301.

7. On this point, see Lisa Young, "Fulfilling the Mandate of Difference: Women in the Canadian House of Commons," in Jane Arscott and Linda Trimble, *In the Presence of Women: Representation in Canadian Governments,* pp. 85–86.

8. Committee for Aboriginal Electoral Reform, *The Path to Electoral Equality,* pp. 7–12.

9. Daiva Stasiulis, "Deep Diversity," pp. 200–204.

10. Iris Marion Young, "Justice and Communicative Democracy," in Roger S. Gottlieb, ed., *Radical Philosophy: Tradition, Counter-Tradition Politics* (Philadelphia: Temple University Press, 1993), p. 133.

11. Anne Phillips, *The Politics of Presence* (Oxford: Clarendon Press, 1995), pp. 67–68.

12. Ovide Mercredi and Mary Ellen Turpel, *In the Rapids: Navigating the Future of First Nations* (Toronto: Penguin, 1993), p. 36.

13. For an extensive discussion of this point, see Anne Phillips, *The Politics of Presence,* ch. 2.

14. Iris Marion Young, "Justice and Communicative Democracy," p. 136.

15. Anne Phillips, *The Politics of Presence,* p. 152.

16. Will Kymlicka, *Multicultural Citizenship: A Liberal Theory of Minority Rights* (Oxford: Clarendon Press, 1995), p. 192.

17. Anne Phillips, *The Politics of Presence,* p. 47.

✗ **NO**

Group Representation in Parliament Would Be Dysfunctional for Canada
JOHN H. REDEKOP

INTRODUCTION

Various critics rightly assert that the Canadian Parliament does not accurately reflect Canada's social diversity. They are also correct when they say that Canada's electoral system plays a major role in producing unrepresentative legislatures. What is at issue in the present discussion is not whether the Canadian Parliament, specifically the House of Commons, should be reformed and the electoral system improved but whether the proposal to adopt group representation, as explained by Tim Schouls, constitutes a desirable and workable change.

As I understand it, the proposal under consideration seeks to remedy the alleged major flaw in Canada's electoral system by guaranteeing parliamentary seats for "disadvantaged groups such as women, Aboriginal peoples, ethnic and visible minorities, and people with disabilities." While additional categories are suggested by the phrasing, we will limit this discussion to these five groups; they encompass about 75 percent of Canada's population. We will also limit this analysis to the House of Commons. Senate reform needs to be discussed in its own right.

It should be noted that the proposal emphasizes the need for "political equality," which apparently means "equal representation" or mathematical proportionality. Thus, since females constitute about 51 percent of the population, they would, in the proposed scheme of "proportional parliamentary inclusion" and "proportional presence," be guaranteed 51 percent of the seats in the elected House of Commons. The other four groups would similarly be guaranteed a percentage of seats in this "identity-based" system of representation.

This essay will demonstrate that identity-based group representation in Parliament, with guaranteed seats, as described by Tim Schouls, is neither desirable nor workable in Canada. On balance, I believe, it would not be an improvement over our present single-member plurality electoral system.

One can think of several reasonable and democratic ways in which our present system could be reformed. One way would be to have half of the House of Commons seats filled by our present form of election—which would enable all Canadians to retain the benefits of having their own MP—with the other half being filled by a proportional representation system as is presently practised in Germany, Japan, and New Zealand. Having half of the MPs elected according to the second system would promote unity and goodwill, for example, by allowing a nationally victorious party to have at least some representation from a province where it got a large number of votes but did not come first in any riding. Such was the situation for the Liberals in the general election of 1980, for example, when they received 24 percent of the popular vote in Saskatchewan and 22 percent in each of Alberta and British Columbia but failed to elect even one member in those three provinces. In those three provinces, thus, the Liberals were unrepresented in the national cabinet.

ARGUMENTS BASED ON IDEOLOGICAL CONSIDERATIONS

In part, the case for group representation, as presented in the preceding article, rests on faulty assumptions; we will review seven.

1. **The five groups under consideration are all definable entities with basically clear boundaries.** This assumption is important because we would need to be clear about who belongs to a particular group if we want to assign guaranteed seats to that group. While there is no difficulty in identifying the women in Canada, the situation is problematic for the other four groups. Who should be in the Aboriginal group? Would a person who is one-eighth Aboriginal and seven-eighths French-Canadian—and there are many such people—be part of the Aboriginal group or the French-Canadian group or both? What fraction of Aboriginal blood would be required? Would Aboriginal people be allowed to decide on fractions for themselves? Such kinds of problems are legion. The actual membership and boundary problems boggle the mind. Also, should we include in the Aboriginal group those Aboriginal people who don't want to be part of this racially segregated group but would rather participate in the category of general voters? Would we force them to be racially categorized?

Similarly, who would belong to a given ethnic minority? Would we require some racial tests? And what about the millions of Canadians who identify with more than one ethnic group? To ask the question is to think of enough problems to keep a small army of bureaucrats happy for years. Further, would a Chinese-Canadian husband and his Jamaican-Canadian wife vote for different slates of candidates, and would their twenty-year-old daughter living at home vote for a third slate of candidates? Would she have a choice?

Moreover, which ethnic groups and which visible minorities would qualify for separate and guaranteed representation? If we want to accommodate all organized ethnic groups in Canada, we would have to deal with at least 160 of them. If they each got even one seat—and the larger groups would insist on getting more—then more than half of the seats in the House of Commons would be assigned to these ethnic groups. And let us not wiggle out of this dilemma by suggesting that only the larger ethnic groups would be assigned seats. They already tend to win seats on their own. It's the scores of smaller groups that systematically and regularly get no representation. Perhaps one could argue that ethnic groups could be lumped together, for example, East Europeans, people from the

Middle East, Blacks from Africa, and so on. But often the greatest animosities exist between neighbouring groups, such as Serbs and Croats, Jews and Arabs, Taiwanese and mainland Chinese, and so on.

Even agreeing on who in Canada should belong to the group termed "disabled" would be very difficult. Are we thinking only of paraplegics or quadriplegics? Do we include the blind? What about the hearing impaired? What about the mentally impaired? What about those with perpetually sore backs? Do we include those who have AIDS? Would people with chronic fatigue syndrome qualify? And what about the thousands who are terminally ill with cancer or some other disease? They are certainly disabled and permanently so. Should these and others who could be listed all be included? They certainly all have disabilities. Furthermore, how much impairment creates disability? Who would decide? And would it be logical to assume that this diverse spectrum of groups would have a common political agenda?

2. Voters can be represented well only by representatives who share their social traits. Schouls states that "parliamentary representatives must share central experiences and assumptions with those they represent if those representatives are to understand their constituents' needs and interests." I find his argument unconvincing.

If we look at the professions of teaching, medicine, and law, for example, we find that effective representation and service do not require social similarity. I am confident that if members of the five identity-based groups were given the choice, the vast majority would rank competence as more important than social similarity. When people are sick, it is more important that they have a competent physician than that they have one from their own ethnic group. Similarly, people generally look for competent teachers, lawyers, mechanics, accountants, photographers, and other professionals and tradespeople. Why should we assume that it would be different when we turn to the profession of politics? Granted, social similarity is a significant asset, but it is not the most important criterion.

3. Parliamentary input will shape parliamentary output. The Canadian political system grants power and authority to a majority party or coalition, not to minority groups whose support is not needed by governments in order to retain office. Clearly, identity-based minorities would influence what is said in legislative debate, but why should we assume that such minority voices would affect legislative output, the policy decisions? (The special situation with the majority composed of women will be discussed later.) In fact, it would likely be the case that the majority rulers, either one party or a coalition, would be inclined to discount and marginalize the input of identity-based MPs with their narrow agenda because the rulers cannot realistically hope to win them over to the perspective of the governing majority. There is nothing to be gained by acceding to the requests of opposition minorities. Majorities can safely ignore such minorities.

Conversely, if these same identity-based MPs were members of the governing party, or even of the official opposition, they would have some hope of influencing policies and platforms, but only if they were prepared to accept substantial compromises.

As I see it, the error in Schouls's apparent assumptions in this regard is that voice equals influence. A second apparent assumption is that representation in itself, even having one or a few MPs advocating a certain perspective, constitutes power.

Both assumptions, in my view, are faulty. All the eloquence one can imagine and a total sharing of social traits with one's constituents carry virtually no weight in legislative debate if there is not a political reason for the decision makers, generally the cabinet, to take such input seriously. A few eloquent MPs may achieve publicity, even popularity, but generally do not have significant influence on legislative output.

4. Political decisions grow out of parliamentary debate. In earlier times, generations ago, public policies may actually have had their genesis in parliamentary debate, but those days have passed. It is now erroneous to assume that important public policies, the type that the five identity-based groups would like to see enacted, are actually shaped in Parliament and are the result of MPs' input and debate. It seems safe to say that at least 98 percent of public policies in Canada are generated by the cabinet—which may get its ideas from many sources including pressure groups—and are not formed or changed to any significant extent by parliamentary debate. An identity-based group having 5 or 10 percent of the MPs does not mean that it has 5 or 10 percent of the influence on public policies.

Schouls states that "marginalized groups," including the five we are considering, "want to be more fully included in the political discussions that shape the political identity of Canada as a whole." I seriously question whether parliamentary debates play a significant role in shaping Canada's political identity. It seems more accurate to say that these five groups would achieve more success in influencing Canada's political identity if they contributed informed input to cabinet members and senior officials before cabinet decisions are made. In this way they could also, with greater credibility, threaten voter retaliation, if need be, a tactic they cannot employ if the constituency they represent votes in its own elections or at least for its own set of candidates and the decision makers have nothing to gain by accommodating them. A group that is electorally hived off by itself should not expect to gain concessions from decision makers who have nothing to gain by making such concessions.

It could be that MPs who represent identity-based groups would become part of a governing coalition. In such a situation they might be able to influence policy decision but, in virtually all cases, only by making compromises, which is exactly what we have under our present system. In rare instances, such MPs might actually be able to topple a government. Such action would perhaps give the key MPs a sense of power, but it would not bring about the implementation of their political agenda.

5. Women do not participate in politics as much as men do because the women "have been ignored and marginalized by the male hierarchy". In earlier times this assumption was valid, but today it has little validity. My experience and observation lead me to conclude that in most situations, political parties, still dominated by males, bend over backward to get qualified women to stand as candidates. They do so for the same reason that they often seek out ethnic and other minority people to stand as candidates—they believe that having such candidates increases their chances of victory.

If we want to find out why women remain relatively underrepresented in Parliament (although the situation is gradually improving), we must probe more deeply. Simply blaming men will not do. Electoral results and various studies have shown, as former prime minister Kim Campbell and many others could verify, that women do not necessarily or even disproportionally vote for women. Most female voters, just like most male voters, tend to vote for the candidate or party that they believe to be the best of the options. People are more sophisticated than to vote, blindly, for a candidate on the basis of which bathroom that candidate uses.

It is also the case, of course, that most of society, including many women, still believes that women can make their greatest contribution by providing a strong home setting. As long as that view is dominant, there is likely to be a relative shortage of qualified women standing for office and being elected. This point ties in with another important reality, namely, that women have babies and men don't.

Any remaining societal barriers hindering political success by women should, of course, be removed. These barriers may include inadequate child care in Parliament, inadequate leave policies for pregnancy, or inappropriate financial policies. We should not delude ourselves, however, by assuming that if we guarantee women a certain number of seats in Parliament we are thereby eliminating barriers.

6. "The primary qualification to become an MP is purely and simply the ability to represent". This assumption strikes me as being false. The primary qualification, in our electoral system, to become an MP is to find a way to get more people to vote for you than for any other candidate. Often the person who appears to have the greatest "ability to represent" is not elected. Many explanations come to mind as to why such an outcome is commonplace. For a variety of reasons, a candidate may get a huge sympathy vote. The strongest candidate may not belong to the most popular party or even to a credible party. The incumbent may have done so many favours and created so many IOUs that he can defeat all other candidates even if they are obviously more capable. And a certain party or party leader may sweep a lamentably weak candidate into office by promising major benefits to the candidate's constituency.

Once we acknowledge the fact that "simply the ability to represent" is not the primary qualification to become an MP, then we realize that there are key factors other than sharing social traits that shape political outcomes and that we should not concentrate primarily on social traits.

7. "The presence of women in Parliament ensures that all the diverse and quite possibly conflicting interests of women will actually be heard and debated in Canada's central representative political arena". For better or worse, such an assumption does not bear up under scrutiny. For one thing, no one can ensure that "all" interests will be presented. The significant subgroups of women, as well as of many other groups, are far too numerous to allow us to accept such an assertion as valid. In our parliamentary system, debate in Parliament will continue to be dominated by differences between government and opposition agendas, not by diverse values and perspectives among men or among women or among Aboriginal people or among ethnic groups. Those differences will, in the main, need to be debated elsewhere.

Moving beyond these ideological assumptions, we need to consider several basic ideological issues:

1. Identity-based representation would increase social fragmentation in Canada. That's exactly the opposite of what Canada needs at present. The biggest question we face is whether we have enough commonality to remain united. The country may not survive the injection of additional cleavages that pit some Canadians against other Canadians. In a free society, having a plethora of organized groups—religious, social, ethnic, economic, athletic, professional, and so on—is a sign of political health. But if these groups are elevated to the point of formal and official electoral competition, then differences tend to overwhelm commonalities.

This country would be dangerously weakened if social differences were incorporated into electoral struggles. We do not need the religious animosities that dominate Irish or Israeli party politics, the ethnic tensions that destroyed Yugoslavia and that perennially threaten Belgium and various other countries, the race-based policies that have bedevilled South Africa and other countries, or a parliamentary division that pits women against men simply because some MPs are women and some MPs are men.

Indeed, I would go so far as to argue that Canada has evolved into a stable, free, and tolerant country largely because our national legislature has not reflected the major cleavages in society and has not let these divisions become dominant in our national political agenda.

2. Identity-based group representation raises insoluble problems of boundary and number. Once we start categorizing people according to their personal traits instead of their possession of citizenship, where do we stop? Groups will quickly realize that to be assigned guaranteed seats is the easiest, indeed, for some the only, way for them to be assured of gaining representation in Parliament. If we guarantee seats for women, we can safely assume that soon homosexual women will want to have the authorities guarantee them a quota of seats because as a small minority group among women, they probably would otherwise not get any.

Quite apart from the long list of groups, especially ethnic groups, that would quickly clamour for guaranteed seats, we would soon see a series of divisions and further divisions within the groups initially assigned seats. This problem raises another key question. Who would decide which groups and subgroups would be guaranteed seats? And would the same authority or authorities decide how many seats each group would get? The whole exercise would undoubtedly generate widespread disappointment, resentment, frustration, and anger.

3. The proposal to move to identity-based representation is condescending toward the five groups under consideration. Today, members of all of these five groups have the right to stand for office and to vote. Increasing numbers do, in fact, stand for office, vote, and win seats. Now, with progress well under way, we are being told that these groups are not good enough to make it on their own.

This proposal is condescending in that it assumes that women, who constitute 51 percent of Canadian society, do not know their own best interests or are too incompetent to vote according to their own best interests. They cannot be trusted to decide which candidates, be they male or female, will be the best representatives for them. They need to be told by the dominant male "hierarchy," to use Tim Schouls's term, that they should vote only for women. That's an insult. Why don't we let them decide for themselves who can best represent their interests? If they want to organize a women's party or if they want to vote for women, let them do so. But surely they do not have to be instructed by men or by our mostly male Parliament what they should do.

The same line of reasoning can be applied to the other groups. It may well be that some categories of voters in some parts of the country will not elect people who are their best advocates. But that's how democracy works. Democracy does not ensure that the wisest and most competent and the most effective representatives will be elected; it can only ensure, generally speaking, that the truly uninformed and the seriously incompetent and the utterly ineffective and those who would seek to destroy freedom do not become representatives in our legislatures.

4. The proposal would create first-class and second-class MPs. Presumably, in an electoral system that incorporates identity-based group representation, some women, some Aboriginal people, some visible minorities, some members of ethnic groups, and some disabled people would still be elected in the open segment of the electoral process in the way that they are elected now. Others would be elected by their own kind to fill guaranteed seats. It seems to me that very quickly a situation would develop in which those who were elected to guaranteed seats would be deemed to be second-class MPs because they were elected with special governmental facilitation. They could not make it on their own the way the others did.

One result of such a development would likely be that those who were elected to guaranteed seats would have less credibility in Parliament. Such a result would, of course, undermine the whole reason for embarking on the exercise in the first place.

5. To a significant extent, immigrants should be assimilated into Canadian society; Canada should not serve only as a receptacle for transplanted societies from around the globe and should not tolerate the transplanting of tensions and animosities that exist in many of those societies. Generally speaking, ethnic groups in Canada should not expect governmental assistance in the perpetuation of their ethnic communities. Analogous to the shifting popularity of religious groups, the survival or disappearance of ethnic groups in Canada is properly the concern of the private sector.

This is, after all, Canada, not the immigrants' former country. Ethnic groups should, as I see it, expect gradual assimilation. In any event, they should not expect the Canadian Parliament to make provision for their segregated survival. Above all, we do not want ethnic cleavages and rivalries built into our Parliament. Guaranteeing ethnic seats would, in my view, seriously increase ethnic antagonisms. Let us assume, for example, that the responsible authorities would guarantee two seats to Indo-Canadians; it could hardly be more, given that half of the total seats would be assigned to women and many other groups would need to be accommodated. Immediately there would be fierce rivalries concerning who should be selected. Should Indo-Canadian Hindus, Buddhists, Sikhs, Muslims, and Christians all be given seats, with the groups taking turns electing their MPs? And what about the growing nonreligious subset?

Would the Canadian government, in trying to be fair, undertake to count the members of the various Indo-Canadian subgroups? It would be a mammoth task to decide which Indo-Canadian groups would get the assigned seats.

Surely it would be much wiser to let Indo-Canadians take their place as Canadians and eventually make their political contributions the way the majority of Canadians do. As a matter of fact, Indo-Canadians have already made important political contributions in various jurisdictions in Canada, even at the cabinet level. The same situation prevails for many other ethnic groups, including Chinese-Canadians and other visible minorities.

What multiethnic Canadian society and its government should promote is the identification and strengthening of areas of commonality. We need all the glue we can find to keep this country united. We do not need an electoral system that emphasizes and reinforces ethnic cleavages and thus also ethnic tensions and rivalries. To put it very candidly, Canadian multicultural policies, in electoral matters and in other areas, should guarantee freedom, tolerance, and respect, but in a truly free society, these policies should not underwrite the political costs of ethnic group perpetuation, and they certainly should not undermine democracy in a futile attempt to guarantee ethnic group survival.

6. It would be very unwise to agree with the proposal that "no effort should be spared to get more minority representatives into the House. "No effort spared" means exactly that. These words may be a popular slogan, but the fundamental idea they convey is a great threat to democracy. Do we want the effort made to ban the nomination of nonminority candidates so that the minorities can win? Do we want quotas applied along racial and ethnic lines for the general elections? These and numerous other efforts should not be undertaken.

7. The term *political equality* needs to be clarified and then to be understood and applied appropriately. I have difficulty understanding what Schouls means by this term, one which seems to be central to his thesis. If he means equality of opportunity, then he is on solid philosophical and political footing. If, on the other hand, he means equality of influence or, even worse, equality of political outcome, then we have a serious problem.

Democracy cannot guarantee ideal outcomes. Freedom of choice means choice, including the right to make unwise or less than ideal decisions. It includes the right to make choices—in politics, religion, economics, and so on—that are not the most advantageous to oneself. It includes the right to make illogical choices. In the area of religion, for example, freedom does not ensure even the survival, let alone the good health or expansion, of any one faith. Concerning ethnic group survival in Canada, guarantees of freedom should only provide a climate of opportunity and perhaps some general tax and other minor concessions. They should not attempt to ensure or guarantee anything more.

With reference to the proposal for identity-based group representation, one needs to ask in what way would minority representation create political equality?

It would create minority representation and not much more than that. It certainly would not create equality of influence on legislative outcomes.

8. The liberal approach to representation does not insist that MPs represent individuals only. I question the statement that in the liberal perspective "representatives are elected to advance the individual interests of their individual constituents." Liberalism assumes more than that. Certainly Canadian MPs do more than represent individual interests. Even a brief reading of *Hansard* should correct such a misconception. Individual MPs from both sides of the House and from all parties frequently urge policy changes or initiatives to assist companies, towns and cities, ethnic and other groups, categoric groups such as families, women, taxpayers, or the unemployed, and, of course, the country as a whole.

For me, however, the main issue in this regard is not whether individuals or groups should be represented and promoted—clearly the interests of both categories must be upheld—but whether national well-being is being advanced. With Edmund Burke, I believe that though individual representatives have specific responsibilities to their own constituencies, they should always balance constituency well-being with national well-being.

9. The election of MPs representing identity-based groups would likely produce chronic governmental instability. Most proportional electoral systems have some means, usually a 1 percent or a 5 percent clause, as in Japan and Germany respectively, to prevent the appearance of numerous one-person, two-person, or three- person parties in the legislature. Under the proposal advocated by Schouls, there could be no threshold exclusion clause. In fact, the whole intent would be to have a series of mostly small, special interest groups in Parliament that would be likely to soon become special interest political parties.

Such a situation would, of course, almost certainly produce a series of Parliaments without a majority party, and, therefore, a sequence of shaky and short-lived governments, unless the 153 or more women decided to govern as a bloc. Thus, in trying to address a problem of underrepresentation, we would, in fact, be creating much more serious problems for Canadians.

One of the major reasons for general Canadian political and economic stability, even when separatists threaten to break up the country, is our majority cabinet system with its stability and predictability between elections. If no one party is permitted to field its own slate of candidates in all constituencies in an effort to form a majority government, we might well regularly produce minority governments consisting of numerous groups and parties and, therefore, vulnerable to disintegration in the face of separatist threats or various economic and political crises. We should not toy with such risks.

In passing, we should also note that small ethnic or other groups invited to join coalitions should not expect to make substantial headway with their particular agendas. The larger party or parties leading the coalition would likely have at least several small groups to appease, as best they could, so that each small group would likely get very little of what it wanted.

Such a situation reminds us again that in a democracy, compromise is a crucial ingredient. The desire to implement narrow, doctrinaire agendas is not an important component.

10. Political accountability is greater when half or more of the members in a legislature are elected in single-member districts. Single-member districts, as in Canada's present electoral system, tend to create majority governments by disproportionally rewarding that party or those parties that are the most popular. While this system tends thus to distort public preferences, it also tends to produce governmental accountability.

If one believes, as I do, that an effective system of political accountability is a very important factor, then one is prepared to accept the distortion that the system creates. The distortion can, of course, be greatly reduced by the adoption of the dual German electoral system.

Given the broad economic and social scope of governmental activity in our day, it is surely important to know whom to thank and whom to blame. It is much easier to do so if a majority government is in place than if a broad coalition governs. Since most governments tend not to change greatly the general political direction and policies that they inherit when they take office, it seems more important that we should be able to hold governments accountable than that the composition of a legislature accurately reflect the social composition of society.

Furthermore, in the identity-based system of representation being advocated, it is not clear how voters could identify the official loyal opposition, that is, a "government in waiting," the likely alternative to the government of the day. The important distinction between two relatively clear sets of policies and politicians, offering clear alternatives to voters, would become very blurred or even disappear. That would be a serious loss.

11. Social, religious, or racial fragmentation of society probably constitutes a greater threat to political stability than does the geographical division of the electorate for purposes of electing a legislature. The proposal makes much of the supposed division of the electorate into geography-based constituencies. Schouls suggests that such a method of dividing voters "rests on the assumption that voters' primary political identity flows from their attachment to geography." As I see it, such an assertion misstates the point. The division of voters into constituency groups is a pragmatic and utilitarian means of getting MPs elected by approximately the same number of potential voters per riding, with special provisions made for sparsely inhabited regions. As I see it, this system does not imply primary attachment of voters to territory or to anything else, although in some cases there is considerable racial or religious homogeneity. It is only a convenient way to divide voters, most of whom likely have nongeographic primary attachments, into groups of the desired size.

Above all, these constituency groupings are not based on social, religious, or other social tests, do not reinforce cleavages or animosities, and do not exacerbate tensions.

ARGUMENTS BASED ON PRACTICAL CONSIDERATIONS

1. The categories and percentages presented in the proposal raise numerous important problems and dilemmas. In the early sections of the article, Schouls emphasizes the importance of the "new Canadians with origins in the Caribbean, Africa, Middle East, Central and South America, and Asia." If, in his ethnic categories, he includes, as he logically should, all ethnic groups, including those not part of the visible minorities, that come from these regions, then the total becomes considerably greater than the 6.3 percent that he cites. Further, when he introduced his five categories, he listed "ethnic and visible minorities" as two groups. What has happened to the ethnic groups that are not visible minorities? Having acknowledged that "numerous visible minority and ethnic groups in Canada are able to put forward a very strong case," Schouls seems to have forgotten about the nonvisible ethnic minorities.

In the scheme before us, 153 seats in the current 301-seat House of Commons would be assigned to women. An additional twelve seats would be assigned to Aboriginal people. Given Schouls's strong commitment to equality, one must conclude that six of these twelve would be given to Aboriginal women. Of the nineteen seats he would guarantee to visible minorities, we ought to conclude that at least nine would be given to women. The result would be that 168 seats would be assigned to women, which means that the male voters, with 133 seats, would be seriously underrepresented. Or maybe the six Aboriginal females would be part of the 153.

The situation becomes additionally complicated if we factor in the people with disabilities, who seem also to have been forgotten somewhere along the way, and, of course, the large groups of ethnic minorities who belong to distinct and cohesive ethnic groups but who, in most cases, are not physically recognizable.

Other complicating factors come to mind. Where would one place an MP, elected to a nonguaranteed seat, who is female, disabled, and Aboriginal? Would she be counted in one or all of those categories, or in none? Even more important, who would decide? And would the number of guaranteed seats be reduced if significant numbers of women and several Aboriginal people and members of visible minorities, or even any of them, managed to get elected to nonguaranteed seats? Surely the authorities could not simply let the number of seats allocated to the "others," the presumably nonvisible minority males, be markedly reduced, or the whole scheme would go out of whack in that direction.

The assigning of individuals to the several voting groups would be a national nightmare. How would one categorize spouses in mixed marriages? How would the authorities categorize the children of these marriages? Would every Canadian have to carry a racial or ethnic identity card, a Canadianized version of apartheid? Presumably so, or the overall registering of voters could not be carried out in a way to facilitate the achievement of the stated percentage goals.

Additional major problems would involve the allocation of the twelve Aboriginal seats to the numerous competing groups, the allocation of the nineteen visible minority seats to at least twenty-five visible minority groups, and the allocation of whatever the appropriate number of seats is to people with disabilities. The challenges and problems boggle the mind.

2. **We are not told how the electoral system would be altered to ensure that the guaranteed seats would be filled as intended.** This is no small matter. Since relatively well-paid, high-status positions as members of Parliament are at issue, we can be assured that there would be a great clamouring for the occupancy and control of these seats. Who would handle the nominations? For example, concerning the women, would various organizations each be assigned certain seats? Would the National Action Committee on the Status of Women be given a bloc? Would Real Women be assigned a large segment, since they seem to represent a high percentage of nonorganized women? Would the women's organizations be allowed to nominate candidates who would compete against one another? Would there be primary elections? If so, who would pay the costs? What about all of the other women's organizations? Would the guaranteed women's seats be spread across all of the provinces?

And what happens if most of the voters in a given riding don't want to be part of such a guaranteed constituency? Will they simply be told by whoever has the authority to tell them that their MP will be a woman, like it or not? What happens if all of the established parties in one of these ridings refuse to nominate anybody in such an authoritarian situation, but a small women's pressure group manages to nominate a woman? Would that female candidate automatically become that riding's "elected" MP?

And what happens if, in a guaranteed woman's riding, a party nominates a male? Would the sex (or gender) police declare the nomination invalid on account of a candidate being of the wrong sex? How would such a ruling be upheld given Canada's commitment to equality? How could such a ruling or policy be justified given all of the official legislative and judicial decisions, not to mention constitutional provisions, spelling out equality of the sexes?

If, perchance, the assumption is that the guaranteed women MPs, more than half of the House of Commons, would not be elected in existing ridings, then how would they be chosen? Would they be selected by women's groups, or one women's group, such as the National Action Committee on the Status of Women, without any connection to a given territory such as a riding? And how could this be seen as fair in that the women get to vote twice, once in the general election and, presumably, once in a women's election? Or are the 153 "guaranteed" female MPs not even going to be elected? If that is the intent, then how could this be done given the stipulations in the *Elections Act* and the relevant equality provisions of the Charter of Rights and Freedoms?

Furthermore, if it is fair to guarantee a specified number of seats to women, why is it not fair also to specify a number of seats for men? Surely that would be more equitable than giving special guarantees to members of only one sex. Would men be allowed to vote in the women's elections? Would parties still be allowed to nominate women in all of the nonwomen's seats? And what happens if, after all of the ballots are counted, the total number of female MPs comes to 60 or 65 or 70 percent of the House of Commons? That would be a distinct possibility. Would that constitute equality? Would that be more democratic than what we have now?

3. Who will administer the incredibly complex and probably unworkable scheme advocated in the proposal? Somebody will have to make many very controversial, often very unpopular, decisions. Some of the dilemmas would involve policy and others would involve implementation and administration. Is it assumed that the last freely elected House of Commons would try to implement this Orwellian manipulation? Is it assumed that the cabinet would issue an order-in-council or that the legislature would enact a statute, perhaps relying on article 33 of the Charter, the notwithstanding clause, to get this whole venture under way without having it aborted by the courts?

CONCLUSION

Tim Schouls is to be commended for urging that the barriers that many women and other groups face in politics be removed. Unfortunately, guaranteeing seats does not in itself remove barriers. In fact, the proposal being advanced as a remedy creates more barriers than it removes.

Perhaps the major flaw in the proposed scheme is that it fails to accommodate the fundamental principle that democracy cannot, and should not attempt to, guarantee outcomes. Democracy cannot ensure that the ideal will be realized or even that the best option will be chosen. Freedom of political choice, like freedom of religion, includes the right to make wrong choices, wrong as some people or even the majority might define wrong. It includes the right to make choices that are not self-serving, self-advancing, or even well informed.

Throughout history, ideologues have tried to combine idealistic outcomes with democratic means—to do so cannot be ensured and no coercive attempt should be undertaken to try to achieve that goal. Political leaders and common citizens alike must rely on education and persuasion. Either the voters have free choice, within very broad and reasonable limits, or they do not. All else is undemocratic manipulation, even if done in the name of democracy and equality. The French Revolution bears solemn witness to that fact. The proposed plan for representation based on group identity ultimately takes away choice, specifically the option to choose that which ideologues and true believers of various sorts deem to be improper and unwise.

The proposed plan, however laudable its genesis and honourable its intent, must be rejected as both undemocratic and unworkable. It risks the achievements that have been made in assisting the politically marginalized groups, and it undermines the prospect for further democratic progress. We must look elsewhere for the agenda for further success.

POSTSCRIPT _____

In reading this debate, it is interesting to note the absence of discussion of class issues, especially in the article by Schouls. While he is concerned about increasing the representation of those marginalized in society, marginalization is identified primarily with the identity politics of ethnicity and gender. What role does class play in this analysis? Is the issue of class merely subsumed or transcended by issues of ethnicity and gender? What relevance, if any, does class analysis have to this debate?

Will Kymlicka is one theorist whom Schouls uses to develop the philosophical basis for his argument. See Kymlicka's *Multicultural Citizenship: A Liberal Theory of Minority Rights* (Oxford: Clarendon Press, 1995) for a defence of granting differentiated rights to ethnic groups based on their vulnerability. For an interesting critique of this position, see Brian Walker, "Plural Cultures, Contested Territories: A Critique of Kymlicka," *Canadian Journal of Political Science* 30, no. 2 (June 1997), pp. 211–234.

A number of good references are useful for pursuing this issue further. For two books that deal with the philosophical dimensions of this debate, see Jane Arscott and Linda Trimble, eds., *In the Presence of Women: Representation in Canadian Governments* (Toronto: Harcourt, Brace & Company, 1997), and Anne Phillips, *The Politics of Presence* (Oxford: Clarendon Press, 1995). For a book that tackles some of the practical difficulties of implementing proportional representation for social groups, see Committee for Aboriginal Electoral Reform, *The Path to Electoral Equality* (Ottawa: Committee for Aboriginal Electoral Reform, 1991).

When the territory of Nunavut was being created, an interesting experiment in gender representation was contemplated. The Nunavut Implementation Commission proposed the creation of electoral districts that would elect one man and one woman each in order to create the world's first legislature with full gender parity. However, the proposal received only 43% of the vote in a referendum and therefore was not implemented. To learn more about this potential experiment in equitable social representation and why it failed to win support, see Jackie Steele and Manon Tremblay, "Paradise Lost? The Gender Parity Plebiscite in Nunavut," *Canadian Parliamentary Review* (Spring 2005), pp. 34–39.

Jocelyn Praud, who teaches women in politics at the University of Regina, examines some reforms undertaken in France to increase gender parity and discusses their relevance to the Canadian situation. The article, entitled "The Facts Ma'am: Looking to France for Ways to Improve Canada's Representative Democracy?" (May 30, 2002) and can be found at http://www.equalvoice.ca/facts-democracy.htm. Also useful is Linda Trimble and Jane Arscott, "Barriers to Women: Why Are We So Far from Gender Parity in Our Legislature?" *Alberta Reviews* (June 5, 2005). This article can be found at http://www.albertareviews.ab.ca/issues/2005/Jun05/ABJuneBarriers.pdf.

Should the Court Challenges Program Be Reinstated?

✔ **YES**

A. WAYNE MACKAY, DANIEL MCGRUDER, AND KENNETH JENNINGS, "Why the Government Was Wrong to Cancel the Court Challenges Program"

✘ **NO**

TASHA KHEIRIDDIN, "Why the Government Was Right to Cancel the Court Challenges Program"

Few government programs with such modest budgets have generated as much controversy as the Court Challenges Program. When the Conservative minority government of Stephen Harper eliminated the program in 2006, the announcement caused dramatically different reactions. Some lauded the government's courage in cutting a program that had benefitted a small number of very vocal special interest groups. Others decried the move as both a major setback in the promotion of equality in Canada and a negative reflection on Canada's international status as a promoter of human rights. At the heart of this debate have been important differences in how justice is conceived and how to ensure that the equality provisions of the Charter of Rights and Freedoms are met.

The roots of the Court Challenges Program go back to the Liberal government of Pierre Trudeau in 1977. The government of Quebec had passed the controversial Bill 101, which was intended to strengthen the protection of the French language in the province while curtailing the usage of English. Rather than challenging the provisions of the bill directly, the Trudeau government chose an indirect approach by establishing the Court Challenges Program. This provided funding to minority language groups so they could challenge provincial laws that threatened the guarantee of minority language rights under the *Constitution Act, 1867*. In order to appear balanced, in the first three years, the program funded three cases defending English language rights in Quebec and three cases defending French language rights in Saskatchewan and Manitoba. When the Charter of Rights and Freedoms was adopted in 1982, the mandate of the Court Challenges Program was expanded to allow challenges to government policies under the language provisions of the new Charter.

When the equality provisions of section 15 of the Charter came fully into effect in 1985, there was growing pressure on the government to expand the range of challenges that could be funded by the program beyond linguistic rights. A special parliamentary committee examining the issue of equality rights noted that, within a very short period of time, a significant number of cases had been launched by individuals against various government departments and agencies. However, the committee expressed concern that "the imbalance in financial, technical and human resources between the opposing parties constitutes a serious impediment to those who might wish to claim the benefit of section 15, thus reducing the effectiveness of resorting to the courts as a means of obtaining redress" (*Equality for All: Report of the Parliamentary Committee on Equality Rights*, Ottawa: House of Commons, 1985, p. 133). The committee feared that the equality provisions of the Charter would be without real substance if disadvantaged or marginalized groups within Canadian society were not provided with the resources to mount real challenges to government policies.

As a result, the Conservative government of Brian Mulroney expanded the program, opening the door to funding of court challenges based on sections 15 (equality), 27 (multiculturalism), or 26 (sexual equality) of the Charter. In 1989, the program was renewed with a five-year budget of $12 million and moved to the Human Rights Centre at the University of Ottawa in order to make the management of the program and the selection of groups and cases funded more at arm's length from the government.

Despite these changes, the Conservative government had a change of heart in 1992. While Minister of Justice, Kim Campbell terminated the program, justifying the move as part of a series of cost-cutting measures the government was implementing. The decision invoked widespread criticism and became an issue in the run-up to the 1993 election. In response to growing pressures, all federal parties went on record stating that they would reinstate the program if elected to office. When the Liberal government of Jean Chrétien came to power in 1994, the Court Challenges Program was reinstated with an annual funding of $2.7 million. Although funding was provided by the federal government through the Department of Canadian Heritage, the program itself was re-created as an independent national nonprofit organization. Its supporters hoped that this arrangement would make it more difficult to cut the program in the future. During the Chrétien years, the Court Challenges Program funded a number of significant challenges under the equality provisions of the Charter, especially in the area of women's rights.

However, changing political tides suddenly placed the Court Challenges Program in doubt when the Conservative minority government came to power in 2006. One of the program's harshest critics, Ian Brodie, was now part of the new government's inner circle, serving as chief of staff to Stephen Harper. Thus, it came as no surprise to many observers when the new government announced that it was eliminating all funding to the Court Challenges Program in its first government budget, effectively killing the program.

Critics of the program hailed the Conservative decision, arguing that the move was long overdue. Others expressed alarm that the cut was a major setback for human rights in Canada and represented a shift away from fundamental Canadian values of equality. This debate is taken up in the two readings that follow. Law professor Wayne MacKay and law students Daniel McGruder and Kenneth Jennings argue that it was a fundamental mistake to cancel the program. They argue that this has made justice and real equality less accessible for many poor and marginalized Canadians. In contrast, writer Tasha Kheiriddin argues that the Harper government made the right decision. She believes that the decision brought a justifiable end to an ideologically driven program that had too long favoured a few special interest groups, while excluding others whose views were less popular.

✔ **YES**
Why the Government Was Wrong to Cancel the Court Challenges Program
A. WAYNE MACKAY, DANIEL MCGRUDER, AND KENNETH JENNINGS

In cancelling the Court Challenges Program in September 2006, the federal government, headed by Stephen Harper, made justice less accessible for many disadvantaged Canadians and thereby struck a blow against equality—one of Canada's core values. This was not a cost-saving reduction but, rather, a statement of policy and ideology that should alarm Canadians. To its credit, the government did admit that it was attacking the program on its merits and not just to save money. There were even some statements that the liberated funds would be used in other more effective ways. The truth of that claim remains to be proven. What is clear is that Canada has lost a valuable and effective program that helped to make the promises of equality in the Charter of Rights a reality for more people. The program was not perfect, but its elimination is radical surgery that is not justifiable. We would go so far as to assert that the program cancellation significantly detracts from one of Canada's core values—the pursuit of a more egalitarian society.

SUPPORTING CANADA'S CORE VALUES OF JUSTICE AND EQUALITY

It was American founding father Alexander Hamilton who said, "The first duty of society is justice." It was this kind of thinking that animated the late prime minister Pierre Trudeau's pursuit of a "just society"—a society in which governments are actively involved in promoting the welfare of all of its citizens. In a society as privileged as Canada, it is sometimes easy to take for granted the promise of justice for all citizens of our country. However, these freedoms are usually hard-won, and come at a price. We should be proud to live in a country that cherishes fundamental freedoms for all its people, and we should be proud to live in a society where our legal and political systems strive for justice and fairness. Accordingly, we should be saddened at the cancellation by the current federal government of the Court Challenges Program (CCP), which allowed some of Canada's most disenfranchised citizens to pursue justice in our courts.

The Court Challenges Program, created in 1978, provided funds to support test cases of national significance to dispute and clarify the constitutional rights of Canadians. The Court Challenges Program is not a big program (its funding being a miniscule fraction of the federal budget), but it is an important one, both substantively and symbolically. To realize this, one need only consider the question, what does it say about a government that it is willing to help fund citizens in challenging its own laws? We think it says positive, not negative, things about the country and those who govern it.

The cancellation of the CCP, though minor in budgetary terms, represents a significant loss for all Canadians. It is a subtraction from the human rights of every citizen. Fundamentally, this is a question of access to justice. When we enshrine constitutional rights, we should be able to expect that if Canadians believe the government is violating their rights, they can challenge that infringement. But if citizens or other residents, due to financial constraints, cannot enforce respect for their rights by having their day in court, then our constitutional democracy is a hollow shell, and the rights enshrined in the Canadian Charter of Rights and Freedoms are thereby diminished.

Commitment to the protection of Charter rights for disadvantaged individuals and groups is one of Canada's core values. As the Supreme Court of Canada indicated in the *Quebec Secession Reference* (1998), this is true both before and after 1982. If we wish to continue to enjoy these rights, and maintain our place as a leader in human rights on the world stage, it is the duty of every Canadian to call for the reinstatement of the Court Challenges Program.

THE COURT CHALLENGES PROGRAM—BENEFITS OF JUSTICE AND FAIRNESS

The Canadian Constitution establishes important constitutional rights, including the rights of everyone to equality before and under the law, and to equal protection and benefit of the law without discrimination. However, these rights are empty unless the individuals and groups they are designed to protect can exercise and enforce them. Since the Charter was adopted twenty-five years ago, successive federal governments have recognized that they have the responsibility to ensure that disadvantaged minorities have funding to take Charter cases to the courts. The Court Challenges Program, by providing modest contributions to the cost of important test cases dealing with language and equality rights, has made constitutional rights more accessible to all Canadians. Without the Court Challenges Program, Canada's constitutional rights are real only for the wealthy—this is unfair, and it does not comply with the rule of law, which is also a fundamental principle of Canadian society and our Constitution, as recognized in the *Quebec Secession Reference* and in other judicial and political venues, as well as in the preamble to the Charter of Rights.

Since its inception, the Court Challenges Program has funded numerous court challenges that have helped to give meaning to the Canadian Charter of Rights and Freedoms for many Canadians who would otherwise have been unable to assert their constitutional rights. This is achieved through partially funding the court costs of select, needy Canadian individuals or groups who are allegedly being disadvantaged through laws passed by the Canadian government.

The Court Challenges Program has advanced the constitutional rights enshrined in the Charter. An example of this is the CCP-funded case of *Canadian Newspapers Co. v. Canada (Attorney General)*, in which a victim of a sexual assault was at risk of having her name published in a newspaper. Relying on the funding of groups through the Court Challenges Program, the victim successfully defeated the threat of disclosure and confirmed the right to privacy for future victims. Other cases, such as *Egan v. Canada* have furthered the doctrine of substantive equality in Canadian society. This particular case brought about the recognition of sexual orientation as a ground of discrimination.

The real contribution of the Court Challenges Program stems from just these sorts of cases, which demonstrate the CCP's facilitation of substantive equality. Unlike formal equality, which overlooks personal differences, substantive equality is concerned with the impact of the law on different groups of individuals. Substantive equality requires that there be equal impacts on persons affected by a law, while formal equality insists that all people be treated identically. The fundamental problem with formal equality is that people are not identical—to treat them identically is actually to treat them unequally, based on the inherent disadvantages that an individual or group faces. Thus, justice requires that in order to value people equally, we must sometimes treat them differently. The challenge is to know when to take account of differences, but both judges and academics now provide guidance to facilitate this difficult task.

The case of *Eldridge* (as mentioned on the CCP website) provides a good context in which to illustrate the benefits of substantive equality. In that case, a number of deaf patients challenged the British Columbia medicare system for failing to ensure that sign language interpreters were available for medical appointments and procedures. The formal equality approach would see no problem here, since every patient that comes into a hospital is getting the same medical services delivered without the aid of interpreters. However, the substantive equality mode of analysis adopted by the Supreme Court recognizes that the impact of not having interpreters adversely affects deaf people. Without interpreters, deaf patients cannot adequately communicate with doctors and medical personnel, and are more likely to be improperly diagnosed and receive inferior treatment. By virtue of their disability, deaf people did not receive the full and equal benefit of the British Columbia medicare system. The substantive equality approach ensured that the deaf minority were able to access the same level of care as that enjoyed by the hearing majority, by providing interpreters for the deaf in hospitals.

A substantive approach to equality recognizes that patterns of disadvantage and oppression exist in society and requires that lawmakers and government officials take these systemic factors into account when drafting laws and formulating policies.[1] One of Canada's fundamental values is the rule of law: the principle that no one is above the law. Law only mirrors justice when it is based on fundamental principles that are known and applicable to all. By doing away with the Court Challenges Program, the federal government has weakened the rule of law by limiting access to an essential enforcement mechanism—the court challenge. By so doing, it has in effect placed itself and its actions "above the law" in the sense that the great majority of Canadians cannot afford to challenge the laws and policies of the government, as is their constitutional right. In a democracy, we demand that our politicians and lawmakers be accountable to the polity. The Court Challenges Program, by funding citizens in challenging their laws and policies, was a shining example of the government's commitment of accountability to all its constituents, particularly those minorities whose views are not always reflected in a majoritarian democracy.

Canada has long been recognized as an international leader in human rights and a beacon of hope to the disenfranchised and the oppressed on the larger world stage. By cancelling the Court Challenges Program, the government has not only tarnished its international human rights record and reputation but also shrunk from its role as an exemplar of freedom and hope. As recently as May 2006, Stephen Harper's Conservative government appeared before a United Nations committee in Geneva to defend its commitment to human rights in Canada, citing the Court Challenges Program as evidence of this commitment. As stated by the government, "[t]his uniquely Canadian program has been successful in supporting a number of important court cases that have had direct impacts on the implementation of linguistic and equality rights in Canada." Canada vouched to remain a society that values transparency and equal access to basic human rights and benefits of the law. The cancellation of this program flies in the face of the government's public position on human rights and its commitment to the protection of the Charter rights of disadvantaged individuals and groups. To be an effective world leader, Canada must walk the talk and lead by example.

CRITIQUES OF THE PROGRAM—CHALLENGING THE CHALLENGER

It has been said that the Court Challenges Program, while once an important part of the Canadian justice system, is no longer needed. After twenty-five years, critics say, how can there still be any novel challenges left to fund? This criticism shows disrespect to all Canadian residents who may need protection of their equality rights, including women, Aboriginal peoples, people with disabilities, members of racialized minorities, immigrants, refugees, lesbians and gay men, children, and seniors. The government itself has publicly stated that there remain dimensions of the constitutional provisions currently covered by the CCP that still require clarification. The CCP has a proven track record of facilitating the realization of the promise of justice enshrined in the Charter for these sometimes disadvantaged groups. Even if the annual numbers of cases funded by the CCP are fewer, ensuring that this promise remains real and accessible to all Canadians should be just as important now as it was in the early years of the Charter.

The Court Challenges Program has been attacked on the charge that it is not accountable. This is not a sustainable objection. The CCP has an established track record as an effective and accountable institution that promotes access to justice.

It provided quarterly reports on its activities to the government and published an annual report with statistics on the number and types of cases that it had funded. The annual report and public documents were available on the CCP's website. On several occasions, independent evaluators have furnished the program with high praise, most recently in 2003–2004. The only information that the CCP does not divulge for the purposes of public and government oversight is information legally restricted by solicitor–client privilege. In this way, the CCP has remained accountable while protecting its beneficiaries and their personal information.

But what of these beneficiaries? The Court Challenges Program has been the subject of two criticisms in this regard. Critics of the CCP dislike some of the cases that it has supported: cases related to same-sex marriage, voting rights for prisoners, and *Criminal Code* provisions regarding hitting children. The fact that some individuals and groups do not agree with some of the test cases funded by the Program is no reason to cancel it. No one among us is likely to agree with every single test case that appears. But it is important to let such cases proceed on their merits to the courts to be decided on the basis of our Constitution and our laws. The point of a constitutional human rights regime is to ensure that diverse claims, perspectives, and life experiences are respected and taken into account in the design of laws and policies. The equality guarantees and the language rights in the Constitution were designed to help minorities, whose views and needs may not always be respected by governments, to be heard on issues that affect them. Cancelling the Court Challenges Program mutes their voices further, and makes Canada a less open and tolerant society.

In a similar vein, critics have pointed out that the program is too selective in whom it represents. But the CCP only has limited funds for important test cases. Therefore, it stands to reason that these limited resources go to those who need them most—those whose cases are the most promising, and those whose rights have been the most seriously infringed. Considering that the CCP issues a full report on every case it funds, thus alleviating the accountability issue, this criticism actually indicates the need for further funding, not cancellation, as some opponents of the program would like.

CONCLUSION—OUR VISION FOR CANADIAN SOCIETY

Fyodor Dostoyevsky once intimated that a society must be judged by how it treats its weakest members. In the final analysis, then, an assessment of the Court Challenges Program turns on what sort of vision we have for Canadian society. Are we willing to relegate our weakest and most vulnerable citizens to second class constitutional status? Or should we give them the means and encouragement to pursue the elusive promises of the Canadian Charter of Rights? The Court Challenges Program, while not perfect, was certainly a step in the right direction. Those who need to point out the imperfections in our laws in order that they may live on equal footing with others deserve to be heard. By cancelling the Court

Challenges Program, the government has made it more difficult for those on the margins of Canadian society to be heard. The role of governments should be to reduce economic barriers to the exercise of our constitutional rights; not to increase the height of those barriers. Canada has been rightly applauded for its record on human rights at home and abroad, and we hope that this rather mean-spirited cancellation of the Court Challenges Program is not a sign of a policy shift with more surprises yet to come.

NOTE

1. The first part of this sentence is paraphrased from the CCP website, http://www.ccppcj.ca/e/rights/rights-charter.shtml.

✗ NO

Why the Government Was Right to Cancel the Court Challenges Program

TASHA KHEIRIDDIN

In the words of the late, great American economist Milton Friedman, "Nothing is so permanent as a temporary government program." By targeting groups with specific characteristics—such as sex, race, disability, or income bracket—government programs create political constituencies, and in a democracy, constituencies vote. Whenever the state terminates a program, it inevitably generates howls of protest from the affected group, which claims that its "rights"—usually code for "financial benefits"—have been taken away. The pressure exerted by interest groups is frequently so strong that governments back down and maintain the programs, especially when faced with the prospect of an imminent election.

That is why the Conservative government exhibited remarkable courage last fall when it cancelled a spate of ineffective and outdated initiatives. It put an end to the One-Tonne Challenge (an environmental program which gave comedian Rick Mercer considerable airtime but did little to improve the environment), closed 12 Status of Women offices (instead of paying bureaucrats to keep the lights on, the government decided the money would be better spent by women working in their communities) and terminated the Court Challenges Program (an initiative which funded legal challenges to government legislation, led mostly by interest groups).

It is on this last program that we focus our attention, because the decision to end it represents more than just sensible policy, but a potential turning of the page in Canadian politics. Even if the concept of the CCP was defensible when the Charter of Rights and Freedoms was new, few can say that 25 years later, the Charter needs testing at the taxpayer's expense. In an interview in 2005, excerpted in *Rescuing Canada's Right*, former federal justice minister John Crosbie, who renewed funding for the CCP 20 years earlier, agreed that the time for the program "is long past. . . . If the civil rights advocates want to, let them pay for their own challenges."

In that same interview Crosbie also made a more disturbing comment. He affirmed that the Progressive Conservative government renewed the CCP in 1985 because of "political correctness. If we had discontinued the program we would have received very bad publicity . . . reinforcing our image as not being 'with it' on social issues." And therein lies the most compelling reason to cancel the CCP. The program survived all these years not on its merits as a program, but as part of a larger agenda of left liberal special interest politics.

How did this agenda come about, and how did the CCP fit into it? For the answer, we must cast our eyes back to 1968, when newly elected prime minister Pierre Elliott Trudeau began shaping what he called the Just Society. His project was profoundly interventionist, seeking to use the power of government to "correct" social inequalities, whether of means, status or rights. It would ultimately culminate in the entrenchment of equality rights in the Charter some 13 years later.

In Trudeau's first term in office, however, his strategy was more subversive. It involved using the state's resources to fund external actors, chiefly special interest groups, to lobby in favour of the type of interventionist policies he wanted to implement. These lobbying efforts mobilized the public and created the impression of widespread support for his government's initiatives. The funds were disbursed mainly through the Citizenship Branch of the Secretary of State, which journalist Sandra Gwyn, writing for *Saturday Night* magazine in 1972, colourfully described as "a freespending *animateur sociale....* Massive grants went out to militant native groups, tenants' associations and other putative aliens of the 1970s."

At the same time, in response to the rise of separatism in Quebec, Trudeau sought to dilute the tension between Canada's two solitudes by implementing state-funded multiculturalism. Former civil servant Bernard Ostry, who headed the Citizenship Branch at the time, confirmed that "millions of dollars were made available to the branch to ensure justice and fairness to every ethnic group that wished to preserve and celebrate its cultural heritage."

Trudeau also brought in official bilingualism, in part to reassure French Canadians outside Quebec and Anglophones inside that province that their language rights would be protected. Between 1970 and 1982 official language minority groups received $76 million in funding from the federal government; not surprisingly, during that time the number of these groups doubled, to 370. Sociologist Leslie Pal, in his seminal work *Interests of State,* chronicled how the federal cabinet authorized a new "Social Action Program" to "animate" French-Canadian minorities in "desired directions." This support was then extended to women's groups, ethnic groups, native and youth groups as well.

The CCP formed part of this state-supported interest group strategy. Trudeau initially set up the CCP in 1978 to sponsor minority language law challenges, in particular to Quebec's Bill 101. Between 1978 and 1982 it funded six cases, three in Quebec and three in Manitoba and Saskatchewan, with a total annual budget of $200,000. But with the equality provision of the Charter, section 15, coming into force in 1985, interest groups began demanding direct government funding of minority rights litigation of all kinds, not just linguistic.

Trudeau had departed the political scene, but as Crosbie pointed out, the new Progressive Conservative government wanted to be seen as "with it" on social issues. Crosbie also claimed, in a 2001 interview with Ian Brodie (now chief of staff to Prime Minister Stephen Harper), that the Tories wanted to promote a progressive agenda without creating new entitlement programs. An expanded CCP was seen to fill that need, and in 1985 the program's budget was increased to $9 million over five years.

In his book *Friends of the Court,* Brodie reported that, by 1989, 15 percent of that budget was being used for "community outreach" to encourage litigation and in some cases even create new interest groups. Furthermore the program was spending $1,421 per application on "public information," more than 10 times what it spent deciding which application to fund. Yet when the CCP came up for renewal again in 1989, the Progressive Conservatives increased its budget to $12 million over five years, and outsourced its management to the Human Rights Centre of the University of Ottawa.

What did taxpayers get for their money? In its first decade, the CCP funded equality rights challenges by a variety of groups, including LEAF (the Women's Legal Education and Action Fund), the Charter Committee on Poverty Issues, Equality for Gays and Lesbians Everywhere (EGALE), the Canadian Prisoners' Rights Network, the Canadian Committee on Refugees and the Equality Rights Committee of the Canadian Ethnocultural Council. Of the 24 equality rights judgments the Supreme Court handed down between 1984 and 1993, 9 had a party or intervenor that was funded by the CCP, and most of these were successful.

While these groups battled for different causes, they all had one thing in common: they sought to advance the doctrine of substantive equality. Unlike formal equality, which requires that the law treat all persons equally, substantive equality posits that to treat people equally, the law must actually treat some people differently. This "different but equal treatment" is said to compensate for discrimination suffered as a result of belonging to a "disadvantaged group," such as women, Aboriginal people, immigrants, gays and lesbians, etc.

The CCP was instrumental in advancing the concept of substantive equality through its funding of two LEAF-led cases, *Andrews v. Law Society of British Columbia* and *Schacter v. Canada.* Ironically, in both cases the plaintiffs were white males. In *Andrews,* a British lawyer argued that the B.C. Law Society's refusal to admit him because he wasn't a Canadian citizen was discriminatory; being a "non-citizen" made him part of a disadvantaged group. In *Schacter,* an adoptive father sought the same paternity leave benefits as a natural father, claiming that adoptive parents should be treated the same as parents with biological children.

In both cases, the plaintiffs were successful, entrenching the doctrine of substantive equality in Canadian jurisprudence. The cases also advanced what is known as "political disadvantage theory," which advocates that minority groups whose interests are excluded from the executive or legislative branches of government can resort to the courts to defend those interests. It implies an ever-growing range of "discrete and insular minorities," to quote former Canadian Supreme Court Justice Bertha Wilson in *Andrews.* These minorities may not have been envisaged by the framers of the Charter, but if they are analogous to other minorities that do enjoy protection, the argument goes, they should be given the same rights. This line of reasoning led to the establishment of the "reading-in" doctrine in *Schacter*, which established that courts could read in (i.e., rewrite) Charter provisions to protect this growing list of disadvantaged minorities. Possibly the most controversial use of this doctrine was to later read in sexual orientation as a prohibited ground of discrimination under section 15, as analogous to race, sex, religion or age.

By funding these types of cases, the CCP had a profound impact on the courts' interpretation of section 15. The *Andrews* decision laid the foundation for more successful challenges down the road involving freedom of speech, abortion, gay rights, prisoners' voting rights and pornography. Politically speaking, in most of these cases, the causes advanced were "progressive" or of a left-liberal persuasion. They furthered Trudeau's Just Society project, with the state as social engineer, constantly deploying its power and resources to accommodate differences and "correct" inequalities.

Not surprisingly, whether a litigant received funding from the CCP depended on where he or she stood on the political spectrum. In *The Charter Revolution and the Court Party,* authors Ted Morton and Rainer Knopff concluded, "The CCP has been a funding bonanza for LEAF and other equality seeking groups on the left." In some cases, CCP grants appear to have had little to do with financial need and much to do with connections and ideology. For example, in the late 1980s, Toronto lawyer Beth Symes received a CCP grant to challenge the fact that she couldn't deduct the expenses for her nanny. At the time, Symes was a practising lawyer and was one of the founders of LEAF.

Litigants who were not bent on advancing the doctrine of substantive equality or other left-liberal views were not as warmly received by the CCP. Morton and Knopff reported, "Nonfeminist groups such as REAL Women and Kids First saw their applications for litigation funding either ignored or rejected." A group of Native elders in British Columbia who wished to challenge the constitutionality of the Nisga'a agreement were refused funding as well; their lawyer, John Weston, ended up setting up an autonomous foundation to fund their case. In 1992, as part of a general package of restraint measures, the Progressive Conservative government terminated the CCP. The outcry was immediate. Interest groups, together with powerful supporters including Supreme Court Justice Wilson and Max Yalden, Chief Commissioner of the Canadian Human Rights Commission, lobbied for the CCP's reinstatement and made it an election issue in the 1993 federal campaign. Liberal leader Jean Chrétien vowed to reestablish the program, and Prime Minister Kim Campbell softened her position and promised to create a new Charter Law Development Fund. A year after sweeping to power in 1993, the Liberals inaugurated a new CCP with annual funding of $2.75 million. After 1997, according to Brodie, the beneficiaries of the CCP were also given a direct role in the management of the program.

Overall, the effect of the CCP has been to privilege some litigants over others, and advance those litigants' particular view of equality in the courts. It has helped further a statist political agenda by institutionalizing it in the form of government-sponsored interest group litigation. The 2006 decision to scrap the CCP is thus justifiable and long overdue. It is completely inappropriate for government to favour one side of the debate on the Charter by funding it to the exclusion of other voices. While groups should be able to use all the levers at their disposal, including the courts, to make their case for social change, no group has the right to do so at taxpayers' expense.

Worse yet, by entrenching substantive equality as a doctrine in our courts, CCP-funded cases have perversely made it an advantage to be disadvantaged. As long as one remains a member of a disadvantaged group, one is entitled to use the resources of the state to improve one's position. Instead of encouraging individuals to advance themselves on their merits, this type of politics fractures society into rent-seeking groups, which look to the state to correct perceived inequalities. This increases people's dependence on government, and expands the power of the state in the life of the citizen. The result is not a more equal society, just one with a different set of rules as to how you get ahead: who can best curry favour with bureaucrats doling out government grants, who has the better lawyer to assert their "disadvantaged group" status, who has the better lobbyist to pressure the state to do its bidding.

In sum, if the government rigs the game to give some a greater say in the legal debate, it is not furthering equality—it is just creating a new inequality. For all these reasons, Canadians are better off without the CCP, and the government should hold firm in its decision to cancel the program.

POSTSCRIPT_____

Both critics and supporters of the Court Challenges Program acknowledge that the Charter of Rights and Freedoms is not a self-enforcing document. Without judicial review and litigation, the Charter would have little effective impact. Thus, supporters of the Court Challenges Program argue that government funding of litigation is not to be feared but to be seen as a healthy antidote to some of the weaknesses of democracy. Such programs give voice to those individuals and causes that might otherwise not be heard and therefore contribute to the achievement of a more substantive form of equality within society. For an argument along these lines, see Gregory Hein, "Interest Group Litigation and Canadian Democracy," *Choices*, 6(2) (March 2000), pp. 3–31.

However, critics of the Court Challenges Program do not see it necessarily as a sign of a healthy democracy. Ian Brodie has argued that the Court Challenges Program was more of a sign of an "embedded state" in which the distinction between "public" and "private" break down. By deciding who to fund, the government can often choose to favour those groups that reflect its own agenda while denying funding to those that do not. For a more extensive treatment of Brodie's concerns about the Court Challenges program, see Ian Brodie, "Interest Group Litigation and the Embedded State: Canada's Court Challenges Program," *Canadian Journal of Political Science*, XXXIV, no. 2 (June 2000), pp. 357–376, and Ian Brodie, "The Court Challenges Program," *Fraser Forum* (October 2002), pp. 15–16. Further criticisms of the Court Challenges Program can be found in Barry Cooper, "Some Implications of the Embedded State in Canada," in Alain Cairns, Philip Resnick, and Gerald Kernerman, eds., *Insiders and Outsiders: Alan Cairns and the Reshaping of Canadian Citizenship* (Vancouver: University of British Columbia Press, 2005), and Robert I. Martin, *Most Dangerous Branch: How the Supreme Court Has Undermined Our Law and Our Democracy,* (Montreal and Kingston: McGill-Queen's University Press, 2003).

An important element in the defence of the Court Challenges Program, as reflected in the second reading in this issue, is the concept of "substantive equality." According to this concept, implementation of the goal of equality is not achieved simply through the neutral application of formal rules of law. A focus on formal legal equality may result in outcomes that are unbalanced and unfair. Therefore, for the concept of equality to have real substance, it is necessary for the law and public policies to take into account the different social and political situations of specific groups. Supporters claim that the Court Challenges Program does this by assisting those who may not have adequate resources to challenge discriminatory laws. Without such assistance, genuine or "substantive" equality will not be achieved. For a discussion of the importance of this concept to the development of the women's rights movement in Canada, including the role of the Court Challenges Program, see chapter two, "The Path to Substantive Equality," in Christopher Manfredi, *Feminist*

Activism in the Supreme Court: Legal Mobilization and the Women's Legal Education and Action Fund (Vancouver: University of British Columbia Press, 2000). This study is of particular interest since the Women's Legal Education and Action Fund (LEAF) has been one of the principal beneficiaries of the Court Challenges Program. For further discussion of the problems that arise when people have differential access to the justice system, see Lynn Smith, "Have the Equality Rights Made Any Difference?" in Philip Bryden, Steve Davis, and John Russell, eds., *Protecting Rights and Freedoms: Essays on the Charter's Place in Canada's Political, Legal, and Intellectual Life* (Toronto: University of Toronto Press, 1994).

For further material in defence of the Court Challenges Program, see Kathleen Ruff, "Final Appear," *Canadian Forum*, 17 (June 1992), p. 14 and the websites "Save Court Challenges" at http://www.fafia-afai.org/en/node/365 and "Save the Court Challenges Program of Canada" at http://www.savecourtchallenges.ca. The official website of the Court Challenges Program is http://www.ccppcj.ca.

Contributor Acknowledgments

The editors wish to thank the publishers and copyright holders for permission to reprint the selections in this book, which are listed below in order of appearance.

Issue 1

Paul Nesbitt-Larking, "Canadian Political Culture: The Problem of Americanization," © Nelson Education Ltd., 1994, 2008.

Michael Adams, "Canada and the United States—Separated at Birth," excerpt from Michael Adams, *Fire and Ice: The United States, Canada and the Myth of Converging Values* (Toronto: Penguin Books, 2003), © Michael Adams, 2003. Reprinted by permission of Penguin Group (Canada), a Division of Pearson Canada Inc.

Issue 2

Roger Townshend, "The Case for Native Sovereignty," © Nelson Education Ltd., 1994, 2008.

Thomas Flanagan, "Native Sovereignty: Does Anyone Really Want an Aboriginal Archipelago?" © Nelson Education Ltd., 1994, 2008.

Issue 3

Nelson Wiseman, "Going Nowhere: Conservatism and the Conservative Party," © Nelson Education Ltd., 2005, 2008.

Faron Ellis, "Twenty-First Century Conservatives Can Succeed," © Nelson Education Ltd., 2005, 2008.

Issue 4

Robert Martin, "The Canadian Charter of Rights and Freedoms Is Antidemocratic and Un-Canadian," © Nelson, a division of Thomson Canada Limited, 1994, 2008.

Philip L. Bryden, "The Canadian Charter of Rights and Freedoms Is Antidemocratic and Un-Canadian: An Opposing Point of View," © Nelson, a division of Thomson Canada Limited, 1994, 2008.

Issue 5

Andrew Heard and Daniel Cohn, "The Federal Government Should Stay Involved: The Case for a Strong Federal Role in Health Care," © Nelson Education Ltd., 2005, 2008.

Paul Barker, "The Case against a Strong Federal Role in Health Care," © Nelson Education Ltd., 2005, 2008.

Issue 6

Michel Seymour, "Quebec and Canada at the Crossroads: A Nation within a Nation," *Nations and Nationalism* 6:2 (2000), pp. 227–256, © ASEN 2000, Blackwell Publishing.

Michael Chong, "Canada as One Nation," © Nelson Education Ltd., 2008.

Issue 7

Hugh Mellon, "Coming to Terms with Political Realities: Exploring the Breadth of Prime-Ministerial Power," © Nelson Education Ltd., 2008.

Paul Barker, "Limits on the Power of the Prime Minister," © Nelson Education Ltd., 2002, 2008.

Issue 8

© Peter W. Hogg, 2006.

H. Patrick Glenn, "Constitutional Law, Politics, and Supreme Court of Canada Appointments," © Nelson Education Ltd., 2005, 2008.

Issue 9

David Kilgour, "Discipline versus Democracy: Party Discipline in Canadian Politics," © Nelson Education Ltd., 1994, 2008.

Robert J. Jackson, "The Imperative of Party Discipline in the Canadian Political System 2007" © Nelson Education Ltd., 1994, 2008.

Issue 10

John L. Hiemstra and Harold J. Jansen, "Getting What You Vote For," © Nelson, a division of Thomson Canada Limited, 1994, 2008.

Nelson Wiseman, "Not Knowing What You'll Get," © Nelson Education Ltd., 2008.

Issue 11

Jacquetta Newman, "Small-p Politics: Women Working Outside Formal Political Structures," © Nelson Education Ltd., 2008.

Jacquetta Newman, "Say It Five Times Fast: The Pitfalls of Small-p Politics and a Plea for Large-P Politics," © Nelson Education Ltd., 2008.

Issue 12

Justices Beverley McLachlin and John Major, "Opinion in *Chaoulli v. Quebec*," [2005] 1 S.C.R. (Supreme Court Review), pp. 586–597.

Justices Ian Binnie and Louis LeBel, "Opinion in *Chaoulli v. Quebec*," [2005] 1 S.C.R., pp. 597–611.

Issue 13

Justice Mary Saunders, "Opinion in *Chamberlain v. Surrey School District #36*," B.C.S.C. Doc. No. Vancouver A972046, retrieved Sept 19, 2001, from http://www.courts.gov.bc.ca.

John von Heyking, "Against the Edwardians: Why Religion Has a Place in Public Debate," © Nelson Education Ltd., 2008.

Issue 14

Tim Schouls, "Why Group Representation in Parliament Is Important," © Nelson, a division of Thomson Canada Limited, 1998, 2008.

John H. Redekop, "Group Representation in Parliament Would Be Dysfunctional for Canada," © Nelson, a division of Thomson Canada Limited, 1998, 2008.

Issue 15

A. Wayne MacKay, Daniel McGruder, and Kenneth Jennings, "Why the Government Was Wrong to Cancel the Court Challenges Program," © Nelson Education Ltd., 2008.

Tasha Kheiriddin, "Why the Government Was Right to Cancel the Court Challenges Program," © Institute for Research on Public Policy, 2007.